D0304005

INVESTIGATIVE JOURNALISM

Praise for the first edition:

> 'A surprising book. I'm surprised that it hasn't been done before, and I'd also be surprised if anyone did it better.'
> Roger Cook, *The Cook Report*, Central Television

> 'a book that no aspiring student of the subject can do without'
> Jon Snow, *Channel 4 News*

Investigative journalism has helped bring down governments, imprison politicians, trigger legislation, reveal miscarriages of justice and shame corporations. Even today, when much of the media colludes with power and when viciousness and sensationalism are staples of formerly high-minded media, investigative journalists can stand up for the powerless, the exploited, the truth.

Investigative Journalism provides an unrivalled introduction to this vital part of our social life: its origins, the men and women who established its norms and its achievements in the last decades. Two chapters describe the relationships with the law, bringing us up to date, and others deal with the professional techniques, the sociology and the teaching of investigative journalism. A further new chapter examines the influence of the blogosphere on investigative journalism.

The case studies of the first edition have been supplemented by new chapters: the investigators and methods which revealed the subcontracting of the torture of Iraqi prisoners; how the murder of Stephen Lawrence was treated in the *Daily Mail*; the tabloids and their investigations; BBC *Panorama*.

Contributors: Paul Bradshaw, Michael Bromley, Mark D'Arcy, Hugo de Burgh, Ivor Gaber, Roy Greenslade, Mark Hanna, Chris Horrie, Paul Lashmar, Gavin MacFadyen.

Hugo de Burgh is Professor of Journalism at the University of Westminster, London and Special Professor of Investigative Journalism at Tsinghua University, China.

INVESTIGATIVE JOURNALISM

Second Edition

Hugo de Burgh
with Paul Bradshaw, Michael Bromley,
Mark D'Arcy, Ivor Gaber,
Roy Greenslade, Mark Hanna,
Chris Horrie, Paul Lashmar,
Gavin MacFadyen

Routledge
Taylor & Francis Group

LONDON AND NEW YORK

First published 2000
Reprinted 2001

This edition published 2008
by Routledge
2 Park Square, Milton Park, Abingdon, Oxon OX14 4RN

Simultaneously published in the USA and Canada
by Routledge
711 Third Avenue, New York, NY 10017

Routledge is an imprint of the Taylor & Francis Group, an informa business

© 2000, 2008 Hugo de Burgh for editorial matter, his chapters,
and selection
© 2000, 2008 contributors for individual chapters

Typeset in Bembo by
RefineCatch Limited, Bungay, Suffolk

British Library Cataloguing in Publication Data
A catalogue record for this book is available from the British Library

Library of Congress Cataloging in Publication Data
Investigative journalism / [edited by] Hugo de Burgh.
p. cm.
Includes bibliographical references and index.
1. Investigative reporting.   I. Burgh, Hugo de, 1949–
PN4781.157 2008
070.4′3—dc22
2007049634

ISBN10: 0–415–44143–9 (hbk)
ISBN10: 0–415–44144–7 (pbk)
ISBN10: 0–203–89567–3 (ebk)

ISBN13: 978–0–415–44143–8 (hbk)
ISBN13: 978–0–415–44144–5 (pbk)
ISBN13: 978–0–203–89567–2 (ebk)

CONTENTS

CONTENTS

CONTENTS

NOTES ON CONTRIBUTORS

Paul Bradshaw is a Senior Lecturer in Online Journalism and Magazines and New Media at Birmingham City University. His professional background includes editing consumer magazines, managing news and feature-based websites, and freelance work as a journalist and print and web designer. His writing on online journalism has appeared in Press Gazette, Journalism .co.uk, Poynter Online and Telegraph.co.uk. He was recently named on of the UK's 'most influential journalism bloggers' and his 'Online Journalism Blog' attracts tens of thousands of visitors every month. He has contributed to a number of books about the internet and journalism.

Michael Bromley is Professor of Journalism and head of the School of Journalism and Communication at The University of Queensland, Australia. A former daily newspaper journalist, he has taught at a number of universities in the UK, USA and Australia. He has published widely on journalism and the media, and was a founding editor of the journal *Journalism: Theory, Practice and Criticism*. He is co-editor of *A Journalism Reader* (Routledge 1997) and *Journalism and Democracy in Asia* (Routledge 2005).

Mark D'Arcy is a Parliamentary Correspondent with BBC News, he is one of the presenters for *Today in Parliament*, an occasional presenter for *The Westminster Hour* and the presenter of BBC Parliament's *BOOKtalk*. He is a former BBC Local Government Correspondent in the East Midlands and Political Correspondent for the *Leicester Mercury*. He is the co-author of *Nightmare! The Race to Become London's Mayor* (Politico's 2000), co-author of *Abuse of Trust, Frank Beck and the Leicestershire Child Abuse Scandal* (Bowerdean 1998) and most recently, *Order! Order! Fifty Years of Today in Parliament* (Politico's 2005).

Hugo de Burgh is Professor of Journalism at the University of Westminster and Director of the *China Media Centre*. In 2007 he taught *Investigative Journalism* at Tsinghua University under the Chinese Ministry of Education's International Leading Scholar Programme. His books include *Investigative Journalism* (Routledge 2000), *The Chinese Journalist* (Routledge 2003),

Making Journalists (Routledge 2005), *China: Friend or Foe?* (Icon 2007) and *The China Impact* (McKinsey & Co. 2007). He is Co-editor of *Can the Prizes still Glitter? The future of British universities in a changing world* (University of Buckingham Press 2007) and Chairman of AGORA, the higher education think-tank.

Ivor Gaber is a broadcaster, researcher and consultant. As an independent producer he makes programmes for Radio 4 and the World Service. He is Research Professor in Media and Politics at the University of Bedfordshire and Emeritus Professor of Broadcast Journalism at London University's Goldsmiths College. He has authored three books and numerous articles on political communications and served as a media and politics consultant to governments and international bodies. He has held senior editorial positions at the BBC, ITN, Channel Four and Sky News. He has just helped set up Uganda's first national news agency. He is Deputy Chair of the Communications Section of the UK UNESCO National Commission and is on the organising committee for World Press Freedom Day.

Roy Greenslade is Professor of Journalism at London's City University, writes a media column for the *Evening Standard* and runs a blog on the *Guardian* media website. He has been a journalist for 42 years and has worked for most of Britain's national newspapers, notably as assistant editor of the *Sun*, managing editor of the *Sunday Times* and editor of the *Daily Mirror*, 1990–91. He is on the board of the academic quarterly, the *British Journalism Review*, and is a trustee of the media ethics charity, MediaWise. He is the author of three books, including a biography of the late press tycoon, Robert Maxwell and a history of British newspapers entitled *Press Gang: How Newspapers Make Profits From Propaganda* (Pan Books 2004).

Mark Hanna is a lecturer in the Department of Journalism Studies at the University of Sheffield. He worked for 18 years on newspapers, including the *Western Daily Press, Sheffield Morning Telegraph* and *Sheffield Star*, specialising in crime reporting and investigations, and also for the *Observer* as northern reporter. He won awards, including Provincial Journalist of the Year in the British Press Awards. He is a co-author of *Key Concepts in Journalism Studies* (Sage 2005). He chairs the media law examinations board of the National Council for the Training of Journalists, and is an official of the Association for Journalism Education.

Chris Horrie is a lecturer, author and journalist, and a former staff reporter, writer and editor for *News on Sunday*, The *Sunday Correspondent*, the *Sunday Times Magazine* and BBC *News Online* and, in addition, diarist for the *Independent on Sunday* and the *Observer* business and media sections. He is a contributor to numerous TV and radio discussion programmes and a frequent radio commentator and broadcaster. He is the author or co-author of ten books, mostly about the media and popular culture. He leads journalism courses at the University of Winchester and specialises in teaching and researching media law, media history, journalism practice, multimedia journalism production and related subjects.

Paul Lashmar is an investigative journalist, TV producer, author and lecturer. He covers the war on terror for the *Independent on Sunday*. Since entering journalism in 1978 he has been on the staff of the *Observer* (1978–89), Granada TV's *World in Action* current affairs series (1989–92) and the *Independent* (1998–2001). Since 2001 he has been a part-time lecturer in postgraduate journalism at University College Falmouth where he set up the successful MA in Investigative Journalism. He is also a part-time lecturer at Solent University.

Gavin MacFadyen is Director of the Centre for Investigative Journalism at City University in London and has directed the annual Summer Schools in London and training programmes in South Africa, Serbia, Norway and Columbia University since 2003. A London Film School graduate, he first joined BBC New York to work on *24 Hours* and *Panorama*. In the UK he was a Director of the BBC *Money Programme* and of Granada Television's *World In Action* where he worked on 30 investigative documentaries. He has researched eleven feature films for Paramount, the Michael Mann Company and Lucas Films and directed the BBC investigation into DeBeers, The Diamond Empire which was the subject of major litigation. He has directed and produced investigative programmes for C4 *Dispatches*, ITV, Australian Television and PBS *Frontline*.

ACKNOWLEDGEMENTS

This book is dedicated to

David Lloyd
Creator of C4 *Dispatches* and Head of Current Affairs at C4 Television (1987–2003) in appreciation of his remarkable contribution to journalism and to public life.

Thanks are due, and willingly rendered, to those who helped with the first edition, and whose words are used again here. For their more recent thoughts and advice I thank Andy Bell, Robin Esser, Paul Kenyon, Philip Knightley, Alja Kranjec, Professor Li Xiguang, Donal McIntryre, Julian O'Halloran, Kevin Sutcliffe, Count Nikolai Tolstoy, Xiao Lili, Teaching Assistant, and my students at Tsinghua, Xin Xin and Zeng Rong (translating the book into Chinese). Research was undertaken by Katie Byrne, Steven McIntosh, Mandy Garner and Lam Laihan.

Part I

CONTEXT

1

INTRODUCTION

Hugo de Burgh

In the first edition of this book there was enthusiasm about investigative journalism: as a distinct genre of journalism; as a vital means of accountability, almost the fourth estate itself; as the first rough draft of legislation. Then, it was widely thought that investigative journalism was a valuable public service endangered by new technology and crass management. Now, when every medium trumpets its work as investigative journalism, it is often written off as just another squalid trick up the sleeves of money-grubbing media moguls. Fashions change.

Although I do not buy the characterisation of the media as the enemy of all decent society, a debate which I introduce in Chapter 4, I am less confident of the idealism expressed in the first edition. In the United Kingdom we have lived through ten years of an experiment in government by spin, in which wars have been waged, the constitution subverted, public services distorted and civil servants corrupted in the cause of feeding the media in the hope that they can thus be diverted from attacking politicians. The techniques of investigative journalism, it is now more clearly seen, can be put to partisan, commercial or corrupt use as much as to right wrongs or overcome evil. That this happens in many different countries today was becoming evident to me as I assembled the international essays that went into *Making Journalists: Diverse Models, Global Issues* (Routledge, 2005).

Nevertheless investigative journalism still has the potential to make a worthwhile contribution to society, as the recent examples cited in the pages below show us. It does so by drawing attention to failures within society's systems of regulation and to the ways in which those systems can be circumvented by the rich, the powerful and the corrupt.

The motives may be various, the limitations obvious, yet the tasks still need to be done. And how and why they are done is increasingly discussed and studied in universities and colleges all over the world, where the first edition of this book, translated into many languages, has for eight years provided the only available introduction to the phenomenon in Britain. This second edition keeps many of the previous case studies but replaces all of the original part 1, except for the history chapters (2 and 3). The examples are still relevant, although change is accelerating such that it looks as if a further edition, in say 2015, will start afresh. For the moment, I have added several new case studies, described below.

For whom is this book?

Although we hope that it will have wide appeal, our work is written with media studies students in mind. For them, investigative journalism is one genre of journalism; hence we seek to place it in context, to see how investigative journalism is seen by its practitioners and how it may appear within the wider contexts of public affairs and the study of the media. It is not a 'how to' book.

By contrast, we aim to provide an introduction to the subject for students who need to understand it as an influential social phenomenon, whether or not they ever practice journalism. While several of the writers of this book teach vocational journalism courses, they believe that student journalists should not merely absorb professional conventions without understanding their limitations; equally they hope that media studies students will ground their analyses in knowledge of what media people actually do, how they do it and what influences bear down upon them as they do it. This book will also, we believe, be useful to students of disciplines other than media studies for whom some background knowledge of investigative journalism is needed. It assumes little prior knowledge. We have attempted to write it in such a manner that students from other Anglophone countries, and from other European countries, will follow the cases cited and be able to relate what is discussed to their own situations, and this may account for some explanatory remarks which would be otiose for an English audience.

How this book is organised

In this chapter, after explaining the book, I attempt a definition of investigative journalism that can be useful at least for the duration of the read. Through it, and within other chapters too, you will find references to established incidents in the recent life of investigative journalism that illuminate different aspects in different ways. These include the 'Thalidomide', 'William Straw', 'The Connection', 'Goodwin', 'The Committee', 'Lawrence', 'Gilligan' and 'Rendition' stories.

With Chapter 2 we go to history, with an attempt to show how, gradually, the figure of the investigative journalist emerged. Behind this is the belief that a failure to see journalism as the product of particular historical circumstances, which men and women have the power to influence, condemns us to accepting the common-sense notion that journalistic freedoms have come to stay because they are a free gift provided with modernity. It is easy for Britons or North Americans to fall into this error, but German, Italian or Polish journalists would be unlikely to do so, given the way journalism lost hard-won rights in the last century when totalitarian socialist regimes came to power. There are other lessons of immediate relevance to be taken from history; the undermining of the radical press by mass advertising earlier this century, as analysed by Curran and Seaton (2005), has its echoes and its equivalents today.

Although technology and political economy change dramatically, cultural responses to new circumstances have an eerie familiarity. Once you have read this book you will be familiar with the names of some individual journalists and can decide for yourself whether Pilger is our Cobbett; whether Murdoch, the media prince we love to hate, is the Harmsworth, and Whittam Smith the Renaudot of our era; perhaps England's Paul Foot, in his radical instincts and reasoned research, was the Ida Tarbell of the twentieth century. What cultural stereotype does Gilligan represent? Was he not in the same tradition, in that famous 2003 radio broadcast, as Winston Churchill writing in the *Daily Mirror* of the 1930s? Both were pointing up the dangerous deficiencies of our political masters and drawing upon sources and techniques that contemporaries thought reprehensible. It may be that cultural context is here at play, more enduring than economic determinists would have us believe.

Chapter 3 looks at recent investigative journalism. Yet journalism, even investigative journalism, is ephemeral. How can you make interesting revelations of misconduct or the uncovering of crookery that excited people in 1972? By demonstrating that the act of investigation had bearing upon wider social developments that still impinge upon our lives, by evoking historical empathy, by using them as case studies for skills and techniques or by offering them as examples to emulate or avoid.

The task of selecting specimens and of providing some orderly account of investigative journalism is made more difficult by the shortage of preliminary studies. True, journalists write up their cases into books, and they write memoirs, such as Andrew Marr's *My Trade* (2005); there are books on wide questions of journalism's impact upon society. There are a few books like *More Rough Justice* by Peter Hill and his colleagues (1985) that look at genres or journalistic phenomena, yet analyses of investigative journalism hardly exist.

A new Chapter 4 brings the story up to date; in 2000 we were much exercised by the apparent need for journalism, in a democracy, to function as the opposition. We were also debating the 'journalism of attachment'. More recently the issue has been whether the media are damaging to democracy, or whether it is our politicians that are at fault. Chapter 4 looks at these matters and also provides an overview of investigative journalism in the period, which will give context to the later case study chapters, although the connection between the political debates and the stuff of investigative journalism seems tenuous, unless the increasing boldness and brazenness of investigative journalism is to be interpreted as a function of the decline of the authority of politicians and institutions.

Perhaps the biggest change in the environment for journalism to take place in the period is in the way the internet and mobile phones are now used. 'On the day of the July 2005 London tube bombings the BBC received 22,000 emails and text messages about the bombings and 300 photos, of which 50 were within an hour of the first bomb going off, and several video sequences.'[1] The implications of participatory journalism are dealt with in Paul Bradshaw's Chapter 5, which looks at the relationship between investigative journalism and blogs, beginning with a brief history of the technology and its journalistic uses, before exploring three areas where blogs have become important tools in investigative journalism: in sourcing material; in disseminating the results of fieldwork; and as a source of funding. He proposes that blogs provide an opportunity to revitalise journalism. He looks at the amateur–professional debate; regular monitoring of blogs as leads and sources including sector expertise; Crowdsourcing; Journalistic Transparency; Gatewatching; Fundraising; and the new ethical issues raised by new newsgathering techniques.

American and British journalism share historical and cultural origins and yet display differences that illuminate both. The most significant differences are in the legal and political framework within which journalists operate. Horrie's first chapter explains how the law shapes both the methods employed and editorial agenda pursued by investigative journalists and their publishers. He deals with the key concepts of *public interest*, its relationship to sourcing and privacy, and *qualified privilege*, whereby investigative journalists can use persuasive and accurate, but legally inadmissible evidence, subject to a number of conditions. In recent years a number of cases have clarified these matters as well as endorsed the specifically investigative role of the press in initiating stories, in addition to the less controversial role of public 'watchdog' and the 10-point test for standards of 'quality journalism'.

Horrie's second, short, chapter deals with Freedom of Information in Britain and the uses to which it has been put since a 2000 Act ostensibly handed important opportunities to journalists.

The law is only one way in which investigative journalism is framed; another influence is professional practice. Gavin MacFadyen's *The practices of investigate journalism* is a very clear exposition of the techniques and practices that constitute Investigative Journalism, with illustrations. He covers the main elements, reporting, whistle blowing and protection of sources, researching (which he calls 'digging'), establishing proof and self protection in the age of very sophisticated surveillance. Britain is possibly the best country in which to base such a discussion, since the standards of required proof and the fear of prosecution are considerably greater than in many other countries, because of the severity of UK libel law.

As the title suggests, Hanna's *Universities as evangelists of the watchdog role: teaching investigative journalism to undergraduates* not only describes some of the practicalities of teaching investigative journalism, but alerts us to the role that universities now play in the media. The paucity of industry training programmes and the willingness of the media to take on younger journalism staff mean that the universities have become the main vehicles for the teaching of journalism skills and the transmission of public service values.

Journalists tend to see themselves as free agents. The media studies approach is an essential corrective to this and Michael Bromley's *Investigative journalism and scholarship* looks at the ways in which investigative journalism has been understood and interpreted. He starts with a workaday illustration of the different views of journalists, moralising their profession as a public service essential to the just running of society, and the media businessman. The businessman judges journalism by audience appeal, stop. Reading the pontificating defences of investigative journalism that Bromley shares with us, we shouldn't forget that the revival of the genre in recent years in many countries has been just as much about money-making and democratisation as about social responsibility. More people participating in the public sphere in Latin America and China, for example, means bigger audiences for current affairs and therefore competition by newspapers to satisfy them, often with what is cheerfully labelled 'investigative journalism'. When much of it is manifestly neither properly researched nor much more than sensationalism, the public's disenchantment with the journalists, and mistrust of their public service pretensions, is not surprising.

Bromley brings up other issues, such as the paradox of digitalisation at once giving more opportunities to government to avoid or traduce journalists, and at the same time providing us with 'we media', in which heretofore passive consumers now originate or modify material online and compete for attention with commercial media. He touches on explanations of journalism styles as expressions of culture, something discussed in the 2005 book *Making Journalists*, in particular by Schudson (de Burgh, 2005).

The second half of the book, professional practices, introduces the reader to some of the topics that have been investigated in recent years and some of the vehicles deployed. We start with the 'War on Terror' because of its importance in our lives.

The single most important phenomenon of the last few years, and the one which continues to bear upon public affairs, and thus of course on journalism, is the attack on Iraq of 2003. In his chapter, *From shadow boxing to* Ghost Plane: *English journalism and the War on Terror*, Paul Lashmar both examines the particular story of Rendition, and goes back to look at how the media dealt with the event which triggered off the so-called War on Terror, the Twin Towers Atrocity of 11 September 2001, and their reactions to subsequent events, notably the assault on the Afghan government and the attack on Iraq. Both of these wars are continuing as we go to press.

At first, probably still influenced by the shock of the Twin Towers and the resistance of the Taliban in Afghanistan, the media largely fell for the line that Iraq was a direct threat to the United States, Great Britain and all good people generally. Gradually it became apparent that the citizens of both countries had been deceived and that the war was being pursued for inadmissible reasons rather than for those declared publicly. In Chapter 11, Lashmar gives us the story of how realism and then scepticism returned to the media. He reminds us of the great damage done to our polities and to the relationships between media and politicians by the out and out dishonesty, in such a grave matter, of our leaders and by the revelations of incompetence and irresponsibility in the prosecuting of their policies. But he ends with the disturbing reminder that no matter that the media finally rumbled the politicians and exposed them, the electorates took very little notice.

Chapter 12 deals with 'high politics', the chase of the big beasts by the peoples' tribunes; by way of concrete illustration, we look at the now historic 'Arms to Iraq' scandal and the way in which such a topic is seen as the rightful purview of the investigative journalist. We look at the vehicle for a minister's exposure, the *Sunday Times* Insight, which has the most illustrious pedigree of all the media of investigative journalism. In some ways this example may now seem quaint, because we have, since 1997, become used to a degree of deception and corruption in politics that was then unimaginable.

File on Four remains a powerful exponent of what its editor prefers to call 'evidential journalism' and has made a particular strength of its examination of business issues. We therefore peg a brief survey of business investigations here. Since this chapter was written, BBC *File on Four* has continued to flourish and to undertake an increasingly diverse and daring range of topics, made feasible by the relative economy of radio, as compared with television.

Gaber's *Due impartiality? BBC* Panorama *and the case of 'IVF Undercover'* is a strong attack on the programme that BBC *Panorama* has today become. He starts by pointing out that, although *Panorama* is the world's longest running current affairs programme, it now describes itself as the 'longest running investigative TV show'. He connects this to changes in the objectives of the programme, which he illustrates by examining the types of programmes produced since the re-launch of *Panorama* in January 2007.

All this is a prelude to his case study, in which he examines a programme which had a very high profile as it launched *Panorama* in its new Monday–night slot and which is also high profile because it is still subject to legal action. It is a good example of a *Panorama* investigation, using undercover filming, the successful exploitation of the Freedom of Information Act, and some imaginative production ideas. However, it raises questions. Gaber not only considers whether extensive use of secret recording was justifiable, but also suggests that the treatment of the subject was anything but fair. He smells bad practice by the investigators of bad practices, and also finds that at least two of *Panorama*'s leading lights are concerned both by the techniques and by the topics of the re-launched 'flagship'.

Since the analysis of the investigative critique of social policy, pioneered by Channel 4 (C4) *Dispatches* and examined in Chapter 15, that series has changed yet continues to be a very important vehicle of investigative journalism. As a result there are a large number of references to it in Chapter 4.

Just as BBC *Panorama* has moved to brand itself an investigative programme, the *Daily Mail* has sought to identify itself as an investigating newspaper, by increasing the number and quality of such stories. In Chapter 16, *Journalism with attitude*, we find that the newspaper continues to live up to its campaigning, anti-government, conservative traditions while using investigative teams to throw light on areas of national life that it identifies as of concern to its readers and editorialising forcefully to drive home the points made through the investigations.

In the USA in the 1950s Erle Stanley Gardner, creator of the *Perry Mason* courtroom dramas, first put on television the *Court of Last Resort* which reviewed claims of flawed conviction. Its modern British successor has been BBC's *Rough Justice*, and now *Trial and Error*, made by 'Just Television' for C4. The genre has an impressive history of righting wrongs through the application of investigative procedures. We look at that history in Chapter 17, and at one recent programme.

One of the most important fields for inquiry is surely public administration at the local level, where huge amounts of money are expended, all citizens are involved and opportunities for corruption frequent, in no matter what society. For years commentators have lamented the dreadful decline of the regional and local press, the 'silent watchdog'. In Chapter 18 Mark D'Arcy points out how easy it is for the local reporter not to notice the big stories on his doorstep. He also argues persuasively that investigative journalism is very much needed out in the provinces where state power in particular is hardly regulated. The case of Frank Beck and the child abuse scandals provides lessons in journalistic failure, but it also shows what opportunities await the daring reporter and proprietor.

In Chapter 19, *Subterfuge, set-ups, stings and stunts*, Roy Greenslade tells us how the 'red-tops' go about their investigations. First, he gives us a history of investigations by the popular papers, which is an invaluable supplement to our brief general history in Chapter 2. He shows how, since the 1980s the *News of the World* has become the leading investigative newspaper, and its reporters have taken full advantage of the developing technological advances in order to satisfy a changed agenda. Crime has remained an important component, but sex and celebrity predominate. In order to uncover secrets about people the journalists have also pushed at the ethical boundaries. Subterfuge has become the norm, as has use of concealed audio and video recorders, by the best-known operator of these methods, Mazher Mahmood, now the *News of the World*'s investigations editor.

Roger Cook has done more than any other reporter to bring home to large numbers of people what investigative journalism can do and can be. He is criticised for being populist, but he is also immensely popular for it, so he doesn't care. He covers every conceivable subject matter so no one programme is typical; the example chosen for Chapter 20 deals with a rather emotive aspect of environmental degradation in an engaging and exciting way which reveals Cook at his dramatic and ironic best.

Some years ago Phillip Knightley examined the Gallipoli Myth (he calls it 'the blood icon') which originated from Rupert Murdoch's father, journalist Keith Murdoch, and which represents the Australians of the First World War as 'outstanding troops negligently commanded by British idiots'. The myth has been put to good use by many Australians looking for sticks with which to beat Britain (Knightley, 1997: 254–7) and has possibly been an inspiration for Rupert Murdoch's own well-documented assaults on aspects of this country. Knightley's efforts were not welcomed in Australia but his research is a good example of what investigative journalists can do with history; Chapter 21's example is less influential and more ambiguous. It concerns a widely-known case, generally referred to as 'The Cossacks', from the Second World War. It illustrates the relationships between history, politics and journalism and also some of the pitfalls of investigation.

In the final example, Chapter 22, we glance at how British investigative journalists examine other countries' sins and the moral and political pitfalls into which they might fall; specifically we look at another piece of television journalism, made possible by the researches of a lone Chinese investigative journalist, Harry Wu.

What is investigative journalism?

An investigative journalist is a man or woman whose profession it is to discover the truth and to identify lapses from it in whatever media may be available. The act of doing this generally is called investigative journalism and is distinct from apparently similar work done by police, lawyers, auditors and regulatory bodies in that it is not limited as to target, not legally founded and usually earns money for media publishers. This book will account for this assertion by referring to the way investigative journalism is described in popular culture and professional discourse and by providing concrete examples of how it is realised in society.

In John Grisham's novel and film, *The Pelican Brief*, the character of Gray Grantham is as romantic an idealisation of the journalist as one might hope to meet in popular culture. Not only is he a meticulous desk worker but he is also skilled in the practical arts; his dedication to the public weal is irreproachable, no matter that he is up against powerful and unscrupulous politicians and high officials who will have no compunction in ruining or killing him. Gray Grantham, although fictional, is not so very far from the genuine investigative journalists portrayed in two factual books *The Typewriter Guerrillas* (Behrens, 1978) and *Raising Hell* (Chepesiuk *et al.*, 1997) and in the 1999 film *The Insider*.

The heroic depiction of the journalist, similar to the depiction of heroes of Henty's novels of imperial mission and youthful adventure[2] that were so popular before the Second World War, contrasts with earlier cameos, ranging from the ludicrous Boot in Evelyn Waugh's *Scoop* to the fatuous Hildy in Hecht's *The Front Page* to the repulsive Totges in Heinrich Böll's *The Lost Honour of Katerina Blum*. The idealisation of the reporter is puzzling too because journalists are generally held in the low esteem so appropriately represented by these earlier fictions; yet very large numbers of young people nevertheless want to be journalists, or at least work in the media. Perhaps the low esteem – and, generally, poor wages – is overridden by other considerations such as sense of adventure, being in the thick of 'events' or fame. It is also, if the anecdotes of teachers of journalism are worth anything, because journalists are conceived of, at their best, as being idealists. The icons of British journalism most often mentioned by students are Martin Bell, Kate Adie, Veronica Guerin, Paul Foot and John Pilger. Of them, the first two are noted for their courage in adversity and unbending principle, while the latter three are associated with investigations. There are, of course, very many other distinguished investigative journalists, but their names are known more to aficionados of the genre or fellow journalists than to the community at large. Names such as Phillip Knightley, David Leigh, Nick Davies, Michael Gillard, Dominic Turnbull and Stephen Grey are mentioned regularly. What differentiates their work from that of other journalists? What are their motivations? What skills do they deploy? What significance does their work have for the rest of us?

Investigative journalism and dissenting journalism

It is useful at the outset to distinguish dissenting journalism from investigative journalism, although they are often closely connected. It is a long tradition in Anglophone societies to tolerate disagreement with authority and it is a tradition for which writers have fought since at least the seventeenth century.[3] Campaigns on behalf of this or that oppressed party, polemics for a better way of doing things, dissension from the accepted line are usually tolerated, although not easily in wartime, as the BBC's John Simpson discovered when he found himself out of step with the mainstream media during NATO's attack on Yugoslavia in 1999 (Gibson, 1999) and as many journalists have found since the start of the Iraq War in 2003. The wartime examples aside, for important qualifiers as they are, they belong to a category where other factors such as national security, negotiating positions and the safety of personnel may confuse the issue, few would argue today that dissent should be curtailed. Investigation, however, is quite another matter. You may disagree with authority, but you may not necessarily find the evidence of authority's misbehaviour, i.e. investigate.

On the other hand, Dorothy Byrne, a former editor of C4 *Dispatches*, believes that it is increasingly difficult to surprise audiences with investigative journalism because they increasingly assume corruption to be endemic (Byrne, 1999). If she is right, then it is quite possible that the target audience for this book believes that investigative journalism is in principle 'a good thing', even if it also believes that it does not exist! However, there are respectable people around who believe that investigative journalism is 'a bad thing'. It may be that the latter belong to a generation which prefers to believe that authority is usually trustworthy and only occasionally falls into dereliction, whereas the former are convinced that everyone is on the make and that the honest are the exceptions.

One of the most cogent critics of investigative journalism ('the lowest form of newspaper life') believes that it is not a discipline but a cast of mind which is typical of arrogant, privileged and sneering journalists in current affairs who dress up their desire for high ratings and fat salaries in 'nauseating' assertions about 'their responsibilities to society, the nation, the viewers, the truth', assertions in which he sees no justice (Ingham, 1991: 355). Bernard Ingham, former Chief Press Secretary to Mrs Thatcher, has diagnosed a number of journalists' diseases, of which the first is pertinent to investigative journalism: the conviction that government is inevitably, irrevocably and chronically up to no good, not to be trusted and conspiratorial. This is known as the 'le Carré syndrome' and so sours and contaminates the judgement of otherwise competent journalists as to render them pathetically negative, inaccurate and unreliable. In this context, Watergate has a lot to answer for here – and across the world (Ingham, 1991: 363). Ingham believes that the scepticism of investigative journalism is wrong and harmful, but it is not only at the national level at which he worked that politicians and officials question investigative journalists' right to delve. In 1999 Nottingham City Council invested considerable effort in taking C4 *Dispatches* to court to prevent a film being made about children in care; it then began a campaign advocating a change in the law to require that journalists investigate areas of council competence only with council permission and that the police institute checks on them (Lloyd, 1999; NCC, 1999). In Chapter 4 we look at the debate about the media and its effects on society and polity that has developed since the turn of the century.

Aside from the *justice* of investigative journalism, or its *right* to exist, some challenge its *competence* to undertake the tasks of scrutinising authority on the basis that where these tasks are necessary there should be legislation to create offices sufficiently skilled and resourced to do that work properly (Kedourie, 1988) and this is an interesting critique which deserves to be examined further. Another view of investigative journalism is represented by Charles Moore, a former editor of the *Daily Telegraph*, who sees it as a distraction from the proper functions of journalism, which are to report and to analyse. He has said, 'there is a higher aspiration than exposing corruption. . . . It is to tell people the news, and to interpret it in a way they find interesting, honest and helpful' (Page, 1998: 46).

We might see a contradiction in Moore's views. After all, if the work of the investigative journalist is to be lauded, then surely this is an acknowledgement that it is necessary. It is necessary to those who acknowledge that, sometimes at least, reporting what authority says, or even analysing it, is not enough; because authority may have an agenda that is counter to the general interest; because there are officials and politicians who are swayed by ignorance or self-interest; because there are systems that work to the detriment of people who have no voice. Where there are no institutions capable of performing the functions which investigative journalism has taken on, then to deny the need for investigative journalism is to deny either that these things are possible or that they matter. After all, as the eminent journalist and former editor of the (London) *Evening Standard*, said approvingly that he was advised as a young journalist, 'They lie, they lie, they lie' (Max Hastings on the BBC's *Any Questions?* 1 May 1999). If they lie, then someone must uncover the truth.

Investigative journalism and the news agenda

News journalism, which has been much written about by academics, has a broadly agreed set of values, often referred to as 'newsworthiness': a typical textbook for trainee journalists states that those events are suitable for news which have proximity, relevance, immediacy, drama and so forth (Boyd, 1994). The news journalist makes his or her selection from a range of conventionally accepted sources of information, sources which are in effect the providers of the 'news agenda' and whose regular production of information is diarised; selection from them is made according to these and other criteria of 'newsworthiness'. The multitude of factors that tend to condition his or her acceptance of sources as bona fide and the way in which he or she treats the information has been extensively studied and is reviewed in Shoemaker (1996) and McQuail (1994) among others.

Investigative stories are different in that they may not be on the same agenda. They involve a subject that the journalist has to insist is something we should know about, in effect, by saying 'look at this, isn't it shocking!'; the basis of the insistence is a moral one. In common among the eight cases dealt with in this book is that they cover happenings that journalists believed, or, in the case of Mark D'Arcy, later realised, required attention because they amount to a dereliction of standards. The topics have varying distances from established public moral consciousness; you might say that the subject of cruelty to animals and environmental degradation is well established and that the *Cook Report* programme described below merely satisfies existing moral assumptions. At the other extreme *Dispatches*, in the Chapter 15 example, sought to extend the audience's ideas of what is acceptable, as did Tolstoy's research of war crimes.

John Pilger considers that the term investigative journalism 'came into common parlance some ten years ago in correlation with the decline of inquiry, curiosity and mission among journalists' (Pilger, 1999). This decline he attributes to the domination of media conglomerates by their entertainment interests, changes in employment practises which have made journalists frightened to push, multi-skilling in the newsrooms and the 'corporate solitary confinement' or isolation from the population that has come about thanks to the relocation of news centres and to time pressures. He would like to see the term investigative journalist rejected as a tautology since 'all journalists should be investigative' but does not believe that the conditions at present exist for any but specialists to be so.

Relationship to reporting and analysis

News reporting is descriptive and news reporters are admired when they describe in a manner that is accurate, explanatory, vivid or moving, regardless of medium. Analytical journalism, on the other hand, seeks to take the data available and reconfigure it, helping us to ask questions about the situation or statement or see it in a different way. Clive Edwards, of the BBC's flagship current affairs programme *Panorama*, argues that even though his programme is not always investigative in the sense of resulting from long-term investigation and revelation of the hidden: in some sense every week's *Panorama* is telling you about things that you do not know enough about. Even a relatively innocuous subject such as house prices will be treated in such a way as to show you how they are affecting society and to bring to your attention the problems caused by the situation that most people take for granted. We are trying to get to the bottom of exactly what is happening, the forces behind it (Edwards, 1999).

Going further than this, investigative journalists also want to know whether the situation presented to us is the reality, as for example in 'Inspecting the Inspectors' (Chapter 15); they further invite us to be aware of something that we are not hearing about at all, as in *File on Four*'s 'Insolvency Practitioners' (Chapter 13) or to care about something that is not being cared about (as in the Chinese prisoners in Chapter 22). At its furthest extent investigative journalism questions the basis of orthodoxy, challenging the account of reality that the powers that be wish us to accept. In Lloyd's words: modern information suppliers are very powerful and sophisticated; they create an image of what they want us to believe by taking some aspects of the truth and weaving it into an image that is a denial of the truth. Journalists must not be lulled into believing that this is the truth. We really have got to show that we are up to the task of demonstrating that there are other ways of seeing things, that their premises are wrong (Lloyd, 1998).

Definitions of significance

Whereas news deals very rapidly with received information, usually accepting what is defined for it by authority (ministries, police, fire service, universities, established spokesmen) as events appropriate for transformation into news, investigative journalism selects its own information and prioritises it in a different way. The distinction is not by any means absolute and neither are news editors as passive nor investigative journalists as active as this simplification suggests. Moreover there are great differences between commercial and public channels, national and regional ones, nevertheless the distinction is broadly true. Taking the events supplied for them, news journalists apply news values in prioritising those events; investigative journalism picks and chooses according to its own definition of significance. What are those definitions? Investigative journalism comes in so many shapes and sizes that it is not easy to generalise.

14

That stories affect many is the criterion of one journalist; another is content to reveal what has been done to only one victim. There is, though, always a victim and, even if it is collective, always a villain to blame. Usually there is a failure of the system, whether that of the administration of justice, or of bureaucratic management, or of the regulatory bodies of this or that sphere. The villains may be so because they stand to make money, as in the business stories sketched in Chapter 10, because they are brutal xenophobes, as in Pilger's revelations of East Timor, or because they are ignorant and deluded as the *Dispatches* series claimed policy-makers and managers to be in an investigation of age discrimination in employment (C4 *Dispatches*: 'An Age Apart', 1993).

All the villains want to stop the story coming out, or at least control its presentation. A common definition of investigative journalism is 'going after what someone wants to hide' although not everything that someone wants to hide is worth going after. Jonathon Calvert, of *Insight*, the *Observer*, and the *Express*, says 'I want to expose a bad practice, not a bad person'; the founding Head of C4 News and Current Affairs, David Lloyd, wants the investigative journalist to ask 'What individual, what institution, does not want this story told, and of what potency are they? The more important the answer, the more engaging the task' (Lloyd, 1998). Similarly, Alan Rusbridger, Editor of the *Guardian*, suggests that the quality of target is what defines investigative journalism from mere exposure journalism. He says: 'What's the public interest in a cricketer having a love romp in a hotel room or a rugby player having smoked cannabis 20 years ago? But if elected representatives are arguing a case in Parliament but not revealing that they are being paid to do so, then that strikes at the heart of democracy. That's public interest; this is an easy distinction' (Rusbridger, 1999).

The *Daily Mail* argues the same:

> The *Daily Mail* is generally conservative but not necessarily Conservative. Our natural inclination is to be critical of governments and sceptical of the claims of politicians. In the Major years the *Daily Mail* was fervently critical of the Conservative government, while the *Mail on Sunday* supported it. At the 1997 election the *Evening Standard* supported Labour, the *Mail on Sunday* the SDP and only the *Daily Mail* the Conservatives. At that time our proprietor Lord Rothermere sat on the cross benches of the House of Lords but said that were he able to vote he would vote Labour. The point is that if someone needs investigating, we don't care what their party is.
>
> (Esser, 2007)

The moral impetus

The urge to get at the truth and to clarify the difference between right and wrong is most clearly evident in the miscarriage of justice stories, where every possible trick has to be used to encourage the audience to see an event as a contradiction of equity and where the audience, if anything, must be presumed to be sceptical of claims of innocence by murderers and thieves. In the revelations of ministerial misconduct over 'Arms to Iraq' (Chapter 12) the context of wars in which extreme suffering was taking place was used to demonstrate the moral dimension to what would otherwise have been minor dishonesties by people in power. Today the Rendition story (Chapter 11) highlights the same moral defectiveness.

Usually investigative journalists appeal to our existing standards of morality, standards they know that they can rely upon being held by people they know will be shocked by their violation. In this sense they are 'policing the boundaries' between order and deviance, in which case the image of the investigative journalist as intrepidly stepping outside the established order and accusing society is a romantic one; he or she rarely if ever does that. Even in the case of, say, a Serb journalist condemning atrocities by his 'own side' in Kosovo, we must assume that the Serb is appealing to moral standards that he or she believes to be more fundamental to his compatriots than current xenophobia. The *Dispatches* on ageism (C4, 1993) can be construed as an attempt to step outside the orthodoxy of the society and appeal, similarly, to a higher moral law. Animal Rights activists might say that they too were trying to extend our moral boundaries. The fact that much investigative journalism ends with legislation or regulation being promised or designed is not therefore an accident.

Ettema and Glasser (1988) have argued that investigative journalists are also telling stories to fit moral types, rather as I have described in news. At the risk of simplifying an extensive argument, I summarise their position in their words: 'The task is accomplished by cueing the audience's response to these characters through the emplotting of events as recognisably moralistic stories and, more specifically, through the skilful use of such story elements as point of view, ironic detail and ritual denial' (Ettema and Glasser, 1988). To say that investigative journalism fits into cultural categories is not necessarily to diminish it. Even if investigative journalists are less autonomous in identifying wicked things and inspiring moral umbrage than popular culture might have us believe, they may nevertheless be expanding our ideas of what we should think or care about, making us think in a certain way about an event or an issue. Moreover, the claim that they are reaching for 'the truth' is not necessarily rendered absurd by the acknowledgement that there is no truth, in the sense of an absolute hard fact against which to measure their own versions, because what the investigative journalist is after, as with the historian, is a more complete version of the truth.[4] In 1938 Dobrée put it better than I can: 'Most of us have ceased to believe, except provisionally, in truths, and we feel that what is important is not so much truth as the way our minds move towards truths' (cit. in Houghton, 1957: 430). Our minds can move towards a more complete truth by collecting good evidence and by corroborating accounts of people who can either be shown to be disinterested or who speak from different vantage points. Thus, while moral purpose may be a defining characteristic of investigative journalism, so is attention to the evidence used to support that purpose. In fact, Jonathon Calvert defines investigative journalism by the attention paid to the evidence:

> Some stories you make five calls on, some twenty. When you are making a hundred, that's investigative journalism. The story may land in your lap – it's the substantiation that makes it an investigative story, because when you realise people are lying to you, blocking you, then you have to find different ways of getting hold of the information and it can take a lot longer. Also you have to be very careful when you are making serious allegations against people, then the evidence really matters.
>
> (Calvert, 1999)

Alan Rusbridger:

> All journalism is investigative to a greater or lesser extent, but investigative journalism – though it is a bit of a tautology – is that because it requires more, it's where the investigative element is more pronounced.
>
> (Rusbridger, 1999)

When asked what skills are of most importance to the investigative journalist, those as diverse as Phillip Knightley, Steve Haywood and David Leppard put first the desk skills. By this they mean the thorough knowledge of information sources and types and the rules that govern them, the ability to read documents for significance, and an understanding of statistics. There are good descriptions of the relevance of these skills in Eddy's (1976) and Knightley's (1997) chapters on the thalidomide story. In the cases selected in this book at least eight different families of documents are required research material, and the ability to master them precedes any employment of the interpersonal skills often cited as being essential too; the empathy with others that will get them to talk; the ability to take account of potential impediments to truth such as false memory and question formulation; the gall and wit to doorstep and the ability to efface oneself sufficiently to go undercover if necessary. The most amusing description of those last mentioned skills is probably by the German investigative journalist, Gunther Wallraff (1978).

Motivations

What are their aims? With clash after clash between journalists and government during the eighteen years of Conservative rule in Britain (1979–1997) it was an understandable assumption made by some that investigative journalism was merely a tactical weapon of the left. The then government was very happy to fuel this prejudice in order to justify its resistance to criticism; however there is no reason to assume that investigative journalism is a prerogative of the left. Scepticism about powerful institutions and privileges has also been an aspect of the attitudes of conservatives; indeed the leading writer on modern Conservative thought identifies skepticism as *the* conservative trait (O'Hara, 2007).

Nevertheless its most prominent practitioners, as with their colleagues in general journalism, have preferred to associate themselves with the left (Weaver, 1998: 151). Paul Foot has long been associated with revolutionary socialism but, since we are neither undertaking a psychological profile of Foot nor trying to understand how aspects of English culture manifest themselves through him, this fact can be separated from his work as an investigator of injustices through the *Daily Mirror* column that he wrote for thirteen years. His books alleging injustice include *Who Killed Hanratty?* (1971), *The Helen Smith Story* (1983), *Who Framed Colin Wallace* (1989) and *Murder at the Farm: Who Killed Carl Bridgwater?* (1993); none can have seemed very promising cases at the outset. According to another journalist, Peter Jay, Foot's motivation is moral: 'He has a natural, decent sensitivity to the oppression of the underdogs in society, the less fortunate' (Langdon, 1993). Foot himself said he felt 'revulsion at the notion of people being locked up for something they did not do, and the obvious injustice done to them as individuals' (Preston, 1999: 3).

He went on:

> It is the responsibility of the individual journalist to find the truth. There are things always to be discovered, never believe anything until it is officially denied; there is another story which is normally more accurate. [It is the job of the investigative journalist] to start the ball rolling, be inquisitive, ask questions independently of the government and every other power structure inside society. Unless people are there asking questions of those establishments, they become stronger and more reckless.
>
> (Preston, 1999: 5)

John Pilger has painted on a larger canvas, making around 50 documentary films as well as writing extensively. His principal theme has been how our governments pursue policies abroad which not only corrupt or wreck other societies but which damage us too, and that they do these things for personal glory and to line the pockets of rich men who hide behind them. As he puts it 'the prime role of journalists is to tell people when they are being conned'. His first well-known revelation was of the extent of rebellion in the ranks of the US army in Vietnam in the late 1970s, a fact that had not been reported but was having, and would have, an enormous effect upon the prosecution of the war. Later his film *Year Zero* showed what Pol Pot's crazed idealism had done to Cambodia after the slaughtering of millions and the destruction of the cities. He also made an unexpected film on poverty in Japan that gave a very different angle on that country to the take offered by most other journalists who concentrated upon its wealth and power. In the 1990s Pilger returned repeatedly to the sufferings of the East Timor population under Indonesian rule, a rule established by Portuguese and Australian government collusion. In the preface to one of Pilger's books, writer Martha Gelhorn (1992) says:

> [Pilger] has taken on the great theme of justice and injustice. The misuse of power against the powerless. The myopic, stupid, cruelty of governments. The bullying and lies that shroud *realpolitik*, a mad game played at the top, which is a curse to real people.
>
> (Gelhorn, 1992)

Other established investigative journalists are seen in the same way and have the same view of their aims. They want to affect the way we see events or to make us care about something we have not thought of before; tell us what is and is not acceptable behaviour; champion the weak; accuse the guilty. Phillip Knightley explained why he felt motivated to spend five years of his life on the thalidomide investigation:

> At first journalistic interest . . . then, when I had met a victim, moral indignation, outrage . . . at the sheer effrontery of men who could put pecuniary interests before their victim's lives.
>
> (Knightley, 1999)

From another generation, Dorothy Byrne, appointed editor of *Dispatches* in 1998 after working on *The Big Story* and *World in Action*, attributes her interest in investigative journalism to the shock she felt when, as a student, she went to West Africa on VSO (Voluntary Service Overseas). She says, 'I knew I couldn't do anything about the suffering, but at least I could tell people who might'. She continued:

> There are really important things in the world that people must know about, and if you don't tell them about them then they won't know and they won't be able to do anything about them.
>
> (Byrne, 1999)[5]

As we discuss in Chapter 4, there has been a very great change in attitudes to public affairs over the past ten years which has, if anything, increased the intensity of the investigatory urge among the kind of people who have always wanted to hold the powerful to account. The epitome of the new inquisitor may be Peter Oborne, some of whose work is described in Chapter 4. Like his predecessors he appears moved by an indignation against the brazenness of the powerful.

To summarise, investigative journalists attempt to get at the truth where the truth is obscure because it suits others that it be so; they choose their topics from a sense of right and wrong which we can only call a moral sense, but in the manner of their research they attempt to be dispassionately evidential. They are doing more than disagreeing with how society runs; they are pointing out that it is failing by its own standards. They expose, but they expose in the public interest, which they define. Their efforts, if successful, alert us to failures in the system and lead to politicians, lawyers and policemen taking action even as they fulminate, action that may result in legislation or regulation. How this situation arose is the subject of the next three chapters.

Notes

1 Lee, Sangbok (2007) The Impact of Video UGC Expansion on Participatory Journalism, unpublished dissertation for the *MA Global Media*, London: University of Westminster.
2 Here is a subject of study: are there any similarities between the heroic stories of boys' fiction 1850–1950, of which Henty is the most famous exponent, and this new phenomenon?
3 Andrew Marr, *My Trade* (2005).
4 This is discussed extensively by Ettema and Glasser (1998: 132). See also two very relevant works, R. J. Evans (1997) and Fernandez-Armesto (1997).
5 However, Byrne is not naive about the motivations of some of those pitching programme ideas to her and claims to take great care to check out the facts she is given lest there has either been deliberate misrepresentation, or journalists are not careful enough or too afraid to tell her when stories do not stand up, or simply do not have the skills. In a casualised industry with no agreed training, investigative journalists may have neither the skill formation nor the hinterland of advice and support provided by the larger current affairs establishments of the past.

Bibliography

Behrens, J.C. (1978) *Typewriter Guerrillas*. Chicago: Nelson Hall.
Boyd, A. (1994) *Broadcast Journalism, Techniques of Radio and TV News*. Oxford: Focal.
de Burgh, H. (1998) Audience, journalist and text in television news. Paper delivered at the Annual Conference of the International Association for Media and Communications Research, 27 July 1998.
Byrne, D. (1999) Talk to the students of the MA Investigative Journalism course at Nottingham Trent University, 29 April 1999.
Calvert, J. (1999) Interview with Hugo de Burgh, 28 May 1999.
Central TV (1990) *The Cook Report*: 'Where did the Money Go?' Birmingham: Central TV. Transmitted 5 March 1990, producer Clive Entwhistle, reporter Roger Cook.
Channel 4 (1993) *Dispatches*: 'An Age Apart'. London: Channel 4 TV. Reporter/producer Hugo de Burgh.
Chepesiuk, R., Howell, H. and Lee, E. (1997) *Raising Hell: Straight Talk with Investigative Journalists*. London: McFarland.
Curran, J. and Seaton, J. (2005) *Power without Responsibility: The Press and Broadcasting in Britain*, 5th edn. London: Routledge.
Dorril, S. and Ramsay, R. (1991) *Smear! Wilson and the Secret State*. London: Fourth Estate.

Eddy, P. (1976) *Destination Disaster*. London: Granada.

Edwards, C. (1999) Interview with Hugo de Burgh, 25 June 1999.

Esser, R. (2007) Hugo de Burgh interview with Robin Esser, Managing Editor of the Daily Mail, 151107.

Evans, H. (1997) Prometheus unbound. Iain Walker Memorial Lecture, Green College Oxford, May.

Evans, R. J. (1997) *In Defence of History*. London: Granta.

Faulkner, R. (1998) Tolstoy pamphlet. On the internet at www.tolstoy.co.uk.

Fernandez-Armesto, F. (1997) *Truth: A History*. London: Bantam.

Foot, P. (1973) *Who Killed Hanratty?* St Albans: Panther.

Foot, P. with Ron Smith (1983) *The Helen Smith Story*. Glasgow: Fontana.

Foot, P. (1989) *Who Framed Colin Wallace?* London: Macmillan.

Foot, P. (1993) *Murder at the Farm: Who Killed Carl Bridgewater?* London: Penguin.

Fukuyama, F. (1993) *The End of History and the Last Man*. London: Penguin.

Gelhorn, M. (1992) Introduction. In J. Pilger (1992) *Distant Voices*. London: Vintage.

Gibson, J. (1999) BBC veteran denies bias. On the internet at http://www.newsunlimited.co.uk/BBC/story/0,2763,43185,00.html.

Gillmor, Dan (2006) *We the Media: Grassroots Journalism by the People, for the People*. Sebastopol, CA: O'Reilly.

Hill, P., Young, M. and Sargant, T. (1985) *More Rough Justice*. London: Penguin.

Houghton, W. E. (1957) *The Victorian Frame of Mind*. New Haven: Yale University Press.

Ingham, B. (1991) *Kill the Messenger*. London: Harper Collins.

Kedourie, E. and Mango, A. (1988) Talking about the BBC. *Encounter*, 71 Sep/Oct: 60–4.

Knightley, P. (1997) *A Hack's Progress*. London: Jonathan Cape.

Knightley, P. (1999) Interview with Hugo de Burgh, 22 May 1999.

Langdon, J. (1993) High noon at the Holborn oasis. *Guardian*, 29 March 1993.

Langer, J. (1998) *Tabloid Television*. London: Routledge.

Lee, Sangbok (2007) The Impact of Video UGC Expansion on Participatory Journalism, unpublished dissertation for the MA Global Media, University of Westminster.

Liu, B. (1990) *A Higher Kind of Loyalty*. London: Methuen.

Lloyd, D. (1998) Talk to the students of the MA Investigative Journalism course at Nottingham Trent University, 19 February 1998.

Lloyd, D. (1999) Information passed to Hugo de Burgh, 10 June 1999.

McQuail, D. (1994) *Mass Communication Theory*. London: Sage.

Marr, A. (2005) *My Trade: A Short History of British Journalism*. London: Pan Books.

Media Center of API (2003) *We Media: How Audiences are Shaping the Future of News and Information*. Stanford, CA: The American Press Institute.

Milne, S. (1995) *The Enemy Within: The Secret War Against the Miners*. London: Pan.

Northmore, D. (1996) *Lifting the Lid: A Guide to Investigative Research*. London: Cassell.

NCC (1999) City wins fight. Press release from Nottingham City Council (NCC), received 8 June 1999. (Further information was requested but not received.)

O'Hara, Keiron (2007) *After Blair*. Cambridge: Icon.

Page, B. (1998) A defence of 'low' journalism. *British Journalism Review*, 9 (1).

Pilger, J. (1992) *Distant Voices*. London: Vintage.

Pilger, J. (1999) Interview with Hugo de Burgh, 29 June 1999.

Prentice, Eve-Ann (1999) My nights under fire in Pristina. *Times*, 22 May 1999.

Preston, Louisa (1999) Paul Foot: the role of the journalist in the surveillance of justice. An unpublished essay for Broadcast Practice 3, BA BJ, Nottingham Trent University.

Rusbridger, A. (1999) Interview with Hugo de Burgh, 25 May 1999.

Shoemaker, P. (1996) *Mediating the Message*. London: Longman.

Silvester, C. (1994) *The Penguin Book of Interviews*. London: Penguin.

Tuchman, G. (1973) Making news by doing work: routinizing the unexpected. *American Journal of Sociology*, 79.

Ullmann, J. and Colbert, J. (1991) *The Reporter's Handbook: An Investigator's Guide to Documents and Techniques*, 2nd edn. New York: St Martin's Press.

Wallraff, G. (1978) *The Undesirable Journalist*. London: Pluto.

Weaver, D. H. (ed.) (1998) *The Global Journalist*. New Jersey: Hampton Press.

Weir, D. (1983) *How the Center for Investigative Journalism Gets a Story*. Reading, MA: Addison-Wesley.

Further reading

de Burgh, Hugo (ed.) (2005) *Making Journalists: Diverse Models, Global Issues*. London: Routledge.

Ettema, J. S. and Glasser T. L. (1998) *Custodians of Conscience: Investigative Journalism and Public Virtue*. New York: Cambridge University Press.

Evans, H. (1997) Prometheus unbound. *Iain Walker Memorial Lecture*, Green College Oxford, May.

Gaines, William C. (1998) *Investigative Reporting for Print and Broadcast*, 2nd edn. Belmont: Wadsworth.

Gillmor, Dan (2006) *We the Media: Grassroots Journalism by the People, for the People*. Sebastopol, CA: O'Reilly.

Media Center of API (2003) *We Media: How Audiences are Shaping the Future of News and Information*. Stanford, CA: The American Press Institute.

Spark, David (2003) *Investigative Reporting, A study in technique*. London: Focal Press.

CONTACTS

Contact details of some organisations, sites and publications useful to investigative journalists

Compiled by Steven McIntosh

British Journalism Review
A forum for analysis and debate, submit the best and the worst to scrutiny, and raise the level of dialogue.

www.bjr.org.uk

editor@bjr.org.uk

020 7324 8500

British Journalism Review,
SAGE Publications
1 Oliver's Yard
55 City Road
London EC1Y 1SP

Broadcast
The UK's leading television & radio publication.

www.broadcastnow.co.uk

bro@subscription.co.uk

0870 830 4965

Broadcast
Tower Publishing Services
Tower House
Sovereign Park
Market Harborough
LE16 9EF

Campaign for Freedom of Information

A non-profit organisation working to improve public access to official information and ensure that the Freedom of Information Act is implemented effectively.

http://www.cfoi.org.uk

admin@cfoi.demon.co.uk

020 7831 7477

The Campaign for Freedom of Information
Suite 102
16 Baldwins Gardens
London EC1N 7RJ

Campaign for Press Freedom

Established 1979, an independent voice for media reform. Promoters of diverse and democratic media.

www.cpbf.org.uk

freepress@cpbf.org.uk

020 8521 5932

Campaign for Press Freedom
Vi & Garner Smith House
23 Orford Road
Walthamstow
London E17 9NL

The Center for Public Integrity*

A non-profit organisation dedicated to producing original, responsible investigative journalism on issues of public concern.

www.publicintegrity.org

(202) 466–1300

The Center for Public Integrity
910 17th Street, NW, Suite 700
Washington, DC 20006

Centre for Investigative Journalism*

A University based, non-profit organisation in London, which offers advice on legal, publishing and source protection for international journalists and whistleblowers.

www.tcij.org

gavin.macfadyen@tcij.org (director)

020 7040 8224

City University
G215 Gloucester Building
Gloucester Way
London
EC1V 0HB

Chartered Institute of Journalists

The oldest professional body for journalists in the world, one of two trade unions in the UK that can boast a Royal Charter.

www.cioj.co.uk

memberservices@cioj.co.uk

020 7252 1187

The Chartered Institute of Journalists
2 Dock Offices
Surrey Quays Road
London
SE16 2XU

Committee to Protect Journalists

An independent, non-profit organisation dedicated to defending press freedom worldwide.

www.cpj.org

info@cjp.org

212–465–1004

Committee to Protect Journalists
11th Floor
330 7th Avenue
New York
NY

Commonwealth Press Union

An association whose members are newspaper groups (some with several hundred newspapers), newspapers and news agencies in 49 countries of the Commonwealth.

www.cpu.org.uk

020 7583 7733

Commonwealth Press Union
17 Fleet Street
London
EC4Y 1AA

International/European Federation of Journalists
Established 1926, the world's largest organisation of journalists. Promotes international action to defend press freedom.

www.ifj.org

efj@ifj.org

(+32)–2–235 22 02

International Federation of Journalists
IPC-Residence Palace, Bloc C
Rue de la Loi 155
B-1040 Brussels
BELGIUM

International Journalists' Network
Set up to help connect journalists with the opportunities and information they need to better themselves and raise journalism standards in their countries.

www.ijnet.org

editor@icfj.org

202–737–3700

ICFJ 1616 High Street
NW Third Floor
Washington, DC 20006
USA

Journalism UK
An extensive directory of links that journalists might find useful in their everyday working lives.

www.journalismuk.co.uk

editor@journalismuk.co.uk

Media Standards Trust
An independent, not-for-profit organisation that aims to find ways to foster the highest standards of excellence in news journalism and ensure public trust in news is nurtured.

www.mediastandardstrust.org

info@mediastandardstrust.org

020 7608 8149

Media Standards Trust
Ground Floor, Discovery House
28–42 Banner Street
London
EC1Y 8QE

Media Watch
A group devoted to campaigning for decency and accountability in the media.

www.mediawatchuk.org.uk

info@mediawatchuk.org

01233 633936

Media Watch UK
3 Willow House, Kennington Road
Ashford
Kent
TN24 ONR

National Union of Journalists
Founded 1907, the trade union for journalists working in the UK and Republic of Ireland.

www.nuj.org.uk

info@nuj.org.uk

020 7278 7916

NUJ Head Office
Headland House
308–312 Gray's Inn Road
London
WC1X 8DP

National Whistleblower Center*
An American nonprofit, tax-exempt, educational and advocacy organisation dedicated to helping whistleblowers. Since 1988, the Center has used whistleblowers' disclosures to improve environmental protection, nuclear safety, and government and corporate accountability.

www.whistleblowers.org

contact@whistleblowers.org

202–342–1903

P.O. Box 3768
Washington, DC 20027

Ofcom
The independent regulatory body and competition authority for the UK communication industries. Ofcom has responsibility for television, radio, telecommunications and wireless communications services.

www.ofcom.org.uk

020 7981 3000

Ofcom
Riverside House
2a Southwark Bridge Road
London
SE1 9HA

POLIS

A forum where journalists and the wider world can examine and discuss the media and its impact on society. Joint venture of the London College of Communication and the London School of Economics and Political Science

www.lse.ac.uk/collections/polis

polis@lse.ac.uk

LSE
Houghton Street
London
WC2A 2AE

PR Watch

Website and weekly e-mail bulletin. Strengthens democracy by investigating and exposing public relations spin and propaganda, and by promoting media literacy and citizen journalism.

www.prwatch.org

editor@prwatch.org

(608) 260–9713

Center for Media & Democracy
520 University Avenue, Suite 227
Madison
Wisconsin 53703

PR Week

The UK's leading Public Relations publication.

www.prweek.com

020 8267 4150

PR Week
174 Hammersmith Road
London
W6 7JP

Press Gazette
A weekly publication aimed at journalists, featuring up-to-date news and information from the industry.

www.pressgazette.co.uk

pged@pressgazette.co.uk

020 7566 5777

Press Gazette
Wilmington Business Information
6–14 Underwood Street
London
N1 7JQ

Privacy International
A human rights group formed in 1990 as a watchdog on surveillance and privacy invasions by governments and corporations.

www.privacyinternational.org

privacyint@privacy.org

0208 123 7933

Privacy International London Headquarters
6–8, Amwell Street
London
EC1R 1UQ

Project for Excellence in Journalism
A research organisation that specialises in using empirical methods to evaluate and study the performance of the press.

www.journalism.org

mail@journalism.org

202–419–3650

Project for Excellence in Journalism
1615 L Street N.W. 700
Washington, DC 20036

Reporters Without Borders
Founded in 1985, an international company that operates in five continents; Reporters Without Borders fights for press freedom on a daily basis.

www.rsf.org

rsf-uk@rsf.org

0790 689 3048

Head Office:
Reporters Sans Frontières
47 Rue Vivienne
Paris
France

Reuters Institute for the Study of Journalism
Established 2006, a university research centre for international comparative journalism.

http://reutersinstitute.politics.ox.ac.uk

reuters.institute@politics.ox.ac.uk

01865 611090

The Reuters Institute for the Study of Journalism
Department of Politics and International Relations
University of Oxford
13 Norham Gardens
Oxford
OX2 6PS

Society of Editors
The Society of Editors works to protect the freedom of all sectors of the media to report on behalf of the public.

www.societyofeditors.co.uk

info@societyofeditors.org

01223 304080

Society of Editors
University Centre
Granta Place
Mill Lane
Cambridge
CB2 1RU

Spinwatch
A nonprofit organisation specialising in information and whistleblowing in the role of the media, genetic engineering, the oil industry, tobacco smuggling, farm and food and the war in Iraq.

www.spinwatch.org

whistleblower@spinwatch.org

07939 529 349

University of Westminster
Britain's leading undergraduate media course at BA level; Westminster University provides degrees in Journalism, PR, Television, Film and Radio.

www.wmin.ac.uk

course-enquiries@wmin.ac.uk

020 7915 5511

School of Media, Arts & Design
University of Westminster (Harrow Campus)
Watford Road
Northwick Park
Harrow
London
HA1 3TP

Voice of the Listener and Viewer
VLV represents the citizen and consumer interest in broadcasting and works for quality and diversity in British broadcasting.

www.vlv.org.uk

info@vlv.org.uk

01474 352835

Voice of The Listener & Viewer
101 King's Drive
Gravesend
Kent
DA12 5BQ

Note

* Information provided by Gavin MacFadyen

2

THE EMERGENCE OF
INVESTIGATIVE JOURNALISM

Hugo de Burgh

By the mid-nineteenth century the conditions had been created for the appearance of a concept of journalism that has been a model ever since and whose relationship to the polity has been an aspiration and an archetype.

Journalism rapidly developed some professional norms; its own techniques; a variety of genres, of which investigative journalism would be one. Moreover it fed upon the increasing rationalism of intellectual discourse in the period and upon that scientific approach of finding truth from facts which was the Enlightenment's greatest gift; in so doing it advanced the idea of objectivity, or at least impartiality. As with the great popular novelists, investigative journalists married rational observation with moral empathy and made exploitation and abuse an ever more likely topic of analysis, discussion and investigation.

However, when in the early years of the twentieth century, the media became big business, journalism as here defined was threatened. Just as their writings became 'the spaces between the ads' so the moral agenda became merely another commodity, or, like pictures of naked girls, another tool with which to attract a buyer. Public Service Broadcasting (PSB) in the 1960s to 1980s gave investigative journalism a new status, but the decline of PSB has been a severe blow.

Before the nineteenth century

Tales of *Perseus*, *Horatius* or *Beowulf* and chronicles such as the *Odyssey* or *Leila and Madjnoun* predate writing. With writing there emerged quite rapidly a distinction between stories like these and facts, as the 'Record of Events' was created, a distinction which, in the light of current debates about journalism and reality, may seem to us artificial.

Traditional histories of journalism usually start their tales early, some even as early as 500 BC, because the Egyptians were then producing news reports by writing their hieroglyphics onto papyrus. Around the same time, before the Caesars, the Roman Republic published *Acts Diurnia*, daily events, in the forum. Here is the kind of thing:

Fourth of the Calenda of April. The fasces with Livinius the Consul. It thundered; an oak was struck with lightning on that part of Mount Palatine, called Summa Velia, early in the afternoon. A fray happened in a tavern at the lower end of Bankers Street, in which the keeper of the Hog-in-Armour Tavern was dangerously wounded. Tertinius the Aedile fined the butchers for selling meat which had not been inspected by the overseers of the markets.

(cit. in Andrews 1859: 11)

In China, from very early times, government sent out investigators to report on economic and social conditions and on the opinions of the populace. By AD 700, Chinese central government officials had established their own records of events which were sent out to the provincial and county officials. In Europe too, though 700 years later, governments tried to ensure that information on events supported their case both by suppressing alternative views and by publishing their own accounts. King Henry VIII of England (1509–47), in his disputes with Rome and with rebels at home, published his own accounts for wider distribution (Andrews, 1859: 23), made possible by the diffusion of paper-making and printing.[1]

One of the earliest reports known in England is that of the Battle of Agincourt in 1415. Its fantastical style was reproduced with the European news pamphlets of the succeeding two centuries, as printers began to publish accounts of current events that were dramatic and also staunchly patriotic and pro-government. Reporting was often vivid, luridly describing, during the time when England was threatened with an invasion from Spain, the 'strange and most cruel whippes which the Spaniards had prepared to whippe and torment English men and women' (cit. in Cranfield. 1978) and another detailed the massacres and rapes carried out by Spanish troops in The Netherlands:

James Messier being stricken over his belly, so that his intrailes did issue forth, dyed a few dayes after. The wife of the said Messier was so sore beaten, that she can never be her owne woman again. Peter Riondet, killed as he came out of his bed, although he was seventie yeares olde, his wife is sore hurt, and is hardly likely to recover it.

(cit. in Cranfield, 1978: 3)

Gradually, these kinds of accounts translated themselves into announcements of what was going on in the present rather than what had happened, or into records that were intended to influence the present, produced in pamphlet form; in both cases their intentions were political.

The expansion of commerce in the sixteenth and seventeenth centuries created a different demand; the most interested customers of all media were now the traders. In medieval times most trade had been dominated by the state, rural communities were self sufficient, cities tiny, artisans local and traders the appendages of royal and noble households, but this changed over the following centuries and there was a tremendous growth in business. As early as the 1500s the more important trading families of Europe such as the Fuggers and Rothschilds already had their own private information networks. By the 1600s they were selling their news to other traders and by 1700 *Lloyds List*, a newspaper of business information, was established as a commercial venture. The concept of news as something distinct from chronicle, story or record, therefore, is at least 400 years old.

The career of the Frenchman Theophraste Renaudot (1586–1683) is instructive because it demonstrates both the new entrepreneurship in information and shows an interest in communication distinct from that of the pamphleteers. A fashionable medical practitioner in Paris whose clients included Cardinal Richelieu, he was tasked with inquiring into the health of the urban poor and then to be (in effect) government minister for the poor. He was convinced that one reason for poverty was the inability of people with work to offer to find those who needed it. Towns had grown too large for word of mouth to work, so he set up the *Bureau of Addresses*, a kind of job centre cum notice board cum free advertisement newspaper (Sgard, 1976).

It was as a byproduct of his *Bureau of Addresses* that Renaudot found himself collecting news. From collecting information about events, he went on to establish correspondence with knowledgeable people in different parts of the country and he noted what was being said in the pamphlets of the day. The government was concerned about scurrilous pamphlets and decided to license him to produce a digest of the information that he was obtaining which could be laced with information direct from the government, giving its point of view on events domestic and international (Smith, 1979).

The first edition of Renaudot's *Gazzette de France* was published in 1631. This kind of newspaper had existed in Holland and Germany for some time under the name of *corantos*. They had little editorial input, were dependent upon state approval and often subsidies and their circulations were limited to ruling class members and approved recipients. Like his less accomplished equivalent in England, the English printer–publisher Muddiman, he was first and foremost a businessman. They can be described as being of the first generation of information entrepreneur.

While Renaudot was at his most active, England was fighting a civil war. Ideas of equality and human rights canvassed by the Levellers and other radical factions during that war were gaining wide currency, and old authorities were challenged. More than this, the English Civil War provided the opportunity for competing interpretations of events, therefore competing newspapers and therefore polemic and partial propaganda. Conflicting interpretations and competition to get out the news first were very good for news entrepreneurs and by the early 1700s controversy and scathing critique of people in high places were more and more common, with Daniel Defoe and Jonathan Swift epitomising the style.

The English newsletters of the period, or *newesbookes* as they were called, were full of polemic. There was little gathering of news as we would understand it, although the glimmerings of the idea that truth should be sought from facts can be discerned. It was in England that what may be the first theory of the media was adumbrated by John Milton (1608–74) in his *Areopagitica* of 1644; according to Hartley (1992: 150), Milton argued the case that liberty is a condition of national greatness and journalism the means by which that liberty is to be assured. Hartley also makes the point that the idea of the reporter as someone identifying truth, what he calls the 'ideology of the eyewitness' predated the scientism normally associated with the Enlightenment. As the century wore on, there developed that scepticism of the religious mindset and attraction to scientific method, historical investigation and the questioning of all and every institution in ways that had been known to no previous civilisation; this was the basis for the idea of impartial evidence and of the reporter as being the one who gathers such evidence.

There were also economic reasons for the development of the media towards journalism. Printers needed to produce and sell ephemera since books often took a long time to shift and thus tied up their capital in stock. The increase in trade meant that there were well-established means of news distribution via the ports and posting systems that were developing rapidly. There was a growing market. The intellectual and cultural revolution in Europe was both a function of and the stimulus for publishing. Readership was limited to a minority, but by no means as small a minority as in the ancient civilisations. Thanks both to the relative simplicity of the Roman writing and Arabic numeral systems that Europeans now used, to the Protestant Reformation that had encouraged reading in indigenous languages and to other factors promoting literacy, that minority grew and probably grew faster in Northern Europe than anywhere else,[2] except perhaps America. There, Protestant settlers with an intense belief in the value of literacy and a passion for disputation as well as a need to get information from the Europe they had left behind, developed their own periodicals. They created, as in England, an audience, often based upon the coffee house where merchants and officials sat and read and talked; the first modern 'public' which was to be steadily enlarged over the course of the following two centuries and to which journalism became, as in Hartley's characterisation of the *Spectator*, 'an active agent in the *representation* of the imagined public to itself' (Hartley, 1992: 153).

Therefore, by the time of William Cobbett (1763–1835) and of the American Revolution (1775–83) there existed not only the newspaper as a conduit of business intelligence but also the idea of the newspaper as a vehicle of political polemic in competition with other propaganda and, inchoate but there, the ideal of truth-seeking. There was a readership, even an embryo public opinion. The Enlightenment had established well the idea of ideas, in other words that there was not one true factual answer to everything based upon religion, but that there were things to be discovered by observation, and upon which opinions might legitimately differ.

The influence of personality may be as important as that of material factors in accounting for the particular direction taken by Anglophone journalism. Why Milton, Defoe, Swift or Cobbett were to reason or act as they did is outside the scope of this survey, but the fact that they did so has influenced journalism. If one of the features of investigative journalism is the fearless uncovering of facts unpalatable to the powerful, then Cobbett is a distinguished precursor. Between 1810 and 1812 he spent two years in jail because he had denounced the flogging of militiamen who had protested against unjustified deductions from their pay (Green, 1983: 350). In the past, information entrepreneurs had gone to prison for offending someone high and mighty or for blasphemy or for getting the official line wrong – but Cobbett went to prison for defending the voiceless. It was an important moment in the development of journalism. How did he arrive at it?

Twenty years earlier, in 1780, Cobbett, the adventurous 17-year-old son of a small farmer signed up as a Redcoat instead of staying around home and labouring. He was sent to North America to fight in the war against the colonists and, while there and doing so well as to be promoted to sergeant major, amused himself with the study of English grammar. That study was to serve as the academic basis for the career of a great early journalist; but it was his own character that supplied the catalyst. Cobbett may have been a conservative in politics, but his journalism was intensely radical and his message was social revolution. He championed the oppressed, the exploited, the marginalised and the cheated.

His first act upon returning to England from America after army service in 1791 was to charge his officers with peculation; he had become outraged by the corruption of the army. However, he had not got his facts correct and the officers invented counter charges so that he had to flee to revolutionary France and then back to America, where he spent several years as a passionate pamphleteer condemning the failings of the new democracy and founding periodicals, including *Porcupine's Gazette*. America, too, became too hot for him and he fled back to England where he founded a magazine that launched attacks on corruption and misuse of public funds, unjust laws, low wages and absentee clergy, *Cobbett's Weekly Political Register*, which survived until his death. The quality of his invective found him loyal readers for his investigations and there are good examples in Derry (1968), from which the following is taken. Given the hue and cry created by people in rich countries over population in poor countries over the past 30 years, it is topical, as the article from which it is taken exposes Malthusian ideas as theoretical covering for attempts to prevent the poor from breeding because of the cost to the Poor Rates:

> In your book you show that, in certain cases, a crowded population has been attended with great evils, a great deal of unhappiness, misery and human degradation. You then, without any reason to bear you out,

predict, or leave it to be clearly inferred, that the same is likely to take place in England. Your principles are almost all false; and your reason, in almost every instance, is the same . . . It must be clear to every attentive reader of your book on *Population* that it was written for the sole purpose of preparing beforehand a justification for . . . deeds of injustice and cruelty.

(cit. in Derry, 1968)

In 1831 Cobbett was prosecuted for defending striking farm labourers and at the time of his death was being accused of encouraging rioting and rebellion by his championship of rural workers (Green, 1983: 164). His career illustrates some important social changes taking place in English society, as well as the connections between ideas, business and politics in France, England and the American states. He was a man who began without any establishment connections; he came from nowhere. It was issues, rather than entrepreneurship, that brought him to journalism. He wrote for a public for whom nobody had written before and in order to communicate with them translated the radical thinkers into simple language that ordinary people could understand when it was read out at inns and street corners. In the past journalists had been more concerned with court and religious politics than with social conditions; Cobbett wrote about matters that affected ordinary people. Among his achievements are the organisation of an efficient distribution system and the begetting of *Hansard*, the first published account of Parliamentary debates. Most of all, he created a new kind of journalism, providing a model for the radical journalism of the nineteenth century such as that of the *Black Dwarf*. Here is an example:

> The people of England have long been in error, it seems, upon the subject of the condition of the *Irish peasantry*; and Lord Castlereagh and Mr Curwen have stepped forward to set them right. It is not true, they say, that Ireland is the most debased and degraded and unhappy country in the world. They are a contented, a *high spirited* and a happy race of mortals . . . True it is, that they are almost in a state of nature, as it respects clothing and habitation: true it is, that their wretched cabins, built of mud, and destitute of cleanliness and convenience, are the very images of the abode of misery and desolation, that the inhabitants of these horrid looking receptacles, which a hottentot would disdain to dwell in, look forth from them in rags and tatters, staring like an unhappy bedlamite looking after some visionary beam of comfort; true it is, that their appearance only excites disgust; yet notwithstanding all this, they are *contented* and *cheerful* and *happy*.
>
> (cit. in Cranfield, 1978: 95)

A vigorous, sceptical and irreverent social journalism had appeared, the proclivities of which are demonstrated in the title of one of its most famous mastheads, *The Poor Man's Guardian*.

The nineteenth century

Journalism and the public sphere

In the first years of the nineteenth century newspapers in England could still be bullied by the authorities through taxation, threats of prosecution, offers of help and exclusive information, and the subsidy of government advertising. By 1860 this had changed. Newspapers became relatively independent of politicians. The radical press survived attempts to stifle it. It has often been remarked that the *Times* and a few other papers became the modern equivalents of the Ancient Greek *agora* or places where opinion-formers and decision-makers met to make public opinion. How had this come about?

Different historians give different weight to the various factors at play. Traditional English histories saw the easing of government restrictions on the press as the result of the struggles of progressives (Williams, 1957); others have preferred to emphasise the burgeoning power of the new business classes who resisted attempts by the political elite to dominate information (Harris, 1996: 106). To Franklin 'undoubtedly the most necessary change was the removal of what opponents dubbed "the taxes on knowledge" ' (Franklin, 1997: 78), by which he means advertising, newspaper stamp duty and duties on paper all repealed between 1853 and 1861. Technological change made it possible to print and distribute more – and larger – newspapers, and thus satisfy the growing demand. In today's parlance, moreover, the stakeholders in newspapers were many: first, the capital required was large and distributed, such that there were many ready to defend their interest; the revenue from advertisements rendered other sources of funds such as political subvention unnecessary; the readers were influential in guiding the policy of the paper; the inland transport revolution provided a much more extensive market and wide distribution gave to the opinions of the writers an influence that politicians began to fear to contravene.

The pre-eminence of the *Times* was clear; between 1800 and 1860, as Britain's position in the world consolidated a very large class of ascendant internationally aware, information hungry and influential bourgeois, it became their debating chamber. Thomas Barnes (editor of the *Times* 1817–41) was their spokesman and informant and he earned new readers by championing causes such as Parliamentary Reform and the victims of the Peterloo Massacre. Rising revenue meant he could spend more on investigation and he and his successors prided themselves on their access to information and their independence from pressure.

A flavour of the situation is conveyed by this well-repeated anecdote. In 1851 the *Times*, edited by John Delane, attacked the French Prime Minister Prince Louis Napoleon. Angry, he demanded that his Ambassador to London either put pressure on the British government to punish the *Times*, or buy a better press through bribery. His Ambassador tried to explain to him that life in England just wasn't like that:

> Someone has told you, Prince, that the hostility of the *Times* and the *Morning Chronicle* was provoked by pecuniary subsidies. Nothing could be more false than such an assertion and, believe me, on such an important subject I would not make a statement without being absolutely certain. . . . Although less than in France, political men in England are sufficiently anxious about newspaper criticism to have tried often to buy an organ so widely circulated as the *Times*: but they have always failed . . .
>
> (cit. in Cranfield, 1978: 160)

That ambassador had correctly noted that, as early as 1851 the *Times* was not amenable to the kind of influence proposed by his Prince. Whereas in the eighteenth century much of the political conflict had been about personalities, cliques and corruption, now with economic development at home and an empire to exploit abroad, and new classes depending upon both, government policies were of intense interest, both those which touched upon business affairs (foreign treaties, trade policy) or which had a wider constituency (social conditions and taxation). One 1832 paper gave as its aims:

> The abolition of tithes, the repeal of the Corn Laws; a more equitable system of taxation; the abolition of the hereditary peerage; an equitable reduction of the national debt; . . . a reform in the expenditure of the crown; and the abolition of all unmerited pensions and sinecures; the doing away with an expensive state religion, and causing society to maintain its own ministers; remodelling the laws, and making the same law for rich and poor; a still more extensive franchise, etc.
>
> (cit. in Cranfield, 1978: 134)

Editors welcomed journalists who could identify the issues of the day, analyse them and communicate their relevance to a critical public. These abilities and the new power of the media are illustrated well in the career of a well-known war correspondent.

The idea of the reporter

In 1853 the Crimean War started and William Howard Russell was appointed the *Times* correspondent. As soon as he arrived he reported on the inadequate preparations, insufficient food and lack of shelter for the troops. He did this in two ways, as articles for the paper and as backgrounders for the leaders. Russell's reports revealed that the British navy was far less efficient than the French; that the French medical services were superior; that the British wounded suffered appallingly; that the officers, through inadequate training, could not cope; that the staff at the headquarters in Britain were negligent and ignorant; that what Raglan and his often brave officers could not do – get changes, get supplies – Russell could. By some accounts (Snoddy, 1992) the consequences of such revelatory reporting were that the government fell; a new post, that of Secretary of State for War, was created; conditions for the troops were improved; the *Times* in London got a fund set up to provide medical services; influenced by his journalism Florence Nightingale and others went to the war and built the foundations of a war nursing profession; in time the army commissioning system was reformed thanks to his revelations, a change that would have an important influence on Britain's ability to wage wars. However, the extent of Russell's success is disputed in *The First Casualty* (Knightley, 1975). For tyro journalists it is nice to know that, as an investigator, he had a presence which today's victims would recognise in Captain Clifford's description:

> . . . a vulgar low Irishman . . . but he has the gift of the gab, uses his pen as well as his tongue, sings a good song, drinks anyone's brandy and water, and smokes as many cigars as foolish young officers will let him, and is looked upon by most in camp as a Jolly Good Fellow. He is just the sort to get information, particularly out of the youngsters. And I assure you more than one 'Nob' has thought best to give him a shake of the hand rather than the cold shoulder *en passant*, for [he] is rather an awkward gentleman to be on bad terms with.
>
> (cit. in Wilkinson-Latham, 1979: 59)

The Crimean War was significant for the development of journalism in that it showed that the profession was earning respect and that the occupation of reporter, as someone who goes out and finds out what is happening, was established. As Stephens (1988) writes, one of the first known to have gone out in search of information rather than merely writing up whatever fell into his lap was Tyas, whose reports of the Peterloo Massacre were influential. Stephens points out the interesting difference between Tyas and his professional successors, in that he did not regard it as part of his duties to meet or interrogate the organisers of the public meeting which was to turn into the Peterloo Massacre of 1819, but simply went as a spectator (Stephens, 1988: 243). By the time of Russell, reporters were bearding generals and ministers, to say nothing of more accessible decision-makers, and requiring of them that they clarify their intentions or at least dissemble well.

Sympathy and morality

Before Charles Dickens the novelist came Charles Dickens the journalist who campaigned to ameliorate the condition of the Oliver Twists and Little Nells of his fictional pantheon (Philip, 1986: 6). An exhortation typical of Dickens opened a feature article in his own journal, *Household Words*, in 1852:

> Umbrellas to mend, and chairs to mend, and clocks to mend, are called in our streets daily. [But] who shall count up the numbers of thousands of children to mend, in and about those same streets, whose voice of ignorance cries aloud as the voice of wisdom once did, and is as little regarded; who go to pieces for the want of mending, and die unrepaired!
> (Dickens, 'Boys to Mend' in *Household Words*, 11 September 1852)

Charles Dickens's literary antecedents lie in the novels of social life that had arisen in eighteenth-century England and in the novel that spoke of ordinary people rather than just the upper classes, more or less a creation of Walter Scott. What he added to the observation and social comprehensiveness of his predecessors was an awareness of the domestic and working conditions in which the poor lived. He shared this with his continental equivalents, Manzoni, Balzac and Zola among them. Emile Zola (1840–1902) was to take a step further; he fused Dickens's awareness and compassion with techniques of observation that we would now call sociological. Like Dostoevsky in Russia, Zola went into the slums and made careful observations of conditions which he then revealed in his writings. The movement born from this was *documentary realism* (Keating, 1991). If method defines the investigative journalist then arguably the documentary realists were the first investigative journalists; they also shared an obsession with the condition of the poor,[3] an intense awareness of the miseries caused by the industrial revolution. Old communities had been uprooted, but, much more immediately evident, people had piled into cities in which there was neither the knowledge nor the skill to make their lives bearable by providing decent water, sanitation or food retailing, let alone education, a ready supply of work and protection from exploitation and criminality. Sharing the tasks of taxonomy and revelation of these phenomena were the early social scientists; the most famous product is probably the seventeen volume *Life and Labour of the People of London* by Charles Booth, published between 1889 and 1891. Keating reminds us (1991: 305) that, in keeping with the increasing obeisance paid to science and scientific methods, both journalists and scholars claimed objectivity, but there was little that was objective about their *aims*; it was the *method* that was supposed to be scientifically detached. The idea that a distinction can be made between subject selection and method such that commitment or partiality in the former is consonant with impartiality in the latter is an interesting one, with an obvious bearing upon investigative journalism.

The urge to identify and tell of suffering and exploitation cannot be attributed solely to a spirit of inquiry; scientism provided the tools but the motivation came from a combination of that evangelical belief that to do good works is to worship; the optimism that inspired people to believe that a utopia could be built for all (Houghton, 1957: 33); the earnestness which infused Victorians to deny themselves pleasures that they might be active in the great struggle to build a better world; a patronising sensibility to the sufferings of the unwashed, born of romanticism, something akin to the sentiments of Dorothea Brooke in *Middlemarch*.

In the latter half of the nineteenth century many writers were both novelists and journalists but around the 1880s there began a gradual bifurcation.[4] H.G. Wells announced that he preferred to be considered a journalist (Parrinder, 1972: 297) and his, and others' documentary realist novels were written as adjuncts to journalism. Other kinds of novel, what we might call 'art house' novels, were written by 'artists' and a familiar distinction occurred, bridged in our own day only by American writers such as Tom Wolfe or Gore Vidal.

Objectivity

Between the early years of the century and 1853 the *Times* developed such independence of political influence that it could claim to be reporting object-ively and without reference to the interests of the powerful. The date 1853 is significant, because it is then that the Crimean reports of Russell were printed in the *Times*. What had happened to make this possible?

There are four main approaches to the emergence of objectivity: the political, economic, technological and institutional, and they are complementary. Jurgen Habermas holds that impartial or objective information, by contrast with the heavily political and biased news of earlier times, came about with the rise of an informed public opinion in Anglo-America which demanded impartial news. This 'public sphere' consisted of competing groups debating the issues of the day, and these groups wished to be supplied with the same information on which to base their often differing analyses of their interests and the interests of their polities. This public sphere itself was fed and helped to grow, and to grow better informed, by the media which thus enabled a process of political development that culminated in modern democracy (Dahlgren and Sparks, 1991).

Schiller (1981) argues that objectivity developed in response to commercial imperatives, i.e. the need to sell to as many people as possible and therefore offend as few as possible; he also emphasises the scientific attitude of empiricism that gradually took hold throughout the nineteenth century and influenced communication as it did intellectual enquiry.

Desmond (1978) largely attributes impartiality to a technical development which had an instant influence upon writing, the telegraph, and a commercial one, the news agency. Before the telegraph, writing was by modern standards long-winded and full of subjective comment and detail. After all, much writing by foreign correspondents was done while waiting several days for a ship. The American Civil War (1862–5) attracted more journalists than any previous war and they were the first to employ the telegraph. Transmission charges were high;[5] every word had to be paid for. Thus the more concise the report, the less it cost to transmit. Correspondents were urged to chop down their material to the minimum of facts and to clarify so that the main points could be identified instantly. When the report was received it could be expanded, and illustrative or subjective material added by the recipient editor. This new way of reporting very soon led to other changes, in particular the introduction of 'the inverted pyramid'. Copy had to start with the key fact or facts, without preliminaries. Enlargements, filling out, followed sequentially and in the reverse order of importance such that the sub-editor might chop off the lower paragraphs without detriment to the meaning, hence 'the inverted pyramid'. Story-telling, by contrast, leads up to the climax from detail whose relevance is not always clear at the outset. As to the content of that pyramid, they are 'the Five Ws and an H', a codification of essential facts for a story that every news journalism student learns: What happened; Where it happened; When it happened; Who was involved; Why it happened; How it happened. These requirements, forced upon journalists by the telegraph, resulted in much greater accuracy and in better reader comprehension; it became a given of journalism that this kind of objective information, news, was different from more discursive, subjective material.

The next major change was the introduction of news agencies. As Desmond says 'while a reporter might write a report that would be acceptable to his own newspaper, a news agency report on the same subject, going to scores of newspapers, might be wholly unacceptable to some' (Desmond, 1978: 217). Agencies had therefore to produce copy that consisted of little more than commonly acceptable facts. Their work provided a check on what newspapers' own correspondents were doing, and a source of comparison. This further accentuated the emphasis upon accuracy and unembroidered fact in news, and the distinction between such news and those parts of newspapers and broadcast schedules where subjectivity was permitted. It also encouraged the idea of the eyewitness as the key to knowledge, which launched the careers of many more special correspondents and inserted the testimonial interview among their tools. Realistic photography, appearing at the same time as the above developments in the 1850s, probably encouraged the belief that there was a reality that journalists could capture. More recent factors in the underpinning of objectivity as a journalistic norm, and the current critique of objectivity, are discussed in the next chapter.

The idea of evidence

The adoption of objectivity as a journalistic norm was simultaneous with the development of the idea that reporters (as we may now call them) used specific techniques particular to their profession — observation of events, enquiry of sources. We can imagine that they were boastful of their accuracy because they saw that not only did this guarantee them a following but also established their status as experts and professionals.

This helped to transform the way journalism was seen – originally seen as mercenary and unreliable polemicists, journalists were being consulted and courted by princes, not only because of their ability to influence opinion but because they were often more knowledgeable than the supposed experts. Such knowledge was also valued by the argumentative Victorian business and intellectual circles whose members increasingly championed the evidential approach, the rational dissecting of outdated institutions and ideas (some of them) and the concept of a public interest (Houghton, 1957: chap. 4). A distinction emerged between those writing the editorials in the office and those gathering news in the field. The report became differentiated from the analysis, as it is today; feature articles appeared, distinct from either, and included what we now call 'human interest'; 'hard' news was distinguished from 'soft' news; literary journalism was introduced; the interview was invented; newspapers campaigned.

The idea of investigation

In 1885 the journalist W.T. Stead sought a girl in the East End of London for sexual purposes, found a 12 year old and bought her. Stead was arrested, tried and imprisoned. However, since his motive had been to stage a publicity stunt and not to take advantage of his purchase his sentence was a short one and he made the whole affair the sting that finally brought success to the campaign to stop child prostitution (Crossland, 1996).

William Stead had started life as a 14-year-old clerk in a Newcastle business. He freelanced for the Darlington *Northern Echo* and in 1871, aged 22, he became editor (Griffiths, 1992). He was brought up in a Protestant sect devoted to good works and believed that journalism gave him the opportunity to save himself. He was first noticed nationally when he was active in a press crusade in exposing atrocities allegedly carried out by Turks in Bulgaria. He was invited to be assistant editor of the then very influential *Pall Mall Gazette*, of which he became editor in 1883. With that he campaigned for a proactive policy over the Sudan (to save the benighted Sudanese), for the London poor and for modernisation of the navy. Much later he was to campaign for peace and to support the Boers in the Boer War.

The scoop for which Stead is best remembered is 'The Maiden Tribute of Modern Babylon'. The background to the story is that, over a year before Stead's first article on the subject appeared, tradesmen serving brothels in Brussels had tipped off an English Quaker human rights campaigner, Josephine Butler, about a slave trade in young English girls. Butler managed to find a Belgian police witness but neither British police nor diplomats were interested. The trade was well established, horrifically cruel and well documented by Butler, yet she made no headway in her efforts to raise the age of consent and to get the police to take action.

It was only when W.T. Stead, then editor of the *Pall Mall Gazette*, became involved that the authorities were to take notice. After buying his girl, on 6 July 1885 he published *The Violation of Virgins, The Report of Our Secret Commission* consisting of five pages of detail under such subheadings as 'Strapping girls down' and 'Why the cries of victims are not heard'. It contained a drawn-out account of his own personal investigation:

> The woman of the house was somewhat suspicious, owing to the presence of a stranger, but after some conversation she said she had one fresh girl within reach, whom she would take over at once if they could come to terms. The girl was sent for, and duly appeared. She was told that she was to have a good situation within a few miles of London . . . [but] seemed somewhat nervous when she heard so many inquiries and the talk about taking her into the country. The bargain however, was struck. The keeper had to receive £2 down, and another sovereign when the girl was proved a maid.
>
> (*Pall Mall Gazette*, 6 July 1885: 5)

The first thing to note about Stead's journalism is that his explicitness was quite novel. We have seen how, two centuries before, newsheets pandered to people's taste for sex and violence, and these kinds of stories continued to be produced but under wraps and in specialist periodicals such as *The Pearl*, which provided stories with such titles as 'Lady Pokingham, or, They all do it' (Cranfield, 1978: 212). There had, until Stead, been no place for this kind of stuff in the respectable press, which was full of moral seriousness. Stead changed the style of reporting by conjoining high moral tone with sensational description, the favoured style of many newspapers in Britain today. Stead got attention not only by prurience, but also by revelation. That this kind of trade existed was almost certainly news to most of his readers. His undercover, investigative style was premonitory. With the help of the specialist, Josephine Butler, Stead carried out detailed preliminary research and undertook a sting, in much the manner favoured by modern investigative journalists. The treatment of the story increased the sensationalism. Stead published it in segments over several weeks, cliff-hangers attracting customer loyalty. His story was talked of everywhere and commented upon by innumerable other papers, circulation rose and touts sold copies at two hundred times the cover price.

Investigative journalism had been invented,[6] just as great changes were about to be demanded of journalism.

Mass media beginnings

As Stead wrote, the conditions for journalism were about to undergo a fundamental development. Although by their own standards their sales figures were impressive, Stead and his admirers failed to notice some of the relevant changes that were taking place in society, or at least failed to capitalise upon their crusading zeal. As with other highbrow editors, Stead had high ideals and great abilities but used them in providing only for a restricted social class – their language still betrayed this, as did the assumptions of culture, knowledge and interests that pervaded the press. Had they been better businessmen they might have noticed that the market was expanding dramatically. They didn't and so, despite all that sensation, they lost out to a different kind of journalist (Williams, 1957).

The population explosion that had started in the eighteenth century had continued, with exponential rise in the birth rate and a vastly higher proportion of people living in cities. The money economy was all but universal and retailing outlets had developed everywhere; distribution by road, canal and rail had advanced tremendously. There were better printing presses, cheaper paper and illustrations. Advertising had developed to such an extent that it reduced dependence upon other forms of revenue, reduced the cover price and thus further enlarged the potential market.

As to readership, universal male suffrage and the trades' union movement politicised the masses; public education had been introduced and literacy was spreading rapidly; football developed from the 1870s and provided a focus for newspapers, enlarging the market further. By choice and professional formation, few existing journalists were appropriate to take advantage of the opportunities these developments offered. Yet professional journalism and the importance it had gained for newspapers, together with the mass market made them commercially successful, and as the media became big business so it attracted people who were first and foremost entrepreneurs rather than journalists. Hence the arrival of the second generation of 'information entrepreneur', epitomised by Alfred Harmsworth (Taylor, 1996).

In 1881 a magazine called *Titbits* was born, launched by George Newnes, not a journalist but an entrepreneur. *Titbits* was a collection of short, amusing cuttings from other publications, supplemented with some original gleanings from hosts of stringers; perfectly suited to young people who could read but had no stamina for high culture or wordy, elite newspapers. Among its admirers was the 16-year-old Alfred Harmsworth, a keen cyclist who toured the country with other cycling enthusiasts, mainly youngsters who worked as clerks or in shops and who probably read *Titbits* too. Harmsworth became one of the earliest contributors to *Titbits*, and went to work for *Wheel Life*, the cyclists' paper (Williams, 1957: 136).

By the age of 21 he was editor of *Bicycling News* and ready to launch his own paper, pretty much a copy of *Titbits*, called *Answers*. Over the next ten years he launched eleven more publications, including *Home Chat* for the housewife, *Chips* and *Pluck* for the errand boy, *Forget-me-not* for factory girls, *Union Jack*, *Halfpenny Marvel* and *Comic Cuts* (Taylor, 1996: 19).

In May 1896 Harmsworth's business had a capital of a million pounds and he could attempt to launch into daily newspapers. By that time he had proved, through his commercial success, that he knew what the masses wanted to read.

Moreover, he knew how to attract readers through stunts and competitions, selling his publications the same as any other article. When he was offered the failing *Evening News* for a low price he bought it and applied the same principles that had made him successful as a periodical publisher. In time Harmsworth would add many other profitable papers to that one, and become the first modern media mogul.

Several press entrepreneurs were to build their media empires out of the mass market created in the 1870s. Typically they ruled them as despots, but, although as individuals they had strong political views that they sometimes chose to promote, their first consideration was commercial success. Rupert Murdoch is in exactly this mould. When in 1986 the *Sunday Times* was hoaxed over the Hitler's Diaries fraud, the journalists felt ashamed, even humiliated. Rupert Murdoch said: 'Circulation went up and stayed up. We didn't lose money, or anything like that' (cit. in Harris, 1996: 567). As far as he was concerned 'we are in the entertainment business' (ibid.) and other proprietors think the same, for example Lord Matthews of the Express Group 'that's how I look at newspapers . . . as money' (cit. in Porter, 1984: 153). With Harmsworth in the 1920s providing for the newly literate classes, ever expanding in numbers, circulation became the most important factor. The broadsheets wanted small select audiences and were increasingly advertising backed as the cost of providing high standard journalism rose; initially advertisers did not influence the content of broadsheets greatly, although in comparison to politics the quantity of feature material grew.

Similar changes took place among the populars, but for different reasons. Advertising was less important – advertisers pay less per capita for advertising to poorer people – but circulation mattered greatly since the populars needed a higher proportion of the cover price and would get what advertising they could only through having large circulations. In order to get them they popularised and sensationalised and simplified. The process of simplifying copy itself, reducing stories to key points, started with the introduction of the telegraph, accelerated with the new populism. Political content was rapidly diminishing in favour of human interest (Curran and Seaton, 1997: chap. 5). Intense competition in the period accelerated this trend and brought stunts and the introduction of market research to check that what was being provided was what the masses wanted. As a by-product of this the radical press died. Political mass market papers could not compete on price, particularly when advertisers were reluctant to advertise in them, or on sensationalism (ibid.). An exception was the *Manchester Guardian*, supported by a Manchester business and professional community whose members tended to share a religious and liberal political outlook. It was able to remain highbrow and independent in a way that was not open to mass circulation papers. There were others like it, although most were eliminated by the mergers of the 1930s or 1950s.

In summary, the era of the press barons had consequences both positive and negative for British journalism. Many more people read the papers but there was a sharp division between popular and broadsheet journalism in both style and concerns. That the information media could be made into big, profitable businesses was now quite clear, as was the fact that when media are seen first and foremost as businesses, this influences their content. Content is also influenced when advertising is more important than sales. Curran and Seaton argue that business-driven media are different from journalism-driven media (1997). They believe that the press barons limited the range of voices that were heard by ordinary people to those that were acceptable to a few selfish businessmen. Thus the economic depression in the 1930s was not properly analysed and people were allowed to think of it as an Act of God; strikers were calumnied and their ideas marginalised as those of a minority; bogies were created in the public mind – Russia, Jews – and enthusiasms were fostered that were not necessarily healthy, for example empire jingoism (Spurr, 1994) and, in the case of the *Daily Mail*, fascism. Curran and Seaton's observations have a particular resonance today, in view of the widespread anguish about journalism's subjection to commercialism and to the power of managers who have no criteria of success but profit.

Commodification

We have seen how the journalism we recognise as such was established by the end of the nineteenth century; Chalaby (1998), building on the ideas of Jurgen Habermas, which are touched upon in Chapter 5, argues that it also came to an end when the media became industrialised.

To Chalaby, in the decades before the mass market, news selection was morally grounded. The press had been polemical, tied to specific parties and points of view; the repeal of the Stamp Acts released the media from these ties and made it possible for a relatively independent and impartial journalism to establish itself. The press no longer needed to kow-tow to narrow sectional interests, whether of the industrial capitalists of Manchester, for example, or the working class, whose press he examines in detail, but sought to serve a much wider constituency. However, as this constituency became much wider, as it became a mass market, it became clear that there were opportunities for profit, and indeed that a greater degree of capitalisation was required to enter such a market.

In the process the media were driven to compete fiercely and this competition pushed them into adapting norms and techniques which greatly changed the nature of the journalism. Journalism, from providing a forum for debate and the wherewithal, unbiased factual information with which to debate, became product to attract audiences, commodities with values according to their power of attraction. The job of the journalist became not to elevate discussion or educate the readers to participation in the *res publica* but to produce such product; unmediated political documents such as the printing of parliamentary debates, disappeared; serious matter was downgraded with the introduction of coverage of a much wider range of activities.

In other words, Chalaby's theory provides an explanation of how journalism adapted as the mass market press became lucrative, attracting entrepreneurs who further commercialised the media businesses and commodified the product. He sees the late nineteenth century as the beginning of a long process of which we see the fruits today in the trivialisation of journalism that is regularly denounced. Postman's aptly named *Amusing Ourselves to Death* (1987) argued that the entertaining, undemanding and ephemeral were distracting us from or just squeezing out important issues.

McManus (1994) gives detailed examples of what he calls 'junk journalism' displacing informative journalism and in Chapter 8 provides evidence from case studies of how little effort was made to gather or present background, context or explanation and how reporters are more likely to use emotional or amusing content than the information required to make sense of the story. He explains trivialisation as the result of increasing market-orientated journalism, which he contrasts with normative journalism, and argues that, as with junk food, this 'pap' creates unhealthy desires and dislodges the better quality. Even though profit-seeking business has been the enabling foundation of journalism here ever since entrepreneurs succeeded political parties as operators of the press 150 years ago, it has usually been kept in the basement. Now the business of selling news is being invited upstairs, into the temple (McManus, 1994: 1).

Sparks (1991) identified a widening gap between the informed elite and the entertained masses; others (Golding, 1998) argue that all media, including élite media, are becoming more entertainment orientated.

So far so good. Research had long established that various biases were endemic in 'hard' news; a bias in favour of authority, for example, or towards selecting stories that privileged stereotypes. 'Soft' news or those entertaining bits that had gradually supplanted hard were relegated. However, once researchers had grasped the increasing preponderance of soft (also called 'human interest') stories[7] then they began to try to understand them too. As we have seen in Chapter 1, Brundson and Morely (1978), Rutherford Smith (1979), van Poecke (1988) and others all found that events tended to be fitted into existing categories and were made to perform certain functions such as reassure us about authority, or amuse us, or pander to our prejudices; at one extreme was the Charles Stuart case, in which a murder was packaged by reporters neatly to fit conventional stereotypes (young black male, car thieving, white woman, traffic) bearing no relation to reality but every relation to expectation (Berkowitz, 1997: 498).

Why is this? News is a genre of journalism; every genre has an identity recognised by producers and consumers, both of whom require obedience to conventions of structure, grammar and vocabulary as well as adherence to the repertoire of themes deemed appropriate to the genre (McQuail, 1994). Various studies, including Mazzoleni (1987) and Bell (1991) have all come broadly to the conclusion that journalists take events and format them in accordance with the requirements of the genre, themselves rooted in cultural assumptions and commercial requirements.

At its extreme, we might say therefore that journalism so reconstructs the world as to ensure that it fits with its reading of what its audience wants to hear, rather than with reality, and that this has various social implications. Bourdieu has gone much further in his critique, specifically of television journalism, arguing that television journalism, far from enriching the public sphere, is having a number of dangerous effects. Television journalism, he believes, contains and limits ideas and argument; classifies people and forces us to see the world through its classifications (Bourdieu, 1998: 22). For institutional, technological, economic and sociological reasons television journalists are able to, and do, impose their own particular constructions and framing upon people and issues: 'the journalistic field is based upon a set of assumptions and beliefs, which reach beyond differences of position and opinion . . . the effect is censorship' (Bourdieu, 1998: 47).

Chalaby's large-scale thesis referred to above appears to be born out by a variety of studies of specific cases of journalism such as Keeble's examination of the way in which the Gulf War was 'created' by the media (Keeble, 1998), certain studies of local TV news (de Burgh, 1998 and Langer, 1998), Cao's comparison of Chinese and British coverage of the Hong Kong handover (Cao, 1997) and others. Are these saying that there is no such thing as truth, or that news journalism has nothing to do with truth? No, but that there are tendencies in commodified journalism that make it naive to assume that journalism reflects 'reality'.

Where does investigative journalism fit into this? It may be that investigative journalism, propelled by its moral impulse, is on a quite different plane from the highly conditioned news journalism that the writers above have sought to interpret, circumscribed by the requirements of format that is itself a requirement of a marketing approach; perhaps investigative journalism is a relic of Chalaby's and Habermas's nineteenth century, with its different values; perhaps, on the other hand, it is just a product (satisfying a desire for pleasurable indignation!), or simply a marketing technique for selling the main product, as with any other media artefact. Suspending judgement, it is now appropriate to look at the investigative journalism of the last 30 years.

Notes

1 Invented in China in AD 105, paper-making was brought to Europe in the twelfth century. Printing, well established in China in the Tang Dynasty (618–907), was developed in Europe in the 1450s with enormous consequences for the Church, politics and knowledge.
2 For a discussion of the causes of literacy and its influences, see Todd (1987).
3 For more on Zola see Keating (1991: 15–6 and 306).
4 Aspects of these issues are discussed in Dr Lynne Hapgood's unpublished doctoral thesis, 'Circe among the cities'.
5 Desmond (1978) provides fascinating detail on these charges and their influence on the media in history.

6 There were other examples of investigation but more research needs to be done. One that something is known about is the exposure by the *Manchester Guardian* of Kitchener's concentration camps for Boer civilians during the Boer War. See Ayerst (1971).

7 The trend had been identified by Mead in 1926, by Hughes in 1968 and by Barthes in 1977; Fiske and Hartley (1978) noted that they had increased as a proportion of stories. However, the main focus of research remained hard news.

Bibliography

Andrews, A. (1859) *The History of British Journalism*. London: Richard Bentley.

Ayerst, D. (1971) *The Guardian: Biography of a Newspaper*. London: Collins: 285.

Barthes, R. (1977) Structure of the faits divers. In R. Barthes (1977) *Critical Essays*. Evanston: Northwestern University Press.

Bell, A. (1991) *The Language of News Media*. Oxford: Blackwell.

Berkowitz, D. (1997) *Social Meanings of News: A Text Reader*. Thousand Oaks, CA: Sage.

Bourdieu, P. (1998) *On Television and Journalism*. London: Pluto.

Brundson, C. and Morley, D. (1978) *Everyday Television: 'Nationwide'*. London: British Film Institute.

de Burgh, H. (1998) Audience, journalist and text in television news. Paper delivered at the Annual Conference of the International Association for Media and Communications Research, 27 July 1998.

Cao, Q. (1997) Ideological versus cultural perspectives: the reporting of the handover of Hong Kong in the British printed media. Lecture to the International Political Science Association 17th World Congress, August 1997, Seoul, Korea.

Chalaby, J. (1998) *The Invention of Journalism*. London: Macmillan.

Cranfield, J. (1978) *The Press and Society*. London: Longman.

Crossland, J. (1996) Belgium's first child sex scandal. *Sunday Times*, 25 August 1996.

Curran, J. and Seaton, J. (1997) *Power without Responsibility: The Press and Broadcasting in Britain*, 5th edn. London: Routledge.

Dahlgren, P. and Sparks, C. (1991) *Communication and Citizenship: Journalism and the Public Sphere*. London: Routledge.

Derry, J. (ed.) (1968) *Cobbett's England*. London: The Folio Society.

Desmond, R. (1978) *The Information Process: World News Reporting to the Twentieth Century*. Iowa City: University of Iowa Press.

Fiske, J. and Hartley, J. (1978) *Reading Television*. London: Methuen.

Franklin, B. (1997) *Newszak and News Media*. London: Edward Arnold.

Fussell, P. (1975) *The Great War and Modern Memory*. New York: Oxford University Press.

Gitlin, T. (1980) *The Whole World Is Watching: The Mass Media in the Making and the Unmaking of the New Left*. Berkeley: University of California Press.

Golding, P. (1977) Media professionalism in the third world: the transfer of an ideology. In J. Curran, M. Gurevitch and J. Woollacott (eds) (1977) *Mass Communication and Society*. London: Edward Arnold.

Golding, P. (1998) The political and the popular: getting the message of tabloidisation. Paper delivered at the Annual Conference of Media, Cultural and Communications Studies, Sheffield. 12 December 1998.

Green, D. (1983) *Great Cobbett*. London: Hodder and Stoughton.

Griffiths, D. (1992) *Encyclopaedia of the British Press*. London: Macmillan: 532.

Hapgood, L. (1990) Circe among cities: images of London and the languages of social concern 1880–1900. Unpublished doctoral thesis. University of Warwick.

Harris, B. (1996) *Politics and the Rise of the Press*. London: Routledge.

Hartley, J. (1992) *The Politics of Pictures: The Creation of the Public in the Age of Popular Media*. London: Routledge.

Houghton, W. (1957) *The Victorian Frame of Mind*. London: Yale University Press.

Hughes, H. (1968) *News and the Human Interest Story*. New York: Greenwood.

Keating, P. (1991) *The Haunted Study*. London: Fontana.

Keeble, R. (1998) *Secret State, Silent Press: the New Militarism, the Gulf and the Modern Image of Warfare*. Luton: John Libbey.

Knightley, P. (1975) *The First Casualty*. London: Hodder and Stoughton.

Langer, P. (1998) *Tabloid Television*. London: Routledge.

McManus, J. H. (1994) *Market-Driven Journalism: Let the Citizen Beware?* London: Sage.

McQuail, D. (1994) *Mass Communication Theory*. London: Sage.

Mazzoleni, G. (1987) Media logic and party logic in campaign coverage: the Italian general election of 1983. *European Journal of Communication*, 2 (1): 81–103.

Oliner, S. (1992) *The Altruistic Personality*. New York: Free Press.

Parrinder, P. (1972) *H.G. Wells: The Critical Heritage*. London: Routledge and Kegan Paul.

Philip, N. (1986) *Charles Dickens: A December Vision*. London: Collins.

Porter, H. (1984) *Lies, Damned Lies and Some Exclusives*. London: Chatto and Windus.

Postman, N. (1987) *Amusing Ourselves to Death*. London: Methuen.

Reader, W. J. (1988) *At Duty's Call, a Study in Obsolete Patriotism*. Manchester: Manchester University Press.

Rutherford Smith, R. (1979) Mythic elements of TV news. In D. Berkowitz (1997) *Social Meanings of News: A Text Reader*. Thousand Oaks, CA: Sage.

Schiller, D. (1981) *Objectivity and the News*. Philadelphia: University of Pennsylvania Press.

Sgard, J. (1976) *Dictionnaire des Journalistes 1600–1789*. Grenoble: Presses Universitaires de Grenoble.

Smith, A. (1979) *The Newspaper: An International History*. London: Thames and Hudson.

Snoddy, R. (1992) *The Good, the Bad and the Unacceptable*. London: Faber and Faber.

Sparks, C. (1991) Goodbye, Hildy Johnson: the vanishing 'serious press'. In P. Dahlgren and C. Sparks (1991) *Communication and Citizenship: Journalism and the Public Sphere*. London: Routledge.

Spurr, D. (1994) *The Rhetoric of Empire*. Durham, NC: Duke University Press.

Stearn, R. T. (1992) War correspondents and colonial war. In J. M. Mackenzie (ed.) *Popular Imperialism and the Military*. Manchester: Manchester University Press.

Stephens, M. (1988) *A History of News*. New York: Viking.

Stocking, H. (1989) *How Do Journalists Think?* Bloomington: Indiana University Press.

Taylor, S. (1996) *The Great Outsiders: Northcliffe, Rothermere and the Daily Mail*. London: Weidenfeld and Nicolson.

Todd, E. (1987) *The Causes of Progress*. Oxford: Blackwell.

van Poecke, L. (1988) The myths and rites of newsmaking. *European Journal of Communication*, 1 (14): 23–54.

Walker, M. (1982) *Powers of the Press*. London: Quartet: 116–20.

Wilkinson-Latham, R. (1979) *From Our Special Correspondent*. London: Hodder and Stoughton.
Williams, F. (1957) *Dangerous Estate*. London: Longman.

Further reading

Cranfield, J. (1978) *The Press and Society*. London: Longman.
Curran, J. and Seaton, J. (1997) *Power without Responsibility: The Press and Broadcasting in Britain*, 5th edn. London: Routledge.
Franklin, B. (1997) *Newszak and News Media*. London: Edward Arnold: especially Chapter 4.
Hartley, J. (1992) *The Politics of Pictures: The Creation of the Public in the Age of Popular Media*. London: Routledge.
Smith, A. (1979) *The Newspaper, An International History*. London: Thames and Hudson.
Snoddy, R. (1992) *The Good, the Bad and the Unacceptable*. London: Faber and Faber.
Stephens, M. (2006) *A History of News*. New York: Oxford University Press.

3

FORTY YEARS

A tradition of investigative journalism

Hugo de Burgh

In the 1960s British newspapers faced competition from television and, simultaneously, because of the consumer boom, found advertisers demanding more media space. So the newspapers became bigger, and filled the space with big feature and picture reporting. At the same time Doig (1997) has suggested that there was a climate conducive to scepticism and irreverence that made investigative journalism attractive. These factors may account for its eruption. There had always been 'exposés', understood as real or claimed revelations of something that had been hidden from us but the investigative traditions of reporting that had led, for instance, to exposés of poverty and exploitation in Victorian Britain had fallen into disuse in the serious newspapers. They left that kind of thing to the populars, mainly the Sundays, with their regular 'I made an excuse and left' revelations about prostitution, or 'I name the guilty man' pieces on small-time fraudsters (Leapman, 1992: 19). Now similar techniques were to be used for 'socially responsible' journalism in the manner of W.T. Stead.

In 1963 there were two major investigations that have continued to be cited as exemplars: the first was of the triangular relationship between a government minister, Profumo, a Russian secret agent and a call girl. It was extensively researched by *News of the World* investigative journalist Peter Earle, who managed to hide the girl and her associates in a country cottage until he was ready for his story to break (Earle, 1963), and also was developed into the first of many Insight books, *Scandal '63*. The second was an exclusive by *Sunday Times* Insight, whose reporter Ron Hall detailed the methods used by a criminal landlord, Rachman, to terrorise tenants (Leapman, 1992: 23). By 1969 the *Times* was using bugging devices to gather evidence of Metropolitan Police corruption (Tompkinson, 1982). These examples set a trend and by the late 1960s there were many new vehicles for investigative reporting in the national media, aside from the regional and local press that made forays into investigation.[1] Of the three most distinguished, *Sunday Times* Insight is dealt with in some detail later in this book. Two other important and long-lasting vehicles,

54

Private Eye and *World in Action*, are not and will therefore be mentioned briefly now.

Private Eye was launched in 1961, then as now funded principally by circulation, and run by a group of well-connected young men whose associations were as varied as arch-Conservative (Auberon Waugh), conservative romantic (Christopher Booker) and left radical (Paul Foot). What they shared was scepticism, lack of deference and satirical wit; brought together they produced a magazine that has been unpredictable, daring and iconoclastic of most shibboleths. As a result it has been despised and hated with fervour; rich men have wasted pots of gold and much energy trying to destroy it, particularly business tycoons and editors. In view of its predominantly satirical approach and the fact that it appears to be read in particular by the moneyed people whom it examines, Richard Keeble has suggested that *Private Eye* is more of a court jester than an investigative medium; however, it has included forensic investigation as part of its repertoire.

Among other achievements, it is claimed that *Private Eye* exposed the shady relationships and manoeuvrings of Prime Minister James Callaghan, corruption in the buildings contracts issued by Wandsworth Council, the Poulson case (see below), the false claims of Dr Christiaan Barnard, a heart surgeon, sanctions busting by the major UK company British Petroleum in Rhodesia (now Zimbabwe), Irish politician (and later Prime Minister) Charles Haughey's involvement in gun-running for the IRA, the bribing of BBC disc jockeys and many financial and business scandals. In fact it may be in financial circles that *Private Eye*, thanks originally to the expertise and accuracy of Michael Gillard, has its greatest following (Marnham, 1982: 134–7) although its 'Rotten Boroughs' column was in the 1990s believed to be required reading for all local authority decision-makers (see Chapter 11).

> Granada Television, a leading company among the holders of UK terrestrial TV franchises known collectively as Independent Television, launched *World in Action* in 1963. When *World in Action* (*WiA*) began it was the first weekly filmed current affairs series on British television: For *World in Action*, current affairs meant anything from Government to guilty men, politics to pop. It was a series that was serious in its purpose . . . Hewat [the first Editor] operated on the assumption that few viewers would willingly subject themselves to 30 minutes of 'current affairs' unless grabbed by their lapels . . . Hewat's achievement was that he created a mass audience for what had till then seemed a preserve of elites.
>
> (Granada, 1993)

It was in 1967 that David Plowright set up the 'Investigation Bureau' and *WiA* set out specifically to make investigative programmes. This carried further the Poulson local government corruption scandal of the 1970s, revealed the mass murders of President Idi Amin of Uganda, sickness among employees of the UK asbestos industry, the export of UK arms to Argentina while the UK was at war with that country in the Falkland Islands, corruption in the Irish beef processing industry, the Pin Down policy by which force could be used on youths in prison and a notorious miscarriage of justice, the Birmingham Six, also mentioned in Chapter 13 (Fitzwalter, 1998). *World in Action* claims to have undertaken one of the earliest investigations of the safety of nuclear power and therefore to have been influential in the decline of that industry; to have been the first to examine the question of the British Royal Family and taxation which resulted in 'the Queen agreeing to pay tax as had her ancestors' (Granada, 1993). It has been widely agreed that *World in Action* has been an influence upon UK public life and its abolition by Granada Television in 1999 was lamented by many as an indication of diminished commitment to public service, increasing greed and a diminution of the UK public sphere.

Among the many individual investigations of the period, three have come to be regarded as classics of the genre: the cases of Poulson, thalidomide and the DC10 Disaster. All of them are well documented in very competent books so that no more than a brief summary is needed here.

In 1970 a young English reporter, Ray Fitzwalter, wrote an article in his local paper, the *Bradford Argus*, on the bankruptcy of architect and public works contractor Poulson. It was picked up by Paul Foot who then did a two-page spread on the subject in *Private Eye*. In time this became an enormous investigation, spawning several broadcast programmes and many articles, and was instrumental in the establishment of the *Royal Commission into Standards in Public Life* in 1974. What the journalists achieved was the revelation of corruption in public administration from the smallest of local authorities right up to the most senior of national politicians and, in particular in his second film, Ray Fitzwalter demonstrated every step in the process by which politicians had used, and been used by, Poulson to obtain public contracts by corrupt means, carry them out incompetently and profit from them greatly (Granada, 1973).

In 1972 the *Sunday Times* started a long campaign to get admission of liability and thus proper compensation for thalidomide victims. Around 1960 a large drug company, Distillers, had supplied the drug thalidomide to pregnant women, which had resulted in 451 babies being born deformed. Despite considerable publicity, after ten years still no compensation had been paid and Distillers was trying to impose a settlement upon claimants representing the families affected. Harold Evans and colleagues at the *Sunday Times* decided to investigate the case. As Lord Denning, the judge who refused the request by Distillers that the *Sunday Times* be forbidden to publish on the case on the grounds that it was *sub judice*, put it:

On September 24 1972, the *Sunday Times* published an article headed

'Our Thalidomide Children: A cause for national shame'. It drew attention to the long-drawn out legal proceedings, and said: 'It seems clear that in the new term lawyers acting for Distillers . . . will appear with lawyers acting for the children, to seek court approval for a settlement which has been worked out in private over the last few months. Unhappily the settlement is one which is grotesquely out of proportion to the appalling injuries the thalidomide children suffered . . . it is little more than 1 per cent of the money made in the last ten years since thalidomide'.

(cit. in Smith 1974: 133)

The investigation mounted by the *Sunday Times* and the campaign based upon it, a campaign which continued for many years, resulted in a better deal for many of the victims of thalidomide than would otherwise have been possible and acceptance by the courts of a public interest argument in the matter of contempt (Evans, 1983: chap. 4). Knightley (1997: chap. 10) has however written that the investigation demonstrated failings of British journalism and that, of itself, it achieved little but keeping the issue alive; he believes that it was the campaign among shareholders of Distillers, the company accused, that frightened its board into making the settlement. The issue of what role investigative journalism really played is discussed in Page (1998) and Knightley (1997: chap. 10), which also contains a useful description of the painstaking research necessary for the Insight team to get to grips with the subject. References to the other books on this investigation are to be found elsewhere in this volume.

Another of the major investigations of the period was also undertaken by the *Sunday Times*, that of the DC-10 air crash of 1974. There is a synopsis in Chapter 11, as well as references.

The profession was impressed by such feats of reportage but established interests and their political representatives were not necessarily impressed in the same way. When journalists looked at the private business interests of UK Prime Minister Harold Wilson's inner circle, the Labour government of the 1970s reacted angrily. A Royal Commission on the Press was set up in 1977 and, among other things, criticised journalists for trying to 'seek discreditable material which can be used to damage the reputation of Labour ministers' (Doig, 1997: 196).

In the mid- to late 1970s the UK went through an economic slump; with the print media facing financial problems and upheavals in staffing, newspaper investigations appear to have declined in number. An important vehicle for dissenting journalism gave up that role in the face of populist commercial competition, according to admirers of the *Daily Mirror*, now the *Mirror* (Pilger, 1997; Molloy, 1997). By the 1980s it appeared that more investigations were being undertaken by television. ITV companies competed to demonstrate dedication to the remits which had been placed upon them by the national regulations covering scheduling and content (Gibbons, 1998: 72). The BBC established *File on Four*, the radio investigative series, of which more later (see Chapter 11).

Investigative journalism and Thatcherism 1979–97: years of fear, years of farce

The relationship between British politicians and the media is the subject of other books; however, an overview of British investigative journalism in the period of the Conservative government 1979–97 cannot avoid touching upon it. Roughly speaking, until Mrs Thatcher fell many investigative journalists felt menaced; within three years of John Major's taking her place fifteen ministers had been obliged to resign as there emerged unending risible details of philandering, greed or petty corruption, and fear (at least from the perspective of the journalists) had been replaced by farce.

On the whole the tabloids concentrated upon the smut (there was plenty) while the broadsheets angled on dereliction of public service. The extramarital affairs of insignificant members of the Royal Family (*News of the World*, 7 July 1985) were typical of tabloid obsession;[2] in 1986 the Deputy Chairman of the Conservative Party and successful novelist Jeffrey Archer was exposed as having paid £2,000 to a prostitute to go abroad; more seriously, in 1988 the *News of the World* revealed that another, notorious call girl, with friends who included many politicians and the editor of the *Sunday Times*, had been issued with a Parliamentary pass. Unjustifiable on any grounds but those of prurience were exposés of the extramarital affair of a football manager, Bobby Robson, and the three-month long investigation of a then well-known television interviewer, Frank Bough (Bainbridge and Stockdill, 1993: 319); the absurd fact that, unbeknown to the then Chancellor of the Exchequer (Norman Lamont), a madam was renting his apartment and details of sundry liaisons of businessmen and soap stars filled up the pages.

More easily justified on the grounds of public interest were the *News of the World* (*NoW*) 1984 exposure of corruption at the government's Property Services Agency, which, as its name suggests, managed the largest real estate portfolio in the kingdom (Macaskill, 1984). Other *NoW* investigations resulted in revelations that an IRA bomber was employed in the House of Commons (1987); that some illegal immigrants were paying to get married to local women (who were sometimes married already), stung at the ceremony in 'Operation Gold Ring' (1990), and that a cosmetic surgery clinic which caused disfigurement as well as pain was operating (Bainbridge, 1993: 331). Equally, Gary Jones' discovery that the jury had made its guilty decision in a murder case by reference to a Ouija board and an extensive investigation of paedophiles were stories that any medium would be happy to own (Jones, 1999). Perhaps the story that was of greatest popular interest was 'Soccer Chiefs and the Vice Girls' (Mahmood, 1998) which described in lurid detail the behaviour, attitudes and crookery of the two bosses of one of the UK's leading soccer clubs, all faithfully recorded by their partner in vice who happened to be the head of *NoW*'s investigations bureau, Mazher Mahmood. Mahmood is one of the most colourful characters in modern British journalism, celebrated for his impersonations of Arab Sheikhs in particular.

An important theme of the period was nuclear power, and the casuistry with which its promoters were alleged to have made their case (Foot, 1990: 57–63). Notable among the many revelations of duplicity and danger was the Yorkshire Television series and book by James Cutler and Rob Edwards, *Britain's Nuclear Nightmare* (1988). It was the first investigation to attend to the high incidence of cancer around nuclear installations, starting a scientific debate that is still ongoing. On the day that it was broadcast, 1 November 1983, Prime Minister Thatcher responded to it in the House of Commons and promised that the claims made by it would be examined urgently. The Black Inquiry was set up and initiated a series of studies which continue today (Edwards, 1999) and the (government advisory) Committee on Medical Aspects of Radiation in the Environment resulted. Unfortunately for the intrepid journalists, their efforts were to an extent overshadowed by war, by Ireland and by the unending battles between the media and the government. As far as the broadsheets were concerned the government's relations with the media started extremely badly with the 1982 Falklands War, when even routine efforts at impartial analysis of the situation were seen as treachery (Meyer, 1998). The story of how the government reacted to level-headed analysis has been effectively written up by Harris (1994) and by Adams (1986). Attempts to dig into the mysteries surrounding the Argentine ship, *General Belgrano*, were furiously resisted and the government brought a case against a civil servant, Clive Ponting, who passed to journalists evidence of ministerial duplicity in this matter towards Parliament (Thornton, 1982: 15). The government was frustrated over Ponting, though not in the 1983 case of Sarah Tisdall who had passed information about the arrival in Britain of Cruise Missiles, and this almost certainly stimulated the introduction of a new Official Secrets Act in 1988.[3]

In 1984 John Stalker, a senior police officer sent to investigate alleged criminal behaviour by the Northern Ireland police, was removed from his job; his treatment, and that of Colin Wallace, another apparent victim of government dirty tricks in Northern Ireland, were exhaustively investigated by Paul Foot (Foot, 1990: 191; Pincher, 1991: 178). There is a long list of programmes dealing with Northern Ireland which were stifled or nobbled in the 1980s (Thornton, 1989: 9); *Real Lives* was banned in 1985, and Thames Television censured by the government for questioning its killing of IRA terrorists without trial in its investigation 'Death on the Rock', later exonerated by a public inquiry (Bolton, 1990). Of this notorious case Bailey *et al.* say:

> In 1988, Thames Television broadcast a *This Week* documentary, 'Death on the Rock', investigating the circumstances of the shooting of three, as it transpired unarmed, members of the IRA in Gibraltar

earlier in the year. Government explanations were that the killings were of members of an active service unit of the IRA intent on planting a bomb on the island and that they were shot by members of the SAS acting in self defence. The documentary, however, included evidence from a 'new' witness to the events who asserted that those killed had been shot without warning and with their hands in the air. The documentary rekindled debate about the existence of a 'shoot to kill' policy on the part of the security forces in dealing with terrorists. The documentary was strongly denounced by the Prime Minister, Mrs Thatcher.

(Bailey *et al.*, 1995)

These cases alone indicate the climate of hostility between broadsheet journalists and the government; indeed insults impugning the veracity of journalists in general or the BBC in particular issued almost daily from the mouths of senior politicians. More materially, the government obtained an injunction against the 1987 BBC Radio 4 series *My Country Right or Wrong* on the security services, and had the police raid the offices of BBC Scotland and seize a series of six programmes researched for the BBC by Duncan Campbell, *Secret Society*, going so far as to break into the homes of Campbell and two other journalists. This extraordinary example of government paranoia and the violent behaviour that resulted has become known as the Zircon Affair and has been written up in, among others, Ewing and Gearty (1990). The late 1980s were also enlivened by the undignified spectacle of Her Majesty's Government trying to ban the memoirs of a former British secret agent (Peter Wright: *Spycatcher*), notwithstanding that the ensuing publicity ensured that the book immediately became available and attractive to large numbers of people who would otherwise have taken not the slightest interest in a rather specialist memoir. The escapade did further demonstrate that the Conservative government continued the policy of its Labour predecessor in trying to make scrutiny of its activities even more difficult by increasing secrecy and censorship. Illustrations of this are too numerous to detail (Ewing and Gearty, 1990) but one more must be mentioned. In October 1991 Channel 4 Television (established by the Conservative government in 1982, see Chapter 11) broadcast *Dispatches*: 'The Committee' to the ire of the police who obtained an injunction to hand over all the production documentation under the 1974 Prevention of Terrorism Act in an attempt to discover the sources of allegation that terrorists and police cooperated in Northern Ireland to liquidate other terrorists. The following year C4 was fined £75,000 (US$124,000) for its refusal to name the sources of the revelations in 'The Committee'.

As much as any ideological commitment to the free market, it may well have been loathing of journalists, and investigative journalists in particular, that was behind the impetus to dismantle the BBC (which did not succeed) and make the broadcast media increasingly commercial (which has to an extent succeeded) (Goodwin, 1998: 166; Gibbons, 1998). Some of those Conservative politicians most hot for deregulation had been themselves investigated in a 1986 documentary, *Maggie's Militant Tendency*.

The 1990s boom

Nevertheless, contradictory though it may seem, the atmosphere of constant conflict that I have sketched above in fact appears to have stimulated a resurgence of investigative or quasi-investigative journalism, especially on television. An unsystematic trawl of a database for 1995 (*Programme Reports*, 1995) suggests that in that year alone on UK terrestrial television there were 300 discrete programmes that could be classified as investigative, this total excluding magazine programmes with investigative elements. As to the media for them, during the 1990s several new current affairs series were born, all of which from time to time did investigative work:

- BBC *Inside Story*
- BBC *Public Eye*
- ITV *Big Story*
- ITV *Network First*
- C4 *Cutting Edge*
- ITV *First Tuesday*
- BBC *40 Minutes*
- C4 *Street Legal*.

The history series BBC *Timewatch* and C4 *Secret History* commenced and C4's *Witness* sometimes undertook historical investigations, for example on the relationship between Sinn Fein, the Irish nationalist political party, and Nazism (C4, 1997). Series or strands claiming to be exclusively investigative that were launched in the 1990s included:

- ITV *The Cook Report*
- C4 *Countryside Undercover*
- BBC *Taking Liberties*
- ITV *Beam and Da Silva*
- ITV *Disguises*
- C4 *Undercover Britain*
- BBC *Here and Now*
- BBC *Rough Justice*
- BBC *Private Investigations*.

Predictions made in 1990 that investigative journalism would not survive increasing commercialisation seemed in 1995 not to have been borne out, indeed it was booming. Investigative journalists suffered some setbacks – *Panorama* withdrew an investigation of corruption by Westminster (local government)

Council until after the elections with which it dealt, Central TV cancelled a *Cook Report* on political lobbying (but left the field open to the *Guardian*), possibly under pressure from the lobbyist under investigation, and Paul Jackson, Managing Director of Carlton Television notoriously declared, apropos of the *World in Action* which had increased the awareness that eventually led to the release from prison of the Birmingham bombers, that 'It isn't part of the function of the TV system to get people out of prison. Its function is to make programmes that people want to watch' (Fitzwalter, 1999). Nevertheless, investigative journalists also came to grip public attention with a series of investigations into corruption ('sleaze') which involved colourful personalities and well-known institutions.

Sleaze

The 'Cash for Questions' saga kept 'sleaze' in the public eye from 1994 to 1997 and is widely credited with having so damaged the Conservative government as to ensure its defeat in the 1997 General Election. From the point of view of a student of journalism, the main points are these. Soon after the *Sunday Times* had established, in the sting on MPs described in Chapter 1, that Members of Parliament would do favours for money, Mohamed al Fayed, businessman and owner of Harrods, the London store, revealed[4] to the *Guardian* that Members of Parliament with responsibilities related to his interests had been bribed, both by him personally and through a then well-known lobbyist, Ian Greer, to present his case in a variety of ways. It was the fact that, in his view, they had failed to defend his interests while thoroughly enjoying his money that seemed to embitter him. The services for which he had paid included parliamentary questions to ministers and pitches to their colleagues with appropriate ministerial responsibilities. Such representations had been made as if impartially so that those undertaking the lobbying had cheated their colleagues in government as well as Parliament as a whole. In the course of a lengthy investigation of the lobbyist and his stable of hired politicians the journalists uncovered further unsavoury details of many other lobbying activities, in particular of how Greer had attempted to influence government policy in favour of commercial operators wanting to market drugs to youngsters (Leigh and Vulliamy, 1997: 126) and in favour of the Serb leader and President of Yugoslavia Slobodan Milosevic at the time that his troops were carrying out atrocities in former Yugoslavia (ibid.: chap. 8).

Much of the investigation was to be confirmed by details obtained only thanks to the libel case attempted, but then abandoned, by Member of Parliament Neil Hamilton. Hamilton was a second rank government minister who, appropriately, had responsibility for those areas of national life in which he had been deeply involved as a covert lobbyist for Ian Greer. The detail of the *Guardian* investigation and of the legal battles that took place are certainly of interest to the student of the media; from a wider perspective what the 'Cash for Questions' saga exposed were the familiar failings of the English legal system; the inability of the British Parliament to regulate itself with the clarity and transparency of its US counterpart; the tenuousness of UK journalists' freedom to investigate and the failure of politicians to resist Party pressure even when faced with obvious mendacity and even criminality (Leigh and Vulliamy, 1997: 244). On the other hand its achievements were important: journalists considered themselves vindicated for their widely-maligned investigations when Hamilton and Greer withdrew their suit, although they did not admit liability, and before long disappeared from public life. The first major revelations of corruption were published by the *Guardian* on 20 October 1994; soon thereafter the government appointed an independent committee, the Nolan Committee on Standards in Public Life. This committee subsequently established new rules for Parliamentary behaviour; its first on-the-ground investigation was to be of Hamilton himself, published by the first Parliamentary Commissioner for Standards, Gordon Downey (Leigh, 1999).

The Jonathan Aitken story also turned on the revelation of petty details of expense accounts which, we infer from the effort and energy deployed in hiding them, potentially led to something grander and more shocking, could that something but be pinned down. It was established by meticulous investigation that Aitken, the Minister of State for Defence Procurement,[5] had maintained while a minister a long-standing commercial relationship with princes of the Saudi royal family, a relationship which appeared to make him the servant of one of those princes. The sordid details of that servitude are catalogued in Harding *et al.* (1997). As in the Hamilton case, the target's position was made worse through litigation that both concentrated the minds of the journalists and made it possible for other facts, including in this case some tangential but damaging details about Aitken's personal life, to emerge. In 1999 it was finally established which companies were doing what deals and providing how much in commission to Aitken's associate, who relied upon Aitken's position as minister in the British government responsible for such deals (Pallister *et al.*, 1999).

David Leigh, involved in the investigation from the start, has summarised his view of the story and the achievement: 'Its abiding irony is that – largely because the *Guardian* exposed Aitken's murky trip to the Paris Ritz Hotel – none of the deals came off, and none of the conspirators made a penny' (Leigh, 1999). Aitken did, however, go to prison for perjury committed during his attempts to deny his activities.

The extent of the subject matter

From the account above it may appear that UK investigative journalists were obsessed with (1) security matters and (2) sleaze. These were two areas where public authority was touched to the quick, but investigations looked at other areas, broadly classifiable as corporate corruption, public administration, social policy, miscarriages of justice, historical, the environment, high politics and foreign affairs.

Corporate corruption covered such diverse areas as investigations of landlords making fortunes by ripping off the housing benefit system (ITV: *Beam and Da Silva*, 18 January 1994) or landlords who harass and illegally evict tenants (C4: *Living in Fear*, 25 January 1994). Private security companies were found to be potentially dangerous (ITV: *The Wrong Arm of the Law*, 31 October 1994; BBC1: *Out of Order*, 21 October 1997). Financial fraud was the subject of several programmes, including C4's documentaries on the Bank of Credit and Commerce International (13 August 1991) and the Barlow Clowes Affair (27 February 1992) and BBC2's on creative accountancy and price-fixing (1 March 1992). The *Observer*, with Michael Gillard as main reporter, tackled corruption in the Inland Revenue (tax authority) (Gillard, 1996) and banking scandals at Deutsche Morgan Grenfell (Gillard, 1997); Gillard again, but writing in the *Guardian*, looked at how the oil giant British Petroleum assisted the police in Colombia, police with a long record of human rights abuses. Public administration was examined in a multitude of programmes on education, some more thorough than others, from 'Do Schools Fail Children?' (BBC2, 16 November 1993) to 'Inspecting the Inspectors' (C4, 1998), discussed in Chapter 11. Serious allegations were made against the police in the matter of crack cocaine (*WiA*, 23 November 1992) and we found out how criminals get a new identity (*WiA*, 11 March 1996).

Reporters quite regularly posed as the unfortunate or exploitable, starting with a *WiA* on 9 March 1992 in which a reporter posed as one of the homeless and notably in a series called *Undercover Britain* (C4) and *Disguises* (ITV).[6] There are many media dealing with health issues in one form or another. Perhaps the most notable actual investigations in this period dealt with the surprising number of deaths during surgery at a British hospital, whose staff were later charged; shoddy practices among operating theatre assistants (BBC1: *Public Eye*, 21 March 1995); there were several programmes on physical abuse of the elderly (C4: *Dispatches*, 21 January 1992) or insane (C4: *Cutting Edge*, 7 December 1992). Much discussed were investigations into the dangers of contraceptive pills (*WiA*: 'Safe Sex?', 10 July 1995) and cancer clusters near military bases (*WiA*: 'Shadow of the Bomb', 9 September 1996). C4's *Dispatches* claims to have been the first medium to reveal the effect of Creutzfeld Jakob Disease on humans in 1994 (Lloyd, 1998).

Revelation that paedophiles had infiltrated charities working with the young in Eastern Europe caused a sensation (*WiA*: 'In the Name of Charity', 3 April 1995); a series of programmes on Indonesia's treatment of its (in effect) colony of East Timor and Australia's complicity in the genocide there was made by John Pilger and screened by Carlton Television (for example on 26 January 1999). A good example of investigative journalists taking up difficult subjects and subjects unpopular to many people is the programme made by *WiA* about the gypsy refugees from Slovakia and the Czech Republic (Index, 1998).

Professional accolades were showered upon two 1995 productions by C4 *Dispatches*: 'The Drilling Fields' by Kay Bishop and Glenn Alison and 'The Torture Trail' by Martin Gregory; it is the folk wisdom of the industry though that such programmes excite only that specialist minority of people unusually interested in foreign affairs which are not salacious. That minority was also interested, if space in the *Guardian* is a guide, in the historical investigations into the treatment of persecuted minorities in the 1930s–1950s by Swiss banks and German industries, started by journalist Oskar Scheiben (in the Swiss *Wochenzeitung*). Among many historical investigations undertaken by UK journalists in the 1990s, some touched upon in Chapter 13, one of the most distinguished is surely that by then *Guardian* reporter Jaspar Becker, who researched the 1958–61 famine in China for his book *Hungry Ghosts*.

No survey of investigative journalism can avoid mentioning *Panorama*, Britain's longest running current affairs television programme and the BBC's 'flagship', and yet this programme is probably not widely regarded as principally investigative. It provides reportage, a lot of analysis and some investigation; its decision-makers have always to be careful to remember that politicians will read its programmes as the voice of the BBC. Clive Edwards, deputy editor, describes the programme thus:

> *Panorama* is probably the most famous current affairs programme in the world and is also the BBC's flagship programme. It is under pressure to produce some level of ratings that helps to justify its place on BBC 1, yet at the same time it is also there to be the centrepiece of the BBC's News and Current Affairs operation so that we have to, and want to, do the world's major stories. We will therefore do 'the euro' even though it will not thrill many viewers; we will do it because the programme helps fulfil the BBC's 'mission to explain' serious issues which are going to affect peoples' lives dramatically. You have to work very hard to make some issues entertaining and, no matter how well you do that, they may still get only a small audience. This applied to the Scottish elections, to Rwanda, to the euro.
>
> (Edwards, 1999)

Whenever something becomes a major public concern, a 'contentious issue in the public gaze' – mobile phones ('The Mobile Mystery', 24 May 1999); genetically modified foods ('Frankenstein Foods', 17 May 1999), working mothers ('Missing Mum', 3 February 1997) or meningitis ('Every Parent's Nightmare', 22 February 1999) – *Panorama* covers it; but, as Edwards suggests, it also takes on the task of dealing with matters that are not of widespread interest, though by any standard of public importance such as the Scottish elections ('The Battle for Britain', 26 April 1999), biological warfare ('Plague Wars', 13 and 14 July 1998) or Rwanda ('When Good Men Do Nothing', 7 December 1998). Its investigative journalism of the last ten years has included a revelation of government abuse of the rules on public information ('Getting the Message Across', BBC 1989). Reporter Vivian White examined a public service advertising campaign on television about the retraining of unemployed young people and found that the times that the advertisements had been booked to run were not those that you would use to reach the young unemployed, but ABC1 opinion formers, whose view of the government's approach to youth unemployment, and therefore their votes, might be swayed by such a campaign.

In 'The Great Pensions Gamble' (14 October 1996) the team put a secret camera into a flat and let salesmen from different companies pitch to a member of the *Panorama* team presenting himself as the client (with the same biographical details each time) to see which companies were mis-selling. Early in the life of the 1997 Labour government *Panorama* made a programme about the state of the London Underground system, commonly agreed to need new investment ('Down the Tube', 16 June 1997). The incoming Labour administration had committed itself to the previous government's spending totals but also to modernisation of the Underground. 'Logically, that left only one solution – privatisation' (White, 1999). However, the government minister and his associates were against privatisation. After the ministerial interview standard to such an analytical programme, one of the *Panorama* team found a file marked 'Panorama' on the floor of the office in which the interview (with the minister who was hostile to privatisation) had taken place. When the reporter opened it he realised that it contained the minister's briefing notes, which revealed that the government was indeed considering privatisation. Once this useful documentary evidence had been incorporated into the programme and made the desired stink, the programme might well be described as investigative journalism, albeit by chance. Despite the limited interest in foreign affairs, *Panorama* does many foreign stories. One which was rated highly by the critics was Tom Mangold's investigation of the UN weapons inspectors in Iraq and whether they had been penetrated by the CIA ('Secrets, Spies and Videotape', 22 March 1999).

Given the relatively small proportion of the available viewers that watches current affairs television, investigative journalism probably meant, for most British people, 'sleaze'. From 1992 the *News of the World* investigated the private lives of minister after minister, six of whom were forced to resign on account of some intimate entanglement. Nevertheless the scope of investigative journalism was quite extraordinary and became a well-established feature of British public life in the 1990s, thanks to developments in the organisation and economics of the press, consumer demand and broadcasting regulation, the consequences of which were to become only too apparent in the Blair years.

Notes

1 In the late 1960s national media with dedicated investigative personnel included: **press** *Sunday Times* (Insight), *Observer* (Daylight), *Guardian*, *Daily Telegraph* (Closeup),

New Statesman, Leveller, Private Eye, News of the World, Daily Mirror; **television** *World in Action, Panorama, TV Eye, Man Alive, The London Programme.*

2 The particular member was Princess Michael of Kent. When I taxed Bob Warren, Executive Editor of *NoW* to justify such an intrusion into privacy (the princess and her lover had been endlessly trailed, deceived and photographed) he replied that since she was 'on the Civil List', i.e. in receipt of public funds, she should behave impeccably or expect to be exposed (Warren, 1999).

3 Harold Evans makes a telling point about the difference between the US and UK when he compares the contrasting experiences of Mr Robert MacFarlane in the Iran Contra Scandal and Mr Clive Ponting in the *Belgrano* affair. In America, MacFarlane, President Reagan's National Security Adviser, was prosecuted for deceiving Congress. In Britain it was the whistle-blower Ponting who revealed the deception of Parliament, not the deceiving Minister of the Crown, who was prosecuted (Evans, 1997: 9).

4 Fayed did not reveal everything at once, by any means. The whole exciting story of how the reporters built up their case and fought for it is in Leigh and Vulliamy (1997). Because of what it teaches about journalistic methods, the British polity today and the legal framework for journalism, this book is essential reading for all students of British journalism.

5 Astoundingly, in retrospect, Aitken was promoted to Cabinet rank in 1994 even as information about his behaviour was surfacing.

6 There is no space to discuss the German master of these techniques, Wallraff, here, but his methods and general approach are well described in his book *The Undesirable Journalist.*

Bibliography

Adams, V. (1986) *The Media and the Falklands Campaign.* London: Macmillan.

Bailey, S. H. and Jones, B. L. (1995) *Civil Liberties: Cases and Materials.* London: Butterworths.

Bainbridge, C. and Stockdill, R. (1993) *The News of the World Story.* London: Harper Collins.

BBC (1989) *Panorama:* 'Getting the Message Across' (reporter: V. White). London: BBC.

Becker, J. (1996) *Hungry Ghosts: China's Secret Famine.* London: John Murray.

Bolton, R. (1990) *Death on the Rock and Other Stories.* London: W. H. Allen.

Brown, G. (1995) *Exposed!* London: Virgin.

de Burgh, H. (1998) Audience, journalist and text in television news. Paper delivered at the Annual Conference of the International Association for Media and Communications Research, Glasgow, July 1998.

Byrne, D. (1999) Talk to the students of the MA Investigative Journalism course at Nottingham Trent University, 29 April 1999.

Carlton TV (1997) 'Breaking the Mirror: The Murdoch Effect' (reporter: John Pilger). London: Carlton TV.

Channel 4 TV (1997) *Witness:* 'A Great Hatred'. London: Channel 4 Television.

Channel 4 TV (1998) *Dispatches:* 'Inspecting the Inspectors' (Sarah Spiller). London: Channel 4.

Clarke, D. (1983) *Corruption: Causes, Consequences and Control.* London: Frances Pinter.

Clarke, N. (1998) Spindoctors and the *World at One.* Talk to third year students on the BA Broadcast Journalism course at Nottingham Trent University, 13 November 1997.

Curran, J. (1997) *Power without Responsibility.* London: Routledge.

Cutler, J. and Edwards, R. (1988) *Britain's Nuclear Nightmare*. London: Sphere.

Doig, A. (1997) The decline of investigatory journalism. In M. Bromley and T. O'Malley (eds) *A Journalism Reader*. London: Routledge.

Dynes, M. (1995) *The New British State: The Government Machine in the 1990s*. London: Times Books.

Earle, P. (1963) Enter the blackmail syndicate. *News of the World*, 23 June 1963.

Eddy, P. (1976) *Destination Disaster*. London: Granada.

Edwards, C. (1999) Interview with Hugo de Burgh, 25 June 1999.

Edwards, R. (1999) Information to Hugo de Burgh by telephone 10 June 1999.

Evans, H. (1983) *Good Times, Bad Times*. London: Weidenfeld and Nicolson.

Evans, H. (1997) Prometheus unbound. Iain Walker Memorial Lecture, Green College, Oxford, May.

Ewing, K. D. and Gearty, C. A. (1990) *Freedom Under Thatcher: Civil Liberties in Modern Britain*. Oxford: Oxford University Press.

Fennell, P. (1983) Local government corruption in England and Wales. In M. Clarke *Corruption*. London: Frances Pinter.

Fitzwalter, R. (1998) Investigations. Talk to students on the MA Investigative Journalism course at Nottingham Trent University, 26 February 1998.

Fitzwalter, R. (1999) Interview with Hugo de Burgh, 18 March 1999.

Fitzwalter, R. and Taylor, D. (1981) *Web of Corruption: The Story of J. G. L. Poulson and T. Dan Smith*. London: Granada.

Foot, P. (1990) *Words as Weapons*. London: Verso.

Franklin, B. (1997) *Newszak and News Media*. London: Arnold.

Gibbons, T. (1998) *Regulating the Media*. London: Sweet and Maxwell.

Gillard, M. (1996) Revenue paid. *Observer*, 1 December 1996. See also Sadaam's banker. *Observer*, 23 February 1997.

Gillard, M. (1997) DMG – the agony goes on. *Observer*, 19 January 1997.

Gillard, M. and Tomkinson, M. (1980) *Nothing to Declare: The Political Corruptions of John Poulson*. London: John Calder.

Golding, P. (1998) The political and the popular: getting the message of tabloidisation. Paper delivered at the annual conference of the Association of Media, Cultural and Communications Studies, Sheffield, December 1998.

Goodwin, P. (1998) *Television under the Tories*. London: British Film Institute.

Granada Television (1973) *World in Action*: The Rise and Fall of John Poulson (reporter: Ray Fitzwalter). Manchester: Granada.

Granada Television (1974) *World in Action*: Business in Gozo (reporter: Ray Fitzwalter). Manchester: Granada.

Granada Television (1993) *World in Action: 30 Years*. Press Information issued by Granada, 7 January 1993. Manchester: Granada Television Ltd.

Harding, L., Leigh, D. and Pallister, D. (1997) *The Liar, The Fall of Jonathan Aitken*. London: Penguin.

Harris, R. (1994) *The Media Trilogy*. London: Faber and Faber.

Index on Censorship (1998) *Gypsies: Life on the Edge*. No. 4. London: Writers and Scholars.

Jones, G. (1999) Investigations and the Tabloids. Talk to students on the MA Investigative Journalism course at Nottingham Trent University, 4 March 1999.

Kingdom, J. (1991) *Government and Politics in Britain*. London: Polity.

Knightley, P. (1997) *A Hack's Progress*. London: Jonathan Cape.

Leapman, M. (1992) *Treacherous Estate*. London: Hodder and Stoughton.

Leigh, D. (1999) Aitken, the fixer and the secret multi-million pound arms deals. On the internet at http://www.icij.org/investigate/leigh.html, dated 28 May 1999.

Leigh, D. (1999a) Cash for Questions: A case study in media activism. Talk to members of the Chinese National Media Legislation Working Group held at Nottingham Trent University, 23 February 1999.

Leigh, D. and Vulliamy, E. (1997) *Sleaze: The Corruption of Parliament*. London: Fourth Estate.

Leppard, D. (1997) The Watergate model in UK journalism. Talk to students on the MA Investigative Journalism course at Nottingham Trent University, 27 November 1997.

Lloyd, D. (1998) Talk to the students of the MA Investigative Journalism course at Nottingham Trent University, 19 February 1998.

Macaskill, I. (1984) Scandal in the sun. *News of the World*, 11 November 1984: 10.

Mahmood, M. (1998) Soccer chiefs and the vice girls. *News of the World*, 15 March 1998: 1.

Marnham, P. (1982) *The Private Eye Story*. London: André Deutsch.

Meyer, Sir A. (1998) Talk to the students of the MA Investigative Journalism course at Nottingham Trent University, 10 March 1998.

Molloy, M. (1997) The mirror crack'd. *New Statesman*, 14 February 1997.

National Union of Journalists (1994) *Rules of the National Union of Journalists*. London: NUJ: 50.

Neil, A. (1996) *Full Disclosure*. London: Macmillan.

Nolan, Lord (1995) *First Report of the Committee on Standards in Public Life*, Command: 2850– I. London: HMSO.

Page, B. (1998) A defence of 'low' journalism. *British Journalism Review*, 9 (1).

Pallister, D. *et al.* (1999) Aitken, the fixer . . . *Guardian*, 5 March 1999: 1 and 21.

Pilger, J. (1997) Gutted! *Guardian*, 15 February 1997.

Pincher, C. (1991) *The Truth about Dirty Tricks*. London: Sidgwick and Jackson.

Programme Reports (1995) London: The Programme Report Co. (Held at library of Nottingham Trent University.)

Smith, A. (1974) *The British Press since the War*. London: David and Charles.

Thornton, P. (1989) *Decade of Decline: Civil Liberties in the Thatcher Years*. London: NCCL.

Tompkinson, M. (1982) *The Pornbrokers*. London: Virgin.

Wallraff, G. (1977) *The Undesirable Journalist*. London: Pluto.

Warren, R. (1999) Earle and Mahmoud: a comparison of two styles of investigative journalism. Talk to students on the MA Investigative Journalism course at Nottingham Trent University, 11 March 1999.

White, V. (1999) *Panorama*'s place in the Polity. Talk to members of the Chinese National Media Legislation Working Group held at Nottingham Trent University, 11 February 1999.

Williams, F. (1957) *Dangerous Estate*. London: Longman.

Further reading

Harris, R. (1994) *The Media Trilogy*. London: Faber and Faber.

Knightley, P. (1997) *A Hack's Progress*. London: Jonathan Cape.

Leapman, M. (1992) *Treacherous Estate*. London: Hodder and Stoughton.

Marr, A. (2005) *My Trade: A Short History of British Journalism*. London: Pan Books.

4

THE BLAIR YEARS

Mediocracy and investigative journalism

Hugo de Burgh

Mediocracy and political corruption

Little did the journalists who congratulated each other on their revelations of sleaze realise that much, much worse was to come, such that the Major years of the mid-1990s would seem in retrospect a period of probity and disinterestedness.

It took them a little time to grasp what was going on. Many if not most in the media welcomed the election of Tony Blair and co. There is the famous and oft repeated story of the manager at the BBC who announced that questioning politicians was now out of date:

> Just after the 1997 general election, Peter Horrocks, the editor of Newsnight, told his staff that the days of digging up facts that might disconcert the powerful had passed. 'Labour has a huge mandate,' he wrote. 'Our job should not be to quarrel with the purpose of policy but question its implementation. Ennui is over for now.' In the unlikely event of his minions mistaking his meaning, Horrocks deployed the English establishment's most condescending put-down to get them on message. 'Clever-clever' questioning of the warm, new consensus was inappropriate. Newsnight's tradition of skeptical inquiry was mere 'trickiness and world-weariness'. What the show needed was a 'lighter feel'. And, by God, it quickly got it.
>
> (Cohen, 2000: 123)

While Blair and company were at first taken at their own valuation, even the most gullible of journalists found it difficult to swallow the Ecclestone affair, the first of many examples of corruption that were to taint the Blair decade. When the much-respected BBC presenter Nick Clarke lectured students in 1998 he was livid that a Prime Minister's spokesman had threatened to 'wreck his career' if he allowed the *World at One* team to make inquiries into the propriety of Minister, and leading Blair ally, Tessa Jowell's business affairs.[1]

As far as I am aware no systematic study of corruption under Blair, still less of the media's approaches to it, has been made. Nevertheless coverage grew and grew as it dawned on the press that they faced a government that was not merely not perfect, but one whose leaders' behaviour was unquestionably worse than those of its much mocked and investigated predecessor. Examples are given when we consider investigative journalism in the period, below.

Meanwhile in what politicians and journalists often refer to derisively – and perhaps occasionally, in awe – as 'the real world', the prestige of politics and the media had both plummeted remarkably. It is well established that trust and confidence in politics has declined, and that fewer people participate (Bromley and Curtice, 2002). Among the many explanations for this that are abroad are two particularly common ones: first, that the media are responsible for fostering scepticism about politics, and, second, that this scepticism is the cause of reduced turnout at elections. The fact that turnout has reduced markedly since 1997, and only since 1997 (Miller, 2004), has given rise to the theory that the Blair government's notorious belief in image over substance, in media manipulation, has been the causes of widespread disenchantment with politics, but most of all that the media themselves have undermined respect for political institutions and office holders.[2]

Debates

There has developed a new theory of the media, which differs from that of 'the media as the real opposition' discussed in the first edition of this book. In retrospect it now seems that although leading Editors, from Alan Rusbridger of the *Guardian* to David Lloyd of Channel 4, claimed for themselves that they had to replace a weak opposition and offer the only serious analysis and critique of government,[3] the media were arguably at least as cooperative as they were confrontational. The government, with its now famous media management system,[4] managed to control the agenda to an unprecedented degree, and bamboozled the media where they should have been most skeptical, for example with its dishonest claims over the Iraq War. When the media bayed for the blood of the leading BBC executives over the Gilligan affair (see Chapter 11) they were dancing to a tune played by the Blair government.[5] In a series of books arguing the case that the media and political elites are in fact collaborators, Peter Oborne has indicted the media for their failure properly to hold government to account.[6] Some of his work is discussed as an example of investigative journalism later in this chapter.

Yet at the beginning of the century, what caught the imagination of politicians in particular was a different theory, that of the media as a destructive power, eroding faith in public institutions and civil life through its relentless negativity and scepticism. The principal proponent of this theory was John Lloyd, although equally distinguished exponents of it were Onora O'Neil and the American author Phillip Bobbitt.[7]

The fact that John Lloyd is a well-established Labour Party supporter might be thought to weaken his credibility as a critic of the media's antagonistic treatment of the government. Writers less associated with Labour viewed things from another angle, though not entirely differently. However, Lloyd deflected attacks as a partisan of government when he, *pari passu*, also took issue with the media for being 'institutionally leftist', rejecting outright the old canard that the media are naturally Tory:

> . . . the left bias in the broadcast media − dominated as it is by the BBC, with some 40% of market share in television and a much higher share of radio − is perfectly clear. At a formal level, the chairman of the board of governors and the director general, Gavyn Davies and Greg Dyke, were both active Labour supporters and donors; although this is scandalous, it is doubtful whether either would seek to inject bias into the BBC's coverage. More germane is that the reflexes of the BBC, and of most broadcasters, are culturally and politically on the liberal left . . .
>
> (cit. in Aitken: 193–4)

Another leading journalist, Ian Hargreaves, agreed. He reported, for example, that in a 1995 poll, only 5 per cent of journalists questioned said they would vote Conservative and 57 per cent expressed support for Labour (Hargreaves, 2006: 232). Regular research around the world by Weaver (2000) has confirmed that this is not just a British phenomenon.

Returning to the BBC, Robin Aitken, a BBC reporter of 25 years standing, in an evidenced polemic, by a journalist evidently committed to the ideals of impartiality, fairness and truth espoused by the BBC, shows us how far he believes 'the most famous media brand in the world' has drifted from its principles. He argues that the BBC require that its people conform to an ideology suspiciously close to that of New Labour; gives the benefit of the doubt to a whole range of assumptions and beliefs with which it sympathises; that it is partial, cynical and unfair with those with whom it does not. Aitken's book was written before the mid-2007 revelations of dishonesty in the making of programmes, which included changing the meaning of an event involving the Queen by tampering with a filmed sequence, and cheating participants in quiz shows.

Aitken makes very firmly his point that the BBC has become institutionally biased, the transmitter of a political ideology. He holds that this ideology is that of the metropolitan political elites, originally only of New Labour. He makes no bones about his disenchantment with this ideology and his anger at the BBC for failing to interrogate it, or to admit that it is only one among competing views of the world. But his more general critique, of the standards of modern journalism, has been presaged by a notable series of studies by Steven Barnett, Peter Golding and others from a different perspective. There is commonly felt distress at the lowering of standards of reporting and of coverage (Barnett, 2000, 1999; Golding, 1999).

Don't blame the messenger

From this brief introduction to the debates it can be seen that the media have themselves become an important story. Everyone is trying to work out just how bad the media are for democracy, enlightenment and our moral health. It is an orthodoxy that the media are a negative impact on society and polity. But can this be justified? Are the media really to blame?

At one particular convention on the issue, a number of interesting points were made, which I attempt to summarise here.[8] First, a report by Catherine Bromley and John Curtice, presenting empirical research into the role of UK media in influencing voter behaviour, provides a valuable corrective to the premise, and indeed to the *Phillis Report*,[9] which was the government's response to the accusations. They examine whether voters have become more cynical, whether readers are more cynical and whether the cynical are less likely to vote. They go on to seek evidence as to whether consumers of media were more likely to become mistrustful of politics between 1997 and 2001 and whether the mistrustful are less likely to vote. Their findings are counterintuitive.

The decline in trust is no different between media users and non-users; the cynical are not necessarily more likely to eschew voting. There is only weak corroborative evidence to support the claim that newspapers generate cynicism, or that cynicism discourages people from voting. Cynicism had a somewhat greater impact on turnout in 2001 than it did in 1997 because those who had low levels of trust earlier had their inclinations reinforced by 2001, but the decline in voting during that period cannot be blamed generally on cynicism.

Bromley and Curtice suggest that the fall in turnout can better be attributed to the perception that there is no difference between the parties and to Labour's long dominance. They also point out that the influence of newspapers on British public life is diminishing because fewer people, particularly tabloid readers, read them. Moreover, those who have given up reading newspapers are likely to be those who have no interest in politics anyway, so it is hardly the fault of the tabloids that they are not interested in politics. These authors conclude that the media should not task themselves to improve the image of politics but to try to woo back customers.

Yet the media do apparently trivialise politics. Did you know that during the 2001 election in England, a Yorkshire butcher sold sausages in blue, red or yellow? Lots of readers did, although they would have preferred their press to shut up about bangers and tell them more about policies. By contrast with Bromley and Curtice, Bob Franklin tells us that local newspapers' style of coverage of general elections 'may be one factor in explaining the sustained decline in public interest and participation in elections evident since the 1980s'.

In a beguiling corrective to another orthodoxy, Franklin's empirical work shows that journalists' assumptions that they have to localise and personalise politics are wrong and that readers do not necessarily find political coverage 'boring'. Readers were interested in 'Europe' and 'taxation' but journalists were intent on providing quirky and amusing stories or biopics of candidates, dumbing down, in other words. But it is not only the media that are at this; the parties were making the same mistake as the journalists, assuming that they had to emphasise the local, both in news management and in candidate selection.

Political economy is behind the journalists' emphases: the big conglomerates that have gobbled up local newspapers have priorities far removed from education, information and enlightenment. They want a general readership and they do not want to turn anybody off. The staffing is 'leaner' and there is much reliance on ready sources of copy. In 2001, some editors got close to avoiding coverage of the election at all. They asked themselves, 'Can we get value for money out of it?', and the reply was, only just, 'maybe'.

To complement Franklin's research, Andrew Russell's study tears into the media, and particularly media directed at youth, for reinforcing, or perhaps creating, apathy about politics. He demonstrates that there is an assumption among those who work in the media that politics are boring, from the editor of a leading daily newspaper who blames politicians for their dress sense to presenters of children's BBC who, in the preamble to a political story, refer to it as 'pretty dull'. So the media may be, at least in part, to blame for the widespread perception that voting changes nothing, but so are politicians if they give the impression that politics are all about presentation, about tricking people into voting for you. It is this impression that results in such a high proportion of young people (as Russell tells us) claiming to have 'no interest in politics at all'.

The narrower focus of the study by James Thomas, Stephen Cushion and John Jewell provides evidence of the media's tendency to follow the orthodoxy, in this case to allow 'apathy' to dominate its coverage of the 2003 Welsh Assembly elections, to interpret 'apathy' as discontent with devolution and to emphasise these matters to the exclusion of policy issues. They also argue that media representation of political attitudes is, typically, simplified and over emphasises the negative. They also suggest that assumptions about citizens' low level of interest in politics are wrong, if research is taken into account (Worcester and Mortimore, 2001) and probably reflect the media elite's disdain for ordinary people.

Another elite demonstrated awareness of the widespread concerns about spin and its possibly corrosive effects by commissioning an inquiry into government communications, the Phillis Report,[10] the premise of which was that the Blair government's handling of relations with the media was the root of widespread scepticism about politics generally. The one man most associated with that handling was Alastair Campbell. The influence of Campbell upon our political life has yet to be thoroughly assessed.[11] Spin has always existed, but what Campbell did was to bring into public life an obsession with appearance at the expense of meaning, together with a vulgar vocabulary and thuggish approach which infected other government officials, such as Jo Moore,[12] to an extent that these intangibles may have been as important in diminishing public life as his more concrete corruptions of democracy: purging the government information services, swamping ministries with special advisers, subjecting cabinet ministers to the will of press officers, bullying elected representatives and 'enhancing' information. Many may be relieved that the Phillis Report exists as some sort of acknowledgment that what Campbell and co did has to be corrected. Ivor Gaber argues, however, that Phillis misses the point, that its proposals will decrease, rather than increase, transparency in government communications and further reduce accountability to parliament. Gaber considers that it is not tinkering with the roles of information officers, but expanding the power of elected politicians that will 'start to challenge the public's perceptions of deep mistrust'.

David Miller performs the invaluable service of placing the media within the wider context of political economy, showing the distortions in the way the media work and their impact upon politics as reflections of the greater political crisis in representation and participation. He illustrates how the media are blamed for the democratic deficit, the arguments now increasingly associated with John Lloyd (2002, 2004), but argues that it is not the way the media treat politics that is problematic but rather 'what this signifies in terms of decline of democratic process'.

We should be looking at how the media are reflecting the increasing dominance of business interests in 'both style and substance of politics'; the wrecking of cabinet government by Prime Minister Blair's intimates and propaganda machine; the dominance of parliament by government and the failure of parliament to hold government to account; the erosion of the intermediate institutions of democracy (Willetts, 1994: 21); the perception that the Prime Minister can disregard the views not merely of the public as identified by the opinion polls but also of parliament and his party over such a critical matter as an aggressive war; the leeching of power to EU institutions. The so-called 'Americanisation' of political discourse, as with the growing influence of the PR and lobbying industries, brings us politicians who conform to celebrity conventions of deportment, appear more actors than leaders, more commodities than consciences. Miller does not deny media collusion: coverage of international affairs is down, current affairs and documentaries wane, spin and propaganda go uninterrogated, sensationalism wins over reason. He holds these to be symptoms, or parts, of the problem, rather than its cause.

From an international perspective, the theory that the media in Britain have become the enemies of democracy is a curious one, since elsewhere they emancipate, even where they do so against great odds. All over the world, the media are acquiring new functions and demonstrating new types of influence over society and politics. Al Jazeera TV shows the Arab world's new ways of thinking about politics (Sakr, 2005); investigative journalism undermines political authoritarianism in Latin America (Waisbord, 2001); in China, the media hold crooks to account and show (some) politicians in the dock (de Burgh, 2003). Institutional and technological changes that are global combine with local political and cultural circumstances to hand the media new powers.

The UK studies I have quoted suggest that, while something is indeed wrong in the relationship between the media and politics in Britain, to blame the media is to fail to look at the forces framing and driving those media. Politicians get the media they deserve: only they can get us out of the mess they have got us into, perhaps by attending to the forces that influence the media, but certainly by restoring respect for a political system whose significance in their lives, and whose potential, many people no longer understand.

In these circumstances, what has happened to investigative journalism? Is there more or less? What can we say about investigative journalism since the first edition of this book? How did investigative journalists deal with the big issues of the moment? Can we discern any kind of relationship between the big contextual issues of the media and politics and the way investigative journalism has been developing?

Investigative journalism in the twenty-first century[13]

There seems to be much more investigative journalism and a wide variety of topics is dealt with; celebrity investigators and undercover operations are more in evidence than ever before; how much of investigative journalism really qualifies is open to question, following a spate of revelations of dishonesty or error; it is argued that some of the most important stories are avoided.

When asked for their judgments, commissioners and observers put forward several for the accolade of 'best'. John Ware's Omagh programme for Panorama: *Who Bombed Omagh?* in which he named individuals who had been questioned by police over the car bombing. It had been carried out by The Real IRA and claimed 29 lives but nobody had, up to the time of the programme, been charged with the atrocity. Other favourites were *Beneath The Veil*, a C4 Dispatches on Afghanistan. and *Jamie's School Dinners* 'It was a piece of journalism and it had real impact'.

I will first go through some representative examples from the topics which have been covered in investigative journalism and then look at the audiences, approaches and the issues raised by the oeuvre.

Welfare

Interrogation of our health and welfare provision has increased. Goaded first by the promises of reform made by successive politicians, and then by the spectacle of those politicians preferring, apparently, to pour huge sums into public services rather than properly to reform them, journalists have been unflinching in pointing out the failures of the health and welfare systems.

Cruelty and neglect in care homes for the elderly has been revealed by both a BBC *Panorama* investigation and several newspapers. *Panorama*: 'Please Look After Mum' (BBC, 12 February 2007) exposed shocking abuse as did a *Sunday Times* investigation, 'Exposed: filth and abuse in care homes' which contrasted the huge profits made from care homes with the squalid conditions of their residents (Newell, 2007).

The *Observer* revealed 'errors and negligence' in UK hospitals 'that result in stillbirths or disabled babies', following a tradition of investigating hospitals (see first edition).

Another much discussed topic was adoption. Davies (2007) brought a new angle by showing how a way of ensuring that children born to women who, often with regret, could not bring them up, might be given a stable home, has turned into a business in which young women are encouraged to supply babies. While childless couples benefit, so too do lawyers and commercial adoption agencies; the agencies are accused of providing material incentives for and applying moral pressure to, vulnerable young women in order to provide more product, i.e. babies.

MacIntyre Undercover : 'Children's Homes' was an investigation of how homes for sub-normal children are managed, in which the reporter seeks and gets a job working in such a home. He found that many of the children were treated with cruelty and neglect.

Notwithstanding this, there is dreadful evidence that many people in this rich society really are desperate, as Nick Davies' *Dark Heart: The Shocking Truth About Hidden Britain* reported to us in 1996. Davies' book investigates 'the undiscovered country of the poor' in harrowing detail – prostitutes, drug users, children on the streets, thieves, you name it. It is in the tradition of Dickens and you do not have to agree with his apportioning of blame to find his work moving. For he was writing when the assumption was that these horrors were the product of 1980s economic policies. It is difficult to believe that now; there are other interpretations. But the awfulness reported by Davies still exists, indeed by some accounts may be more widely diffused and worse.

Business

Some older business stories are discussed in Chapter 13. Although in recent years there have been bilious attacks on politicians – there have been relatively few on business.

> . . . during the past four decades big corporations, financiers and banks
> have hugely extended their influence over the lives of ordinary people
> who have become more dependent on them for their shopping, their

leisure or their credit. Government itself has co-operated much more closely with the private sector, as the Treasury has delegated more and more projects to commercial consortia. And the professions . . . – lawyers, academics and journalists – who have had a record of proud independence, have all become more interlocked with the interests of big business.

(Sampson, 2004: 244)

Here are some exceptions.

Watchdog is the BBC's main consumer affairs programme, and it investigates at least three stories in each edition, usually small-scale scams. In a pathetic example (Series 21: 9 May 2007) you see a small-time crook being investigated – he offers to provide entertainment for children's parties but does not, probably used because of its popular appeal and attractive images.

In 'The Supermarket that's Eating Britain', C4 *Dispatches* (2006) examined the food business that dominates two thirds of food retailing. It looks at its plans for further expansion, tax avoidance and the way it has made friends with the Labour government and exploits its connections to exert influence.

A business investigation that hit the headlines was *Ryanair: Caught Napping*, transmitted 13 February 2006. Ryanair is Europe's largest low-cost airline, operating 270 low-fare routes to 21 European countries.

> Two Dispatches undercover reporters spent five months secretly filming Ryanair's training programme and onboard flights as members of the cabin crew. The reporters reveal what really takes place behind the scenes: inadequate safety and security checks, dirty planes, exhausted cabin crew and pilots complaining about the number of hours they have to fly.
>
> (www.channel4.com)

Seroxat is an anti-depressant drug that had for a number of years first been prescribed for adults, and then for children. *Secrets of the Drug Trials: GlaxoSmithKline (GSK)*, transmitted in 2007, claims to show not that Seroxat is unsafe, because an earlier BBC *Panorama* programme had already done that in 2006, but that the system supposed to monitor the drug companies is inadequate and that research supposedly written by respected academics can be ghost written by drug company researchers and their PR officers.

The biggest single business story to be investigated – I exclude Enron as a huge story but with no one major investigation of it – was BAE. Of the investigation into bribery by British Aerospace, the judges of the Paul Foot Award stated:

> Four parliamentary debates, the removal of an attorney-general, criminal investigations on three continents, another investigation by the US

78

department of justice and a special investigation of the UK by the OECD under an international bribery treaty – few investigations by British journalists have provoked such widespread international consequences.[13]

David Leigh and Rob Evans' work is available on http://www.guardian.co.uk/baefiles/. At the time of going to press its latest allegation was that BAE secretly paid Prince Bandar of Saudi Arabia more than £1bn in connection with Britain's biggest ever weapons contract.

In his book *As Used on the Famous Nelson Mandela: Underground Adventures in The Arms and Torture Trade* (London: Ebury Press, 2006), Thomas states:

> The easiest way to make contact with people who want guns is to read Amnesty International's annual human rights report, see who comes out worse and then nip round to their embassy. These places often have picket lines of protestors outside, but you can always nip past the chants and candlelit vigils by saying you are going to hand in a letter of protest. Once in the front door, head for the defence attaches office; they will probably have a list of the guns they want written out and waiting.
>
> (Thomas, 2006: 1)

He uses a number of witty tricks to get reactions from and interviews with people in the arms business, but these devices are also to amuse you as you grapple with the statistics and details of the trade. He gets the lowdown on how the UK government guarantees, and often pays for, the country's arms exports to other countries, arms exports which often end up being used to do two things: slaughter the poor, the ethnic minorities or even the people who provided the arms, and enrich corrupt generals and political gangsters. He works out how the government subsidises jobs in the arms trade (every job by over £13,000 a year); how the corruption works; how shackles get sold by a company so historic its started with leg irons for slaves; who sells electric shock torture kits and other 'widgets of barbarity'. He also takes a hefty swipe at the British government's laughable claims of having an 'ethical foreign policy'.

Foreign affairs

> Post 9/11 the world matters and it matters if it's happening outside your front door and if it happens half a world away.
>
> (Sutcliffe, 2007)

It used to be a truism that only a tiny minority cared what happened abroad. Now, apparently, this is not so for English audiences. Kevin Sutcliffe, head of investigations at C4 TV (see Chapter 15) thinks that the Twin Towers of

11 September 2001 made a big difference. Among the programmes he has been able to commission as a result are a series on what has been going on inside Iraq, such as *Iraqi Death Squads*, which claims to be a revelation of how Iraq is really run today – by gangsters who happen to be the police. The programme shows us the trigger-happy thugs at work and secretly films inside an illegal prison.

Sutcliffe increasingly uses film-makers from places inaccessible to his regular UK suppliers, in Iraq, Chechnya and Burma for example. This has the other advantage of 'giving us other voices. Investigative journalism has a tendency to be a middle-aged male domain and it's nice to be able to break that down' (Sutcliffe, 2007).

Other stories use different media. In a careful analysis of painstakingly marshalled facts, Ed Harriman tells us the story of just who has benefited from the 2003–7 Iraq War and how. His saga of the looting of Iraq was published in *The London Review of Books*,[14] a reminder that journalism today, and investigative journalism, flourishes in many diverse places, from ostensibly literary magazines to think-tank pamphlets and blogs.

The best-known work of foreign affairs investigative journalism in the period was probably *Ghost Plane*, Stephen Grey's book discussed in Chapter 11.

> Grey asked *The Guardian* to fund the research but in the end he did so with a publisher's advance and spin-off pieces sold to the newspapers as the investigation went along. He stumbled in the course of doing this on the fact that flights by the CIA were all logged somewhere and managed to crack into the computer system. He and Duncan Campbell were able to trace who was being rendered even down to the hotel at which the CIA guards stayed while they were picking up [the victims]. This was a story of major importance which only his dogged determination got off the ground because no major editorial group would fund it.
>
> (Knightly, 2007)

A feature film (*Rendition*, 2007) later dealt with one, but central, aspect of the many issues raised by Grey.

British foreign policy is today very dependent upon the competence and resources of our armed forces. One of the C4 *Insider* series[15] employed Bob Stewart, a former UN Commander of British Forces in Bosnia, to investigate the Territorial Army, civilians in uniform, in today's military operations. Once upon a time the TA was a reserve, simply to be called on in times of extreme crisis; now 'bank managers, mortgage advisers, road workers and teachers . . . facing an average of five insurgent missile and mortar attacks every day'.

Poor training and equipment, little support for families back home and low morale are all causing a haemorrhaging of membership of the TA. The politicians are in effect using the TA to fill gaps in their provision, and thus destroying it.

Public policy issues

The burgeoning power of the state in Britain, and the accelerating privatisation of functions, and their removal beyond public oversight is a phenomenon widely identified, early on and notably by Freedland in his polemic on England's stymied democratic development.[16] Increasingly journalists look to the making and implementation of public policy in representative areas of state activity.

There have been many programmes on immigration, but one of the most arresting was when *Panorama*'s Richard Bilton went to Slough to find out the effects of immigration on the town's people and the local council's finances.[17] Not only did he find that at least 10,000 Poles had moved in in three years, but also that central government no longer had any idea at all of the numbers; that local government was overwhelmed and that earlier immigrants were frightened of the implications for community of the waves of new arrivals. 'Immigration: How We Lost Count' showed in microcosm what was happening in many other towns and cities but the investigative element was the revelation of the incompetence of the government.

The same government for several years advocated that babies be inoculated with a triple vaccine called MMR because it defended babies against Measles, Mumps and Rubella. There was widespread panic after the media reported that medical researchers at an important research hospital feared that the MMR vaccine was dangerous, that it might cause autism and other problems.

Dispatches: 'MMR' revealed that some medical researchers had deliberately cast doubt upon MMR, because they wanted to develop and sell their own vaccine. The programme showed the research upon which the doubts were based was faulty and exposed that the researchers would have benefited financially from replacement of MMR by their own concoction.

The rather extraordinary claim, commonly bruited about, that the British is the most spied on population in the world, and the unease felt by many journalists and lawyers at the government's apparently heavy-handed anti-terrorism measures, has lead to some good articles, programmes and books on surveillance. Ross Clark tried to make a rather short journey in England without being spied on and made it the hook of his *The Road to Southend Pier*.[18]

Many people have, regardless of their own political views, expressed shock at the 'avalanche of security legislation' promulgated by the UK government in the last few years. In C4 *Dispatches*: 'Stealing Freedom' (27 November 2006) reporter Peter Hitchens examines how the civil liberties of ordinary people have been affected. 'The result', Hitchens explains, 'is that we are sleepwalking into a Big Brother state.' Travelling across Britain, Hitchens meets ordinary people who have suffered needlessly because of new legislation and increased police powers.[19]

Environmental concerns

To 'whitewash' something means to cover something with a coat of white paint so that you cannot see the 'reality' underneath. In this programme, *Dispatches*: 'Greenwash' the reporter reports on how government and companies pretend that they are pursuing 'green' (beneficial to the environment) policies whereas in fact they are not. For example, a car manufacturer pretends its cars are environmentally beneficial, whereas only a tiny number of their cars are; the government introduces regulations on housing construction but does not police their implementation, and so on.

Corruption

It has seemed, over the past ten years, that there has been a new revelation almost every week. The first to hit the public consciousness was the Ecclestone affair, when a racing promoter paid millions to the Labour Party so that his company might be exempted from new legislation. The one that is probably indelibly dyed into the consciousness of the British public is the investigation of Prime Minister Blair over selling seats in the Upper House of Parliament, which dragged on until, at about the same time, politicians managed to squash the inquiry and Tony Blair resigned both from office and from Parliament (2007).

Seizing on a random clutch of clippings from 2006, we note these stories: The multitude of ways in which associates of the government have received rewards; Cherie Blair (the then Prime Minister's wife) receiving fees and gifts; links between big companies who win government contracts and Labour leaders (Turnbull, 2006; Boffey, 2006); planning rewards for Labour donors (Turnbull, 2006a); the greed with which Ministers have hoovered up perks such as apartments, cars and expenses (Turnbull, 2006b); breaking the rules on party funding (Grice, 2006); politicians enriching themselves by exploiting privileges (Buckwell, 2006); by using offshore facilities (Oliver, 2006); how lobbyists influence ministers on contracts (Winnett); links between Blairs' personal financial arrangements, Labour party backers and government contracts (Turnbull and Walters, 2006); defrauding of the taxpayer through sale of public assets (Heathcoat Amory, 2006); allegations of tax fraud and money laundering against the husband of Blair ally Tessa Jowell (Channel 4). Perhaps corruption fatigue set in, perhaps Gordon Brown, the new Prime Minister's, team really did manage to clean up the government, but there seemed less to reveal of political corruption in 2007, when the biggest stories seemed to be how married cabinet ministers Cooper and Balls cashed in on the perks of office (Merrick, 2007) and the scrutiny of the business affairs and political associations of BBC presenter Kirsty Wark and her husband. Aside from those allegations, it was questioned whether, as BBC *Newsnight* presenter she should have had Scotland's First Minister holidaying in her Spanish villa and whether certain commercial advantages had accrued to her because of her Labour Party associations (McKinstry, 2007).

In a thorough examination, Hosken (2006) traced the gerrymandering of the leader of Westminster Council, Dame Shirley Porter, although, that being old and famous news, his efforts are useful more as guide to future would-be investigators of local government than as revelation.

'Labour's Gambling Addiction' is an example of a corruption story that did not quite make it. It started with the premise that somebody in government had to be benefiting from a policy as unpopular as the relaxation of controls on gambling, since it was so obvious in the interest only of big, usually foreign, businesses. It failed to find significant corruption and had to settle for the government's greed for taxes and free-market mania as culprits. In this programme the Freedom of Information Act (see Chapter 7) made a difference. The journalists were able to access documents dealing with the awarding of casino franchises, something which ten years ago would not have been possible, thereby placing the topic beyond bounds.

When is a work of journalism investigative, and when 'merely' analytical or even polemical? This question has often been asked of the work of, for example, John Pilger. Nick Davies' *Dark Heart*, exposed unpleasant facts about British society with a powerful sense of mission in the tradition of W.T. Stead. So too do the very different writings of Peter Oborne, who has produced three books which tell us a great deal about how our country is run; the most powerful of them *The Triumph of the Political Class* was produced just as we went to press.[20] As with Davies, it is the factual revelations that shock, as much as the arguments derived from them. He, and others, have theorised about the rise of a political class in Britain as representing a complete rupture with the politics to which we are accustomed, and which retains only sufficient of the outward forms of past politics to deceive us into thinking that the content remains.

Although he does not spell this out, it seems implicit from Oborne's researches that Britain is developing a version of the politics that took the world by storm in the twentieth century, what we may come to call the century of socialism. Then, cliques came to power, often by revolution, claiming that by sweeping away intermediate institutions – 'bourgeois' law, autonomous universities, adversary politics, impartial civil servants – they would connect directly with, and thus reflect, the will of the people. This is what happened in Hitler's Germany, Lenin's Russia, Mao's China and Mussolini's Italy. Charismatic politics were allowed to replace politics by due process.

Mere polemic would not back these assertions with more than cursory evidence, but Oborne has assembled a good deal of evidence, and examined it within the perspectives of recent past practice in British politics and political theory, so it is much, much more than polemic. He treads a path first marked out by Bob Franklin when he identifies the ways in which the 1997 government sought to politicise the civil service, and by Ivor Gaber and Steven

Barnett, and in several books by Nicholas Jones, when they described its misuse of the media. Oborne goes further, showing how there has been a change in the nature of government and the development of a culture of bullying and manipulation as well as a subverting of normal procedures, which has had a disastrous results.

> This refusal to engage with the normal process of government, to take notes, and to consult with civil servants and others, can be seen in retrospect to be responsible for many of the most grievous policy failures of recent years, above all the fiasco and waste of money surrounding the introduction of tax credits.
>
> (Oborne, 2007: 141)

He shows in authoritative detail the way in which the civil service has been sidelined, and power given to the Prime Minister's political creatures – former flatmates, party donors, sycophants and bouncers. The dividing line between party and state collapsed; that between public sector and market was muddled such that we can almost speak of a 'corporate takeover of British state' and all this resulted not in achievements but a rapid decline in elementary competence (Oborne, 2007: 147–51).

Some of Oborne's best work is his analysis of the behaviour of the Standards and Privileges Committee of the House of Commons, where he reveals how Standards Commissioner Filkin was persecuted and discredited; the techniques used by the leaderships to nobble members; the different standards applied to the cases of compliant and well-connected MPs regardless of political party and those not protected.[21] The complicity of the three parties appears to make clear that the adversarial system of government is in abeyance.

Oborne goes further when he shows how, to an unprecedented degree, leading members of Blair's government 1997–2007 abused their positions to enjoy sexual favours, to enrich themselves and to provide gifts to their friends at public expense; to use civil servants for personal, and sometimes demeaning, tasks; to break rules of conduct that if broken by a civil servant would have resulted in sacking; to extract free holidays and other personal advantages; routinely to lie about their transgressions. He provides further evidence that Mrs Blair herself behaved as 'a member of a privileged elite who [do] not have to adhere to the rules and norms set down for the bulk of the population'. Even if the details are hazy, it is now generally understood that Blair was heavily involved in selling favours, not just honours but also policy, for donations. Furthermore it seems at least plausible that British foreign policy was carried out under the influence of the only man willing to support Blair's greedy lifestyle upon retirement, Rupert Murdoch, and with an eye out for Blair's future earnings in the USA. Unfortunately Oborne's researches stop there; he asks, as have others, why the clandestine and suspicious relationship between Blair and Murdoch has not been investigated properly.[22]

The media

Investigation of the media themselves seems to be a new excitement. Radio 4's *Document* 'letters to *the Times*' reveals how the BBC had been complicit in government propaganda; it had sacked journalists who were sceptical about the EU on the recommendation of a Foreign Office propaganda unit.

The *Sunday Times* investigated, in 'How the BBC dances to an IRA tune' the demonisation of the Irish protestants and sympathy for IRA.[23] In another examination of the BBC, a thorough piece of investigation done by a senior BBC executive on sabbatical, David Kerr, reported that, in one particularly tendentious and influential documentary, the journalist reporting on a particular group was an outright, active opponent of those upon whom he was reporting who chose his evidence partially, excluded facts where they did not suit his case, misused statistics, selected case studies so as to mislead, distorted arguments, traduced interviewees, misrepresented the opinions of interviewees, uttered false statements and made damaging accusations without giving opportunity of rebuttal.[24]

To conclude this brief survey of topics, investigative journalism has covered an ever-wider variety of subject matter, although its critics suggest that it avoids the really difficult though potentially most rewarding subjects, such as the recent Prime Minister's financial affairs, the governing party's relationship with the postal unions, the quangocracy, local government and the doings of all but a very few major businesses.

Format

Looking back to the 1990s it is now clear that a new phenomenon had come about – the investigative reporter became an actor, an entertainer as much as the earnest gumshoe of yore. It started with Roger Cook, a pioneer. By the early years of this century others had taken his ideas much further.

We see those ideas, for example, in Cook's 'Bird Bandits', an investigation into the illegal export of peregrine falcons, an endangered species. The birds were sold mainly in the Arab world where they are used in sport. The team films robbers of birds' nests and secret meetings with prospective Arab buyers. But the tease emphasises Cook the magician. In part of the programme, Roger Cook will disguise himself as a wealthy and be-robed Arab in order to trick thieves into selling him the birds. This is trailed heavily at the start, where Cook is shown being made up and having a false beard attached.

Soon we have other players in this game. Whereas Cook exuded a certain authority, a certain moral gravitas, younger Paul Kenyon, of *Kenyon Confronts*, hams up a 'chirpy chappie' image, making clear that he is just any old bloke, with no more skills than you and I or Maureen by the slot machine might have. He's just employing his citizen wits in 'Bogus Marriage' and his hectic activity is made part of the story. The issue is serious; it seems that there are many tens of thousands of marriages that are false, in the sense that they are undertaken by strangers so that one side can win the UK citizenship of the other. Some of the women – they are usually women – have been married in this way many times and earn a good living at it. He checks out the marriage registers to see who is pretending to a false address; treks around the streets knocking on doors to locate couples he wants to check up on, videos weddings to show how dodgy they are, pretends to be a wedding photographer and, scattering confetti, calls out for the grooms to kiss the brides.

From cheeky chappie to sex symbol. Donal MacIntyre of *MacIntyre Undercover* shows off techniques and torso. In the trailer you see him stripped off to wire himself up for recording, unshaven chin exuding maleness, the deep voice that of the seducer. The *MacIntyre Undercover* series have covered many different subjects, among which football hooligans; homes for subnormal children and the European fashion industry, where MacIntyre found that the people responsible for taking care of young models were both getting them hooked on drugs and enjoying them sexually. At the start of each programme he introduces himself: 'I'm Donal MacIntyre, and I'm a reporter for the BBC'. He then reviews his recent achievements, over clips of himself in dangerous situations, with thugs and rapists and gangsters. You know that, with Donal, you're in for something juicy: violence, sex, corruption, cruelty. It's like those old fashioned horror films that start with the vampire sticking his teeth into the virgin's neck at the very start. Shudder, and enjoy!

By contrast with the butch style, ITV in August 2007 introduced Nina Hobson, the *Undercover Mum*. Hobson is given to us as 'an ordinary mum with two children. She used to be an undercover police officer investigating everything from rape to robbery'.[25] In a three-part series Hobson investigates family issues: children's food, teenage drinking and families who are going thousands of pounds into the red to fund their lifestyles.

Techniques

As MacFadyen and Hanna show us in their chapters, the key skill required in IJ is research. The journalist needs to know how to get information, how to analyse it and how to evaluate it. But whereas a few investigations tell you how they go about that – as does a film such as *Erin Brockovich* – there is more and more emphasis on the entertaining aspects:

- Infiltration
- Impersonation
- Secret filming
- Dramatisation
- Reconstruction.

Infiltration

Donal MacIntyre is the TV master of infiltration; Mazour Mahmood his newspaper equivalent (see Chapter 19). Perhaps the most famous infiltration of the period was Mark Daly's, reported in BBC's 'Secret Policeman' in 2003.[26] He joined Greater Manchester police as a trainee and spent five-and-a-half months posing as a probationary constable.

He secretly filmed at the national training centre in Warrington, Cheshire, recording commonplace racism among police recruits. He was arrested in August and accused of gaining his salary by deception. Immediately after the transmission of the programme, several police officers were dismissed, but the then Home Secretary, David Blunkett, criticised the programme and suggested the BBC intended 'to create, not report' a story.

In C4 *Dispatches*: 'Undercover Mosque' a reporter joins various Muslim communities and claims that he proves that 'An ideology of bigotry and intolerance is spreading throughout our country, with its origins in Saudi Arabia'. The Muslim Wahabi sect of Saudi Arabia is training young imams and activists, then sending them around the world to replace more moderate, peaceful, imams. These imams are taught to believe that all non-Muslims are enemies, that Muslims should overthrow, or at least undermine, non-Muslim states. The documentary secretly films imams stirring up hatred against non-Muslims and advocating war against them. It also finds hidden websites and DVDs for children spreading hatred and encouraging martyrdom. The documentary later came in for criticism – from West Midlands Police, which made a formal complaint to Ofcom, claiming it was 'distorted'. This was rejected by Ofcom.[27]

Impersonation

Zaiba Malik, working for *Guardian Weekend*, spent a month undercover as a hotel cleaner. She described the exceedingly hard work, poor pay, low standards of sanitation and rough working conditions, in particularly of those cleaning luxury hotels (*Guardian Weekend*, 9 December 2006).

A black Englishman goes to Africa to experience the journey that an illegal immigrant must make if he wants to get to the UK from Africa. In *Dispatches*: 'Living with Illegals' he is sometimes accompanied by (an invisible) cameraman, sometimes not. We see him, for example, after he has been smuggled to Spain from Africa, trying to earn some money by selling flowers on the street, and trying to find somewhere to sleep in bank lobbies.

Secret filming

You can trick the audience into thinking they are watching something of some weight, of some importance by putting some secret filming in, perhaps using a couple of doorsteps so using all the old tools that we would have used to do serious investigations and the bonus of course for the TV companies is that's an awful lot cheaper. So you can easily get a house and attract some dodgy plumbers in there and you could probably turn that around in a couple of weeks and put it out on some prime time slot and it will cost you a tiny amount. Whereas we know that a serious investigation would normally take at least a year to do depending on the subject matter. It's become increasingly less viable to do long-term investigations like that and I believe they have been supplanted by some of the broadcasters by things that have the appearance of doing all that work but haven't really.

(Kenyon, 2007)

More and more undercover operations are being undertaken. Technology has been a major factor.

Now your reporters are carrying more or less undetectable and certainly very small pieces of technology that can record for a very long time. That has had an impact on what people expect of investigation – people want to see things now. Whereas before a reporter would tell you things, now often a piece of investigative journalism gets noticed because it's showing you things.

(Sutcliffe, 2007)

Whereas traditionally we had done secret filming for gun crime and serious criminal practice, commissioners realised that viewers come in as soon as they see secret filming because they think it's going to be intriguing. So I think the bar was dropped very much lower to the point where they said 'look we can actually do dodgy builders and dodgy plumbers and dodgy estate agents and we can do all that kind of things, bring in a very good audience, we use all the same tools that we used to use for serious investigative journalism now we use it for this kind of watchdog area, consumer affairsy type journalism and I think they realise it's an awful lot cheaper.

(Kenyon, 2007)

C4 *Dispatches* on postal workers in May 2004 was fiercely criticised by the postal workers union for an unfair and misleading representation of post office workers as lazy, dishonest and inefficient. However the company itself, Royal Mail, was in February 2006 fined £11.7m for 'disastrous failings' which were discovered as a result of investigations by PostComm, the industry regulator. These inquiries were undertaken after the revelations made in the C4 *Dispatches*.

Reconstruction

It is unusual to have more than a few seconds of dramatic reconstruction in a documentary but *Panorama*: 'A Fight to the Death' is almost entirely dramatic reconstruction. Here it was considered necessary, because very few of the events it reveals and analyses could be filmed. The subject is a very sensitive one – exactly what happened over the Kelly Affair, when government scientist Kelly killed himself after he was quoted by BBC reporter Gilligan as having said that the British government knew that its reasons for the war in Iraq were false. There followed an inquiry by a senior judge at which Prime Minister Blair had to defend his behaviour.

Dramatisation

Ghosts illustrates a new trend – investigative journalists using what have traditionally been considered quite separate media. A number have recently branched into comedy, putting on satirical shows based on in-depth research; others have written plays for the theatre. In the USA Michael Moore produces his famous (or notorious) cinema release documentaries and the UK's Mark Thomas publishes a book, *As Used on the Famous Nelson Mandela*, discussed above, though he is best known for evidential stand-up.

C4: *Ghosts* is a drama film of 96 minutes. The reporter, Nick Broomfield, is famous for his observant documentaries. This time he chooses to tell the tale of a group Chinese cockle-pickers who drowned off Morecambe Bay because their gangers did not tell them about the dangers of the sea tides. He wanted to show the dark side of illegal immigration, using this story as a case study. The trailer shows the deaths of the cockle-pickers, desperately crying out for help as the waves engulf them. The young woman in the party uses her mobile to call her little son in China for the last time, and we then find ourselves in South Eastern China a few months earlier, as the same young woman is taking the momentous decision to buy her way to the West so that she can earn the school fees her child will need. We see the whole process, from being sucked in by the promises of a local broker to the appalling journey, smuggled like contraband goods; the tragic squalor of living with other desperate people and the misery of being unable to communicate; the succession of short-term jobs, from the pay of which her Chinese master lifts his share. It is deeply moving, but also well researched.

Another drama based on current affairs investigation which deserves note is Tony Marchant's *The Mark of Cain*, transmitted on C4 in October 2007. Struck by the nonchalance by which a young British soldier had, when home, handed in to be processed a roll of film of the abuse of Iraqi detainees, he decided to try to understand how youths can become so dehumanised. He and a colleague investigated the case, as it became, of abuse by the Royal Fusiliers, and trial of the soldiers. By the time the drama was transmitted, two further cases of atrocities by young British soldiers had been revealed, such that his drama, highlighting the contrast between the high moral sentiments of the commanding officers with the culture of brutality in the ranks, seemed vindicated as a cameo interpreting what appeared suspiciously as if it might be a common phenomenon.

Audiences

In a period of audience fragmentation, those for the relatively small number of investigative shows have held up quite well and yet, perhaps because they are expensive, it seems that broadcasters are chary of commissioning them.

Broadcaster	Programme title	Last series	Audience
BBC	*Panorama*	ongoing	4,000,000
BBC	*Watchdog*	ongoing	4–5,000,000
C4	*Dispatches*	ongoing	1–2,500,000
ITV	*The Cook Report*	30 October 2007	7–14,000,000
BBC	*McIntyre Undercover*	24 February 2003	5–7,000,000
BBC	*Kenyon Confronts*	1 November 2003	4,100,000

According to the BBC the *Panorama* audience varies from subject to subject but the audience at 22.35 tends to be older and more male than earlier audiences for the channel. It is after the 10pm news and people are about to go to bed so it needs to be a good story to keep them up. BBC *Watchdog* gets between 4 and 5 million viewers in an early evening slot.

C4 is targeted at social group AB (wealthier, professional people with higher education). *Dispatches* viewing figures vary depending on the subject matter – generally domestic stories get larger audiences. Figures range from 2–2.5 million to under a million. On average in 2006 Dispatches had 1.1 million viewers. Twenty per cent of viewers were aged 16–34, 29 per cent 35–54 and 47 per cent were aged over 55. More men watch it than women (51 per cent).

The Cook Report is a production by national Independent Television (ITV) and has been one of the most popular factual TV programmes ever with an audience of 14 million at its peak and an average of over 7 million. ITV is planning to screen a retrospective of *The Cook Report*.

MacIntyre Undercover got audiences of 7 million for at least one of the programmes (into abuse at the Brompton Care Home for children). It usually commands rather less, while *Kenyon Confronts* is advertised as the highest performing TV current affairs strand in 2001 with an average of 4.2 million viewers.

Conclusion

One of the most notable developments of recent years has been the prevalence of accusations of bias, misrepresentation or just plain dishonesty. We have seen above how BBC partiality has been called in question, but there is worse.

The Boys who Killed Stephen Lawrence (July 2006) set out to explain why no one had been brought to book for the murder of an 18 year old in 1993. It accused police of taking bribes to shield the boy's killer from justice. Yet an inquiry by the Independent Police Complaints Commission concluded that the BBC claims were false (http://www.ipcc.gov.uk/news/pr050407_lawrenceupdate.htm).

The BBC Trust expressed concern about two editions of *Panorama*, one on the Church of Scientology and one on the health effects of wireless technology (Holmwood, 2007).

C4 *Dispatches* was accused of 'libelling' Sebastian Coe, Chair of the London Organising Committee of the Olympic Games, when it claimed in September 2007 that Lord Coe used his position for personal gain. It was among other accusations, of greed by Board Members, dishonesty by the Secretary of State and suspicious links to the American financier who owns the Millennium Dome (Beard, 2007).

With the huge increase in media of many different kinds which has followed from digitalisation, all have to compete for attention, such that the stories have to be more gripping, so that they compete with drama, and the cutting has to be faster to compete with commercials. All these factors make for more investigative journalism, or apparent investigative journalism, more rapid work and more risk. Thus is investigative journalism affected by market developments; there are other changes.

Issues and stories are personalised, to conform to the culture of human interest which now permeates most journalism. Celebrity culture, or the giving of prominence to individuals because they appear to be glamorous or powerful, requires that journalists too need to compete, so they package themselves – as we have seen with first Cook, then Kenyon, then MacIntyre – as unique and influential.

Increasingly journalists are more assertive, take moral positions and step forward with their own ideas instead of merely reporting or interpreting events. Events in Georgia and Ukraine in particular bear this out. Connecting with all these changes is the fact that journalism is increasingly 'globalised', at least in the limited sense that it is influenced by the international.

Not only does the internet pervade all we do, with the potential that it gives both for international research and for cooperation, but journalists are ever more educated by international educators or themselves travel abroad. They are little by little forming an international community of like-minded people. On the one hand this may make them more detached from their own countries and publics. On the other it may give them valuable contacts and a certain independence. This may result in influences such as journalists abroad helping journalists to reveal a story which cannot be revealed in their own country, as in the case of the revelations of SARS in China, and of other notable stories.

Anna Politkovskaya's bringing to light of the shameful behaviour of the Russians in Chechnya is a main example. Her book is *A Small Corner of Hell:*

Dispatches from Chechnya, and was published a few months before she was murdered. She received worldwide encouragement and her audience was bigger outwith her own country.

Globalisation may simply give a wide audience to something which might in the past have been restricted in its diffusion – Seymour Hersh's stories for example. Veteran American reporter Hersh, famous for his influential reports of the My Lai massacre of the Vietnam War, revealed the torture at the Abu Ghraib prison of the second Iraq War.

Or it may permit hundreds of journalists working together to produce a book such as Stephen Grey's *Ghost Plane*. He relied upon his international colleagues to help track the international story of how prisoners from Iraq were being transported all round the world to be interrogated (see Chapter 11).

All these developments have intensified the relationships between government and investigative journalism, as the number of books dealing with these relationships, and cited here, bears witness. But the most powerful influence upon them may only be just starting to show itself: blogging. It is to this that we turn in the next chapter.

Notes

1 Actually, more her husband's affairs, which have since become very much reported and in 2005 resulted in Jowell and he separating, a move generally assumed to have been made in order to protect her political career, a career that has, astonishingly, continued to prosper under Gordon Brown's premiership.
2 Much of the following is taken from de Hugo Burgh (2004) 'Don't blame the messenger', in Hugo de Burgh, Ivor Gaber and Dominic Wring (eds) (2004) *Can Vote, Won't Vote*, special edition of *Public Affairs*, 4 (4), 322–325.
3 Hugo de Burgh (2000) *Investigative Journalism*. London: Routledge.
4 S. Barnett and I. Gaber (2005) *Westminster Tales: 21st Century Crisis in Political Communication*. London: Continuum; Nicholas Jones (2002) *The Control Freaks: How New Labour Gets its Own Way*. London: Politico's Publishing.
5 Robin Aitken (2007) *Can We Trust the BBC?* London: Continuum.
6 Peter Oborne (2007) *The Triumph of the Political Class*. London: Simon and Schuster; Peter Oborne (2005) *The Rise of Political Lying*. London: Free Press; Peter Oborne (1999) *Alastair Campbell: New Labour and the Rise of the Media Class*. London: Aurum Press.
7 Philip Bobbitt (2003) *The Shield of Achilles*. London: Anchor.
8 In late 2003, Goldsmith's College's Unit for Journalism Research convened a symposium under the title 'Can Vote, Won't Vote: Is the Media to Blame for Political Disengagement?', directed by Emeritus Professor Ivor Gaber, in cooperation with Dr Dominic Wring of the Political Studies Association. The papers reviewed here are a selection of those delivered.
9 R. Phillis (2004) *An Independent Review of Government Communications*. Review Group, Interim Report, London: Cabinet Office.
10 Ibid.
11 Although Peter Oborne (2004) has provided *Alastair Campbell*.
12 Jo Moore, a British political adviser who briefly obtained fame when working for a minister. On the day of the 11th September 2001 terrorist attacks, Moore sent an e-mail to her department, suggesting that the day would be 'a very good day to get out

anything we want to bury' because the media would be preoccupied with reporting events from the USA (http://en.wikipedia. org/ wiki/Jo_Moore). She was later accused of doing something similar on the day of the announcement of the death of the Queen's sister, and was obliged to resign.

13 From April to July 2007 I delivered a course of lectures at Tsinghua University, Peking, on English Investigative Journalism. To help me to prepare for this, Katie Byrne conducted four interviews, obtained audience data and also sourced a number of investigative programmes that I used as examples in the course. This material has since found itself incorporated into this chapter. I am grateful to Katie Byrne, to the interviewees and in particular to Kevin Sutcliffe, who generously supplied me with copies of C4 output.

14 Harriman (ed.) (2005) Where has all the money gone? *London Review of Books,* 7 July 2005, pp.1–21.

15 http://www.channel4.com/news/ontv/theinsider

16 Jonathan Freedland (1999) *Bring Home the Revolution: The Case for a British Republic.* London: Fourth Estate.

17 BBC *Panorama*, 'Immigration: How we lost count', 23 July 2007.

18 2007, London: Harriman House.

19 http://www.channel4.com/news/microsites/S/stealing_freedom/index.html

20. Oborne, Peter (2007) *The Triumph of the Political Class.* London: Simon and Schuster.

21 Compliant and well-connected MPs: Geoffrey Robinson, John Reid, John Major; those not protected: Ken Livingston, Teresa Gorman. See also Kaye (2003).

22 Wheatcroft also makes this point, writing 'insufficient attention has been paid to Tony Blair's finances, which are doubtless linked in some way to his close relationship to Rupert Murdoch' (2007: 141). According to Wheatcroft (2007: 143), Prime Minister Blair spoke to Murdoch on the telephone 13 March 2003 and the next day *The Times* articulated Blair's line; soon after, HMG rejected the media 'plurality test' for the Communications Bill.

23 Robin Aitken (2007: 105) *Can We Trust the BBC?* London: Continuum.

24 Kerr, David (n.d.) 'An investigation into Issues of Impartiality in the Broadcast Media with Special Reference to the BBC' [BBC *Panorama*: 'Sex and the Holy City'], Paper, Wolfson College, Oxford, cited in Aitken (2007: 148). Aitken's book is itself a work of investigation, providing evidence of bias (178) from interviews with BBC executives.

25 ITV promotional material.

26 BBC *Panorama*: 'Secret Policeman', 21 October 2003.

27 Synopses of these events can be found in, for example, North (2007: 109); Aitken (2007: 119–41).

Bibliography

Barnett, S. and Seymour, E. (2000) *From Callaghan to Kosovo: Changing Trends in British Television 1975–1999.* London: University of Westminster.

BBC1 (1999) *MacIntyre Undercover:* 'Abuse in Care Homes', 16 November 1999.

BBC1 (2000) *Panorama*: 'Who Bombed Omagh?', 9 October 2000.

BBC1 (2001) *Kenyon Confronts:* 'Bogus Marriage', 26 February 2001.

BBC1 (2004) *Panorama*: 'A Fight to the Death', 21 January 2004.

BBC1 (2007) *Secrets of the Drug Trials,* 29 January 2007.

BBC1 (2007) *Panorama*: 'Immigration: How We Lost Count', 23 July 2007.

BBC Radio 4 (2006) *Letters to the Times,* 20 October 2006.

Beard, Matthew (2007) Lord Coe 'libelled' by TV Olympics documentary, *Evening Standard*, 11 September 2007.

Boffey, D. (2006) A nice little E-Earner: how Lord Cashpoint's noble friend profits from computers-for-schools, *The Mail on Sunday*, 2 April 2006.

Bromley, C. and Curtice, J. (2004) Where have all the voters gone?, in H. de Burgh, *Can Vote, Won't Vote: Is the Media to Blame?*, special edition of *Public Affairs*, edited with Ivor Gaber and Dominic Wright), London: Henry Stewart.

Buckwell, A. (2006) Blair's £96,000 a year pension to escape raid by the taxman, *The Mail on Sunday*, 2 April 2006.

Campbell, D. (2007) The tragic human cost of NHS baby blunders, *The Observer*, 23 September 2007.

Channel 4 (2001) *Dispatches*: 'Beneath the Veil', 26 June 2001.

Channel 4 (2004) *Dispatches*: 'MMR: What They Didn't Tell You', 18 November 2004.

Channel 4 (2005) *Jamie's School Dinners*, 23 Feb–16 March 2005.

Channel 4 (2006) *Iraq's Death Squads*, 7 November 2006.

Channel 4 (2007) *Dispatches*: 'Undercover Mosque', 15 January 2007.

Channel 4 (2007) *Dispatches*: 'Labour's Gambling Addiction', 22 January 2007.

Channel 4 (2007) *The Mark of Cain*, 5 April 2007.

Chittenden, M. (2007) Quango fat cats reap the price of failure – even more money, *Sunday Times*, 11 November 2007.

Cracknell, D. and Oakeshott, I. (2006) Anger over new Cherie lecture fee, *Sunday Times*, 12 March 2006.

Davies, B. (2007) Billion Dollar Baby Trade, *Daily Mail*, 3 November 2007.

Davies, Nick (1997) *Dark Heart: The Shocking Truth About Hidden Britain*. London: Vintage.

Graham, C. and Turnbull, D. (2006) MoS Investigation reveals horror of hunting trips set up by father of Prince Harry's girl. Slaughter on safari. Safari staff gossip about 'wild' Chelsy, *The Mail on Sunday*, 2 April 2006.

Grice, A. and Brown, C. (2006) Scotland Yard is now investigating Labour's secret loans scandal. So how serious is it for the Prime Minister, a key mover in the affair? Blair and the £14m questions, *The Independent*, 22 March 2006.

Heathcoat Amory, E. (2006) Lord Crony and an orgy of greed. The sale of Britain's defence research centre is proving the most incompetent privatization ever. Worse still is the stench of financial scandal. But don't worry, it's only we taxpayers who've been short-changed, *Daily* Mail, 14 February 2006.

Holmwood, Leigh (2007) BBC Trust expresses concern over Panorama, *Media Guardian*, 15 June 2007

Hosken, A. (2006) Nothing like a dame, *Granta*, 6 March 2006.

Joseph, C. (2007) Uncovered by the makers of Dying Rooms, the scandal of how China's brutal single child policy leads to . . . Babies For Sale, *The Mail on Sunday*, 7 October 2007.

Kaye, R. (2003) 'Regulating Parliament: The regulatory state within Westminster', CARR Discussion Paper Series (DP13). London: Centre for Analysis of Risk and Regulation, LSE.

Kenyon, P. (2007) Interviewed by Katie Byrne 19 February 2007.

Knightly, P. (2007) interviewed by Katie Byrne 16 February 2007.

Lewis, J. (2006) Torture row as Minister backs the use of 'simulated drowning', *The Mail on Sunday*, 12 March 2006.

Lloyd, D. (1998) Head of News and Current Affairs. C4 TV, in a talk to the students of the MA Investigative Journalism, 19 February 1998 at Nottingham Trent University.

Lloyd, D. (2001) Journalism today: the view from Channel 4. Address to the postgraduate students of the Department of Media and Communications, Goldsmiths' College, 28 March 2001.

Lloyd, J. (2002) Media Manifesto. *Prospect*, 79, 48–53.

Lloyd, J. (2004) The news media – is the raw material of democracy in safe hands?, Address to Civitas in London, 1 June 2004.

McKinstry, L. (2007) Kirsty, a nasty case of spying and the story you won't be hearing on Newsnight , *Daily Mail*, 8 November 2007.

Mediawatch UK (2002) Goodbye good taste and decency, *Newsbrief*, Summer 2002, p. 1.

Merrick, J. (2007) The Cabinet couple 'cash in on second homes perk', *Daily Mail*, 24 September 2007.

Newell, C. (2007) Exposed: filth and abuse in care home, *Sunday Times,* 4 November 2007.

Oborne, P. (2004) *Alastair Campbell*. London: Aurum Press.

O'Halloran, J. (ed.) *File on Four,* interviewed by Katie Byrne.

Politkovskaya, A. (2007) *A Small Corner of Hell: Dispatches from Chechnya*. Chicago: University of Chicago Press.

Sutcliffe, K. (2007) Interviewed by Katie Byrne 19 February 2007.

Thomas, M. (2006) *As Used on the Famous Nelson Mandela: Underground Adventures in the Arms and Torture Trade*. London: Ebury.

Turnbull, D. (2006) Revealed: the staggering expense of providing personal perks for John Prescott, *The Mail on Sunday*, 14 May 2006.

Turnbull, D. and Owen, G. (2006) Cash-for-peerage row: tycoon paid Cherie £60,000 to help block critical City Academy report, *The Mail on Sunday*, 23 April 2006.

Turnbull, D. and Walters, S. (2006) Cash for peerages link to Blair Trust. Trustee is business associate of man who lent Labour secret £1m, *The Mail on Sunday*, 21 May 2006.

Walters, S. (2006) Levy U-turn on party funding, *The Mail on Sunday*, 26 March 2006.

Willetts, D. (1994) *Civic Conservatism*. London: SMF.

Winnett, R. and Boles, T. (2006) The nuclear lobbyist plugged into Labour, *Sunday Times*, 14 May 2006.

Further reading

Bourdieu, P. (1998) *On Television and Journalism*. London: Pluto.

de Burgh, H. (2004) 'Don't blame the messenger!' in H. de Burgh (ed.) (2004) *Can Vote, Won't Vote: Is the Media to Blame?,* special edition of *Public Affairs*, edited with Ivor Gaber and Dominic Wring, London: Henry Stewart.

Cohen, N. (2000) *Cruel Britannia*. London: Verso.

Sampson, A. (2004) *Who Runs This Place? The Anatomy of Britain in the 21st Century*. London: John Murray.

5

INVESTIGATIVE JOURNALISM AND BLOGS

Paul Bradshaw

Introduction

This chapter will look at the relationship between investigative journalism and blogs, beginning with a brief history of the technology and its journalistic uses, before exploring three areas in which blogs and new media technologies have become important tools in investigative journalism: in sourcing material; in disseminating the results of fieldwork; and as a source of funding.

In the course of addressing these areas we should recognise how blogging's history has shaped its contents, while being wary of falling into technological determinism. No technology is neutral, and all technologies have their own cultural histories that influence the content, cultures and uses that grow up around them, histories that are influenced by the actors who play a part in their development. This chapter provides a brief overview of those histories, while also recognising that the blog genre and technologies are still in flux.

The question of who can call themselves journalists, and the value of 'amateurism' in reporting, have been recurring themes during the rise of citizen journalism. The second part of this chapter deals with that 'professional versus amateur' debate, arguing that amateur bloggers perform a useful role outside the commercialised, bureaucratised work processes of professional journalists, simultaneously noting how the blog form has been 'co-opted' by the mainstream media.

The section on sourcing looks at the rise of *reader contribution* and *crowdsourcing*[1] as methods of gathering, refining and checking information, and notes the related potential for increased reader engagement from a journalism that previously 'reduced publics to spectators' (Bromley, 2005: 321). The section on publishing then looks at how the potentially limitless time and space of new media technologies have opened up new possibilities for publishing source material and escaping the time-bound nature of traditional news. It is argued that the conversational and iterative nature of new media technologies offers an opportunity to rebuild public trust in journalism through transparent working practices, while networked digital distribution technologies offer a way to circumvent censorship and build international audiences. However, readers should be wary of becoming technologically determinist by falling for the idea that 'everyone is a journalist' or, indeed, no one is.

A final section looks at how the already creaking economic bases for traditional journalism have been further weakened by new media technologies, and how investigative journalists are turning to the internet for new ways of funding – some directly through reader donations or sales of related products; others through foundations, advertising and licensing; most through a mix of all of the above. Finally, the conclusion addresses the strengths and weaknesses of investigative journalism in a new media age, and proposes that its future lies along a number of paths, but that in the end it is the organisational culture, ways of doing things that are entrenched and not likely to simply disappear because of a new technology, and the economic pressures on the boardroom that will dictate what happens next, rather than the technology.

Blogging and journalism

To ask whether blogging *is* journalism is to mistake form for content. Blogs – like websites, paper, television or radio – can contain journalism, but may not. They are platforms, albeit, like other media platforms, with certain generic conventions. Like all conventions, these have advantages and disadvantages for journalism, which this chapter aims to address.

As platforms, blogs are a type of website which is normally built to a template, using content management software, on which entries are dated and arranged with the most recent entry (post) uppermost. Despite their extraordinary range and number, there are shared qualities to blogs which derive from their technology and history. These include a most-recent-post-top structure, a 'blogroll'[2] of related sites, an often personal or subjective writing style, brevity, and, related to brevity, a tendency to link to any source mentioned (which the user can click to find out more).

When they first began to spread in the late 1990s, blogs tended to be lists of links to similar sites, and this 'blogroll' element still remains in many blog systems and templates today. Blog posts, meanwhile, often hinged around a single link, where:

> An editor with some expertise in a field might demonstrate the accuracy or inaccuracy of a highlighted article or certain facts therein; provide additional facts he feels are pertinent to the issue at hand; or simply add an opinion or differing viewpoint from the one in the piece he has linked. Typically this commentary is characterized by an irreverent, sometimes sarcastic tone. More skilful editors manage to convey all of these things in the sentence or two with which they introduce the link . . . Their sarcasm and fearless commentary reminds us to question

97

the vested interests of our sources of information and the expertise of individual reporters as they file news stories about subjects they may not fully understand.

(Blood, 2000)

Although the first blogs were programmed by their authors, it was the launch of free content management systems such as Pitas, Blogger and Groksoup (all in 1999) which facilitated an explosion in blogger numbers as the barriers to entry were lowered to those without HTML coding skills. Rebecca Blood (2000) argues that this change, and Blogger's interface and culture in particular, resulted in a change in the medium itself, in favour of more diary-like blogs, with accompanying cult of personality focusing on the author as a 'star' blogger. It was during this time that blogs received much of their initial exposure in the mainstream media.

The years since, however, have seen a number of supplementary technologies develop that have made the blog more similar to journalistic enterprises. One is the rise of RSS as a distribution method. RSS (*Really Simple Syndication* or *Rich Site Summary*), now routinely included in blog services such as Blogger and Wordpress, is a technology which allows readers to subscribe to a blog through an 'RSS reader', by which they create a personal webpage which 'pulls' the feed from the blog, so that they do not have to visit it.

This removes the requirement for readers to check the blog itself for any new postings, and means they can instead include the blog feed as one among a number to form their personal news service. It also means feeds can be aggregated by publishers or journalists.

A second factor is the rise of *linkbacks* (also known as trackbacks, refbacks or pingbacks). These 'ping' a blogger to notify them when another blogger has linked to their post, while a brief extract of the referring website and a link is often included as part of the comments on a particular post, enabling the blogger to address any response or debate, as well as allowing readers to follow discussion that has taken place on other blogs since the original post was written. This combination of reverse referencing and notification adds to blogging's conversational nature, making bloggers aware of their readers' identities and opinions, and allowing them to correct errors or clarify and refine arguments. Notably, articles which are not written on a platform using *trackback* technology, i.e. most traditional news websites, do not get included in this discussion.

Thirdly, because of the tendency for blogs to link frequently, and because of the importance of incoming links to a webpage's ranking on search engines such as Google, blogs have become a major factor in the profile of particular stories. A story that is heavily blogged benefits from a high visibility on search engines – particularly blog-specific search engines which monitor popular terms and sites. Economically, the advent of services such as *AdSense* and *BlogAds* meant some journalistic bloggers who began as amateurs were able to commercialise their operations and employ full-time staff, as popular blogs such as *Boing Boing* and the *Daily Kos* enjoyed visitor numbers higher than most mainstream news organisations.

Perhaps partly as a result of the significance of blogs to search engine ranking, and therefore readers and online advertising revenue, and partly because of the threat that blogs pose in taking away their audiences, the blog format has been increasingly adopted by news organisations, who have either co-opted the technology for their own journalists, employed bloggers on their staff, teamed up with blogging and citizen journalism operations (Gant, 2007), or targeted them for takeovers (The Outlook, 2007). With this shift into the mainstream media, the pre-existing generic qualities of blogs have, in many cases, been diluted, with some journalists writing blog entries in the same way as a column, disabling comments or linkbacks, or failing to link to their sources (in some cases because of legal concerns or the technical limitations of the content management systems). The blog, in these cases, sometimes becomes a new platform for traditional print content ('shovelware[3]'), or a defensive act of what Susan Robinson describes as 'news repair'. In other cases, however:

> They are now achieving what Gans called for in an 'indirect sharing of responsibilities' with journalists [and] represent the multi-perspectival news that will end up setting more and different agendas as desired by Gans.
>
> (Robinson, 2006: 80)

The amateur–professional debate

Blogs have attracted criticism for being susceptible to mob rule (Allan, 2006), for containing ill-informed and biased opinion, for being an 'echo chamber' of homogenous voices (Henry, 2007), for lack of editorial rigour, and as representing the rise of the 'cult of the amateur'. At the same time, professional journalism itself has been under attack for the rise of a commercial culture (Gant, 2007), with many journalists seeing 'their autonomy diminishing as newsroom standards of ethics, rigour and balance lost out to management goals of saving money and trivializing the news' (Beers, 2006: 113), while under-resourced newsrooms have faced criticism for running unedited PR videos (Henry, 2007), or relying on only one source (Ponsford, 2007), and investigative journalism specifically has been criticised for allowing sources to set agendas (Feldstein, 2007).

Underlying many of these debates are tensions between amateurism and professionalism. By its nature, professional journalism is commercial, required to make money. In order to do this it must either attract very large audiences, or relatively affluent ones that are attractive to advertisers or willing to pay high cover prices. It must also keep costs low where it can, meaning newsgathering is generally routinised, and bureaucratised.

Herman (2005) illustrates this in identifying five things which condition information as it is processed into news: the size, ownership and profit orientation of news operations; the dominance of advertising; dependence on 'official sources'; attempts at control; and ideological pressures.

Herman's framework is useful in illustrating how few of those pressures are applicable to blogs. Most journalism blogs are written by one person, who does not make a profit from their blogging. Advertising, if any exists, is typically sold through a third party such as Google AdSense, and the blogger is rarely dependent on the revenues generated from that – although commercial blog networks are increasing in number.

However, while 'official sources' are not used in the same way that journalists rely on press releases and spokespeople, there is a well-documented reliance on the mainstream media itself for second-hand information, albeit often complemented with reference to alternative versions, deeper information and original documents.

The amateur nature of blogs is often seen as a counterpart to the professional nature of journalism. This is what Axel Bruns calls 'gatewatching' (Bruns, 2005), or Jane Singer describes as an 'antidote to journalistic group think' (Friend and Singer, 2007: 119). As Skinner points out:

> They are guided by a purpose or mandate other than the profit motive and they are often organized to facilitate a broader range of input into production than their corporate cousins [and] provide ways of seeing and understanding that are marginalized or not available there.
>
> (cit. in Beers, 2006: 115)

For instance, a Pullitzer-nominated blog, Michael Yon's reporting from Iraq, expressly rejects commercial assignments in order to remain independent:

> Not as a rabble rouser or as pugnacious individualist reflexively bucking 'the system', merely someone who could buck the system when it needed bucking.
>
> (Yon, 2007)

The subjective quality of blogs is compensated for by their sheer number: objectivity, some commentators argue, is no longer essential in an age and on a platform where publishing monopolies do not exist, and the opposing view is only a click away (Gillmor, 2005), while objectivity as an aspect of professional journalism was motivated by commercial pressures to attract advertisers and large audiences (Friend and Singer, 2007; Gant, 2007). Indeed, objectivity as a value within mainstream journalism is losing its appeal, with some organisations dropping it from their codes of ethics (Friend and Singer, 2007).

Blogs' appearance of being 'unchecked' is misleading. Whereas professional journalism employs editors to check reports before publishing, blogging tends to reverse the process: publishing, then checking. Editing, in this case, takes place 'from the margins', as readers and other bloggers check the facts presented in a process of 'iterative journalism' (Bruns, 2005). This can result in legal problems when erroneous or libellous information is published and distributed without correction. Unlike mainstream journalism, however, which produces a time-bound product that seeks to be definitive, or at least a 'first draft of history', the products of blogging and other forms of new media journalism are forever unfinished: open to comments, rewrites, updates and, in the case of wikis,[4] editing and redrafting by users themselves.

Sourcing material

While the opportunity that blogs provide for anyone to publish has undoubtedly led to a proliferation of new sources and leads, in particular 'Insider' blogs produced by experts and gossips working within particular industries (Henry, 2007) and even 'YouTube whistleblowers' (Witte, 2006), it is the very conversational, interactive and networked nature of blogs which has led journalists to explore completely new ways of newsgathering.

One of the biggest changes that blogging and new media have brought to journalism is the rise of 'crowdsourcing', whereby individual elements of a particular project are spread (or 'outsourced') between members of a particular community. Typically these take one of two forms: tapping into a range of experience and expertise; or simply tapping into distributed manpower.

Attempts to tap into the 'wisdom of crowds' (Surowiecki, 2004) draw on blogs, wikis, social networking, mailing lists and the ideas of the open source movement. These enable journalists to tap into a wider range of knowledge or manpower than exists in the newsroom and to pursue stories that might otherwise not have been covered, or which would have taken longer to cover.

Talking Points Memo, one of the most successful investigative journalism blogs, frequently draws on its readership to pursue big stories. In December 2006 the blog posted a brief piece about the sacking of a US Attorney from the State of Arkansas and, noting that several other US Attorneys were being replaced, asked its readers if they knew of anything similar happening in their area. As the blog, along with sister blog *TPM Muckraker*, accumulated evidence from around the country, the rolling story led to the resignation of a senior Justice Department official and to the cause being taken up by Democrat politicians.

In a different story, owner *Josh Marshall* asked readers to survey their own members of Congress on the issue of the proposed privatisation of Social Security. Marshall says that:

> Hundreds of people out there send clips and other tips . . . There is some real information out there, some real expertise. If you're not in politics and you know something, you're not going to call David Broder. With the blog, you develop an intimacy with people. Some of it is perceived, but some of it is real.
>
> (McDermott, 2007)

Similar approaches have been adopted by *Porkbusters.org* – which invited readers to identify wasteful spending in their state or district, blog about it, and link to it from the *Porkbusters* site (Reynolds, 2005) – while in another example, bloggers and readers mobilised to cover a story about the contamination of pet food ingredients exported from China which they felt was being overlooked by the mainstream news media. Blogs such as *The Pet Connection, PetFoodTracker.com* and *ThePetFoodList.com* provided information ranging from symptoms of poisoning and safe foods, to the latest news on the issue, as well as acting as focal points for pet owners, lawyers, industry groups and reporters. One site, *Itchmo.com*, became so popular that it was banned in China (Weise, 2007).

Hurricane Katrina has acted as a particular focal point for crowdsourcing initiatives, with a number of online operations, including TPM, drawing on reader input to compile 'timelines' for the events leading up to, during and after Hurricane Katrina. One of the best examples came from the *ePluribus Media* community, who gathered information on over 500 events, fact-checked and sourced, documenting 'the devastation, the political shenanigans, and the struggles of the people living on the Gulf Coast' (ePluribus Media, 2006). These range from a 26-year-old report about weak soil under the levee to an article eleven months after the levees broke documenting a tripling in suicide rates.

Once the online world had proved the approach could work, mainstream media began experimenting. And when in May 2006 Florida's *News-Press* received calls from readers complaining about high prices being charged to connect newly constructed homes to water and sewer lines, Kate Marymont, the *News-Press'* editor in chief, decided that:

> 'Rather than start a long investigation and come out months later in the paper with our findings we asked our readers to help us find out why the cost was so exorbitant . . . We weren't prepared for the volume, and we had to throw a lot more firepower just to handle the phone calls and e-mails.' . . . Readers spontaneously organized their own investigations: Retired engineers analyzed blueprints, accountants pored over balance sheets, and an inside whistle-blower leaked documents showing evidence of bid-rigging. 'We had people from all over the world helping us', said Marymont. For six weeks the *News-Press* generated more traffic to its website than 'ever before, excepting hurricanes'. In the end, the city cut the utility fees by more than 30 percent, one official resigned, and the fees have become the driving issue in an upcoming city council special election.
>
> (Howe, 2006a)

In a further example from the Fort Myers *News-Press* in Florida, the newspaper put information online stating which citizens had received government help after Hurricane Katrina, and encouraged readers to look through it.

Within 24 hours, there were 60,000 searches from readers, who then told News-Press journalists about neighbours with wrecked homes who had not received aid. The readers did the investigating and the paper then reported the stories.

(Beckett, 2007)

But there are reservations about using crowdsourcing for covering particular issues – in particular concerning legal issues such as libel and contempt of court, as well as the effect on newspaper staffing, and the potential for abuse.

Gregory Korte, an investigative journalist with the *Cincinnati Enquirer* who has been working to implement Gannett's crowdsourcing policy, says crowd-sourcing holds 'a great deal of promise for certain "pocketbook" [manageable – ed] issues, like the sewage scandal in Fort Myers', but that it will take time and work to discover the best ways of using it. 'The newspaper of the future is going to need more programmers than copy editors, and we're going to have to figure out how to make that transition' (Howe, 2006a). Greg Yardley at Yardley.ca, meanwhile, illustrates the dangers of stories being hijacked by polit-ical groups and agendas, asking what would happen if he organised ten friends to call the paper, asking for an investigation into the local 'Demolican' coun-cilman. 'Can I influence the news? Now imagine the local Demolican party gets wind of this, and they start *paying* some inclined members to counteract this with their own stories and investigations. How much could they in turn influence the news?' (Howe 2006c).

The *News-Press* examples highlight not only how newsgathering but also news consumption and, specifically, engagement, is being changed by new media technologies. Jennifer Carroll, Gannett's Vice President for new media content, notes that, 'We've learned that no one wants to read a 400-column-inch investigative feature online. But when you make them a part of the process they get incredibly engaged' (Howe, 2006a). *Guardian* investigative journalist David Leigh also notes that multimedia elements of the web such as graphics, video and audio can bring stories to life:

> The problem with all these bribery and corruption stories is they are often quite complicated, financial and dry. Because of the legal prob-lems, of which there are many, you have to be quite roundabout with the things you say. But to find ways of doing it online that can bring it alive for people and give them a handle on it is a really exciting thing. You've seen these stories which say 'Complex web of financial trans-actions', and people's eyes glaze over. This is about trying to find a way past that.
>
> (Smith, 2007)

This point is echoed by filmmakers Journeyman Pictures, who state on their website: 'Multimedia developments offer diverse and different broadcast potential in a way never possible before. They offer new platforms to a niche previously too small to justify much airplay on terrestrial TV. . . . A combination of the web's interactivity, a powerful publicity machine and a topical sales focus means films remain easy to discover, and continually on offer' (Journeyman Pictures, 2007).

Added to this potential for increased engagement is a perceived opportunity to revitalise the fourth estate, as the 'unfinished' and conversational nature of blogs has opened opportunities for journalists to test their work in public, fine-tune it for errors, and invite additional information. When science policy blogger Nick Anthis proposed to write about the NASA public affairs staffer George C. Deutsch, for instance, it was one of his readers who suggested that he might not have graduated from university (Revkin, 2006). After confirming this was the case, Anthis published, and the story led to Deutsch's resignation.

Afghanistan-based video journalist Vaughan Smith also posts regular updates to *YouTube*, mini-blogging tool *Twitter*, and a blog, providing a number of spaces for readers to contribute. Colleague Graham Holliday notes: 'A lot of what Vaughan is doing is likely background stuff for longer features including interviews and suchlike. I think he'll be putting that together when he gets back to London, making a longer feature or features' (Jones, 2007).

Journalists who don't post their 'rough drafts' online in the new media age, meanwhile, run the risk of being fact-checked and 'outed' after final publication or broadcast, by bloggers with a keen eye for detail or specialist expertise. The most famous example is 'Memogate' or 'Rathergate', when in 2004 CBS broadcast a programme about George W. Bush's Air National Guard service, and bloggers raised questions about the memos on which the story was based.

> On 7 September, the day prior to [the] broadcast . . . [the] left of centre blog Talking Points Memo [posted] news that the programme was set to present 'documents that shed light on Bush's guard service or lack thereof'. Blogs of all political descriptions were promptly stirred into action in anticipation of the broadcast, especially those on the political right [. . .] Nineteen minutes into the broadcast, the first post calling into question the integrity of the memos appeared on the right-wing blog FreeRepublic.com. Four hours later the documents under scrutiny were decried as a hoax again.
>
> (Allan, 2006: 95)

One blogger in particular, Minneapolis lawyer Scott Johnson, posted an email from a reader to that effect, and returned from work to find '50 emails from experts of all kinds around the country, supplying additional information. And we kept updating our post with that information through the day' (in Allan, 2006: 95).

Publishing

Traditionally, news has always been subject to the pressures of time and space. Today's news is tomorrow's proverbial 'fish and chip paper' – news is required to be 'new'; stories 'have a 24 hour audition on the news stage, and if they don't catch fire in that 24 hours, there's no second chance' (Rosen, 2004). At the same time, part of the craft of journalism in the twentieth century has been the ability to distil a complex story into a particular word count or time slot, while a talent of editors is their judgement in allocating space based on the pressures of the day's competing stories.

In the twenty-first century, however, new media technologies have begun to challenge the limitations of time and space that defined the news media in the twentieth.

The internet provides a potentially infinite space for journalists to publish not only edited articles, but also raw material, while hyperlinks offer the potential to provide important context and background. When David Leigh and Rob Evans decided to investigate allegations of corruption in the arms trade in 2003, for example, *Guardian* editor Alan Rusbridger suggested they think beyond a traditional book and create a website. The result, a broad and deep exploration of the allegations, the details and the figures involved, includes recent news on the investigation's progress; a 10-part investigation into Britain's arms trade; biographies and details on 40 people and how they are relevant to BAE payments; an interactive 'global investigations map'; profiles of BAE's weapons and planes and the company itself; photocopies of the main evidential documents; and video interviews with key figures. Leigh says that the website meant 'We were able to lay everything out with no constraints of space and say "OK guys, here's all the evidence" ' while the website has allowed the two journalists to publish memos, faxes, emails and research passed on to them by other journalists and authors working on the story (Smith, 2007).

The 'public draft' possibilities of blogs can offer a more transparent way of working for journalists. At a time when public trust of journalists is low, the transparency of blogs offers a way to rebuild that trust, while Singer (Friend and Singer, 2007) notes the need for transparency as an ethical principle, allowing audiences to judge the validity of information, the process by which it was secured, and the motives and biases of the journalist providing it. Other theorists point to a need to narrow the widening gap between citizens and journalists (Gans, 2003), or to reappropriate the private discussion sphere that has been hijacked by the mass media in a way that excludes the public (Habermas, 1989). 'By widening the disclosure circle through information sharing', writes Paul Andrews (2003) 'blogs have contributed to the truth-finding process'.

In another example, during the case of the trial of former high-ranking US official and aide to President G.W. Bush, Lewis 'Scooter' Libby, readers of the blog *Firedoglake* funded a team of people to 'live blog' the trial as it took place. The result was a transcript of what was said – too extensive for publication in print, but a resource which became essential for journalists covering the trial, and for anyone interested in reading the detail (Rosen, 2007).

In terms of raw material, the Center for Public Integrity has used databases to create a searchable website on details of government contracts awarded for post-Hurricane cleanup and reconstruction (Center for Public Integrity, 2007), while Wikileaks launched in 2007 as an attempt to use wiki technology to provide an 'uncensorable system for safe mass document leaking and public analysis'. Within a year it claimed to have received over 1.2 million documents from 'dissident communities and anonymous sources' (Wikileaks, 2007), while its first big story was a report on looting by ex-president Moi of Kenya. Doubts, however, have been raised about the security of any website technology:

> If a security hole is found in [the anonymity toolset] in a year's time then it is now distinctly possible that the authorities will be able to go back through their data records and unpick the handshaking and message-passing that currently obscures the trail, and if that happens it would be very dangerous. The fact is that asking people to risk their liberty or even their lives by using software that inevitably has security flaws in it is a reckless and unjustifiable risk, one that is being taken by the posters, not the people writing the code.
>
> (Thompson, B., 2007)

The permanence of material online over time is equally significant. In perhaps the most famous example, a barely reported speech by US Senator Trent Lott was picked up by bloggers and, as more and more posters added detail, finding evidence of previous statements in favour of racial segregation, and expressing indignation that this speech had gone unreported, the story attracted more and more interest, until it was picked up by the mainstream press.

For Rob Evans, meanwhile, it didn't matter where the BAE[5] story went in the paper, as long as it went online and reached a global audience. 'It's taking a very long-term view, which editors don't normally take: you put something out there and 18 months later it will suddenly click' (Smith, 2007).

Finally, new media technologies facilitate new forms and spheres of distribution – instantaneous, and global. RSS allows for instant and replicated distribution; reports can be 'mirrored' – copied and published elsewhere – to avoid being censored; and email, mailing lists and social networking services allow stories to be quickly passed on. As a result, sites like *YouTube* have been used in Iran to denounce state brutality, and in Zimbabwe to expose civil rights violations; and while many countries have attempted to block specific content or social networking sites in general, including Turkey and Thailand (*YouTube*), the United Arab Emirates, China and Iran (*Flickr*), users continue to find ways around this censorship, including using proxy sites and building browser extensions (Woodard Maderazo, 2007).

For Vaughan Smith, distribution technologies like *Twitter* allow him to update a dedicated audience, while postings on his blog are picked up by others (Tomlin, 2007). In the example of the BAE investigation, despite being published by a British newspaper, the story is now followed by journalists in dozens of countries. Leigh and Evans say they openly welcome help from journalists around the world and give it freely to anyone willing to take the story on. 'We're trying to think our way towards a new kind of journalism . . . The thing is, all the criminals are global now, the police forces are gradually starting to go global and now the journalists are global as well. We need to catch up' (Smith, 2007).

Fundraising

Just as new media technologies are challenging publishing and distribution conventions, traditional business models have also been disrupted in a news industry which has, at least in the West, been facing declines in readership and advertising revenue for decades (Meyer, 2004). In this environment investigative journalism has been one of the first to suffer from cuts to staff and resources (Knightley, 2004; Outing, 2005; Freola, 2007), or from reallocation of funds towards the more profitable.

In response to this decline in funding, blogs have offered a new way to finance investigative journalism.

In April 2003 former AP reporter Christopher Allbritton posted a notice on his site, *Back-to-Iraq.com*, asking for readers to donate money so he could cover the Iraq war. In response, 320 people donated $14,334 through the site. As Allbritton filed stories, donors were put on a 'premium e-mail list', receiving stories early – as well as extra reports and pictures. They also passed along story ideas and 'occasionally berated him for overheated metaphors. "Readers were my editors", he says' (Ante, 2003).

Freelance journalist David Appell repeated the experiment successfully when he asked readers of his blog to support him in investigating a sugar lobbying group (Bowman and Willis, 2003), while *Talking Points Memo* also relied on reader donations for its continuing existence before *BlogAds* allowed Josh Marshall to fund his operation through advertising (McDermott, 2007).

Readers of *Firedoglake.com* donated enough money to cover the travel expenses of six volunteer bloggers and $3,500 a month rent on a Washington apartment so that they could report on the trial of Lewis 'Scooter' Libby (Shane, 2007). These donations of both money and time meant the site was able to draw on 'more boots on the ground than any commercial news operation . . . more background, savvy and commitment to the case. And they dominate[d] the coverage of a big news event. Journalists themselves use[d] it to keep up and get their bearings' (Rosen, 2007).

Jay Rosen added of the fundraising:

> What makes it possible are the people who gather at the site, and the falling cost for those people to meet up, realize their number, find a common mind, and when necessary pool their dollars to get their own correspondents to Washington . . . the cost for like-minded people to locate each other, share information, and work together is falling – dramatically. And so things unthinkable or impractical before might be quite doable now.
>
> (Rosen, 2007)

Marshall Kirkpatrick (2007), writing specifically about video journalism, notes three models for financially sustaining investigative work: foundation support, viewer donation and licensing/advertising. Typically, the reality is a mix of all three. *Alive in Baghdad* and *Alive in Mexico*, for instance, aim to finance their work through licensing deals with mainstream media, but the team has also drawn on donations, subscriptions and prize money (Gannes, 2007). *Democracy Now!* is financed by foundations and viewer donations, while *Collateral News*, says Kirkpatrick, 'appear[s] [to] do commercial video production to support . . . investigative journalism'. Michael Yon, on the other hand, has added to reader donations by selling photographs online, and copies of a book (Yon, 2007).

Conclusion

Blogs and new media have undoubtedly changed the landscape of investigative journalism. In terms of its form, journalism as a whole has become more conversational, and iterative, as readers seek to contribute to the story, and journalists open more of their processes to public view. The time and space offered by the internet has provided opportunities for these conversations to take place, and for journalists to make raw material available to fuel them. And the networked nature of the web has facilitated coordination of contributors across borders and industries, along with a now global distribution of material.

The current period offers both significant threats and opportunities to investigative journalism. The sheer quantity and accessibility of information means that quality is becoming a precious commodity. Technological tools have made the investigative journalist's job of gathering and analysing data, and identifying and contacting sources, easier, but when the source of information is a blog, journalists face the challenge of evaluating both the information and the source, sometimes without knowing what partisan, ideological or commercial affiliations the blogger may have (Friend and Singer, 2007). The protection and access afforded to journalists – in particular, access to certain areas or people, and the ability to protect a source – are not routinely offered to those working outside mainstream media (Gant, 2007), while at the same time the past two decades have seen courts being increasingly reluctant to offer protection even to journalists working for large publishers (Henry, 2007).

The use of blogs for investigative journalism raises a number of challenges and ethical issues. Investigative journalists may find it hard to protect their sources in an age where so much is recorded. There are useful tools that help – such as Invisiblog.com for free anonymous blog hosting and the Online Policy Group (OPG) for privacy-protective domain name registration, while the likes of Tor and Anonymizer.com allow bloggers to hide their IP address (location) and Pingomatic allows bloggers to quickly broadcast an entry while making the poster untraceable (Electronic Frontier Foundation, 2005) – but there are always concerns about weaknesses in such technologies emerging in the future.

Equally, for journalists going undercover there are new issues around invasion of privacy – particularly when the distinction between private and public spaces becomes blurred online. Lee Wilkins notes that

> the Web provides journalists (and others) with ways to invade privacy on a worldwide scale . . . Most journalists don't hide in bathrooms to get stories – because hiding in the bathroom means we can't ask follow-up questions or seek multiple and other points of view . . . So lurking and then quoting without first identifying yourself seems, to me, to be a pretty easy call.
>
> (cit. in Friend and Singer, 2007: 85)

Furthermore, new media technologies allow the subjects of investigations to tell their stories, too – as demonstrated by the video released by Scientologists of BBC journalist John Sweeney "losing it" while conducting his investigation into their activities (Sweeney, 2007).

Economically, the traditional support structures for investigative journalism – large news organisations – are, at least in their own terms, struggling, and investigative journalism is having to look elsewhere for funding. While BlogAds and AdSense have allowed some bloggers to operate through traditional advertising-based models, others have relied on reader donations facilitated by technologies such as PayPal and ChipIn, while foundations are playing an increasing role in supporting investigative journalism – but few have found a reliable revenue stream.

The future of investigative journalism is likely to lie along at least three paths. On the one hand, in a new media world of information overload where 'anyone can be a journalist', investigative journalism offers a way for the mainstream media to provide a distinctive product and prevent the readership migrating elsewhere online (Bradshaw, 2007). News organisations with declining budgets but a commitment to public service may be inclined to outsource part of their investigative work, taking advantage of their brand and experience and using crowdsourcing approaches to pursue investigative journalism. Finally, and perhaps more realistically, it is likely that foundations and reader donations will increasingly support investigative journalism as an important contribution to society. For investigative journalists themselves, the biggest concern is lack of job security – or at least an increasing requirement for new skills in managing volunteers or enterprises. For readers, however, the latter two routes, dependent as they are on active public support, offer some assurance that investigations will be undertaken in the public interest rather than the media's own self-interests. For this to happen, however, requires a change in the cultures of news organisations. As journalism becomes less a product – 'what sells' – and more a service – what people want to use – the need for that change will become increasingly pressing.

Notes

1 Crowdsourcing – drawing on the knowledge or manpower of readers to pursue a story or, 'outsourcing' to the 'crowd'.
2 A blogroll is a list of links to other blogs.
3 Shovelware – software that 'shovels' content from print onto the web, without any changes.
4 Wiki – a webpage or collection of webpages that anyone can edit.
5 BAE is Europe's biggest arms company. The story concerns alleged corruption and bribery in selling arms overseas.

Bibliography

Allan, S. (2006) *Online News*. Maidenhead: Open University Press.
Andrews, P. (2003) 'Is blogging journalism?' *Nieman Reports*, 57 (3), Fall 2003, http://www.nieman.harvard.edu/reports/03–3NRfall/V57N3.pdf
Ante, S. E. (2003) 'Commentary: have web site, will investigate', *BusinessWeek*, July 28, 2003, http://www.businessweek.com/magazine/content/03_30/b3843096_mz016.htm
Beckett, C. (2007) 'Networked journalism: for the people and with the people', *Press Gazette*, 18 October 2007, http://www.pressgazette.co.uk/story.asp?sectioncode=1&storycode=39147&c=1
Blood, R. (2000) 'Weblogs: a history and perspective', Rebecca's Pocket, September 7, 2000, http://www.rebeccablood.net/essays/weblog_history.html
Bowman, S. and Willis, C. (2003) *We Media*, http://www.hypergene.net/wemedia/weblog.php
Bradshaw, P. (2007) 'Blogs and journalism', 8th Vienna Globalisation Symposium, May 31, 2007, http://onlinejournalismblog.files.wordpress.com/2007/06/vienna_speech_postdraf.doc
Bromley, M. (2005) Subterfuge as public service, in Stuart Allan (ed.) *Journalism: Critical Issues*. Buckingham: Open University Press.
Bruns, A. (2005) *Gatewatching*. New York: Peter Lang.
Center for Investigative Reporting. Bi-annual Report: Reveal: Results, 2004, http://centerforinvestigativereporting.org/files/2004report.pdf
Center for Public Integrity, 'Katrina Watch: How We Did It', August 31, 2007, http://www.publicintegrity.org/katrina/report.aspx?aid=884

Electronic Frontier Foundation (2005) 'How to blog safely (about work or anything else)', May 31, 2005, https://www.eff.org/Privacy/Anonymity/blog-anonymously.php

ePluribus Media. KATRINA Timeline, 2006, http://timelines.epluribusmedia.org/timelines/index.php?table_name=tl_katr&page=0&function=search&execute_search=1

Feldstein, M. (2007) 'Dummies and ventriloquists: models of how sources set the investigative agenda', *Journalism*, 2007, 8, 499.

Friend, C. and Singer, J. (2007) *Online Journalism Ethics*. Armonk, NY: ME Sharpe.

Frola, L. (2007) 'watchdogs at work', Poynter Online, January 3, 2007, http://www.poynter.org/column.asp?id=83&aid=115844

Gannes, L. (2007) 'Alive in Baghdad: can citizen journalism done right pay the bills?' *NewTeeVee*, August 28, 2007.

Gans, H. (2003) *Democracy and the News*. Oxford: Oxford University Press.

Gant, S. (2007) *We're All Journalists Now*. New York: Free Press.

Gillmor, D. (2004) *We The Media*. Sebastopol, CA: O'Reilly.

Gillmor, D. The End of Objectivity (Version 0.91), 'Dan Gillmor on Grassroots Journalism, etc.', January 20, 2005, http://dangillmor.typepad.com/dan_gillmor_on_ grassroots/2005/01/the_end_of_obje.html

Habermas, J. (1989) *The Structural Transformation of the Public Sphere*. Cambridge, MA: MIT Press.

Henry, N. (2007) *American Carnival: Journalism Under Siege in an Age of New Media*. Berkeley, CA: University of California Press.

Herman, E. (2005) Media in the US political economy. In J. Downing, A. Mohammadi and A. Sreberny-Mohammadi (eds) *Questioning the Media: A Critical Introduction*, 2nd ed. New York: Sage.

Howe, J. (2006) Gannett to Crowdsource News, *Wired*, March 11 2006. http://www.wired.com/software/webservices/news/2006/11/72067

Howe, J. (2006) 'The rise of Crowdsourcing', *Wired*, June 2006, http://www.wired.com/wired/archive/14.06/crowds.html

Howe, J. (2006) 'Gannett Roundup: The Blogs', *Crowdsourcing.com*, November 7, 2006, http://crowdsourcing.typepad.com/cs/2006/11/gannett_roundup.html

Jones, L. (2007) 'Independent journalist blazes a trail from Afghanistan', Freelance Writing Tips, September 13, 2007, http://www.freelancewritingtips.com/2007/09/independent-jou.html

Journeyman Pictures (2007) Journeyman Profile, http://www.journeyman.tv/?lid=4

Kirkpatrick, M. (2007) 'What are the top investigative journalism video series online? How do they pay their bills?' *SplashCast*, September 7, 2007, http://splashcastmedia.com/investigativejourno

Knightley, P. (2004) 'Media: investigative journalism – a great reporter is dead. Who are', *Independent on Sunday*, July 25, 2004, http://findarticles.com/p/articles/mi_qn4159/is_20040725/ai_n12757697

McDermott, T. (2007) 'Blogs can top the presses', *Los Angeles Times*, March 17, 2007, http://www.latimes.com/news/nationworld/nation/la-na-blogs17mar17,0,4018765,full.story?coll=la-home-headlines

Meyer, P. (2004) *The Vanishing Newspaper*. Columbia, MO: University of Missouri Press.

Norton, Q. (2007) 'Wikileaks spilled', *Wired*, January 12, 2007 http://blog.wired.com/27bstroke6/2007/01/wikileaks_spill.html

Outing, S. (2005) 'Investigative journalism: will it survive?' *AllBusiness*, November 16, 2005, http://www.allbusiness.com/services/business-services-miscellaneous-business/4685406–1.html

Outlook, The (2007) Blogs: the next takeover target? October 23, 2007, http://outlook.standardandpoors.com/NASApp/NetAdvantage/i/displayIndustry FocusEditorial.do?&context=IndustryFocus&docId=12491873

Ponsford, D. (2007) 'Survey criticises dailies for single-sourcing', *Press Gazette*, October 19, 2007, http://www.pressgazette.co.uk/story.asp?sectioncode=1&storycode= 38881

Revkin, A. C. (2006) 'A young Bush appointee resigns his post at NASA', *New York Times*, February 8 2006, http://www.nytimes.com/2006/02/08/politics/08nasa. html?pagewanted= print

Reynolds, G. (2005) Instapundit.com, September 18, 2005.

Robinson, S. (2006) 'The mission of the j-blog: recapturing journalistic authority online', *Journalism*, 7(1): 65–83.

Rosen, J. (2004) 'The legend of Trent Lott and the weblogs', *PressThink*, March 15, 2004, http://journalism.nyu.edu/pubzone/weblogs/pressthink/2004/03/15/lott_ case.html

Rosen, J. (2007) 'They're not in your club but they are in your league: firedoglake at the Libby Trial', *PressThink*, March 9, 2007, http://journalism.nyu.edu/pubzone/ weblogs/pressthink/2007/03/09/libby_fdl.html

Rosen, J. (2007) 'The journalism that bloggers actually do', *Los Angeles Times*, August 22, 2007, http://www.latimes.com/news/opinion/la-oew-rosen22aug22,0,4771551. story

Sandburg, B. (2005) 'Lawyers flock to mystery web site's coverage of SCO-IBM Suit', *The Recorder*, September 9 2005, http://www.law.com/jsp/law/LawArticle Friendly.jsp?id=1126170313067

Shane, S. (2007) 'For bloggers, Libby trial is fun and fodder', *New York Times*, February 15, 2007, http://www.nytimes.com/2007/02/15/washington/15bloggers.html?_ r=1&pagewanted=print&oref=slogin

Smith, P. (2007) Guardian investigators share BAE bribery exposé on the web, *Press Gazette*, July 23, 2007.

Surowiecki, J. (2004) *The Wisdom of Crowds*, London: Abacus.

Sweeney, J. (2007) 'Row over Scientology video', *BBC News*, May 14, 2007, http:// news.bbc.co.uk/1/hi/world/americas/6650545.stm

Thompson, C. (2006) 'A timeline of the history of blogging', *New York Magazine*, February 20, 2006, http://nymag.com/news/media/15971/

Thompson, B. (2007) 'Who stands to gain from Wikileaks?', *BBC News*, March 13, 2007, http://news.bbc.co.uk/1/hi/technology/6443437.stm

Tomlin, J. (2007) 'From the frontline to the Frontline Club . . . and back', *Press Gazette*, September 28, 2007, http://www.pressgazette.co.uk/story.asp?storycode=38934

Weise, E. (2007) 'Pet-food scandal ignites blogosphere', *USAToday*, June 4, 2007, http:// www.usatoday.com/tech/webguide/internetlife/2007–06–04-petfood-scandal_N. htm?loc=interstitialskip#

Wikileaks (2007) Wikileaks: About, http://www.wikileaks.org/wiki/Wikileaks:About

Witte, G. (2006) 'On YouTube, charges of security flaws', *Washington Post*, August 29, 2006, http://www.washingtonpost.com/wp-dyn/content/article/2006/08/28/ AR2006082801293.html

Woodard Maderazo, J. (2007) 'YouTube, Flickr become forces for cultural change', *MediaShift*, September 28, 2007, http://www.pbs.org/mediashift/2007/09/breaking_government_blockadesy.html

Yon, M. (2007) 'How this project is funded, Michael Yon', *Online Magazine*, 2007, http://michaelyon-online.com/wp/how-this-project-is-funded

Further reading

Bowman, S. and Willis, C. (2003) *We Media*, http://www.hypergene.net/wemedia/weblog.php

Bruns, A. (2005) *Gatewatching*. New York: Peter Lang.

Friend, C., and Singer, J. (2007) *Online Journalism Ethics*. Armonk, NY: ME Sharpe.

Gillmor, D. (2004) *We The Media*. Sebastopol, CA: O'Reilly.

Rosen, J. (2007) 'The journalism that bloggers actually do', *Los Angeles Times*, August 22, 2007, http://www.latimes.com/news/opinion/la-oew-rosen22aug22,0,4771551.story

Surowiecki, J. (2004) *The Wisdom of Crowds*. London: Abacus.

6

INVESTIGATIVE JOURNALISM AND ENGLISH LAW

Chris Horrie

Investigative journalism has been defined as an attempt to 'discover the truth and to identify lapses from it in whatever media may be available . . . distinct from apparently similar work done by police, lawyers, auditors and regulatory bodies in that it is not limited as to target, not legally founded and it is closely connected to publicity'.[1] To this definition should be added consideration of the way in which the law shapes both the methods employed and editorial agenda pursued by investigative journalists and their publishers.[2]

It might be added that the idea of 'agenda setting' is central to investigative journalism. To borrow Lord Nicholls' famous phrase, used in his judgement of the watershed Reynolds libel case, investigative journalists have the right to behave as 'bloodhounds' as well as watchdogs.[3] Investigative journalism is thus a generic form in which the journalist or newspaper initiates the story, based on a suspicion of wrong-doing, rather than simply reporting in a more passive and disinterested way the routine news of the day, or unscheduled disasters and accidents. Just like Emile Zola's articles about the Dreyfus case, and the *Washington Post*'s Watergate expose, investigative journalists attempt to start or re-ignite debate or provoke political action over some issue that is officially 'closed'.[4]

In terms of legal liability journalists have advantages and disadvantages over official investigators, such as the police, even though they may share the same objectives of exposing wrong-doing. The obvious disadvantage is that they generally lack the resources and investigatory powers available to police authorities.[5] But the corresponding legal advantage is significant and far-reaching. Whilst the police must prove their allegations 'beyond reasonable doubt';[6] the harshest legal test that can be applied to journalists is that their allegations should be true 'on the balance of probabilities'.[7] This is the lower standard of proof required in the civil courts, importantly in libel cases.[8]

The evidence gap: civil and criminal standards of proof

The *Daily Mail*'s famous branding of five young men suspected of killing the London teenager Stephen Lawrence as 'Murderers' is a highly illustrative example of the way in which journalism can operate in the 'gap' between the standards of proof in the civil and criminal law.[9] Police believed they knew the identity of the killers, but did not feel they had sufficient evidence to secure conviction 'beyond reasonable doubt'.[10] Had an arrest taken place, and the 'killers' been found not guilty, they could not have been tried at a later date, when evidence might become available, second time because of the rule on double jeopardy. (The five were in fact never convicted.)[11] A private prosecution of the same five suspects was mounted by the Lawrence family, but collapsed because most of the evidence, including police surveillance video, was circumstantial.[12]

After the collapse of the trial the *Daily Mail* printed front-page pictures of the five youths beneath the block headline 'MURDERERS' and the prominent strapline: 'The Mail accuses these men of killing. If we are wrong, let them sue.'[13] Had the accused been facing trial the paper would have been guilty of the serious crime of contempt of court.[14] But since it was now extremely unlikely that the accused would be facing trial in front of a jury in the near future the only legal risk was an action for libel. Libel is tried in a civil court and so the paper would only have to show that its allegations were true 'on the balance of probability'. In the civil courts the paper would have been able to rely on the persuasive evidence that had been ruled as inadmissible in the criminal courts and must have been very confident of defeating any libel action brought by the accused. A further factor was the cost to the accused of bringing the case and bearing the additional and likely multi-million costs of the *Daily Mail* if, as seemed likely, they lost. It was doubtless a very effective piece of journalism, though it was criticised as a 'cynical stunt' and 'trial by media' by the *Daily Mail*'s critics and rivals.[15]

The BBC *Panorama* programme's investigation into the Omagh bombing is another illustrative example of investigative journalists using persuasive and accurate, but legally inadmissible evidence, gathered by the police (and in this case by the intelligence services).[16] The official investigation was largely based on the then innovative methods of electronic tracking of patterns of mobile phone traffic. This evidence was highly persuasive, but open to challenge as circumstantial and coincidental.[17] Unwilling to mount a criminal trial which they might lose, the police instead gave the evidence to the *Panorama* team who checked it independently, and used it as the core of their programme.[18]

As with the *Daily Mail* Lawrence case the BBC effectively challenged the accused to bring a libel action, during which the police evidence could be used. No such action was started.[19] As was also the case in the Lawrence case the BBC was accused of conducting 'trial by media' and, by some, of having an overly close relationship with the security forces. The programme's reporter,

John Ware, defended his methods and commented: 'Getting people out of jail who have been wrongly convicted has always been recognised as a journalistic pursuit very much in the public interest. By the same token, helping to lock up people who commit crimes as heinous as the Omagh bombing is also in the public interest.'[20]

Absence of malice: common law qualified privilege

In recent years the gap between standards of evidence required for criminal conviction on the one hand and the standard needed to defend an investigative report has widened considerably, and very much in favour of the serious and responsible investigative journalist, who works without malice.[21] The key development is the extension of common law qualified privilege (QP) to cover allegations which are made 'in the public interest'. The right of qualified privilege allows journalists (and others) to make defamatory statements, even if they cannot prove the allegations – and even if they are incapable of proof – subject to a number of conditions, the most important being that by making the allegations the journalist is serving the public interest.[22]

Common law QP dates back to a case in 1834 when a judge dismissed a libel action from a butler whose employer had said in a job reference that he was dishonest. The employer could not prove that the butler had been stealing, but the judge said that so long as he sincerely believed the defamatory remarks it promoted 'the common convenience and welfare of society' that they should be made 'depending on the absence of actual malice'.[23]

Statutory QP was clarified by the 1996 Defamation Act which specifies powerful rights to repeat or publish defamatory remarks made in parliament, court cases and a schedule of other public proceedings subject to some restrictions.[24] It is always better for the investigative journalist to repeat allegations which have been made in parliament or in court rather than make them himself. If the allegations are made in another formal meeting listed in the schedule of the 1996 act, he can repeat them, so long as he points out that the allegations are denied, if that is the case, and – above all – makes every effort to include the accused person's version of events.[25]

Common law QP applies to allegations which are not protected by statutory QP. The right is a very useful one for journalists and it has been strengthened by a series of rulings in court cases, underpinned by the passage of the Human Rights Act (HRA) in 1998, and especially by section 10 of the European Convention on Human Rights.[26] In 2000 Lord Bingham ruled that *The Times* had been justified in common law QP strengthened by reference to the HRA Section 10 in defaming a firm of Northern Ireland lawyers who had been accused of assisting IRA terrorists. The allegations had not been made in a court, or in parliament (and therefore were not protected by statutory QP), but at a public meeting run by an anti-IRA group campaigning in support of a

British soldier, private Clegg, who had been convicted of murder for shooting a Belfast youth he wrongly believed to be a terrorist.[27]

The significance of the Clegg case was that it appeared to extend the protection already available to accurate reports of allegations made in court and parliament (and other official gatherings specified by the 1996 act) to a new range of public meetings and unofficial gatherings. Once again it was crucial for the newspaper to prove that it had acted 'without malice' and had instead worked in a careful and neutral way, as 'the eyes and ears of the general public' as Lord Bingham put it. The point was that anybody in the world could have attended the meeting, which was about a very important public matter, and the newspaper was simply serving the public by saving them the inconvenience of turning up in person.[28]

The press after Reynolds: bloodhound as well as watchdog

In 1994 the *Sunday Times* published the results of an investigation, accusing the Irish Prime Minster Albert Reynolds of misleading the Irish parliament over the case of Father Brendan Smyth and a cover-up of child sexual abuse in the Irish Catholic Church.[29] The scandal brought down Reynolds' coalition government and he sued the *Sunday Times*.[30]

Reynolds won the action in the High Court in London, but was awarded only one penny in damages. The award was derisory because although the *Sunday Times* had not proven its allegation that Reynolds had deliberately participated in the cover-up (even on the basis of balance of probability) and therefore lost the case, the judge thought that public discussion of the way the scandal had been handled by the government was in the public interest. The *Sunday Times* won on appeal to the House of Lords.[31] Lord Nicholls' judgement in the case was seen as a major extension of qualified privilege, giving serious investigative journalism a very great deal of legal protection. Lord Nicholls endorsed the specifically investigative role of the press in initiating stories, in addition to the less controversial role of public 'watchdog' established by Lord Bingham in the Clegg case and elsewhere. He said: 'The press discharges vital functions as a bloodhound as well as a watchdog. The court should be slow to conclude that a publication was not in the public interest and, therefore, the public had no right to know especially when the information is in the field of political discussion. Any lingering doubts should be resolved in favour of publication.'[32]

In the same ruling Lord Nicholls set out a 'ten-point test' of responsible journalism which would, he believed, enjoy the full protection of the courts.[33] The test covers many points that would be considered good practice by journalists and which are covered by points in various voluntary codes of conduct. As such it should be followed as a legally sanctioned guide to the practice of investigative journalism. The ruling, including the test, is highly significant and has been frequently cited in major libel cases since 2001.[34] The advent of the ten-point test and the 'Reynolds defence' has been described by lawyers specialising in libel defence as 'a new dawn for press freedom'.[35]

The public interest and public concern

Central to the ten-point test is the idea of the public good and 'the public interest', and how this is to be balanced against the right of the individuals under investigation to maintain their reputation, as well as their HRA right to privacy.[36] If it can be shown that there is a high level of public interest in making the allegations, and that they are free from malice, then there is a strong QP right to publish them (and perhaps, indeed, even a duty to publish), even if the allegations turn out to untrue, or are incapable of proof.[37]

Some litigation experts, following Lord Nicholls's example, now prefer the term 'of public concern', since 'public interest' (as defined in the various codes of professional ethics) may become confused with 'that which interests the public', which may be a very different thing.[38] Thus 'investigative journalism' which has as its focus purely private concerns such as the state of health or interesting lifestyles of public figures may not enjoy protection even if the methods used to obtain and check information conform to the ten-point test and are otherwise of the highest quality.[39]

In the first seven years since the original Reynolds ruling the defence has been successfully used in court in only three cases, though it is likely that without its provisions many more potential complainants would have started actions.[40] *The Times*, the *Daily Telegraph* and the BBC have all failed with Reynolds defences in recent years, 'essentially because they failed to convince juries that their journalism was good enough'.[41] The most spectacular failure was the *Daily Telegraph*'s attempted Reynolds defence of allegations made against the Respect Party MP George Galloway.[42]

The paper ran an investigative story claiming that Galloway had for a number of years been a paid agent of Saddam Hussein. The story was based on Iraqi foreign ministry documents obtained in Baghdad which, the journalist believed, proved that Galloway had taken money and engaged in subversion as directed by the Iraqi regime. In court Mr Justice Eady said that the story might easily have had Reynolds-type common law QP protection, except for the fact that at least three of Lord Nicholls' points had been flouted. The story certainly was a matter of the highest public concern, since it involved a type of treason.[43] But the paper failed to write the story in the style of neutral reportage,[44] had not taken steps to check the reliability of its sources[45] and, crucially, had not put its allegations to Galloway in full, so that it could balance its report with his full denial.[46] Justice Eady said: 'If the documents had been published without comment or serious allegations of fact Mr Galloway could have no complaint since, in so far as they contained statements or allegations of fact it was in the public interest for the *Telegraph* to publish them, at any rate after giving Mr Galloway a fair opportunity to respond to them'.[47]

American publishers have done much better in British courts, notably the *Wall Street Journal*'s employment of the Reynolds defence in the Jameel libel case. It may be that they have higher standards. The fact that the *Journal* employs fact-checkers[48] and can show it has routine management systems which set high hurdles whereby reporters have to prove the truth of defamatory allegations before publication, weighed heavily in favour of the paper in court. The case concerned a piece of investigative journalism discussing ways in which Saudi Arabian financial institutions based in the USA might be funding terrorist groups.[49]

The appeal judge in Jameel built on Reynolds, emphasising that QP was available to investigative journalists so long as they could show two things were present in their investigations – firstly the 'quality' and type of journalistic techniques that they themselves as well as the publication or broadcaster for whom they were working routinely use; and secondly that stories dealt with matters of public concern. Journalism which can be shown to be of 'high quality' (in consideration of the methods employed by the journalist and publisher) and is *also* about a socially important issue (in consideration of content of the story) will enjoy a high degree of QP protection.[50] The libel lawyer David Price notes that QP defence is essential in stories dealing with corruption in totalitarian countries, where definitive proof may be impossible to obtain because of official censorship, or severe intimidation of witnesses.[51]

'Quality journalism' – a question of methods

The idea of 'quality journalism' is problematic, since it is most commonly used as a self-defined marketing term by national newspapers targeting or servicing an older, wealthier and more highly educated demographic.[52] The reference is to the editorial agenda, and not necessarily to methods. The case law after Reynolds and Jameel sees 'quality' mainly in the methods employed, rather than the editorial agenda.[53]

Quality journalism includes reporting work which is carried out within the Reynolds ten-point test, and within the profession's self-regulatory codes of conduct.[54] The reputation and experience of the journalist doing the story is significant. A journalist with a long track record of publication without reasonable complaint might have more QP protection than one without such a record.[55] A journalist with specialist training, or foreign language skills, or a newspaper which hires or consults specialists (such as accountants in the case of financial investigations), may enjoy more protection.[56] The reporter on an investigative story relying on Jameel-type QP protection would have to show that they had consulted experts, and would need to keep notes[57] or tape recordings of interviews, ideally using sworn statements where appropriate.[58]

The way in which allegations are reported is also significant, including the tone of writing and the style of presentation. Reporting and headlines which are un-sensational in tone will be more protected then those reported in strident tones.[59] Editors must supervise the entire production cycle to ensure that scrupulous, balanced and sober reportage is not 'sexed up' at a later point in the publication process, by journalists trained to relegate detail in favour of impact.[60] The Reynolds-type QP defence is a very strong one, if it can be obtained, but it is likely that in future the courts will restrict it to articles which consist of 'neutral reportage' – simply reporting agreed facts and 'reasonable and moderate comment from unimpeachable sources'.[61] This might result in a 'dull' journalist, but 'dull journalism is safe journalism'.[62] There is a need to keep records of the way in which investigations are conducted, as well as the results of those investigations. The burden of proving that the publisher has been scrupulous remains with the publisher.[63]

Conversely, journalists or publications with a track record of getting things wrong, of having complaints upheld against them, or who can be shown to be reckless or slapdash in any particular case would be less likely to gain QP protection.[64] As one leading libel defence lawyer advised journalists at a conference: 'Always question reliability of your source. Log each step you take in an investigation. Get independent corroboration, and – above all – put the allegations to the accused.'[65] The principles set out in Ben Bradlee's *Ethics and Standards* present tough challenges for journalists, first amongst them the ability to doubt the truth of their own stories. But following these ideals will tend to produce good quality and legally defensible journalism.[66]

Privacy – the 'new libel'

Showing that an investigation has been conducted 'in the public interest' is probably easier than showing that it meets the standards of quality journalism set out in the ten-point test, especially when it comes to details of private lives. Following the Reynolds and Jameel cases libel has become less of a constraint on investigative journalists who are pursuing stories in the public interest, and dealing with matters of public concern.[67]

But this new degree of legal protection has to be set against the growing legal constraint of fast developing judge-made privacy law based on section eight of the Human Rights Act (HRA). This gives legal protection to enjoyment of normal family life without unwanted intrusion, surveillance or investigation by third parties.[68] The original intention of section eight was to give citizens protection from state surveillance, for example from telephone tapping by the police.[69] But it has been developed to constrain the press, especially the tabloid press, celebrity magazines and paparazzi photojournalists to begin with.[70] When the HRA became law in 2002 it was hoped that the 'freedom of expression' provisions contained in section 10 of the act[71] would mitigate any restrictions on the press arising from section eight.[72] Case law has however shown that section eight of the HRA always beats section ten unless there is something highly specific in the facts of the case. Section eight has thus become 'a great restriction on what can be said, and on what photographs can be published, about people when they are not engaged on a clear public duty'.[73]

The danger is that corrupt or anti-social individuals may be able to use privacy law to deter journalists. Detection of corruption often begins by looking at the lavish private lifestyles of public servants apparently living beyond their means.[74] Also, after the 2005 McKennitt case in which the 'kiss and tell' memoirs of a pop star's friend and assistant were held to constitute a breech of confidentiality, it will be much harder for journalists to publish as evidence descriptions of people's lifestyle, no matter how unusual or interesting, given by confidents like butlers, or assistants.[75] The same case may have delivered an official death blow to the 'role model' argument in all but the most clear cut cases of official hypocrisy. The judge ruled that higher standards of professional or ethical behaviour may be expected of priests or school headmasters in their private lives, but (except in the case of the most direct type of fraudulent hypocrisy) not other businessmen, pop stars or professional footballers. Likewise the judge ruled that if a person surrendered the right of privacy in one area of their life, it did not mean they had surrendered it entirely. A self-publicist, such as a pop star, was entitled to say 'that's enough publicity now . . . please stop writing about me'.[76]

The trend in law is for people who might previously have sued for libel to prefer to use privacy law whenever possible, because of the stronger underlying statutory right given by section eight of the HRA. In the past a person who had been falsely accused of having an extramarital affair, or who was simply (wrongly) said to be suffering from a serious medical condition[77] might have sued for libel. Such a person is more likely now to use privacy law. In future, investigative journalists touching on issues like this will have to prepare to fight both types of cases.[78]

Protection of sources

Protection of confidential sources of information is perhaps the key professional duty of the journalist. As one editor recently put it: 'The fundamental ethical principle of journalism is that we have a moral imperative to give a guarantee of anonymity to genuine confidential sources providing bona fide information.'[79] In investigative journalism, in so far as this branch of news involves revealing secrets of one sort or another,[80] this duty is central and can bring the journalist into conflict with the law in two related areas: contempt of court and breach of confidence.

A fundamental principle of justice is that an accused person should be tried before a jury of his peers who will assume that he is innocent until proven guilty.[81] Any action by a journalist, or anyone else, that corrupts this process constitutes the crime of contempt of court. The 1981 contempt of court act defines the offence in several ways, including the publication of any material which creates a 'substantial risk' of prejudicing the jury against an accused.[82] One highly illustrative and fairly recent example was a publication by the *Sunday Mirror* of an interview with relatives of the victims of a violent assault in which the relatives graphically alleged the guilt of defendants in a court case, using evidence which could not be cross-examined in court. The article also made an emotional appeal for judicial revenge against the accused and their severe punishment. Even though the article was not published in direct defiance of the court, it was likely that the jury had read the article and the defendants claimed they were being denied their right to a fair trial without prejudice. The trial collapsed and the paper was fined.[83]

Refusal by journalists to reveal sources of confidential information can lead to prosecution for contempt of court if the journalist defies a court order to reveal those sources. The classic case involves the technology journalist Bill Goodwin. More recently the Attorney General threatened the deputy news editor of the *Manchester Evening News*, Steve Panter, with prosecution after he had refused to reveal protected sources who had helped him name suspects behind the 1996 IRA bombing of central Manchester. The case was dropped amid comment that it would have been politically unwise to turn Panter into an 'instant martyr'.[84] In this case, at least, the political power of an independent press appealing to the common sense of justice and doing a good honest reporting job on a popular issue proved more powerful that any statue.

Notes

1 de Burgh, H. (2000) *Investigative Journalism: Context and Practice*. London and New York: Routledge.

2 Throughout this chapter 'publisher' is used to include both publishers of newspapers, books, magazines and pamphlets and broadcasters alike as defined by section 1(2) of the 1996 Defamation Act. Likewise reference to publication in a newspaper is taken as the same act as broadcasting on TV or radio, or publication on the internet.

3 The news agenda refers to the importance of scheduled events in official and civil public life, such as parliamentary and local government debates, court cases, scheduled statutory meetings and so on. The classical 'fourth estate' definition of the social and political role of journalism involves the accurate and balanced reporting of such events, in so far as they are of interest to a large or sufficiently well-defined group to make such reports commercially viable. This is the 'watchdog' function, endorsed by common law, and referred to by Lord Nicholls in his judgement of the Reynolds libel case. It is quite different to the more proactive 'bloodhound function' which he endorsed as legitimate in the case of responsible and non-sensational investigative journalism.

4 Zola's investigation of a miscarriage of justice which lead to an innocent Jewish army officer being sent to exile on Devil's Island after being framed for treason amid anti-Semitic hysteria is regarded by many as the classic form of modern investigative journalism. For an account see Cahm, E. (1996) *The Dreyfus Affair in French Society and Politics*. London: Longman.

5 Electronic surveillance by private persons (and journalists) was made illegal by the 1997 Criminal Law Act, and the prohibition was strengthened by the Regulation of Investigatory Powers Act (RIPA), 2000. There was concern at the time of the RIPA's passage that it would constrain certain types of legitimate journalistic investigation. January 2007 saw the first prosecution of an investigate journalist using RIPA – *News of the World* investigative reporter Clive Goodman was sentenced to four months in jail after being discovered using an electronic 'bug' to record telephone calls made by the British royal princes. A further concern for journalists is additional powers given to the police by RIPA to demand access to records of phone calls made by journalists, including investigative journalists, where they believe these may be of use in prosecuting criminals.

6 The classic statement of the common law presumption of innocence unless allegations can be proved beyond reasonable doubt was given by Viscount Sankey, LC in *Woolmington v D.P.P.* 1935 AC 462, 481: 'Throughout the web of the English criminal law, one golden thread is always to be seen, that it is the duty of the prosecution to prove the prisoner's guilt.' The Universal Declaration of Human Rights (1948) makes the principle international. Article 11(1) provides: 'Everyone charged with a penal offence has the right to be presumed innocent until proved guilty according to law.' Article 6.2 of the European Convention for the Protection of Human Rights and Fundamental Freedoms (1950) provides: 'Everyone charged with a criminal offence shall be presumed innocent until proved guilty according to law.' The Human Rights Act (1998), Article 6.2 emphasises the same point.

7 The standard of proof in civil courts is that a fact must be proved on the balance of probabilities using the evidence before the court. This means that upon consideration of the evidence admitted by the contesting parties, the account that is more likely will be accepted. The inherent probability of the allegation is considered in the process. Gillham's Legal Dictionary, 2007. See http://www.gillhams.com/dictionary/listB.cfm. Accessed 1 July 2007.

8 See http://www.westminsterjournalism.co.uk/medialawweb.html accessed 1 July 2007. Libel is defamation in a permanent form (for example in a newspaper, but also on the web or in a broadcast that could be recorded). The law on defamation is ancient and not very clearly defined. Libel is the only type of civil case that is normally tried with a jury, and it is up to a jury to decide whether or not the words actually spoken (slander) or published/broadcast (libel) are 'defamatory' or not. The judicial guidelines for juries are that a statement is defamatory if it merely tends to lower their reputation in any (not all) of the following ways. That the statement either:

(a)   Exposes them to hatred, ridicule or contempt, or
(b)   Causes them to be shunned or avoided, or
(c)   Discredits them in their trade, business or profession, or
(d)   Generally lowers them in the eyes of right-thinking members of society.

9 *Daily Mail*, London, 14 February 1997. For a facsimile of the *Daily Mail*'s 'Murderers' front page, see: http://news.bbc.co.uk/1/shared/spl/hi/pop_ups/06/programmes_enl_1146753319/html/1.stm. Accessed 1 July 2007.

10 For details of the police's widely criticised handling of the case, See: MacPherson of Cluny, Sir William (1999) *Report of the inquiry into the death of Stephen Lawrence*. London: HMSO, Cm 4262–I.

11 The Criminal Justice Act 2003 abolished avoidance of double jeopardy as an absolute principle, and allowed re-trail on the basis of fresh evidence in certain limited circumstances. Criminal Justice Act 2003, Part 10, 75: 'new and compelling evidence'.

12 The evidence included police video of the suspects recorded in 1994. The youths were heard to say: 'If I was going to kill myself do you know what I'd do? I'd go and kill every black, every Paki, every mug, every copper that I know. I'd go down to Catford and places like that with two submachine guns and I'm telling you I'd take one of them. Skin the black alive, mate. Torture him, set him alight. I'd blow their two legs and arms off and say: "Go on, you can swim home now".' This was not however a confession to the crime, and so would not have passed the test of being evidence beyond doubt that the man who spoke these words actually did the killing, though together with other circumstantial evidence, such as the discovery of knives buried in the youths' gardens, and their whereabouts on the night of the killing, the evidence was compelling enough for the editor of the *Daily Mail* to be absolutely certain that they had carried out the murder. See: MacPherson of Cluny, Sir William (1999) *Report of the inquiry into the death of Stephen Lawrence*. London: HMSO, Cm 4262–I.

13 *Daily Mail*, London, 14 February 1997.

14 Contempt of Court comes in many forms, including the publication of material which is likely to influence a jury in a particular court, even if that material is true, so long as it has not been given as evidence in the court while it is in session. For more detail on contempt of court see Horrie, Chris and Adamson, Richard (2007) Media Law Web, http://www.westminsterjournalism.co.uk/law/002reportingthecourts.htm. Accessed 1 July 2007.

15 See 'Trial By the Daily Mail', leading article, *The Guardian*, London, 15 February 1997.

16 BBC (2000) *Panorama*: 'Who Bombed Omagh?', 9 October 2000, London: BBC. The bombing took place in August 1998 and killed 29 people. Terrorists used a remotely detonated car bomb parked in the town centre on a busy Saturday morning.

17 The admissibility of this evidence was still being argued in pre-trial tribunals in Northern Ireland at the time of writing in the summer of 2007.

18 BBC News Online, 4 October 2000. http://news.bbc.co.uk/1/hi/northern_ireland/956465.stm The Northern Ireland police were explicit and open about their alliance with the BBC. In the programme the chief constable of the Royal Ulster Constabulary (as the service was then called), Ronnie Flanagan, said that he knew who had carried out the bombing, but he could not prosecute until witnesses came forward. 'We need the final pieces fitted into this jigsaw in terms of evidence', Flanagan said, adding: 'There must be a whole range of people – associates; even friends; people shocked to the core by this atrocity – who have vital pieces of information as to the activity of those who were actually involved in this atrocity. And those people, if given encouragement, might just exercise their judgement properly and come forward'.

19 The terrorists did not bring a libel action but, within a year, the terrorist group named in the *Panorama* programme was accused of being responsible for a car-bomb attack on the BBC television centre.

20 Ware, J. (2000) 'Panorama and the Omagh Atrocity', *British Journalism Review*, 11 (4), London: BJR.

21 For a good working definition of malice see Robertson, G. and Nicol, A. (2003) *Media Law (fourth edition)*. London: Penguin.

22 In addition to common law qualified privilege the 1996 Defamation Act give a schedule of types of statement which have various degrees of protection from libel action, subject to certain conditions. The most protected statements are accurate, verbatim reports of what is said in court or in parliament. It is always safe for a journalist to report what is said in court, no matter how serious or defamatory the allegations, provided that the account is completely accurate, that it is a

fair and balanced account (for example it included the fact that the allegations have been denied) and it is published immediately, or as soon as is practically possible.

23 *Toogood v Spyring* (1834) 1 CM&R 181, 193, The judge in the case said: 'The law considers such publication as malicious, unless it is fairly made by a person in the discharge of some public or private duty, whether legal or moral, or in conduct of his own affairs, in matters where his interest is concerned. In such cases the occasion prevents the inference of malice, which draws from unauthorised communications, and affords a qualified defence depending on the absence of actual malice. If fairly warranted by any reasonable occasion or exigency, and honestly made, such communications are protected for the common convenience and welfare of society; and the law has not restricted the right to make them within any narrow limits'.

24 The schedule of privileged information in the 1996 act is reproduced in Horrie, C. (2007) *Media Law Web*, http://www.westminsterjournalism.co.uk/law/004qualifiedprivilege.htm. Accessed 1 July 2007.

25 The complete protection given to statements made in parliament can be made available to investigative journalists who take care to develop particular MPs as trusted contacts and collaborators on investigative campaigns. A journalist may be able to persuade an MP to make a statement in the House of Commons, and this can be safely quoted. More common is the practice of getting MPs to table written questions to ministers. These may never be read or debated in parliament, but allegations made in this form still enjoy the protection of statutory QP.

26 The article enshrines in British law the European Human Rights Convention, including a constitutional right to freedom of expression (though not, explicitly, freedom of the press). Article 10 has two sections:

10(1). Everyone has the right to freedom of expression. This right shall include freedom to hold opinions and to receive and impart information and ideas without interference by public authority and regardless of frontiers. This Article shall not prevent States from requiring the licensing of broadcasting, television or cinema enterprises.

10(2). The exercise of these freedoms, since it carries with it duties and responsibilities, may be subject to such formalities, conditions, restrictions or penalties as are prescribed by law and are necessary in a democratic society, in the interests of national security, territorial integrity or public safety, for the prevention of disorder or crime, for the protection of health or morals, for the protection of the reputation or rights of others, for preventing the disclosure of information received in confidence, or for maintaining the authority and impartiality of the judiciary.

27 Lord Bingham of Cornhill (2000) *Opinion of the Lords of Appeal for judgement. Turkington and others vs Times Newspapers*. London: HMSO.

28 Op. cit. Bingham (2000).

29 *Sunday Times*, London, 20 November 1994.

30 For an account see Moore, C. (1995) *Betrayal of Trust: The Father Brendan Smyth Affair and the Catholic Church*. Dublin: Marino.

31 Lord Nicholls (2001) *Reynolds v Times Newspapers*. London: HMSO.

32 Op. cit. Lord Nicholls (2001).

33 Henceforth, courts hearing libel cases were told to take into account the following ten-point, non-exhaustive list when deciding if a defence of QP was allowable:

1 the seriousness of the allegation;
2 the nature of the information, and the extent to which the subject-matter is a matter of public concern;
3 the source of the information;

4 the steps taken to verify the information;
5 the status of the information;
6 the urgency of the matter;
7 whether comment was sought from the claimant;
8 whether the article contained the gist of the claimant's side of the story;
9 the tone of the article;
10 the circumstances of the publication, including the timing.

34 For example, *Loutchansky v Times Newspaper Ltd* (2001) – this is a significant case because the *Sunday Times* mounted a common law QP 'Reynold's Defence' (the term is now current) and the presiding judge, Mr Justice Grey at the Queen's Bench applied the ten-point test systematically to the *Sunday Times*' story which accused the eponymous Mr Loutchansky of being a violent member of the Russian and Uzbeck mafia engaged in money-laundering in the City of London.
35 For example, Adrienne Page QC, a libel defence specialist and expert on common law QP, speaking at the Newspaper Society media law conference. Page, A., May 2007, Reuters Centre, London.
36 Human Rights Act (1998) Article eight: 1. Everyone has the right to respect for his private and family life, his home and his correspondence. 2. There shall be no interference by a public authority with the exercise of this right except such as is in accordance with the law and is necessary in a democratic society in the interests of national security, public safety or the economic well-being of the country, for the prevention of disorder or crime, for the protection of health or morals, or for the protection of the rights and freedoms of others.
37 Lord Nicholls (2001) uses the phrase 'public concern' instead of the more usual 'public interest'. In his judgement he spoke of maintaining the 'elasticity' of such common law formulations which, he thought, were more likely to preserve freedom of speech than a specific definition of 'allowed political speech' which would automatically enjoy protection. Nevertheless the existing definition of the public interest given not in law, but in the PCC code of conduct, is likely to qualify for protection under this definition. The definition of a 'protected disclosure' given in section 43B of the 1998 Public Interest Disclosure Act might also serve as a definition of information which, when disclosed, is always in the public interest and therefore protected:

    (a) that a criminal offence has been committed, is being committed or is likely to be committed;
    (b) that a person has failed, is failing or is likely to fail to comply with any legal obligation to which he is subject;
    (c) that a miscarriage of justice has occurred, is occurring or is likely to occur;
    (d) that the health or safety of any individual has been, is being or is likely to be endangered;
    (e) that the environment has been, is being or is likely to be damaged; or
    (f) that information tending to show any matter falling within any one of the preceding paragraphs has been, is being or is likely to be deliberately concealed.

38 Page, A. (2007) op. cit.
39 This trend is more pronounced in the rest of the EU than in the UK itself. For example the Princes Caroline privacy case (*Von Hanover v Germany*, ECHR, June 24 2004).
40 Page, A. (2007) op. cit.
41 Page, A. (2007) op. cit.
42 *Daily Telegraph*, London April 22nd, 2003. The article alleged that Galloway had received £375,000 a year from the Iraqi state in return for furthering Iraqi interests

in the UK. The story was based mainly on documents obtained by the paper which, Galloway successfully maintained, were forgeries.

43 The investigation complied with points 1 and 2 of the ten-point test, in that the allegations were serious, and they dealt with matters of very significant public concern. But the article was deficient in other ways, and so the defence was not available.

44 Note Reynolds point 9 – the 'tone' of the article. 'Neutral reportage' is required, but in this case Justice Eady accused the paper of sensationalism and construction.

45 Reynolds points three, four and five.

46 Reynolds points seven and eight.

47 Justice Eady in the High Court, 2 December 2002. London: HMSO.

48 For an account of 'ingrained ethics' on US newspapers see: Cohen, D. and Elliot, D. (eds) (1998) *Journalism Ethics – A Reference Handbook (Contemporary Ethical Issues)*. New York: Abc-Clio.

49 *Mohammed Abdul Latif Jameel and Abdul Latif Jameel Company Limited v The Wall Street Journal Europe* (Eady J, 1–19 December 2003). The article in question appeared in the *Wall Street Journal* (European edition) on 6 February 2002 and was headed 'Saudi Officials Monitor Certain Bank Accounts – Focus is on those with Potential Terrorist Ties'. Jameel was named and claimed that at least by innuendo he was being accused of providing funds to terrorist organisations. He said this was untrue and defamatory, and that the newspaper had no proof. The *Journal* said that its article had merely reported in neutral terms the fact that various responsible, but un-named, officials were concerned about the situation. Jameel was on a list of potentially suspect financiers and so there were reasonable grounds to suspect and discuss his possible misconduct. The *Journal* therefore defended its article in the High Court pleading Reynolds-type Common Law QP. The *Journal* lost the case, but later won on appeal to the House of Lords. The Lords held that Reynolds had been interpreted too strictly in the past: the 10 criteria, including steps taken to verify the information and the tone of the article, were pointers as opposed to hurdles for the media.

50 Page, A. (2007) op. cit.

51 David Price and Partners, defamation and media law newsletter, November 2006.

52 For example the *Daily Telegraph* claims that it is 'Britain's biggest selling quality newspaper'. But such a claim was of no use in mounting a Reynolds-type QP defence to its George Galloway story.

53 For a discussion see Horrie, C. and Chippendale, P. (2005) *Stick it Up Your Punter*. London: Simon and Schuster.

54 In the UK the NUJ Code of Conduct, the Press Complaints Commission Code of Conduct, the OFCOM guidelines and the BBC's internal editorial guidelines all contain explicit provisions corresponding to the ten points. The difference is that these codes do not have the force of law.

55 A journalist with good sources and who is an expert might have more of a QP defence than a generalist or an inexperienced journalist. Adrienne Page QC (2007), op. cit.

56 The training of journalists within particular specialisms (such as medical journalism) is a trend in journalism education. In many countries journalism is now primarily a graduate-entry profession, with many new entrants also gaining postgraduate training of academic qualifications.

57 Revival of training in the art of shorthand note-taking is a central part of the mission of the BBC College of Journalism, the internal body set up to promote higher standards of journalism at the corporation in the wake of Hutton Inquiry.

58 Affidavits can be sworn for free at a county court; or for a charge of about £10 by any qualified solicitor.

59 In the Galloway case Justice Eady (2003) condemned the *Daily Telegraph* for its sensationalists and judgemental tone. The paper had drawn conclusions and 'embellished' points of fact. For these and other reasons, mainly that Galloway had not been given a chance to rebut the allegations, a story which could not be proved, but which might otherwise have enjoyed QP protection, was found to be libellous and the newspaper was heavily fined.

60 Page, A. (2007) op. cit.

61 Page, A. (2007) op. cit.

62 Page, A. (2007) op. cit.

63 'The complainant's lawyers will crawl over notes, methods, drafts, tapes to see that it was all done in an ethical way. There will a need for positive proof that facts have been independently checked.' Page, Adrienne (2007) op. cit.

64 One example was journalists working for the tabloid *Daily Star*, who were not believed when defending a libel action brought by Jeffrey Archer, the politician.

65 Page, A. (2007) op. cit.

66 See Bradlee, B. C. (1989) in Thomas W. Lippman (ed.) *The Washington Post Deskbook on Style*, Washington DC. Bradlee was the executive editor of the *Washington Post* at the time of the Watergate investigation.

67 Andrew Caldecott QC, a privacy and defamation litigation specialist speaking at the Newspaper Society media law conference, Reuters Centre, London, May 2007.

68 For the actual text of section eight of the HRA see above.

69 The possible restraining effect of section eight of the HRA was discussed in parliament at the time of the passage of the act. Emphasis was given to clause 2 of the section, which emphasised protection by right of the citizen from harassment by the state, rather than civil bodies such as the press.

70 This trend was pronounced after the death of Princess Diana which was attributed by some to pursuit by photojournalists. Significant cases employing section eight, such as *Von Hanover v Germany* in the ECHR, have concerned the work of photojournalists.

71 See above, Human Rights Action section 10(1) and 10(2).

72 An additional section 12(4) was put in to prevent this, but it has not been effective. Section 12(4) of the HRA was designed to inhibit Article 8 interfering with article 10 freedom of expression. But judges have ruled that section 8 and section 10 have equal weight and no additional article can change that. The main significance of section 10 in practice may be to deter courts from awarding punitive damages in libel and privacy cases.

73 Caldecott, A. (2007) op. cit.

74 For example, the murdered Dublin investigative journalist Veronica Guerin's expose of police corruption began by reporting the lavish personal lifestyles and consumer habits of police officers. O'Reily, E. (1989) *Veronica Guerin: The Life and Death of a Crime Reporter*. London: Vintage.

75 In 2005 the pop star Loreena McKennitt sued her former best friend Niema Ash for breach of confidentiality after Ash has published a book called *Travels with Loreena – My Life as A Friend* which contained details of the two women's private lives.

76 Justice Eady in his judgement said: 'There is a significant shift taking place between, on the one hand, freedom of expression for the media . . . and, on the other hand, the legitimate expectation of citizens to have their private lives protected.'

77 The allegation that a person was suffering from a disease would constitute a breach of privacy even if the allegation was not true. If untrue there might also be an action for injurious falsehood or possibly malicious falsehood if the journalist had recklessly overlooked the facts, or not bothered to check them.

78 Page, A. (2007) op. cit.
79 Coulter, J. (2005) *British Journalism Review*, 16 (1), 65–69. See also NUJ code of conduct, article seven: 'A journalist shall protect confidential sources of information'; and the Press Complaints Commission Code of Conduct article 14: 'Journalists have a moral obligation to protect confidential sources of information'.
80 According to some, this definition extends to all journalism. Lord Northcliffe's dictum that: 'News is what somebody somewhere wants to suppress; all the rest is advertising' is displayed on a plaque in the Reuters newsroom in London, and is doubtless dear to the heart of editors around the world.
81 See the discussion of presumption of innocence and the standard of proof required in criminal cases 'beyond reasonable doubt' above.
82 The Contempt of Court Act 1981 bans publication of any material which might prejudice a fair trial; the reporting of opinions expressed by jurors; anything which interferes with the course of justice and any breach of a court order. Section 10 of the Act, however, gives journalists ('a person responsible for publication' in the words of the Act) a limited and counterveiling right to refuse to reveal sources, even when ordered to do so by a judge, unless that refusal would either endanger national security or hinder the police in the investigation of crime or deny justice in a court case.
83 In England conviction for contempt of court carries the threat of an unlimited fine and up to two years imprisonment. The *Sunday Mirror* was fined £75,000 for contempt of court and ordered to pay £100,000 in legal costs following publication of an article that led to collapse of the ten week trial of Leeds United footballers Lee Bowyer and Jonathan Woodgate in 2001. The 1981 Act (section 2(2)) makes contempt of court a 'strict liability' offence, meaning that in a prosecution it does not need to be shown that the contempt was carried out deliberately.
84 For an account of the Panter case see *The Guardian*, London, 22 July 2002.

Further reading

Arlidge, J., Eady, The Hon Mr Justice and Smith, A.T.H. (2005) *Contempt of Court*. London: Sweet and Maxwell.

Armstrong, N. Carey, P. Coles, P. and Lamont, D. (2005) *Media Law*. London: Sweet and Maxwell.

Banks, D., Greenwood, W. and Welsh, T. (2007) *McNae's Essential Law for Journalists*, 19th edition. Oxford and New York: Oxford University Press.

Barendt, E. *et al.* (1997) *Libel and the Media: The Chilling Effect*. Oxford: Clarendon Press.

Caddell, R. and Johnson, H. (eds) (2007) *Blackstone's Statutes on Media Law*. London: Blackstones.

Cornish, W. and Llewelyn, D. (2007) *Intellectual Property: Copyrights, Trademarks and Allied Rights*. London: Sweet and Maxwell.

Crone, T. (2002) *Law and the Media*, 4th edition. London: Focal Press.

Duodu, K. and Price, D. (2003) *Defamation*. London: Sweet and Maxwell.

Keenan, D. (2007) *Smith and Keenan's English Law*, 15th edition. London and New York: Pearson Longman.

Nicol, A. and Robertson, G. (2002) *Media Law*, 4th edition. London: Penguin.

Toulson, The Hon Mr Justice and Phipps, C. (2006) *Confidentiality*. London: Sweet and Maxwell.

7

THE ENGLISH FREEDOM OF INFORMATION ACT

Chris Horrie

All forms of journalism, including comment as well as reportage and observation, depend on reliable sources of information. Journalism dealing with public affairs depends on state information, and all official information in the UK belongs, in the first place to the state. It follows that ways in which the state controls the release of this information determines the nature of journalism in any particular country. In this context investigative journalism can be thought of as a type of news reporting based on official information which has been obtained through unconventional (and possibly illegal) means; or information which has been proactively obtained by a journalist using Freedom of Information legislation in countries where such legislation exists.

At least some degree of secrecy is the starting point for any state, and this may be justified for much of the routine working of government. State control over official information can be asserted in common law simply by way of Crown copyright.[1] Beyond this all civil servants owe a common law duty of confidentiality to the state, their employer, meaning that they can not release information to any third party (journalist or member of the public, it makes no difference) without permission. This obligation is clearly expressed in the Civil Service Code of Practice which states: 'Civil servants . . . must not, without relevant authorisation, disclose official information which has been communicated in confidence within Government or received in confidence from others . . . (section 4.2.2)' and 'Civil servants must obtain the prior approval of their Head of Department or Agency Chief Executive before entering into any arrangements regarding the publication or dissemination of any Crown copyright protected material by private sector publishers or information providers. (UK Civil Service Code section 4.2.12)'.[2]

In addition, almost all employees of the state or a public body will have specific obligations of confidentiality or secrecy written into their contracts of employment.[3] Finally, a large number of public employees are, in addition to all of this, subject to the draconian restrictions of the Official Secrets

Act.★ Employees of companies with government contracts, especially in the field of defence and security, may also be subject to the stringent restrictions of the Official Secrets Act.[4]

At least until the passage of the 2000 Freedom of Information Act into law the premise of the government and the permanent departments of state was that everything is secret, unless there is specific approval for information to be released by an appropriate authority. One Freedom of Information advocate has written that long after other modern democracies had bestowed intrinsic rights of access to information 'Britain continued along the path of secrecy and scandal'.[5]

The state monopoly on official information meant that the news agenda was set by what information the government chose to release and debate in parliament, supplemented by other glimpses into the world of official information provided by the courts, Royal Commissions (of investigation) and planning inquiries. Indeed periods of the year when parliament is not in session are still referred to by some journalists as 'the silly season' – when no reliable or sensible official information is available.[6]

Thus the classic form of modern journalism has awarded a lot of space to parliamentary proceeding and parliamentary reporters (along with crime reporters, specialising in covering the courts) achieved high status as having access, however limited, to the monopoly of reliable official information.[7] For the local press, access to local government council debates played the same role. Indeed the traditional training of journalists, as set out in the curriculum and examinations of the National Council for the Training of Journalists, was based almost entirely on an understanding of official local and national government structures, together with skills such as shorthand which would enable the reporter accurately to record local government and court proceedings and then rapidly produce large quantities of highly accurate summary reporting of the

---

★ Certain types of public information such as details of military or intelligence operations are 'official secrets'. The Official Secrets Act 1911 (and various amendments) contains schedules of secret information. Revealing any of this information can lead to criminal prosecution.

    The main practical danger here is for photographic or TV journalists who may inadvertently break the Act by, for example, taking wallpaper shots of military bases and so on, which are covered by the Official Secrets Act. Normally at a military base (or for example a nuclear power station) there will be a notice saying: 'This is a prohibited place under the Official Secrets Act. Persons entering here may be arrested and prosecuted'. If this is the case you can not take photos, or make a drawing or anything of that sort without permission. Prosecutions under the Official Secrets Act are relatively rare. Recent cases included revelations made by the former MI6 officer David Shayler about MI6 operations in Libya and elsewhere. Shayler claimed, for example, that MI6 had contemplated the assassination of Colonel Gadaffi of Libya. The official secrets act can be read at the following UK government website: http://www.opsi.gov.uk/acts/acts1989/ Ukpga_19890006_en_1.htm. State information protected by the OSA is also automatically excluded as accessible material under several specified exemptions set out in the 2000 Freedom of Information Act.

information state authorities had chosen to make public in these forums, written without comment or analysis.[8]

The reality had always been that the government could subvert the significance of parliament by 'leaking' official information directly to selected journalists in order to by-pass parliamentary scrutiny and gain political advantage.[9] Civil servants (and, as in all of this discussion the same points apply in the relationship between local government and the local press) would 'leak' directly to journalists in order to gain advantage or, sometimes, obey the dictates of conscience.[10] The effective down-grading of parliament as an original source of information (by the sheer volume and complexity of information processed by the modern state and executive agencies if nothing else) led inevitably to a loss of status for formal 'objective' parliamentary (or local council) reporting. Newspapers invested instead with a new breed of reporters whose status was based on their 'contacts' – meaning the number and seniority of civil servants and politicians who would regularly 'leak' to them.

Unsurprisingly demands for 'freedom of information' – the establishment of extra-parliamentary rights to see and publish official records – generally come as part of wider discourse on government corruption, waste, inefficiency, and are made by opposition political parties and activists and opposition newspapers.[11] After a long period in opposition the promise of a Freedom of Information Act formed a key part of the 1997 election campaign which brought New Labour to power in the UK. The Freedom of Information Act (FOIA) passed through parliament in 2000 and came into force in 2005. Originally the act was hailed as a huge step towards open government. It was also a powerful tool for journalists on all types of media. It also gave a boost to the new phenomena of 'citizen journalism' coinciding with the spread of internet use. One activist group claimed that in its first year of operation the FOIA had enabled journalists to produce more than 500 articles, all of which were clearly on matters of public concern, and none of which originated with traditional off-the-record contacts.

There were forces at work long before 1997 which made freedom of information legislation in some form overdue. Faith in the effectiveness of parliamentary scrutiny was in decline, replaced by a new emphasis on individual rights. And underlying all this was the huge increase in the amount of information gathered and generated by the modern state: the idea that all of this information could be scrutinised by parliament and its committees was increasingly untenable. The FOI enthusiasts come out of the tradition of consumer investigative journalism, for example the journalist Heather Brookes who writes:

> Most of us are not that interested in party politics. We just want good solutions to common problems: safe public transport, reliable and competent healthcare, good schools for our children, safe streets and a just and efficient legal system.[12]

The US has had a Freedom of Information Act since 1966, which was strengthened in 1974 following the Watergate scandal. US legislation was comprehensively updated in 1996, extending access to electronic records. For many years British investigative journalists could find out about British organisations (including the military and private companies) by ordering searches of US records using US legislation. Such searches sometimes turned up information gathered by the US about British subjects (such as the safety of British sourced consumer products) which was unavailable in the UK itself.

Under the 2000 FOIA more than 100,000 public authorities were required to give a legal right to the public, including journalists, to inspect their records. They are also required to publish a schedule setting out the type of information which they hold. They must also help process inquiries within certain time limits. The whole process is overseen by a national Information Commissioner to whom appeals can be made. Public bodies which do not help the public exercise their rights under the act could, in theory, lose their right to keep records at all which, in practice, would mean they could no longer function. The Commissioner's office publishes a straightforward guide to the provision of the Act. Several independent 'how to guides' have been published, both by campaign groups and by journalists. Websites associated with these guides are frequently updated, since this is a developing area of law and state practice where precedent is important. An application for official information in a sensitive area is more likely to succeed if a similar but previous application was accepted. Campaign groups such as Friends of the Earth and the Campaign for Freedom of Information draw attention to important cases as they arise.[13]

In summary, under the 2000 Act any person making a request for information to a public authority is entitled to be informed in writing by the public authority whether it holds information of the description specified in the request, and if that is the case, to have that information communicated to him.[14]

The form of the request would be to ask, for example, the department of transport if it kept records relating to the relative cost of road construction in different parts of the country. The department would have to reply confirming that it does have such records (if this is the case) and provide a list of all the documents that the department honestly thinks the inquirer might want. In some circumstances a public body might confirm that it has the information, but then refuse to release it, citing one of a long list of exemptions included in the act (for example that release of the information would endanger national security; or was otherwise illegal because, for example, it would involve a breach of confidence). But unless one of these exceptions is invoked the enquirer can ask for the information to be supplied. The department can charge a fee for the time and effort involved or, controversially, claim that the cost of processing the request is prohibitive.[15]

The first potential difficulty for journalists or others using the Act is the definition of 'information' itself. The Act specifies that only information, or records of decisions, which have been written down or electronically recorded, counts as information available to the public under the meaning of the Act.[16] The danger is that once public officials realise that decisions they record will be open to public scrutiny, they will be more circumspect in creating accessible records in the first place. It was alleged in the 2004 Butler report into the decision to go to war in Iraq that under the prime ministership of Tony Blair decisions were often made by unofficial sub-groups. Records of decisions made in Cabinet or other official bodies did not exist, because they had been made in advance and in private.[17]

A public authority (including the government) can refuse to process a request for information on two grounds – the request is too expensive to process[18] or that the requested information is covered by one of the specific exemptions detailed in the act and must therefore remain secret for some good and legal reason. A request can also be refused if it is judged to be too trivial or 'vexatious'.

Exemptions fall into two categories. The first is qualified exemption (meaning that the information is potentially sensitive, but can still be released if, on balance, it can be shown that such a release is in the public interest.[19] Unsurprisingly this public interest qualification is controversial and contested with journalists and campaigners arguing for a broad definition of the concept, and public bodies interpreting it far more narrowly. The second is absolute exemption, meaning that it can never be in the public interest to release the information, normally because to do so would involve breaking some other law, or would prejudice legal proceedings.[20]

The 2000 Freedom of Information Act was widely seen by journalists and constitutional reformers alike as a step forward and one which, notably, would create a rights-based approach to the legal status official information on US lines. However, the state has proved adept at using the long list of exemptions to frustrate investigation into areas of public life, almost at will (at least in the case of central government) by deploying the 'catch-all' exemptions relating to national security and to an ill-defined public good. It seems that the long-running four way battle between democratic politicians, special interest pressure groups, executive officials and journalists will continue for many years yet, despite a slight redistribution of power between the parties. More significant in the long run may be the arrival of individual campaigners or 'citizen journalists' armed with direct access to official information (however parochial), a partisan audience and an effective means of distribution via the internet.

Notes

1 For a discussion see: The Stationery Office (1998) *Crown copyright in the information age: a consultation document on access to public sector information* (Cm 3819). London.
2 The Cabinet Office (2006) *Civil Service Management Code*. London: HMSO.

3 For an introductory discussion of confidentiality law see: Horrie, C., *Media Law Web: Confidentiality and Secrecy* at http://www.westminsterjournalism.co.uk/law/005confidentiality.htm. Accessed 1 November 2007.

4 HMSO, *Official Secrets Act 1989 (c.6)* at http://www.statutelaw.gov.uk/content.aspx?activeTextDocId=1351839, The UK Law Statute Data Base, London: Ministry of Justice. Accessed 1 November 2007.

5 Brooke, H, (2007) *Your Right To Know*. London: Pluto Press.

6 For an assertive view of the continuing importance of 'proper' political and parliamentary reporting, see Letts, Q. (2003) 'The Daily Sketch' in *British Journalism Review*, 14 (3), 39–44. For a historical survey of the relationship between parliament and the early modern press see: Alexander, A. (2000) *The History of British Journalism: From the Foundation of the Newspaper Press in England to the Repeal of the Stamp Act in 1855, with Sketches of Press Celebrities. Volume 1*. London: Elibron Classics.

7 For a fuller discussion see: Marr, A. (2004) *My Trade: A Short History of British Journalism*. London: Macmillan.

8 For the details of the NCTJ's qualification system and definition of a properly qualified professional news reporter see: http://www.nctj.com/qualdisplay.php?qid=8. Accessed 1 November 2007.

9 See: Stone-Lee, O. (2006) 'The time-old tradition of leaks'. London: BBC News Online.

10 For an account of a landmark 'leak' episode see: Norton-Taylor, Richard (1985) *The Ponting Affair*. London: Cecil Woolf.

11 Straw, J. (1999) Speech at the Campaign for Freedom of Information Annual Awards Ceremony, June 1999. London: CFOI. Jack Straw, the Home Secretary, claimed during the public debate on the New Labour government's 2000 Freedom of Information Act that the legislation would change the balance of power between citizens and the state. Straw said: 'for the first time every citizen will have a legal right of access to information held by bodies across the public sector. There will be a duty on public authorities to adopt a scheme for the publication of information about their work, a positive duty on authorities'.

12 Brooke, H. (2007) *Your Right To Know*. London: Pluto Press.

13 See: http://www.cfoi.org.uk for the Freedom of Information Campaign's Website; http://www.yrtk.org/ for campaigning journalist and FOIA author Heather Brooke's website. An updated guide to both the FOIA and the Environmental Information Regulations (2004) which give additional FOIA type access rights to information about the environment is maintained by Friends of the Earth at http://community.foe.co.uk/tools/right_to_know/. All accessed 1 November 2007.

14 The Act applies only to England, Wales and Northern Ireland. Scotland has its own Freedom Of Information regime, which is similar to that in the rest of the UK with, in general, a greater degree of openness. See: http://www.cfoi.org.uk/scotland.html.

15 Various public bodies and campaign groups provide pro-forma standard letters and checklists which, it is asserted, are most effective in obtaining information. Standard letter templates can be viewed at, for example, or obtained from English Nature at http://www.english-nature.org.uk/about/access/docs/StandardLetters.pdf.

16 The difficulties in defining information are to some extent balanced by section 16 of the Act which places on public authorities a general obligation to actively assist enquirers in their attempts to obtain the information to which they are entitled.

17 Lord Butler of Brockwell (2004) *Review of Intelligence on Weapons of Mass Destruction: Report of a Committee of Privy Counsellors*. London: House of Commons. Butler's report criticised the practice of informal decision making at cabinet level, which was memorably described as 'sofa government'.

18 The 2000 Act gives public bodies the right to refuse to process an information request if the work involved in searching for and compiling the information exceeds 24 hours (two and a half working days for a single civil servant) in the case of central government or 16 hours (two full working days) for all other public bodies. (Note: This excludes time or money spent on taking legal or policy advice.) In 2004 these costs were put at £25 an hour, fully chargeable to the enquirer, with a maximum fee of £600 for central government and £450 for other public bodies. If an information request is judged to be too expensive to process (exceeding the maximum number of hours) then the authority does not have to comply with the request, though there is a right of appeal. The relatively high cost of processing FOI requests and the exemption of requests that would take a long time to process is highly controversial and, advocacy groups have alleged, gives authorities an easy way of sabotaging information requests simply by dragging their feet so that processing exceeds the stipulated time and cost limits and can therefore be legally refused.

19 Qualified exemptions (information can be released if the act of doing so can be shown to be in the public interest). The numbers indicate the relevant section of the act and code:

22: Information already scheduled for publication.
24: (information likely to prejudice) national security (in general).
25: (ditto) defence of the UK and colonies, the safety of UK or allied forces.
26: (ditto) UK's international relations.
27: (ditto) relations between government authorities within the UK.
28: (ditto) relationship between branches of UK government.
29: (ditto) the economy.
30: (ditto) investigations and proceeding by public bodies.
31: (ditto) law enforcement functions.
33: (ditto) auditing or assessment of effectiveness of public bodies (while audit or assessment process is progress. Thereafter such information should be available as an absolute entitlement without having to pass a public interest test).
35: (ditto) formulation of government policy.
36: (ditto) effective conduct of public affairs (absolute exemption if the requested information is held by either of the Houses of Parliament, or has been given certified parliamentary privilege by either house).
37: information about honours or communication with the royal family.
38: information likely to endanger an individual's health and safety.
39: information which may be released under other FOI legislation.
40: information protected by legal and/or professional privilege.
43: (ditto) legitimate commercial advantage; trade secrets.

The catch-all section 36 'conduct of public affairs' exemption has proved to be controversial. During the House of Lords debate on the Act, Lord MacKay observed: 'Obviously the draftsmen decided, just in case something escaped and there is one last fish in the sea, let us get it with a grenade; and this is the grenade'.

20 Absolute exemptions (information does not have to be released in any circumstances; numbers refer to sections of the Act):

21: information accessible by other means.
23: information relating to or supplied by the UK security and intelligence services, special forces, the National Criminal Intelligence Service and certain other specified bodies with intelligence or security function (12 specified organisations comprising the UK 'intelligence community').
32: court records.

34: information of any description specifically exempted by parliamentary privilege by means of a certificate signed by the speaker of the House of Commons or the Clerk of the Parliament (House of Lords).

36: Information likely to prejudice the conduct of public affairs in either the House of Commons or the House of Lords (information likely to prejudice the conduct of public affairs in other institutions, such as local government, is only a qualified exemption meaning that the information can be released if shown to be in the public interest. But there is no public interest test in the case of parliament.

40: Information about private individuals protected by the provisions of the Data Protection Act.

41: Confidential information which, by its release, would create a breach of confidentiality (for example by identifying individual patients' medical history without their consent). Claims of confidentiality however can be challenged on grounds of public interest. But any information has to be shown not to be protected by confidentiality law before it can be released.

44: Information otherwise subjected to legal restraint on disclosure. This would include information protected by the Official Secrets Act and the laws of contempt of court relating, or the rehabilitation of offenders.

Further reading

Birkinshaw, P. (1996) *Freedom of Information: The Law, the Practice and the Ideal*. London: Butterworth.

Lord Butler of Brockwell (2004) *Review of Intelligence on Weapons of Mass Destruction Report of a Committee of Privy Counsellors*. London: House of Commons.

The Cabinet Office (2006) *Civil Service Management Code*. London: HMSO.

House of Commons (1998) *Crown copyright in the information age: a consultation document on access to public sector information* (Cm 3819). London: HMSO.

Griffiths, J. and Wadham, J. (2005) *Blackstone's Guide to the Freedom of Information Act*. Oxford and New York: Blackstones.

Northmore, D. (1996) *Lifting the Lid: A Guide to Investigative Research*. London: Casssell.

Rowe, H. (2003) *Data Protection Act 1998: A Practical Guide*. London: Tolley's.

Rowe, H. (2007) *Your Right to Know: A Citizen's Guide to the Freedom of Information Act*, (2nd edition). London: Pluto Press.

Smith, K. (2004) *Freedom of Information: A Practical Guide to Implementing the Act*. London: Facet (Chartered Institute of Library and Information Professionals).

8

THE PRACTICES OF INVESTIGATIVE JOURNALISM

Gavin MacFadyen

Investigative journalism is more demanding both of its subjects and its evidential standards than normal newsroom practice. A range of differing methods has evolved, many aiming at the same result. Practices in some environments are not appropriate in others. In many national institutions, collegial working is uncommon and rarely practiced. In others, often in mainstream current affairs television, it is a frequent practice in complex investigations. For freelancers without major institutional resources it becomes increasingly difficult to replicate the standards of these often wealthy organisations. But some major stories have been broken by single individuals.

In stories for example where there are few if any reports or public documents and little government transparency, different evidence must be sought. In stories which encounter intrusive electronic surveillance, and where there is little security for sources or indeed for the journalist, entirely different working practices have evolved.

Reporting

Reporting in itself implies coverage without lengthy or protracted in-depth research. Reporting in dangerous circumstances or where it is prohibited or frustrated by governments or corporations demonstrates a commitment that is, or is very close to, investigative journalism. It implies that the subject of the report itself may by its revelations or forbidden character be of investigative interest.

The many articles written between 1996 and 2006 by Anna Politkovskaya[1] in the Russian liberal newspaper, *Novaya Gazeta*, concerned the two Chechnya wars, where independent reporting was either banned or made impossibly difficult. Politkovskaya found victims, witnesses and family members in refugee camps, distant cities and hospitals, and investigated the difference between official reports and government statements and the reality on the ground. This entailed hiding from Russian troops while conducting interviews and gathering evidence often in defence of a common Russian soldier or Chechn-yan fighter. This detailed, often illegal, background reporting with eye-witness testimony attracted frequent death threats and her exclusion from official gatherings.

Her particular method involved securing testimony, documents and first-hand descriptions of the prosecution of the wars particularly during the second Chechnyan War, when few reporters were prepared to contradict the official justifications and statements of the Putin government. She returned many times in ever more difficult circumstances to report indiscriminate killings, bribery, protection rackets, the mistreatment of common soldiers, prisoners, and kidnappings by or with the collusion of Russian authorities. Her accounts equally included reports of the brutalities and criminal connections of sections of the Chechnyan separatists.

The focus and tenacity underlying these critical reports of attacks and kill-ings of unarmed civilians, the innocent and the vulnerable, drew increasing hostility from officials. After the publication of *Putin's Russia*, which unspar-ingly criticised the Russian President, she was found shot dead outside her flat in Moscow, in October 2006.

Other constituents of reporting are the use of photographs and video to expose a lie, provide evidence of misleading or unsafe practices, which against the pressure from powerful interests, may constitute a critical element of an investigative report. The video and still photographs of the Abu Ghraib[2] torture and abuse of prisoners in Iraq are a striking example. The power of these images to contradict official pronouncements is reflected in the banning of photographs of US dead or seriously disfigured soldiers, or photography of victims of torture and abuse. Photographic evidence of course can easily apply to more normal environments – industrial accidents, for example, or unsafe or polluted environments. The work of the *Philippines Center for Investigative Journalism* in exposing government corruption and cronyism relies heavily on photographs of officials' palatial houses, luxury cars in gated communities in a country submerged in poverty. It is a curiosity that there are few photographers devoted to capturing this increasingly powerful evidence.

Evidence of medical, industrial or military emergencies, or simply evidence of a person at a place and time, when authorities or officials seek to prevent pub-lication, constitutes a valuable technique to authenticate allegations. Similarly investigative journalists may well seek CCTV evidence which is now available in many cities in the UK and to a lesser extent in the US and Europe.

The publication of a report, which clarifies what may have been an import-ant earlier investigation or concerns a contentious little-known area, may be in itself of substantial investigative interest. These contextual pieces are usually produced by journalists who have a longstanding familiarity with a subject.

Writing and reporting government commissions' findings, or the results of a formal enquiry, would not in themselves constitute an investigation. No matter how valuable, these reports are not the result of the reporter's own work.

Whistleblowers

Whistleblowing remains one of the most important sources of major stories and the cultivation and protection of whistleblowers is a central preoccupation for investigative journalists. Different from 'sources' who may have personal or family connections to the story, whistleblowers are almost always employees and inside. Many of the most important investigations and revelations of the Cold war and after were begun or developed by insiders prepared to risk their professional and personal positions by publicly exposing the criminal or unethical behaviour of their employers.

In what became an icon of investigative journalism, the Watergate scandal was aided invaluably by the anonymous insider, Deep Throat, revealed after his death as W. Mark Felt, a senior FBI official.[3] The 1970–71 scandal forced the resignation of President Nixon and the jailing of Nixon's key White House staff. The *Washington Post* reporters, Woodward and Bernstein, were able to keep the identity of Felt secret for 30 years. Their story became the basis of a motion picture, *All the Presidents Men*.

Anonymous sources provided Seymour Hersh in the *New Yorker* magazine (May 2004) with graphic photographs of the torture and abuse of prisoners at the American military prison at Abu Ghraib in Iraq. Though the evidence was available to CBS *60 Minutes II* for many months, CBS broadcast only after learning that Hersh was publishing. Although the CBS report was book-ended by a US general stating that the tortures were the result of a few irresponsible and unrepresentative soldiers, subsequent disclosures painted a scandalous picture of a standardised programme of institutional brutality and murder that has been a central policy in interrogations for over 40 years. Sparked by the initial reports, the tracking down of witnesses and documents provided depth and certainty to the initial reports. These disclosures resulted in a major change in the public perception of the Iraq war and occupation.

There are dramatic similarities with an earlier investigation by Hersh of the mass murder of between 347 and 500 men, women and children, including the use of babies for target practice, by the US Army on March 16, 1968 in Vietnam. This massacre and the subsequent cover-up and whitewash by senior military and government officials, including a Major who would become Secretary of State, Colin Powell, would shock public opinion and encouraged opposition to the war. Of less interest to the mainstream media, almost all of the officers involved, as with Abu Ghraib, were acquitted; only one Lieutenant was kept under house arrest and was subsequently released directly by President Nixon.

One of the more dramatic cases involved a 1995 CBS *60 Minutes* investigation by Producer Lowell Bergman about Jeffrey Wigand, a US tobacco industry executive who suffered a *crise de conscience* about the links between cigarettes and cancer. Discovering documents, which proved his employer, Brown & Williamson, knew of the carcinogenic effects of their product, his testimony led to one of the most successful legal campaigns in US history.

The urgency of protecting the story from a backsliding broadcaster and from tobacco industry pressure involved convincing and re-convincing a fearful participant, securing critical documents and the legal and physical protection of the source. Handling and protecting an indispensable source were the necessary obligations if the story were not to be suppressed, such that the information never be put before the public.

The broadcaster or publisher is often as much the enemy of investigative journalism as the target. Bergman was forced to resign from CBS following transmission of an edited version of the story. Bergman is now a Pulitzer Prize winning investigator with PBS *Frontline* and the *New York Times*. This story was the basis of a motion picture, *The Insider*, directed by Michael Mann (1999).

Other recent cases have included a former US Military Policemen, Joseph Darby,[4] who first raised the alarm regarding the torture and killing of prisoners at Abu Ghraib prison in Iraq. Another military intelligence officer, Samuel Provance,[5] who exposed the torture of prisoners by interrogators and how senior officials attempted to cover up the abuse, later joined him.

In the late 1980s Indian journalist, Chitra Subramaniam,[6] of the *Hindu* and *Indian Express*, exposed illegal payments from the Swedish arms firm, Bofors AB, to senior Indian government officials, including the Prime Minister Rajiv Gandhi. The scandal involving the sale of 155mm field artillery, led directly to the defeat of Gandhi's National Congress in 1989 and reverberations have continued through 2006–7. Although formally cleared of involvement in bribery, Gandhi was later assassinated while the case was being prepared. A former Bofors engineer, Ingvar Bratt,[7] became known as an important source in the Bofors Arms Scandals, particularly the company's use of forged end-user certificates.

In 2001, an auditor at WorldCom Inc., Cynthia Cooper,[8] conducted a secret investigation into fraudulent bookkeeping designed to hide one of the largest accounting frauds in history. It would total approximately $11 billion and would result in the bankruptcy of the company in 2004, the conviction of CEO Bernard Ebbers and other corporate officials.

In 2003 a British intelligence officer, Katharine Gun,[9] was named as the source of leaks documenting illegal surveillance of members of the UN Security council at the suggestion of the United States, immediately prior to the 2003 invasion of Iraq.

The Israeli scientist, Mordechai Vanunu,[10] in 1986 revealed Israel's nuclear weapons programme to Peter Hounam on the Sunday Times. Probably during negotiations with other newspapers his identity became known to the Israeli secret police. Vanunu was tricked by an Israeli Mossad agent to travel to Rome where he was drugged and kidnapped, smuggled by freighter to Israel where in a closed trial he was jailed for 18 years. Subsequent disclosures confirmed that extrajudicial execution had been considered and rejected, but he was held in solitary confinement for over eleven years.

Andrew Wilkie,[11] an Australian intelligence officer at the Office of National

Assessments (ONA), resigned in March 2003 over concerns that intelligence reports were incorrectly claiming that Iraq possessed weapons of mass destruction.

Protection of whistleblowers

Although some US states have whistleblower protection laws, the strength of which vary with the sensitivity of the exposure, protection of a source is largely down to the journalist. Soldiers in the US military have the military Whistleblower Protection Act, which allows unimpeded communication with any congressman.

In the UK, the Public Interest Disclosure Act 1988 (PIDA) affords a modest degree of formal protection but excludes the security services or the military from its remit. *Public Concern at Work*, an independent UK authority on public interest whistleblowing, provides free advice to those concerned about danger or malpractice in the workplace. Protection of a whistleblower is dependent on a 'good faith' test by a tribunal where it may find that a motive behind making the disclosure was unrelated to the public interest objectives.

It is an important and normally accepted practice for journalists to directly inform the whistleblower of the potential risks they may encounter in taking their concerns or evidence to the public. This will often include advice on secure communications, avoiding corporate or government monitoring of their email and other communications, advice on the law and equally important, the journalists own potential difficulties with their publisher or broadcaster. In important cases involving the government, large corporations or in dangerous circumstances, it would be unwise to record the person(s) name or key details in any potentially subpoenaed or accessible document or electronic file.

Furthermore, once protection to this source is offered, it is incumbent on the journalist to ensure that these assurances are honoured. In exchange for this exclusive arrangement, a journalist may well be confronted with the prospect of imprisonment or contempt of court in refusing to divulge the identity of his source.

It is therefore normal practice to question the source as to their motives, whether there is any financial gain to any party involved in the disclosures and whether anything in the background of the whistleblower might act to discredit their testimony.

There appears to be a variable view in many courts involving journalists' sources, and penalties for their disclosures. Probably because of bad publicity, few journalists in the main industrial countries are jailed or substantially fined.

A list of whistleblower protection organisations is provided below.

Digging

The defining essence of the investigative process is research. Because of the severity of UK libel law, the standards of required proof and the fear of prosecution are significantly higher than in many other metropolitan countries.

Investigations are in many respects the same as ordinary background research but generate greater detail and activities in pursuit of evidence that may be too expensive and time consuming for regular reporting. Allegations made by a plausible witness require the same evidential scrutiny as the denials by the criminal. It is common practice in serious investigations to look for compromising material from ones closest sources, lest that material be used against the investigation as a whole. A last minute surprise with a key witness, that is the result of a failure of research, can damage the credibility of the story and often the journalist's career. It will throw into doubt the solidity of all the evidence and of the professional standards of the journalist.

Government documents therefore have unusual importance as they remain often the most dependable evidence and as most are officially produced, are regarded as safe. Most investigations involving government are 'document led'. The careful perusal of government accounts and financial records may well uncover carefully hidden bribery, corruption or incompetence.

Of particular use are the federal Freedom of Information Acts of the US (1966) and to a lesser extent those of the UK. The US records are available to anyone in any country and the sole charges are for photocopying and mailing. Although widely used by journalists seeking access to records in hundreds of government departments, the Acts main defenders are frequently small businesses. Open transparent bids for government contracts, which the FOIA has enforced, have levelled the playing fields and in these disclosures, forced corrupt practices to new heights of subtlety. Major US scandals have resulted from the publication of Congressional campaign contributions, expenses, gifts, foreign travel and undeclared business interests. Except for the federal and military security organisations, government departments must respond to specific requests and are required to specify which law is cited to justify an exclusion or redaction.

Access to the Act has been streamlined by US journalists' organisations; Investigative Reporters & Editors, Inc has a FOIA & First Amendment Center (http://www.ire.org/foi/), which has useful tip sheets and access advice. The website has links to a myriad of non-profit organisations providing information and advice on using the Act.

The Reporters Committee for Freedom of the Press (http://www.rcfp.org/) publishes a number of valuable guides to information requests. *The Open Government Guide* outlines and explains state open records and meetings laws; *How To Use the Federal FOI Act*, which discusses the Act's exemptions; and *Access to Electronic Records* which provides a summary of state laws effecting records. Of importance however is their Automatic Letter Generator (http://

www.rcfp.org/foi_letter/generate.php), which simplifies requests and actually writes and addresses a FOI request letter.

Documents released under the FOIA relating to intelligence, foreign and economic policy matters can be found at the National Security Archive (George Washington University) http://www.gwu.edu/~nsarchiv/. Disclosures from particular government agencies often have their own reading rooms where previously released material is available.

Almost all of the US organisations which provide handbooks, telephone advice and direct services to investigative journalists are supported by private foundations and universities.

Historical records housed at the extensive and well organised National Archives and Record Administration (NARA) in Maryland (http://www.archives.gov/contact/) have been cited in major European investigations.★

The recently passed UK Freedom of Information Act, though welcomed as a first step, is narrower in its authority than the US Act and the list of exclusions is daunting. According to one authority of the UK Acts, Britain 'does not have open public records, or open meetings laws that mandate the transparent operation of government, so Freedom of Information is one of the only ways to uncover what public officials are doing with public money. In addition, Court records are not considered "public" despite being paid for by the taxpayer.' Barely two years after its passage, the government has proposed financial curbs which effectively curtail its remit and may make the Act unusable.

The present law as it stands however, does require government employees to answer non-vexatious requests within a narrow time frame from any applicant. The reason for the request is not a legitimate concern of the employee. A useful guide to the UK Act is an updated handbook, *Your Right to Know* by Heather Brooke. News of developments and changes in this FOI act are available on http://www.yrtk.org/.

The first campaigning body in the UK pressing for Freedom of Information is the Campaign for Freedom of Information (http://www.cfoi.org.uk/), which publishes a Users Guide.

Despite or perhaps because of increasing privatisation of public services, there are no laws requiring corporations and businesses whose activities affect the public to ensure their records are available to the public.

Powerful examples of digging appeared in a *Guardian* (March 20, 2006) investigation of Iraqi finance by Callum Macrae and Ali Fadhi in what may become one of the greatest financial scandals of the century. Three hundred and sixty three tons of money simply disappeared in corruption, incompetence, swindles and crime. Patching together over several months spreadsheets,

---

★ Local and state level disclosures are more problematic as each state has different ('Sunshine') laws governing disclosure and many have a notable bias against transparency.

whistleblowers, witness accounts and the public record, an extraordinary picture of the human tragedy of the Iraq war emerges.

Michael Gillard's financial and business reporting in *Private Eye*[12] and in other print media does not appear to be the result of government disclosure but reflects continuous, specialised digging over a lifetime. In a range of stories from the strange secrecy of English businessman Sir James Goldsmith's maze of companies through the scandals of Polly Peck and the business practices of Cypriot tycoon Asil Nadir and to the businesses of Russian organised crime, the complex curtain of corporate finance has been pushed aside to show the criminal reality.

Scientific examination of government records and Congressional documents have enabled the *Center for Public Integrity*[13] to expose illicit funding of political campaigns including that of the President, the role of private military companies in water privatisation, chemical industry pollution, tax evasion by the wealthy amongst many. A great deal of the Center's work has concentrated on the acquisition and analysis of contemporary government records.

Digging examples: history

King Leopold's Ghost by Adam Hochschild (1999) extensively investigated the claims of the Belgian King Leopold II to philanthropy, humility and altruism in his private Congo Free State. The official history describes Leopold's colony as a model of Christian charity, where bountiful medicines and sewing machines were sent to grateful natives. What emerged from Hochschild's researches was a tyrant of enormous greed and cruelty who introduced a vast system of forced labour that reduced the population of the Congo from over 20 million to 10 million in 40 years. To obscure the savagery on his exploitations in his private fiefdom, Leopold became the first monarch with a public relations consultant.

In Hochschild's account, the extraordinary violence of Leopold's regime was equalled only by the wealth and corruption which inspired it. The social devastation caused by slavery, and the forced extraction of ivory, gold and rubber would kill over 10 million Congolese and the resultant anarchy and corruption has not today been erased from the Congo.

Earlier investigations by Neal Acheson, in *The King Incorporated*, and others by Jules Marchal and Isidore Ndaywel è Nziem had unearthed important evidence, and intimated much of Hochschilds investigation.

Successful on a par with Gunther Wallraff's books, *King Leopold's Ghost* sold over 400,000 copies and reawakened interest in the life and times of Sir Roger Casement and E.D. Morel, who together drew attention to Leopold's crimes and began what became the first human rights movement. Confronted by a rising tide of anger and demonstrations, Leopold ordered the destruction of the Congo State Archives, erasing the evidence of his complicity and direction.

African scholars, and Joseph Conrad's prescient *Heart of Darkness* support

Hochschild's evidence and description, but it remains a still difficult and controversial subject in Belgium today.

A Question of Torture by Alfred McCoy is an investigation by the author of the *Politics of Heroin in South East Asia* into the long-shrouded history of forced interrogation in US government policy. Long denied by successive governments, or described as aberrations, McCoy has assembled court records, de-classified CIA training manuals, books and truth commission reports. These detail an ongoing programme of research into tortures, which has been disciplined by several considerations. Notably that the pain should be self-inflicted, and be psychologically damaging – isolation, hooding, hours of standing, extremes of hot and cold, loud noise, sleep deprivation, stress positions. Nothing that leaves marks.

These methods were field tested in Vietnam as part of the Phoenix programme, which killed more than 20,000 and tortured unknown thousands more. It was imported to Latin America and Asia as 'police training'. In this context the sadistic tortures of Abu Ghraib and Guantanamo are consistent with the CIA's 50-year programme of mind control and interrogation experiments. McCoy interviewed Asian survivors of the tortures whose testimony was affirmed and corroborated by the released documents and manuals. Confirming what had earlier been strenuously denied, former President Clinton made a public apology over unspecified tortures in Latin America. McCoy has indicated that the investigation went on over almost a decade before publication.

Digging examples: science

Since the success of the *Sunday Times* Insight team's thalidomide investigation in the 1970s,[14] the uncovering of environmental, medical, pharmaceutical and agricultural practices has been an important public strand of investigative journalists. The growth of well-resourced Non-Governmental Organisations (NGOs) has provided significant material that may well not have originated with the journalist but from the NGO's research officers. The current financial cutbacks and the reduction of investigative programming in the mainstream UK media have prevented most journalists from pursuing scientific subjects independently of the NGOs or university departments.

BBC's *Panorama* (January 29, 2007) broadcast 'Secrets of the Drug Trials', the fourth documentary in a series about the drug Seroxat. Shelly Jofre and Ed Harriman broadcast a revealing trail of confidential emails which showed how GlaxoSmithKline manipulated the results of drug trials for its own commercial gain.

One of the current difficulties experienced by journalists without a trained, scientific background is evaluating unusual scientific claims. Even experienced investigators can be misled and some scientifically derived claims remain unsupported.

Current practices suggest confirmation of basic scientific assertions by at least three independent, accredited or peer scientific sources. During the polonium poisoning of Alexander Litvinenko, few journalists appeared to have the benefit of considered scientific opinion. For weeks as the scandal progressed, there was little certainty about the quantities of the radioactive poison that were theoretically available, where was is being produced, at what cost and who was likely to have access to it.

Academics and independent researchers can provide reliable expertise in difficult and highly specialised areas, particularly those in which few journalists have meaningful knowledge. In areas of significant commercial or political interest it is incumbent on enquiring journalists to seek information and judgement from more than one expert.

Digging examples: computer-assisted reporting (CAR)

A current technique widely used and taught in the US and Scandinavia is virtually unavailable in the UK, except in the summer schools of the London based Centre for Investigative Journalism. This technique, which is taught in the US by investigative reporters and editors, National Institute for Computer Assisted Reporting at the University of Missouri, is employed to download, digest and analyse large quantities of statistical data. It uses easily available software and can be taught in several weeks.

With increasing amounts of publicly funded and available data, important stories can be found in these databases, all of which require CAR techniques to extract. The international investigation into the CIA's extraordinary rendition by Stephen Grey[15] and the *New York Times* would not have been possible without the methods developed by CAR.

Major stories effecting airline safety, public health, road transport accidents and some environmental stories in the US, are largely dependent on these methods.

But the technique remains controversial to many older journalists in the UK, where print and broadcast media have lagged behind most developed countries in making use of the technology. As wider use of government databases is brought about through the Freedom of Information Acts, the use of computer-assisted reporting tools is bound to increase.

Digging examples: social network analysis

Another computer-based skill (SNA) maps and measures relationships and flows between people, organisations, animals, computers or other data-processing entities. Widely discussed as the next step in data analysis, it's seen as a way of diagramming and visualising relationships between individuals and businesses and institutions. Its current uses include public health investigators, intelligence and police, sociologists and anthropologists.

It has been used recently for illustrating interlocking directorates of corporate directors, how terrorist cells or criminal groups operate, what ethnic group is disenfranchised and tracking who has the most powerful connections in a community.

Proving

Covert recording

Although controversial in parts of Europe and in mainstream US reporting, it remains a particularly effective means of securing evidence of wrongdoing and danger. For its advocates where the public interest is directly and seriously involved and there are no other methods of acquiring proof, the rights to privacy are reluctantly overridden.

Mark Daly secured taped evidence of police racism in an eighteen-month undercover BBC investigation in October 2003.[16] After a public admission by the Greater Manchester Police that the police were institutionally racist, and a scandal in the murder of Stephen Lawrence, the covert operation was to see what measures were effectively in place to eradicate abuse and discrimination. Immediate attempts to suppress the programme, denounce the reporter and the evidence, suggested that open attempts to penetrate the veil of police secrecy would not be met with sympathy or energy.

One far-reaching eight-month inquiry in 2001 by reporters Aniruddha Bahal and Mathew Samuel from *Tehelka* forced the resignation of the Indian Defence Minister, George Fernandes.[17] Their video recordings of corrupt deals were initially denounced as fraudulent, a sham, and Pakistani propaganda, but quickly sparked a long-running controversy, official inquiries and sackings, involving corruption in defence procurement deals. Released on the internet, the evidence revealed government purchase of military coffins at inflated prices.

One of the most effective disclosures in 2001 recorded the feared head of the Peruvian Secret Police, Valdimio Montesinos, trying to buy a politician's support for $15,000. A congressional commission followed the tapes disclosures and implicated other members of the Peruvian government. They documented a wave of corrupt deals including military purchases where middlemen took cuts of $80million, a death squad, arms trafficking and drugs. It came to light that Montesinos had himself kept approximately 1,000 tapes to blackmail corporate leaders, foreign embassy officials, media moguls and other politicians.

Montesinos fled the country although he was eventually extradited back to Peru and imprisoned. Amongst the evidence uncovered was his confession that he had acted in critical mining deals on behalf of an American mineral giant, Newmont Mining Corporation. The scandal was so popular it resulted in a video game. The president, Alberto Fujimora, fled the country and has not returned.

Undercover and impersonation

A particular method employed by the best-known German undercover journalist, Günter Wallraff, is to enter a subject area by deception and record his experiences.[18] His identity would be constructed to allow him access, which would ordinarily be refused. In disciplined and well-prepared cover, he has become a Turkish guest worker, a tramp, a rightwing tabloid journalist, an alcoholic and a businessman offering funds to a nascent military dictator in Portugal. Wallraff's methods are described by the Swedish word 'wallraffa' which is defined as exposing crimes from the inside by assuming a role.

These methods and the subject of injustice have made Wallraff one of the most popular German authors, his books selling as many as 400,000 copies in Germany and his television documentaries attracting substantial audiences. His targets however have regularly attacked him as an anarchist, a former Stasi agent, a privacy and trades secret violator and falsifier. In many legal actions however, the courts have regularly ruled that his actions are constitutional. A film based on his entry into tabloid journalism, *The Man Inside*, was made in 1990 (director: Bobby Roth).

As noted above, a recent BBC investigation ('The Secret Policeman') into racism in the police involved a reporter, Mark Daly, joining the Manchester Police over a period of eighteen months, and concentrating on the Police National Training Centre in Warrington, UK. With a covert camera, Daly was able to record racist abuse by his fellow officers despite a major government campaign to rid the police of institutional racism. The reporter endured his own arrest by the very authorities he was in effect investigating and the immediate denial by the government of the truth of his evidence. Three officers resigned after the programme was transmitted.

Martyn Gregory impersonated a British businessman supplying equipment to the Lebanese government in his 'Torture Trail' (Channel Four, *Dispatches*, 1995).[19] The impersonation and covert filming demonstrated how British companies evaded export controls on the supply of electric shock equipment to countries where the equipment would be used for torture. The company made a written offer to Gregory to supply £3.62 million worth of this equipment, admitting also the sale of similar equipment to the Saudi government. The government denied the 'Al-Yamamah' arms negotiation of which this was a part. The companies repeatedly denied being involved but Gregory had covertly filmed his meetings with these established arms dealers, including a Manager of Royal Ordnance, part of British Aerospace.

The programme was denounced by government ministers, but unusually Gregory sued and the government was forced to apologise and paid £55,000 damages, which was the first successful libel against the British government. Ironically, the programme was awarded a Freedom of Information Award which was presented by then Member of Parliament Tony Blair.

World in Action, an investigative current affairs series from Granada Television (1963–98), used these methods successfully where ordinary entry was impossible and where there was a demonstrable public interest justification. To enter a guarded steel works where over ten workers had died in industrial accidents, this writer impersonated a local iron worker secretly to film where and how these workers had died. In other undercover films, on corruption and child labour in Hong Kong, he impersonated a Catholic priest from the Holy Carpenter Guest House, and an Indiana doll salesman. Later he would play a right wing American television producer while documenting election fraud by the People's National Congress in Guyana. Other producers secretly filmed while pretending to be anthropologists in Argentina while pursuing Nazi war criminals, and conventional tourists while investigating Czechoslovakia during the Cold War.

Undercover methods, though unpopular in the US and parts of Europe, have no stigma in the UK and are often used by the tabloids for sensational 'disclosures' or in one (unsuccessful) case to entrap a left-wing MP. The undercover reporter was Mazher Mahmood, the 'fake sheik' of the *News of the World*. Mahmood has published the private affairs, homosexual inclinations, drugs, and race fixing of government ministers, celebrities and sports figures.

Undercover methods can provide a sensational look to purely commercial stories of little or no social or public interest. But their use in exposing serious wrongdoing remains an important part of the journalist's toolbox. In serious use and in dangerous environments particular care must be given to the simplicity of the cover, how dangers to the reporter can be communicated to his editors, and the importance of well thought through fall-back plans and means of securing evidence and protecting sources on the ground. Dangers to journalists in many regimes are grave and not to be underestimated.

The sting

The sting is normally an uncover operation to record evidence of wrongdoing and is employed to establish a 'business deal' opportunity where illegal activities would be exposed. It is different from impersonation and other undercover methods as it places the journalist as a participant or potential participant in illegal or criminal acts. It frequently involves setting up a false business or premises where a reporter has reason to believe an illegal act may occur. It is usually attempted when no other method would practically expose the wrongdoing.

The US government frequently deploys stings in organised crime and drug operations. These have not always proven successful. In 1982 John DeLorean was secretly taped in a high-profile case with a government-supplied suitcase full of cocaine but escaped imprisonment.

Sting is frequently denounced as entrapment by its targets, as in the DeLorean case; that is an attempt to induce criminal acts by someone otherwise unwilling to commit a crime. Because of the controversy surrounding the method, serious consideration of the public interest in the enquiry is essential.

In one well-known case, a pair of Chicago journalists, concerned to expose rampant corruption amongst local government and policemen, rented a shop and sent out announcements of the opening. As official after official trooped in to collect their bribes and payoffs, they were all videotaped.

Sting operations require careful preparation in cover stories, documentation and rehearsal and are often expensive, legally complex in many countries and because of corporate liability, require approval from editors and executive producers.

Doorstepping

This is a method of confronting an accused party with the evidence of the investigation. It is rarely used in major investigations as the targets of these enquiries are often wealthy and powerful individuals and institutions who are seldom seen in public and have the means to block any contact with the reporter. It may be an effective, last-resort method of putting key questions to the accused, when they have refused to be interviewed.

There have been cases when contrived doorstepping has been used to secure 'inadvertent' information from an interested party who would not otherwise be willing to appear. This technique has been employed in military stories where soldiers are prohibited from speaking to the press.

In smaller revelations and stories of little public interest, the technique has often been aggressively employed and abused by tabloid reporters. The effect can be viewed as intrusive, often offensive and cowardly, as it is designed to provoke, behind a shield of free speech.

Protection

Electronic

One of the latest threats to the integrity of the investigative process is the increasing fear of government and private electronic surveillance. Stories involving sensitive government or corporate activities or plans may be intercepted, witnesses and sources identified, schedules and legal opinions noted, often without the knowledge of the journalist.

Technical advances in wireless intercepts, recording of computer keystrokes and mass logging of emails for the security services in almost all metropolitan countries now threaten confidentiality to a degree previously never considered. In cases of great governmental or corporate sensitivity, it is impossible for a journalist to be sure that communication with a source is secure.

Encryption and anonymising peer-to-peer software have proven effective defences against normal bugs and taping. Applications like PGP (www.pgp.com)

make routine spying difficult if not impossible, and are used by many investigative reporters, particularly in dictatorial regimes. Communicating in a private environment to share files with known people or small groups is fairly effective though Private P2P software. Some of these applications can effectively mask the users IP addresses.

Other methods include secure email addresses (www.hushmail.com) and software which effectively changes your computer IP address (www.freedom.net). In common with the more innovative areas of the net, much security software is shareware or relatively inexpensive. Many investigators prefer not to draw attention to sophisticated applications on their office machines, where system administrators or the police would notice; or on their home computer, where spyware can record all their keystrokes, but to find distant cyber cafés from which to make their contacts.

Print

Protecting documents often means removing critical or identifiable written material from your office or home to a safe address, which can be another country. In Britain, key affidavits, or sensitive written material or tape are often housed in lawyers' safes. Given the insecurity of mail and electronic communication, reporters might want to consider never mentioning the location or disposition of evidence.

Record keeping

Seldom referred to, this practice is critical in long-term investigations when evidence may well be misplaced, or forgotten in the press of ongoing research. Being unable to produce evidence, critical timelines or carefully vetted narrative exactly when a lawyer requires it, for the defence of a story nearing publication of transmission, might well mean the excision of that material no matter how many weeks it may have taken to find it. The knock-on effects of removing key elements of a forensic argument can sometimes be worse than the original extraction.

This is largely a paper-led process but it is becoming clear that electronic data can be stored and searched faster and more reliably. In a story where hundreds of references, cuttings, book quotations and transcripts may be used, Optical Character Recognition software may be of especial utility. In this technology, all printed documents are digitalised and then 'read' so as to transform the document from a 'picture' into editable text. With normal search engines, thousand of documents in a collection can be found and accessed in seconds.

One Dutch researcher, Luuk Sengers, has developed a shareware Excel-based platform, called Digital Dossier, that very helpfully organises documents and information (nfo@luuksengers.nl).

Whatever the changing technique and practice, the qualities required of an investigative reporter remain simple tenacity, curiosity and a willingness to fight.

Notes

1 Politkovskaya, A. (2003) *A Small Corner of Hell – Dispatches from Chechnya*. Chicago: University of Chicago; Politkovskaya, A. (2001) *A Dirty War*. London: Harvill.
2 Photographs of Abu Ghraib published in the *New Yorker* magazine and on television on CBS *60 Minutes II*, April 2004.
3 Woodward, B. (2005) *The Secret Man: The Story of Watergate's Deep Throat*. New York: Simon and Schuster.
4 Joseph Darby was profiled on the December 10, 2006 edition of *60 Minutes*. On May 16, 2005, he received a John F. Kennedy Profile in Courage Award, recognising his bravery in uncovering the abuse at Abu Ghraib. He was interviewed on NPR *All Things Considered*, August 15 2006.
5 Provance, S. (2004) 'Former Abu Ghraib Intel Staffer Says Army Concealed Involvement in Abuse Scandal', ABC *News*, May 18 2004.
   White, J. and Higham, S. (2004) 'Sergeant Says Intelligence Directed Abuse', *Washington Post* Staff Writers, May 20 2004, p.A01.
6 Subramaniam, C. (1997) *India is For Sale*. New Delhi: UBS Publishers' Distributors Ltd. Chirta Subramaniam received the B.D. Goenka Award and the Chameli Devi Awards.
7 Bratt, I. (1991) 'Ethics in Sweden', IIT, Center for the Study of Ethics in the Professions, *Perspectives on the Profession*, 11 (1), August 1991.
8 Articles about Cynthia Cooper can be found in Colvin, G. (2002) 'Wonder Women of Whistleblowing', *Fortune*, August 12 2002; and Lacayo, R. and Ripley, A. (2002) 'The Whistleblowers', *Time*, December 22 2002.
9 Gun, K. (2004) Interview by Ben Davies, BBC News, 15 September 2004.
   Burkeman, O. and Norton Taylor, R. (2004) 'The Spy Who wouldn't Keep a Secret', *The Guardian*, February 26 2004.
10 Vanunu, M. (1986) 'Revealed – the Secrets of Israel's Nuclear Arsenal', *Sunday Times* Insight Team, October 5 1986. Vanunu, M. (2004) The *Sunday Times* Articles, *The Times* online, April 21 2004.
11 Wilkie, A. (2003) Senior Intelligence Officer, Andrew Wilkie, resigns. Interview for ABC Am (Australia), 12 March 2003. Wilkie, A. (2004) *Axis of Deceit*. Melbourne: Black Inc. Agenda. Martin, B. (2005) 'Bucking the system: Andrew Wilkie and the difficult task of the whistleblower', *Overland*, No. 180, pp.45–48, Spring 2005.
12 The work of Michael Gillard has appeared regularly in the bi-weekly magazine *Private Eye* under the name Slicker. He has written recent exposés of the dubious funding of the Fulham, Manchester City, Chelsea, Portsmouth and Leeds football clubs (*Private Eye* No. 1185, 25 May–7 June 2007).
13 The Center for Public Integrity (http://www.publicintegrity.org) publications: (2007) *City Adrift: New Orleans Before & After Katrina*. Baton Rouge: Louisiana State University Press; (2004) *The Buying of the President 2004: Who's Really Bankrolling Bush and His Challengers – and What They Expect in Return*. London: Harper Paperbacks; (2003) *The Water Barons: How a Few Powerful Companies are Privatizing Our Water*. Washington, DC; (2001) *The Cheating of America: How Tax Avoidance and Evasion by the Super Rich Are Costing the Country Billions, and What You Can Do About It*. New York: William Morrow & Company; (1997) *Toxic Deception: How the*

Chemical Industry Manipulates Science, Bends the Law and Endangers Your Health. Secaucus, NJ: Carol Publishing Corporation; (1998) *The Buying of the Congress: How Special Interests Have Stolen Your Right to Life, Liberty and the Pursuit of Happiness.* New York: Avon Books.

14 Thalidomide: Knightley, P., Evans, H., Potter, E. and Wallace, M. (1979) *Suffer The Children: The Story of Thalidomide.* New York: Viking Press. Nine articles from CBC Archives: *Thalidomide: Bitter Pills, Broken Promises* (http://archives.cbc.ca/IDD–1–75–88/science_technology/thalidomide/)

15 Extraordinary rendition: Grey, S. (2006). *Ghost Plane: The True Story of the CIA Torture Program.* New York: St. Martin's Press. Mayer, J. (2005) 'Outsourcing Torture – The Secret History of America's Extraordinary Rendition program', *The New Yorker*, February 14 2005.

16 Mark Daly – see http://news.bbc.co.uk/1/hi/magazine/3210614.stm

17 George Fernandes: Tehelka – see: http://findarticles.com/p/articles/mi_qn4196/is_20010317/ai_n10667665 http://www.hinduonnet.com/fline/fl1808/18080260. htm

18 Wallraff, G. (1979) *The Undesirable Journalist.* New York: Overlook Press. Wallraff, G. (1985) *Lowest of the Low.* London: Methuen.

19 Martyn Gregory – see: http://www.cfoi.org.uk/awards95pr.html http://www. privacy.org/pi/reports/big_bro/dispatches.html http://www.uow.edu.au/arts/sts/bmartin/pubs/03mcs.html; Wallraff, G. (1985) *Ganz unten.* Kiepenheuer & Witsch, Köln. *BILDerbuch.* Nachwort von Heinrich Böll. Steidl Verlag, Göttingen 1985. *Reportagen 1963–1974.* Mit Materialien und einem Nachwort des Autors. Kiepenheuer & Witsch, Köln 1987.

Whistleblowers protection organisations

Public Concern at Work, Suite 301, 16 Baldwins Gardens, London EC1N 7RJ
Telephone (general enquiries and helpline): 020 7404 6609
Fax: 020 7404 6576
Email: UK enquiries: whistle@pcaw.co.uk; UK helpline: helpline@pcaw.co.uk; UK services: services@pcaw.co.uk

Spinwatch (whistleblower@spinwatch.org) is a non-profit organisation specialising in information and whistleblowing in the role of the media, genetic engineering, the oil industry, tobacco smuggling, farm and food and the war in Iraq. Tel: +44 (0) 7939 52934.

Centre for Investigative Journalism (www.tcij.org) is a university-based, non-profit organisation in London, which offers advice on legal, publishing and source protection for international journalists and whistleblowers.

Whistleblowers Australia Inc. (http://www.whistleblowers.org.au/) is an association for those who have exposed corruption or any form of malpractice, especially if they were then hindered or abused, and for those who are thinking of exposing it, or who wish to support those who are doing so.

Open Democracy Advice Centre (http://www.opendemocracy.org.za/documents/whistleblowing_crisis.htm) is a South African organisation devoted to accountability and transparency and offers advice to whistleblowers and to the Protected Disclosures Act 2000 (PDA). Address: 6 Spin Street, Cape Town 8001, PO Box 1739, South Africa.

US Government Accountability Project (GAP) (http://www.whistleblower.org/content/wsn.cfm) is a non-profit, public interest organisation and law firm in the USA. GAP promotes government and corporate accountability by advocating occupational free speech, litigating whistleblower cases, publicising whistleblower concerns, and developing reforms of whistleblower laws. Address: National Office, 1612 K Street, NW Suite #1100, Washington, D.C. 20006. Tel: 202–408–0034

National Whistleblower Center (contact@whistleblowers.org) is an American non-profit, tax-exempt, educational and advocacy organisation dedicated to helping whistleblowers. Since 1988, the Center has used whistleblowers' disclosures to improve environmental protection, nuclear safety, and government and corporate accountability. Address: P.O. Box 3768, Washington, DC 20027. Tel: 202–342–1903; Fax 202–342–1904

Public Interest Speak-up Advisers (PISA) (http://www006.upp.so-net.ne.jp/pisa/mail.html) advises potential whistleblowers and journalists in Japan.

Whistleblower-Netzwerk e.V. (http://www.whistleblower-netzwerk.de/) is a German organisation devoted to whistleblowers, protection and transparency and offers advice and publications to interested parties.

One directory of international training is: Global Investigative Journalism (tp://www.globalinvestigativejournalism.org/)

Training in Demark in available from: Kaas & Mulvad
Århus | Åbogade 15 | 8200 Århus N | København | Klerkegade 19 | 1308 København K | Tlf. 70 20 07 44 | post@kaasogmulvad.dk

And in the US:
NICAR (National Institute for Computer Assisted Reporting) (http://www.nicar.org/) is the largest CAR training organisation. It maintains a library of 30+ databases containing government data on a wide range of topics from aircraft safety to storm events, problems with medical devices, FBI crime data and government contracts to private companies. It runs regular training programmes primarily in the US but also in Latin America and they collaborate with journalists' organisations in Europe.

In Britain they are partners of the Centre for Investigative Journalism, Summer Schools (www.tcij.org) that runs three-day subsidised workshops in London. One index of the increasing popularity and interest in CAR is the formation of a UK-based training organisation involving the Centre for Investigative Journalism, National Union of Journalists and City University.

They Rule (http://www.theyrule.net/) is a website that allows you to create maps of the interlocking directories of the top 100 companies in the United States in 2001. The data is static, so it is fast becoming out of date, as companies merge and disappear and directors shift boards. A new version of this site is being developed.

Namebase.org (http://www.namebase.org/) contains a database of books and clippings. Users can search for names of individuals, groups and corporations. The search finds books or clippings that cite the name searched. Also available is an option to draw a social network diagram that includes individuals mentioned on the same page as the name searched.

9

UNIVERSITIES AS EVANGELISTS OF THE WATCHDOG ROLE

Teaching investigative journalism to undergraduates

Mark Hanna

Should universities attempt to teach expertise in investigative journalism to undergraduates who have only limited experience of news reporting? Is it – because of developments in the media – increasingly necessary for society, and such students, for university journalism schools to do so?

The way in which I pose these questions, and the chapter's title, betray my viewpoint, which I unfold below. I also argue that any trend towards an increase or intensification in university-based practical tuition in investigative work can be seen in Britain as an earned, as well as a merited, progression in the evolution of journalism education.[1] University journalism educators in Britain, following the historical example set in the USA (Weaver *et al.*, 2007: 35–7, 43) have in recent decades convinced media industries of the employability of graduates as regards basic skills in journalism.[2] Indeed, much of the British media, keen to save on training costs, has grown increasingly and contentedly dependent on university journalism schools as a source of recruits (Hanna and Sanders, 2007). Universities, therefore, because of this acquired centrality in the nation's journalism training, are now well-placed to assert and demonstrate that journalism students should and can, in their studies, go beyond the basics.

A long-running debate about the best form of journalism education lingers – some editors still voice the 'generalist' argument that undergraduate programmes in journalism, compared to those in more general 'academic' subjects, e.g. politics, or English, provide too narrow an intellectual preparation for a journalism career, and therefore that vocational training is best begun at postgraduate level.[3] Also, postgraduate recruits to newsrooms are seen by some editors as having 'greater maturity' (Elliott, 2001) than the (usually) younger graduates with only a bachelor degree.

But financial realities impinge on this debate. For example, the British government's decision to impose annual tuition fees on undergraduates across the range of subjects of study means that the average debt of each British student, by the time they graduate with their bachelor's degree, is expected to rise to at least £15,000, from a previous level of around £8,700 (Department for Education and Skills, 2003: 5–6; Meikle, 2007; for regional and other variations in the fee regime, see Directgov, 2007). Therefore, although in Britain there is growing opportunity to study journalism as a postgraduate – including in recently launched programmes specifically in investigative journalism (City University, 2007; University College Falmouth, 2007; University of Strathclyde, 2007)[4] – there is likely to be growing concern that the prosperous middle or upper classes are over-represented in Britain's journalism workforce, with the increasing costs of postgraduate training being cited as a contributory factor (Journalism Training Forum, 2002: 25; Pecke, 2004: 28; Sutton Trust, 2006: 10, 12–14). For many young people aspiring to be journalists – including those from poorer backgrounds, who are more likely to be 'debt-adverse' (Foskett et al., 2006: 106, 108, 111) – the best financial option is to study journalism as an undergraduate.

Among experienced investigators there are sceptics who ask how effective university teaching of investigative journalism can be, e.g. the late Paul Foot's view was cited to be: 'It's a side of journalism you only really pick up when you are a journalist. People only become 'investigative' journalists when they're established in their own fields' (Adams, 2001). But few young journalists will find themselves, in their first jobs, in newsrooms which foster expertise in investigations, or provide the time needed for such work. Many weekly newspapers, commercial local radio and TV stations, and even some of the smaller city daily newspapers, have no tradition of supporting investigations, because of budget considerations and corporate pressure to produce news cheaply. This model of newsroom is abundant throughout Europe (Van Eijk, 2005: 248–9). To a large degree, this state of affairs is nothing new. But though empirical evidence is, in Britain, in short supply,[5] there can be little doubt that corporate cost-cutting (to ensure increased profit margins) in the nation's regional and local press have made it even less likely over the last two decades for a young journalist to be encouraged to try investigations (Hanna, 2000: 2–4; Pecke, 2004). In 2006, the National Union of Journalists launched its *Journalism Matters* campaign, calling for investment to protect quality journalism and jobs (National Union of Journalists, 2006a; 2006b). In most British national newspapers changes and concentration in media ownership, resultant change in corporate policies, imposition of financial cutbacks and reduction in journalists' autonomy have decreased the amount of investigative journalism being undertaken (Davies, 2000 and 2001; Foot, 1999: 80, 85–9; Marks, 2000; Pilger, 2005: xviii–xx, xxviii). And in British television there are, compared to 30 years ago, fewer opportunities outside the BBC to gain investigative experience, because of greater commercial pressures in a more ratings-driven environment (Barnett and Seymour, 1999: 20–42, 71–3; Beers and Egglestone, 2006; Hanna, 2000: 6–8).

If this view of the media is accepted, it underlines the public interest rationale for universities to teach what many media employers care little to offer – a grounding in investigative methodology and related knowledge.

There is precedent in the USA for other ways in which universities can help safeguard an investigative culture. In 1978 the *Investigative Reporters and Editors* organisation established its base in the University of Missouri (Armao, 2000: 41–3; IRE, 2007). The IRE acts as an evangelist in the field, offering training to students and journalists, and as a community for experienced investigators. It has proved a role model for similar organisations in other countries, e.g. Canada and Denmark (IRE, 2007; Van Eijk, 2005: 60–1, 258–9). The permanent establishment of symbiotic, seminal links between universities and such organisations should perhaps be regarded as marking a distinct stage in the maturing of any nation's journalism education system. Other models exist in universities in the USA to support or teach, or conduct research into, investigative journalism, e.g. Project Censored (2007). In Britain, the Centre for Investigative Journalism, founded in 2006, now has a base at the City University, London (Centre for Investigative Journalism, 2007; MacFadyen, 2006). In the previous decade, there had been other initiatives in Britain to disseminate investigative expertise – events seen by journalists and journalism educators who ran them as helping to compensate for the perceived diminution in such mentoring within mainstream media (Hanna, 2000: 13–16; Davies, 2001).

The challenges of teaching investigative journalism to undergraduates

Some British journalism educators make weary statements about the passivity of some undergraduates; 'When they get to university, they are depressingly incurious about the world around them and sit back expecting you to spoon-feed them. . . . Most want to do sport, music or lifestyle' – a journalism course leader, quoted anonymously by Thom (2004: 29–30). Findings from a survey of British journalism undergraduates from ten universities make, on first sight, grim reading as regards their potential for investigative work (Hanna and Sanders, 2007). Of those who were sure they wanted to be journalists, only 15 per cent of the final year students, when asked why they wanted this career, gave responses indicating a motivation of public service. Only 34 per cent of the final year 'sures' said that they wanted to work in news-oriented subject areas, as distinct from feature or 'lifestyle' journalism, sport or other areas. However, contextualising these findings changes the picture. More than 35 years ago, before any British journalism degrees were launched, a survey was conducted of journalism students – most aged between 18 and 20, and some already employed in newsrooms – training in (non-academic) further education courses. Only 1 per cent cited a career motivation categorised as of public service (Boyd-Barrett, 1970: 186–7, 196). When in 1995 Henningham and Delano (1998: 145–6; Delano, 2001: 292) asked British news journalists the main reason they had become journalists, only 2 per cent made an unprompted 'service to public' response.

At the University of Sheffield, a module I devised and teach – called 'Introduction to Investigations' – is optional for final (i.e. third) year undergraduates. Usually around 30 students choose it, i.e. just under half of the year's cohort. These have already completed several modules in news-gathering and reporting in print and broadcast, e.g. in the first year, each student is given a city district as their 'patch' to find news. They have completed, too, modules in media law and ethics, and therefore recognise, for example, the moral imperative to protect confidential sources. All students, as second years, attend Sheffield criminal courts regularly to learn to produce court reports. This, obviously, deepens their knowledge of vices and virtues, and of how evidence is gathered. Other parts of the curriculum, including the more 'academic' modules, help students consider the media's watchdog role, and its efficacy in it.

In the Introduction to Investigations module there are lectures on how British investigative journalism has developed, e.g. the 1969 exposure of police corruption in London by journalists from the *Times* (Lloyd and Mounter, 1969); the investigation by the *Sunday Times'* Insight team of the DC10 plane crash of 1974, then the world's worst air disaster (e.g. Eddy *et al.*, 1976); and the *Guardian*'s investigation into controversial payments made for BAE Systems to secure the al-Yamamah arms deal with Saudi Arabia (Evans and Leigh, 2003–8). An essay usually comprises 35 to 50 per cent of the module's assessment. Its reading list includes academic works on investigative journalism, books produced from such journalism (e.g. Harding *et al.*, 1997) and autobiographies of relevant editors and reporters (e.g. Evans, 1983; Knightley, 1997). Essay topic options include analysis of whether British investigative journalism has declined in quality and quantity in recent decades; comparison of the work of a variety of investigative journalists – including a few from other countries, e.g. Günter Wallraff (1978), and Carl Bernstein and Bob Woodward (1974); and consideration of how effective the alternative media is in investigations.

Table 9.1 sets out some of the module's content. Some such teaching is directly relevant to tasks students attempt in the module, see below. Other elements offer priming in, and exemplars of, more difficult investigative work, to give them confidence to try it if they become journalists.

For a module in investigative journalism, the ideal, main practical task would be to require students, individually, to research an original story, on an issue they have independently chosen as newsworthy, and to complete it to publishable standard within the module's time constraints. Also, ideally their educators would help them get it published – for example in the local or regional press – to garnish their *curricula vitae*. Producing a publishable news story, not fully-fledged as investigative journalism but using investigative techniques learned in the module, has proved achievable for some students, see below. Instances of actual publication have been rare, but a factor in this has been my choice of

Table 9.1 Some content of Introduction to Investigations module

Week One
Where ideas/tip-offs for investigations come from. Perception of social ills, wrongdoing, scandal. Research into what standards of conduct apply, i.e. what exactly are the alleged contraventions or failings? Basic methodology, time management: early assessment of what can be proved; systematic collection of background information; need for clear, abundant (and legally admissible) proof; primary sources, reliable witnesses; clear provenance of documentation, record-keeping; illustration of typical stages in a lengthy investigation. Use of Freedom of Information Act.

Week Two
Interviewing witnesses and sources; the need to keep them as separate as possible; possible need for signed statements, affidavits; proof by corroboration; proof of 'system'/modus operandi in dishonest conduct. Lecture on 'British investigative journalism: changes in climate' (e.g. discussion of its historical evolution, distinct periods in development, changes in proprietorial support in print and broadcast sectors).

Week Three
'British investigative journalism: changes in climate' (cont). Examples of investigative stories and their proof by documents, witness statements, etc.

Week Four
How to obtain and assess company records of ownership and directorships. Records of court judgements and bankruptcies. Case studies.

Week Five
Use of databases of electoral rolls to find people, and of family records (e.g. birth certificates). Examples of criminal use of false identity.

Week Six
Information available under the Local Government (Access to Information) Act and other legislation; from the Land Registry and other public registries, e.g. the Health and Safety Executive, environmental agencies. Case studies: Review of results of students' initial FOI requests.

Week Seven
Covert techniques to gather evidence for newspapers: taping telephone calls, wearing a 'wire'; going undercover; the technology available; practical problems; ethical considerations, including overview of relevant parts of broadcast codes.

Approaching and questioning the target, e.g. the need to put all relevant allegations to the target, with written questions as a back-up/script. Ethical, legal, regulatory considerations, e.g. fairness; door-stepping as covered in codes of ethics. Case studies of how it can go wrong. The need for different question techniques when interviewing for broadcast.

Week Eight
Consumer investigations – consumer rights, sources of information, common pitfalls. Using other records, databases for background information; helpful 'pressure groups'. Writing up an investigation as a story; the need for fairness and care in assessing what is proved; the need for attribution, exactness and specifics, while maintaining narrative momentum. Case studies of stories cut and altered by media lawyers.

Week Nine
The internet as a research tool, and as a medium for publication. Identifying website publishers through WHOIS registries, etc.

(Continued overleaf)

161

Table 9.1 continued

Week Ten
Local government corruption and malpractice – case studies of how newspapers exposed it;
the National Code of Conduct for Local Government, the Ombudsmen, the role of the
District Auditor.

Week Eleven
Review of module. Review of results of students' further FOI requests.

---

module design, explained below. One barrier to achieving publication is that,
even though, in the module's final assessment, students fairly commonly submit
material which could, with further checks and polish, yield publishable work,
by the time staff see it the degree programme has ended, and the proto-
investigators are already ex-students with other priorities, for example getting a
newsroom job. Also, the complexity of investigative work would mean that
each year, if a publishable story was insisted on for good marks in the assessment, even some of the best students could fare badly by failing to press their
chosen project to a definite conclusion. It is common for students, aged 20 or
21, to be over-ambitious in projects, even after guidance.

So, I have in most years decided:

- that I, rather than the students, should choose the subject of their investigative task, to ensure they have good scope in it to use the methodology, and
  a wide range of the information sources, covered in teaching;
- that for various reasons, which I set out above and below, I should not insist
  that their findings be presented as a piece of journalism, though they must
  prove they have diligently striven to find the required information and to
  identify newsworthy angles;
- that the foci of these tasks should be places in Sheffield, rather than elsewhere, so that students do not face high transport costs, that they have no
  excuse to make inquiries merely by phone or email, that they can use their
  own, acquired local knowledge and contacts, and those of our department,
  and that I can exercise greater supervision;
- that they should work in small teams, to provide mutual support and to
  brainstorm ways through difficulties;
- that, to be fair, each team's task should have similar parameters, in terms of
  difficulty/complexity, to the tasks of other teams.

For example, I have in several years asked each team to identify and interview
the owner(s) of a derelict or neglected commercial or historic building in
Sheffield (i.e. one building per team), and to ascertain why these are derelict,
etc. The reasons may be newsworthy locally, particularly if an historic
building is under threat of further dilapidation, or if neighbouring
properties are blighted by its dereliction (see Table 9.2). I conduct, to select the

buildings/owners, some preliminary investigations myself, gauging the likely level of challenge facing each student team, e.g. ideally the owners would be local too, and to make judgements on what is safe for students to try. They are banned from entering the buildings unless by the owner's invitation and safely equipped. They get clear instructions on risk assessment, and ongoing advice from staff.

In these tasks, students can refine their research use of news databases, and learn how to get information from Companies House (the official, online records identifying the directors and ownership of British companies), from the Land Registry (the database of property ownership, which does not always indicate the home addresses of owners of commercial buildings), from online, electoral rolls (to trace people by name), from council planning registries, court records, historical and other archives. But they also have to hone their 'people skills', e.g. by knocking on doors to question people in relevant neighbourhoods, by seeking other sources, and by adopting the best strategies to gain and successfully conduct an interview with the derelict building's owner(s), who may well be sensitive about controversy concerning it. It becomes clear to students, in class presentations of their findings, that successful teams improvise, gel well, and are energetic, systematic and politely persistent.[6] Students also begin to recognise that however useful databases are, the crucial 'intelligence' is more likely to come from speaking to someone.

So, this type of assignment allows students to experience, in a broad way, what Van Eijk (2005: 21–2) labels 'the input' of investigative work, i.e. its activities, strategies and tactics. Because relevant tuition must be delivered first, this practical task is not given to students until some weeks into the module. Were the assessment to be of the quality, including the possible impact, of journalistic 'output', e.g. a written-up story, and if each student worked individually, choosing his/her own issue/target to investigate, the range of 'input' activities each could experience might be considerably narrower, and 'input' would be curtailed to allow time to write the story. The assignment's design, particularly the requirement for students to describe and assess the investigation's progression (Table 9.2), aspires to embody what Deuze (2006: 27–8, 30) has described as a 'process-focused learning culture'. This, he argues, is at risk in journalism education worldwide, of being overshadowed by 'a product-oriented teaching culture' which, he suggests, may limit how students 'learn to think'.

There is also a local, curricular reason to opt for a task primarily of 'input'. Most of the students, in another module in the same semester, produce a portfolio of news stories and features, of subjects of their own choosing, in either print or broadcast mediums, aiming for that to be of publishable quality. They are, then, being assessed there on 'output'. They can, to compile that portfolio, use the 'input' techniques being learned in the investigative teaching. But it could overload some students – when some are already worried whether they will achieve, in this final semester, a good degree – to insist that, in addition to

Table 9.2 Extracts from derelict building assignment brief

As regards the property allocated to your team, find out what you can about:

- the identity, home and business address of, and a telephone number for, the current owner(s), plus some general information about him/her/them, e.g. age and short resume of their career(s) to date. If the ownership is through a company, then find some general information about it, e.g. business address, telephone number, history and principal business activity, the market it operates in;
- any current leaseholder (same level of details as for owners);
- companies directly connected to the owner, the ownership, leaseholder or recent occupants;
- who the previous owners/occupants/leaseholders were;
- what the site has been used for in recent years, why this use ended;
- the reason it is derelict (if you can, talk to someone who used to work there, other than the owner);
- the longer history of the site, e.g. the building's relevance and place in the surrounding zone as regards the history of the immediate locality or of Sheffield itself;·
- any preservation issues, or community concerns about the site, e.g. what uses or purpose have been envisaged for the site/building in recent years, or for the future;
- the building's relevance and place in the surrounding zone or land as regards current planning considerations;
- any controversy/scandal about it, or about people linked to it.

Explore any newsworthy angles about the site, as print journalists, by interviewing relevant people.

At some stage in your investigation, probably towards the end (when you know more about the property) the team should try to interview its owner(s) or, if more significant, the leaseholder, when seeking or checking information in the categories above. The interview should be pre-arranged. It should be face to face, if feasible.

Each team must produce an initial plan of action (of less than 150 words) indicating who is initially doing what in each team. The thoroughness of each team's initial consideration and allocation of tasks will influence the subsequent assessment of each team's work.

Each team member should compile a personal log, of 1,400–1,600 words, of team meetings and decisions, and what he/she has discovered and how. This must include the names and telephone numbers of sources (unless the information was given in confidence), and the place, time and date you spoke to the source. The log should include information about difficulties encountered, and how you tried to, or did, overcome them.

Each team should produce a basic report of findings (no more than two A4 pages). Each team must explain what it discovered, and how, in a presentation. For each student, 50 per cent; of the assignment's marks will be decided by assessing their team's work as a joint effort – the team mark. This assessment will encompass the overall element of professionalism in the teamwork, and the style and content of presentation. The other 50 per cent of marks will be awarded through assessment of the individual role the student played within the team. Firstly, your personal log will be considered. In addition, as individuals you must each submit a critique of how your team performed in its research and presentation compared with other teams, including an assessment of your own individual role. Your critique, and any views in it, will remain confidential, and be seen only by staff and (possibly) the external examiner.

---

this portfolio, each should also seek to produce a finessed piece of journalism in the investigations module.

Also, strictly to insist that students try to achieve a publishable outcome in investigations could, whether it was published or not, impede learning. British libel laws, though ameliorated by the 2006 House of Lords judgement in the Jameel case, remain potentially harsh for the media compared with laws in other democracies, and therefore demand high standards in finding and recording proof (Welsh *et al.*, 2007: 223–58, 275–84). To insist that students always seek to meet those standards could jeopardise relations with local sources. For example, a community official may be willing to speak out to help a student research a project, but he/she may well demur if asked to sign a witness statement. Worse, if a student attempted covertly to record the target of an investigation, but failed adequately to conceal the recording equipment, this could provoke an angry or even violent response in someone otherwise safe to speak to. Students *are* required, within safety limits, to record their research professionally, e.g. to make notes and to gather copies of documents, as proof. They *are* taught something of the uses and potential pitfalls of covert recording and undercover work (see Table 9.1), and may be given permission to try such activity on a limited scale (though not to be assessed on its technical success per se) in circumstances where it is deemed appropriate ethically, and safe, e.g. taping phone calls.[7]

Although the 'derelict building' assignment is, physically, very localised, it makes students consider wider issues, e.g. the shortcomings of Britain's system of officially 'listing', supposedly for protection from dereliction, buildings of heritage value; and the attempts by city planners and politicians to regenerate rundown areas.

Recent success in regeneration has led to a shortage of derelict buildings. So in one year the students' tasks were changed, and teams were required to identify those running some of the city's 'saunas' as places of prostitution. Such places are tolerated by the authorities, unless creating nuisance or harm. In fact, in 2007 a criminal case – in which John Elsworth, aged 42, owner of the Omega Sauna, in Attercliffe Road, Sheffield, denied living off the earnings of prostitution – was terminated as unfair by a Crown Court judge, on grounds that police had, in effect, previously tolerated 'sauna operators' for several years (*Sheffield Star*, 2007a, 2007b).

The wider social issue here, which the students had to research, is whether brothels should be given licensed, legal status, and whether 'tolerance' zones should be established for prostitutes in some streets, to provide a safer, more regulated environment for them. Debate on such proposals was at one stage led by a Sheffield Member of Parliament, David Blunkett, while he was Home Secretary, but it foundered amid controversy (*Guardian*, 2006).

There are various laws forbidding the running of brothels (Crown Prosecution Service, 2007). So, a phone call by a stranger to such a 'sauna' is often unlikely to yield quickly the full name and details of anyone owning or managing it.

By my own Land Registry checks, by reading local cuttings, and by consulting the city newspaper's crime reporter, I was able to avoid selecting, as the subject of each student team's inquiries, any 'sauna' obviously subject to recent or ongoing police attention. Students were forbidden to 'door-step', but were told to utilise databases and registries covered in the module, and to use other, safe journalistic means, to establish, if possible, the name of the owner or manager, and then to seek, by phone, an interview with him/her about the 'tolerance' debate. Three of the seven teams secured a phone interview of some kind. A further two were invited to conduct the interview at the relevant 'sauna'. They chose to do this, after involving me in the risk assessment. The relevant students attended in pairs, with other team members waiting outside. One owner, who proudly gave the students a tour of the building's 'executive suites', explained he had invested in the brothel because he anticipated the Government would liberalise the vice law, and because he hoped that Sheffield would be chosen by the Government as the site for a regional 'super casino', from which he foresaw custom. Again, this led the students into a political issue, because of controversy over the morality of the Labour Government's plans to secure regeneration by relaxation of gambling laws (Tempest and agencies, 2007).

As mentioned above, the Sheffield module seeks to emphasise that getting interviews is usually the best method of all journalism. For example, though the module includes some tuition on how best to use the internet, it does not set tasks in 'computer-assisted reporting', as pioneered in the USA (Tatge, 2000: 211–28) to analyse statistical data obtained through the Freedom of Information law or otherwise. I feel that, within limited teaching time, students benefit most from continued encouragement for them to seek out, and to learn to question ethically, professionally and cannily, the right people.

The Freedom of Information Act

Britain's long-awaited FOI Act came into force in January 2005 (Brooke, 2007). Since then students have been required to use it in the module (see Table 9.3). For example, one 'sauna' manager was successfully identified by students because they made an FOI request to the city council for all documents relating to inspections of the premises. Records showed that the manager had applied, under the Cinemas Act 1985, for a 'film exhibitions' licence, in order to show pornographic films 24-hours a day to customers, and so a council official made a health and safety check there.

The FOI Act has created greater scope for students to have work published, in that the public authorities/public agencies covered by the Act can hardly contest the veracity of facts they themselves supply. Unless legal exemptions apply, they must meet FOI requests – a requirement which elevates students, and any citizen, in such dealings to something nearer the inquisitorial status of a not-to-be-ignored, experienced journalist. One student, Felicity Hay, used the Act to gain information about the new salary of the then Vice-Chancellor of

Table 9.3 Extracts from brief for Freedom of Information Act assignment

---

A) Make two written requests to public bodies/agencies (i.e. any body covered by the Act's provisions) for documents/data to be supplied, and submit for assessment copies of each of your requests, of any subsequent related correspondence, of the results, and of notes you should make of conversations with any officials about your requests.

B) Submit an analysis – minimum 1,500 words, maximum 1,700 words – on best practise for journalistic use of the Act, and of the Act's utility/effectiveness. This should draw on your own experience, and include an assessment of what you perceive as the strengths and weaknesses of your own use of the Act, with discussion of anything you would have done differently with hindsight. The analysis should include an assessment of the journalistic potential of the information you have received as a result of *at least one* of your FOI requests. For example, is there a potential story in what you have been given? Is there a potential story in what has been withheld? Does the information suggest further lines of inquiry?

By means of your FOI requests, you should aim to obtain information which is:

a) newsworthy to a local or regional or national media organisation
b) not already in the public domain, and not publicly available already under other legislation, and not due to be published routinely by any public authority/body
c) obtainable at no or minimum cost
d) not clearly exempt under the Act's provisions.

Before you make a request under the Act, you should do all you can to meet these aims, and record what those attempts are. It will be good practice, therefore, before you post or email your written requests, to have an initial consultation with the relevant officer at the relevant public authority/body.

Your written requests under the Act should include a query on whether the information is already publicly available.

---

the University of Sheffield, and published this in the students' campus newspaper, a project which, with other work, helped her win two national student journalism awards (University of Sheffield Department of Journalism Studies, 2006a). Another student, Hannah Postles, was told, during a casual conversation with a passenger fleetingly met on a train, that this man's brother was in jail but had just rung him on a mobile phone, smuggled into the prison cell, despite jail regulations forbidding possession of phones. Hannah discovered, in the LexisNexis database of news stories, several references to court evidence that jailed criminals had used mobile phones to organise crime or make threats. She then made an FOI request to establish how many mobile phones had been confiscated in British prisons, and resultant data illustrated the apparent ease with which they had been smuggled in.[8] During internship on the *Yorkshire Evening Post* she gained a front page splash after using an FOI request to reveal what items, including mobile phones, had been confiscated from prisoners in Wakefield's top security prison (which houses murderers, including paedophile killers of children) (University of Sheffield Department of Journalism Studies, 2006b; Postles and Gardner, 2006).

Other FOI requests have helped teach students how officialdom's doggedness in withholding information can be challenged. One such request, initiated in a student project, eventually led North Yorkshire police to disclose that it is paid from the Association of Chief Police Officers Terrorism and Allied Matters budget, rather than from local taxation, for its part in containing pacifists' protests against the Menwith Hill military base, which is run by the USA's National Security Agency and said to be one of the world's largest monitoring stations for eavesdropping on communications. The main lesson here for students was that this innocuous fact was only disclosed after correspondence spanning 21 months, including an appeal to the Information Commissioner (2005–7), who criticised North Yorkshire police for late use of the Act's Section 23 (an absolute exemption for information relating to intelligence services) to justify its refusal to reveal the annual totals of these policing costs, it having previously sought to rely on other exemptions. The Commissioner expressed surprise that the police were previously unaware of the base's status under Section 23.

Conclusions

Sheffield is, of course, by no means the only university to teach investigative journalism to undergraduates. There are other models of such teaching in Britain (Hanna, 2000: 8–12; Hattenstone, 2006) and abroad, including the projects in the USA by final year students at the Medill School of Journalism in uncovering miscarriages of justice (Northwestern University, 2007).

The expansion of Britain's journalism education, and the employment in universities of an increasing number of investigative journalists as educators, almost certainly means that the number of British students learning at least some rudiments of investigative work is at an all time high.

However, career opportunities to gain experience in well-resourced investigative journalism, or in mainstream news journalism, in Britain and other countries seem likely to diminish, at least in the foreseeable future, in the technological upheaval of the internet's growth, which, with other factors – e.g. a multiplication of media outlets, enabled by digitalisation – is causing the audiences of mainstream news media to fragment, and fear that revenue streams may ebb (Anderson and Ward, 2006; Pavlik, 2005: 260–2).

In such a situation, universities become essential in the transmission of the skills and public service values of investigative journalism.

Notes

1 By journalism education I mean a combination of tuition in vocational, practical skills, e.g. reporting, editing; in vocational knowledge, e.g. media law, media codes of ethics; and in 'journalism studies', e.g. academic study of journalism's output, history and culture (Franklin *et al.*, 2005: xiii, 127–8). This chapter signifies some elements of what I consider investigative journalism to be. Contributors of other chapters help define it holistically. See also useful discussion of its definition by Van Eijk (2005), pp. 12–25.

2 In Britain, the first postgraduate programme in journalism was launched in 1970, and the first undergraduate programmes were launched in 1991 (Delano, 2001: 143, 155). The number of students enrolling in such programmes has rapidly increased in recent years (HESA 1994–2005).

3 For expression or quoting of such views, see Cole (2003: 58–9), De Burgh (2003: 102, 104), French and Richards (1994: 85, 92), Phillips and Gaber (1996: 63); Turness (2005).

4 The first British postgraduate programme specifically in investigative journalism was launched in 1997 at Nottingham Trent University (Hanna, 2000: 8–11, 14), another highly regarded centre for journalism training. The programme was discontinued after some students left it (Adams, 2001).

5 For example, there is no longitudinal study of the investigative content of British newspapers comparable to that of Bernt and Greenwald (2000) in the USA.

6 Management at the Land Registry offices in Nottingham, whose territory includes Sheffield, have kindly hosted annual group visits by the students, and given them free access to and guidance on public records there.

7 It is not illegal in Britain to make an audio record of your own phone conversations, even if the other party is not alerted to this.

8 Felicity Hay and Hannah were among students who learned about the FOI Act from my colleague Tony Harcup who, when I was on a research sabbatical, ran the investigative module, helping greatly in its development.

Bibliography

Adams, C. (2001) 'Inside Story', *The Guardian*, 13 March 2001, see http://education. guardian.co.uk/higher/news/story/0,,485022,00.html, accessed 17 July 2007.

Anderson, P. and Ward, G. (eds) (2006) *The Future of Journalism in the Advanced Democracies*. London: Ashgate.

Armao, R. (2000) 'The History of Investigative Reporting', in Marilyn Greenwald and Joseph Bernt (eds) (2000) *The Big Chill: Investigative Reporting in the Current Media Environment*. Ames, Iowa: Iowa State University Press, pp. 35–49.

Barnett, S. and Seymour, E. (1999) ' "A Shrinking Iceberg Travelling South" . . . Changing Trends in British Television: a case study of drama and current affairs', London: Campaign for Quality Television Ltd.

Beers, R. and Egglestone, P. (2006) 'UK Television News', in Peter Anderson and Geoff Ward (eds) (2006) *The Future of Journalism in the Advanced Democracies*. London: Ashgate, pp. 139–56.

Bernstein, C. and Woodward, B. (1974) *All the President's Men*. New York: Simon and Schuster.

Bernt, J. and Greenwald, M. (2000) 'Enterprise and Investigative Reporting in Metropolitan Newspapers', in Marilyn Greenwald and Joseph Bernt (eds) (2000) *The Big Chill: Investigative Reporting in the Current Media Environment*. Ames, Iowa: Iowa State University Press, pp. 51–79.

Boyd-Barrett, O. (1970) 'Journalism Recruitment and Training: Problems in Professionalization', in Jeremy Tunstall (ed.), *Media Sociology: A Reader*. London: Constable, pp. 181–201.

Brooke, H. (2007) *Your Right to Know: A Citizen's Guide to the Freedom of Information Act*, 2nd edition. London: Pluto Press.

de Burgh, H. (2003) 'Skills Are Not Enough: The Case for Journalism as an Academic Discipline', *Journalism*, 4 (1), pp. 95–112.

de Burgh, H. (ed.) (2005) *Making Journalists: Diverse Models, Global Issues*. London: Routledge.

Centre for Investigative Journalism (2007) 'About the CIJ', see http://www.tcij. org/page/about_CIJ, accessed 13 March 2008.

City University (2007) 'Investigative Journalism', see http://www.city.ac.uk/ journalism/courses/postgrad/investigative/index.html, accessed 17 July 2007.

Cole, P. (2003) Escaping From the Timewarp, *British Journalism Review*, 14 (1), pp. 54–60.

Crown Prosecution Service (2007) 'Offences Against Public Morals and Decency', see http://www.cps.gov.uk/legal/section12/chapter_d.html, accessed 19 March 2007.

Davies, N. (2000) 'Keeping a Foot in the Door', *The Guardian*, Media section, 10 January 2000, pp. 8–9.

Davies, N. (2001) 'Digging, but no grave', *The Guardian*, 19 March 2001, see http:// www.guardian.co.uk/media/2001/mar/19/pressandpublishing.mondaymediasection3, accessed 13 March 2008.

Delano, A. (2001) *The Formation of the British Journalist 1900–2000*. PhD thesis, London: University of Westminster.

Department for Education and Skills (2003) *Students' loans and the question of debt*, 15 December 2003, see http://www.dfes.gov.uk/hegateway/uploads/Debt%20-%20FINAL.pdf, accessed 18 July 2007.

Deuze, M. (2006) Global Journalism Education: A conceptual approach, *Journalism Studies*, 7 (1), pp. 19–34.

Directgov (2007) 'How much will university cost? Tuition fees and other expenses', see http://www.direct.gov.uk/en/EducationAndLearning/UniversityAndHigher Education/StudentFinance/FinanceForNewStudents/DG_10034860, accessed 13 March 208.

Eddy, P., Potter, E. and Page, B. (1976) 'The Plane That Fell Out of the Sky', the *Sunday Times*, 17 October 1976, pp. 33–5.

Elliott, G. (2001) 'Money's too tight to mention' ", in 'Journalism Training', a supplement published by *Press Gazette* magazine, May, pp. 4–5.

Evans, H. (1983) *Good Times, Bad Times*. London: Weidenfeld and Nicolson.

Evans, R. and Leigh, D. (2003–8) 'The BAE Files', *The Guardian*, various dates, see http:// www.guardian.co.uk/world/bae, accessed 13 March 2008.

Foot, P. (1999) 'The Slow Death of Investigative Journalism', in Stephen Glover (ed.), *Secrets of the Press; Journalists on Journalism*. London: Allen Lane, The Penguin Press, pp. 79–89.

Foskett, N., Roberts, D. and Maringe, F. (2006) *Changing Fee Regimes and their Impact on Student Attitudes to Higher Education*. York: The Higher Education Academy, see http://www.heacademy.ac.uk/assets/York/documents/ourwork/research/changing_fees_regimes_full_report.pdf, accessed on 30 July 2007.

Franklin, B., Hamer, M., Hanna, M., Kinsey, M. and Richardson, J. (2005) *Key Concepts in Journalism Studies*. London: Sage Publications.

French, D. and Richards, M. (1994) 'Theory, Practice and Market Forces in Britain: A Case of Relative Autonomy', in David French and Michael Richards (eds) *Media Education Across Europe*. London: Routledge, pp. 82–102.

Greenwald, M. and Bernt, J. (eds) (2000) *The Big Chill: Investigative Reporting in the Current Media Environment*. Ames, Iowa: Iowa State University Press.

Guardian (2006) 'Tolerance zones plan in tatters' (no byline), *The Guardian*, 16 December 2006, see http://www.guardian.co.uk/uk/2006/dec/14/suffolkmurders, accessed 13 March 2008.

Hanna, M. (2000) 'British investigative journalism: protecting the continuity of talent through changing times', paper presented to the International Association for Media and Communication Research, 22nd general assembly and annual conference, Singapore, 18 July 2000.

Hanna, M. and Sanders, K. (2007) 'Journalism Education in Britain: Who are the students and what do they want?', *Journalism Practice*, 1 (3), pp. 404–20.

Harding, L., Leigh, D. and Pallister, D. (1997) *The Liar: The Fall of Jonathan Aitken*, London: Penguin.

Hattenstone, S. (2006) 'How To Dig and Keep Digging', *The Guardian*, 11 December 2006, see http://www.guardian.co.uk/media/2006/dec/11/mondaymediasection.highereducation, accessed 13 March 2008.

Henningham, J. and Delano, A. (1998) 'British Journalists' in David Weaver (ed.) *The Global Journalist: News People Around the World*. Cresskill, New Jersey: Hampton Press, pp. 143–60.

HESA (1994–2005) *Students in Higher Education Institutions*, reference volumes for academic years 1994/5 to 2004/5, London: Higher Education Statistics Agency.

Information Commissioner (2005–7) Correspondence between the Commissioner, North Yorkshire police and Mark Hanna. See also http:/www.ico.gov.uk/upload/documents/decisionnotices/2006/fs50074342.pdf, accessed 13 March 2008.

IRE (2007) 'IRE History 1975–1985', see http://www.ire.org/history/30years/decade1.html, accessed 29 July 2007.

Journalism Training Forum (2002) *Journalists at Work: Their Views on Training, Recruitment and Conditions*. London: Publishing NTO/Skillset.

Knightley, P. (1997) *A Hack's Progress*, London: Jonathan Cape.

Lloyd, G. and Mounter, J. (1969) 'London police in bribe allegations', the *Times*, 29 November, pp. 1, 6.

MacFadyen, G. (2006) Mark Hanna's telephone interview, 3 May, in with Gavin MacFadyen, director of the Centre for Investigative Journalism, London, who is a visiting professor at the City University, London.

Marks, N. (2000) 'Uncovering the Secrets of "Real" Journalism', *Press Gazette* magazine, 14 January 2000, p.15.

Meikle, J. (2007) 'University heads warn of £10,000-a-year tuition fees', *The Guardian*, 18 January 2007, see http://guardian.co.uk/uk/2007/jan/18/highereducation.politics, accessed 13 March 2008.

National Union of Journalists (2006a) 'Journalism Matters', see http://www.journalismmatters.org.uk/, accessed 13 March 2008.

National Union of Journalists (2006b) 'Journalism Matters – Campaign Briefing', see http://www.journalismmatters.org.uk/campaign_materials.html, accessed 13 March 2008.

Northwestern University (2007) 'Medill Innocence Project', see http://www.medill.northwestern.edu/journalism/undergrad/page.aspx?id=59507, accessed 13 March 2008.

Pavlik, John (2005) 'Running the technological gauntlet: Journalism and new media', in Hugo De Burgh (ed.) (2005) *Making Journalists: Diverse models, global issues*. London: Routledge, pp. 245–63.

Pecke, S. (2004) Local Heroes, *British Journalism Review*, 15 (2), pp. 26–30.

Phillips, A. and Gaber, I. (1996) The Case for Media Degrees, *British Journalism Review*, 7 (3), pp. 62–5.

Pilger, J. (2005) (ed.) *Tell Me No Lies: Investigative Journalism and Its Triumphs*. London: Vintage.

Postles, H. and Gardner, T. (2006) 'Jailed sex beasts' PlayStation porn', *Yorkshire Evening Post*, 15 June 2005, see http://www.yorkshireeveningpost.co.uk/ViewArticle.aspx?SectionID=39&ArticleID=1566154, accessed 29 July 2007.

Project Censored (2007) 'About Us', see http://www.projectcensored.org/about/index.htm, accessed 24 July 2007.

Sheffield Star (2007a) 'Legal victory for brothel owner', 30 March 2007, see http://www.thestar.co.uk/news/Legal-victory-for-brothel-owner.2193921.jp, accessed 13 March 2008.

Sheffield Star (2007b) ' "We had to take on police", says sauna owner', 30 March 2007, see http://www.thestar.co.uk/news/39We-had-to-take-on.2193332.jp, accessed 13 March 2008.

Sutton Trust (2006) *The Educational Backgrounds of Leading Journalists*. London: Sutton Trust, see http://www.suttontrust.com/reports/Journalists-backgrounds-final-report.pdf, accessed 24 July 2007.

Tatge, M. (2000) 'Taking CAR for a Spin: Conventional News Gathering Goes High-Tech', in Marilyn Greenwald and Joseph Bernt (eds) (2000) *The Big Chill: Investigative Reporting in the Current Media Environment*. Ames, Iowa: Iowa State University Press, pp. 211–228.

Tempest, M. and agencies (2007) 'Brown's U-Turn is latest twist in lengthy casinos saga', *The Guardian*, 12 July 2007, see http://www.guardian.co.uk/politics/2007/jul/12/immigrationpolicy.gambling, accessed 13 March 2008.

Thom, C. (2004) 'Where are the new Pilgers?', Journalism Training supplement, published by *Press Gazette* magazine, 26 March 2004, pp. 29–30.

Turness, Deborah (2005) A contribution within 'Don't Take No For An Answer When You Knock On Journalism's Door', Journalism Training supplement, published by *Press Gazette* magazine, 15 April 2005, p. 5.

University College Falmouth (2007) 'First MA Investigative Journalism students set highest standards', press release, 26 March 2007, see http://www.falmouth.ac.uk/index.php?option=com_content&task=view&id=706&Itemid=312, accessed 17 July 2007.

University of Sheffield Department of Journalism Studies (2006a) 'Felicity triumphs again', see http://www.shef.ac.uk/journalism/news/felicity.html, accessed 27 July 2007.

University of Sheffield Department of Journalism Studies (2006b) 'Freedom of Information – student shows how it's done', 26 June 2006, see http://shef.ac.uk/journalism/news/freedominfo.html, accessed 27 July 2007.

University of Strathclyde (2007) 'MSc Investigative Journalism', see http://www.strath.ac.uk/media/media_62117_en.pdf, accessed 27 July 2007.

Van Eijk, D. (ed.) (2005) *Investigative Journalism in Europe*. Amsterdam: Vereniging van Onderzoeksjournalisten.

Wallraff, G. (1978) *Wallraff, the undesirable journalist*, London: Pluto Press.

Weaver, D. H., Beam, R. A., Brownlee, B. J., Voakes, P. S. and Wilhoit, C. (2007) *The American Journalist in the 21st Century: U.S. News People at the Dawn of a New Millennium*. Mahwah, New Jersey: Lawrence Erlbaum Associates.

Welsh, T., Greenwood, W., and Banks D. (2007) *McNae's Essential Law for Journalists*, 19th edition. Oxford: Oxford University Press.

Further reading

Brooke, Heather (2007) *Your Right to Know: A Citizen's Guide to the Freedom of Information Act*, 2nd edition. London: Pluto Press.

Evans, Harold, (1983) *Good Times, Bad Times*, London: Weidenfeld and Nicolson.

Greenwald, Marilyn and Bernt, Joseph (2000) *The Big Chill: Investigative Reporting in the Current Media Environment*, Ames, Iowa: Iowa State University Press.

Harding, Luke, and Leigh, David and Pallister, David (1997) *The Liar: The Fall of Jonathan Aitken*, London: Penguin.

Knightley, Phillip (1997) *A Hack's Progress*, London: Jonathan Cape.

Van Eijk, Dick (ed.) (2005) *Investigative Journalism in Europe*, Amsterdam: Vereniging van Onderzoeksjournalisten.

10

INVESTIGATIVE JOURNALISM AND SCHOLARSHIP

Michael Bromley

Harold Evans began the account of his editorships of the *Times* and *Sunday Times* in London with a Saturday evening encounter with the newspapers' proprietor Roy Thomson and his son Kenneth, as an issue went to press carrying extracts from the diaries of the former Cabinet Minister Richard Crossman, which the British government would rather did not see the light of day. To Evans, this was a clear case of the watchdog press, the so-called Fourth Estate, exercising the people's right to know; combating 'arbitrary power'; engaging in 'necessary warfare', and invoking a tradition associated with W.T. Stead and the transplantation of 'aggressive' New Journalism from the United States of America to the United Kingdom in the latter part of the nineteenth century (Wiener, 1996: 67–9). As editor, Evans nurtured the 'famous' Insight investigative reporting team at the *Sunday Times* (Neil, 1996: 46) – the 'spearhead' of a decade of investigations at the paper. Under Evans, Insight was charged with naming the guilty, exposing 'evil practices' and identifying failures (cit. in Spark, 1999: 8). Evans argued that 'in the cases we investigated the law and the political institutions had failed the public' (Evans, 1994: 1–8).

The *Sunday Times* of the 1960s and 1970s, like *McClure's Magazine* in the US during the period of muckraking journalism in the opening years of the twentieth century (Serrin and Serrin, 2002; Woodress, 1987: Ch. 9), has been embraced as a prototypical promoter of 'good' journalistic practice exemplified by investigative journalism. A former member of the Insight team, Phillip Knightley (2005), recalled:

> The *Sunday Times* had 350 editorial staff to produce a 48- or 64-page two-section quality broadsheet every week. . . . It spent money like water on investigative journalism – two million pounds on legal costs alone fighting for its right to publish the story about the thalidomide scandal. It was scared of no one. It averaged a libel writ a week. The editor, Harold Evans, was unhappy if a libel writ had not arrived by Tuesday, because he felt that the paper had not been doing its

job – defending people without power from those who wielded it unfairly, exposing corruption, making a difference to the lives of ordinary citizens. Here was a paper that believed in something, which took enormous pains to get things right, and which fought for its editorial integrity.

(Phillip Knightly, 2005)

In this spirit, publication of the Crossman diaries was clearly 'in the public interest'. Lord Thomson, on the other hand, took a more sanguine view: the Crossman diaries were simply 'a good read'.

The potential, identified by Thomson, for journalism which was meant to be 'subversive' to contribute primarily to media popularity (and profitability) and only incidentally to public interest, has since grown rather than diminished (McNair, 1998: 123–4, 164–6). Wrestling with the meaning of 'public interest' has become more a matter of pragmatics. In the 1960s it seemed possible to draw a clearer line between the public's 'right' and its simple 'curiosity', and 'to discriminate between right and wrong motives' (Andrews, 1962: 157). Andrew Neil (1996: 321–2), a successor to Evans as the editor of the *Sunday Times*, was more instrumentalist about the role of investigative journalism: it helped fill the pages of the paper, and it fired journalists with the 'exhilaration of revelation'. When Insight was 'rejuvenated' in the 1980s it was quite a different animal from what it had been a decade or more previously (Doig, 1997: 205–6; Knightley, 1998: 39; Linklater, 1993). For journalists, too, in a more tabloid-inflected era, investigative work was more sheer 'fun' (Clarkson, 1990: 126). Journalism stood accused of having squandered the legacy of Watergate, the quintessential journalistic investigation of the later twentieth century (Hume, 1998: 55).

Yet the assertion of 'golden ageism' in investigative journalism needs to be treated cautiously. For example, Stead's fusion of scoops and sensationalism, 'eye-catching' design and progressivism, investigations and crusades, and the use of cloak-and-dagger techniques, earned him the soubriquet 'a mixture of Don Quixote and Phineas T. Barnum' (Griffiths, 1992: 532). His best remembered 'investigation' into the prostitution of young girls in London was notable for raising the circulation of the *Pall Mall Gazette* from 12,000 to more than one million (Pierce Jones, 1988: 26). At about the same time, the Australian G.E. Morrison, while exposing the Kanaka slave trade for *The* [Melbourne] *Age* to the shame of the Queensland government, was equally content, when working for the *Times* in China, to disguise his identity as a journalist, to provide information to the British government, and to promote political objectives (Thompson and Macklin, 2004: 25–36, 112ff). In 1906 President Theodore Roosevelt was able to deflect investigations into political corruption by condemning journalists as 'muckrakers' for being sensationalist and irresponsible (Dragin, 2001). Later in the century, the account written by Carl Bernstein and Bob Woodward (1974) of their investigation of the conspiracy behind the break-in at Watergate re-established the investigative reporting paradigm and its centrality to Western journalism (Brennen, 2003), but the reputation of journalism, represented in the film *All the President's Men*, was hardly universally accepted; it was more common to portray journalists in a negative light (Page, 2006). Finally, there were those who dismissed investigative journalism altogether as pretentious and claimed it had 'few ardent adherents among practitioners' (Hanna, 2005: 122).

Nevertheless, academics have generally joined journalists in lamenting the supposed contemporary decline of investigative journalism (Doig, 1997; Foot, 1999; Greenwald and Bernt, 2000; Hanna, 2005: 123; Haxton, 2002). This seemed to run counter to the animosity between practice and scholarship evident since journalism entered the academy more than a century ago. This tension even occasionally spilled over into open hostility (as with the Glasgow University Media Group's UK studies of 'Bad News' in the 1970s and 1980s, and the Australian 'Media Wars' of the late 1990s) (for an example, see Leapman, 1993). As a form idealised by journalists (Bromley, 2005: 310–20), investigative journalism might be expected to be a key issue for disputation among practitioners and scholars. This chapter examines approaches to investigative journalism evident in (mass) communication, media, cultural and increasingly journalism studies.

Theoretical approaches to investigative journalism

There have been many, often overlapping, ways in which investigative journalism has been considered theoretically. Together they form a complex matrix of inter-connected ideologies and epistemologies (supported by various methodologies) which cannot be fully explored in a single chapter. Zelizer (2004) suggested that scholars had examined journalism principally through the prisms of sociology, history, linguistics, political science and cultural studies. These studies have engaged with the main theories applied to media, communication and cultural studies, among them Marxism, critical theory, mass culture, political economy, technological determinism, functionalism, feminism, modernism and postmodernism (Stevenson, 1995; Williams, 2003). Nevertheless, it is important to acknowledge the distinction between critical approaches driven by theory and administrative interest in investigative journalism. Halloran (1974: 12) characterised the latter as predominantly 'descriptive rather than analytical . . . and, on the whole, divorced from . . . theory'. In pursuing concerns for the maintenance of the *status quo* and in skirting the (political, economic, social, cultural, institutional, historical) contexts of journalism (two dimensions which are intimately related), administrative research exhibits a tendency to take its object of study for granted, and to ask only how well it is done. Within journalism this has often reproduced itself in the form of 'How to' guides – in the words of one, 'being a better detective' (Ullmann, 1995: 25).

Investigative journalism is thereby reduced to 'the deployment of human, technical or financial resources' (Forbes, 2005: 8) and 'skills and tactics' (Northmore, 1996: 1). Such approaches merely define investigative journalism as 'what investigative journalists say they are doing when they do their job'. As useful as this kind of empirical evidence may be to scholars as research data, by itself it does not provide any analytical understanding of the object of analysis (Van Eijk, 2005: 12–13). It leads to a concentration on practice – 'techniques' and exemplars (Spark, 1999; Ullmann and Colbert, 1991), and debates around the facilitation or obstruction of investigative journalism (Conley and Lamble, 2006: 36–9) from which are drawn 'principles'. By comparison, critical analysis examines 'the contradictory aspects of the phenomena in their systemic context' (Smythe and Van Dinh, 1983: 123). Nevertheless, the two are connected, however tenuously, through normative assessments of investigative journalism which emphasise its 'watchdog' role and its oppositionalism (Forbes, 2005: v; Pilger, 2004: xiv). Therefore, McQuail's (2005: 111–87) broad categories (slightly amended) – normative, socio-economic, cultural and socio-technological – offer a useful template for analysing scholarly approaches to investigative journalism.

Normative theories

At their crudest, normative approaches to investigative journalism start from the assumption that there exists a 'proper role of the news media in society and of the journalist in gathering news' (Ettema et al., 1997: 42). This is commonly derived from liberal ideas of freedom based on rationality in which journalism serves the public good in promoting and sustaining democracy; 'Lockean values – empiricism and rationality in public discourse, government by consent of the governed, a government of laws rather than of individuals, and limitations on governmental power' (Lambeth, 1992: 140). Journalists commit to abide by these values through a sense of 'professionalism' imbued with attributes such as independence, objectivity, accuracy and ethics. Perhaps the clearest modern statement of this position was the Hutchins Commission's injunction for 'social responsibility' in the media which emphasised, 'Civilized society is a working system of ideas. It lives and changes by the consumption of ideas. Therefore it must make sure that as many as possible are available for its examination' (Commission on Freedom of the Press, 1947: vii). The social responsibility approach combined 'freedom' with 'responsibility', arguing that constitutional guarantees of freedom of expression should be tempered with transparent and defensible regulation, and that freedoms should be curtailed to prevent their abuse (Commission on Freedom of the Press, 1947: 82–106). This became the stock tenet of mainstream western journalism in the second half of the twentieth century.

The definition of journalism which found its way into any number of standard textbooks was, to cite one, 'to seek truths and to pass them on to their communities' (Conley and Lamble, 2006: 31), where each element of the equation was determined by the working practices of journalists (Zelizer, 2004: 42–3). Insofar as 'truth' was elusive and not necessarily contained in the simple reporting of facts, but called rather for modes of interrogation, investigative journalism proposed that in many situations 'truth' was more likely to be latent than manifest (Ettema *et al.*, 1997: 43). The expansion of the 'PR state', the manipulation of the media and an increased reliance on 'soft' power of 'international perception management' (Ward, 2007; Knightley, 2005), allied to the technological capacity for governments to address publics directly (Tumber and Bromley, 1998), in which the media could be characterised as 'weapons of mass deception' (Rampton and Stauber, 2003: esp. 161–88), served only to underscore the need for journalism which refused to accept 'the facts' at face value. Thus, for many (particularly in the US) 'serious investigative journalism has become a defining characteristic of the news media' (Aucoin, 2005: 4). Perhaps the most widely read advocate of this approach is the Australian journalist working in Britain, John Pilger (Pilger, 2004: xvi–xvii).

That which investigative journalism confronts, secrecy, is viewed as being indicative of a dysfunctional society (Aucoin, 2005: 3; Van Eijk, 2005: 16–17); that which limits 'independent journalism and freedom of speech' is an assault on basic human rights (Chelysheva, 2007). Ultimately, investigative journalism is regarded as reflecting the society in which it is practised, and as a barometer of democracy embodied in the assertion of the public 'right to know' and in the importance of 'the public interest' (McQuail, 2005: 162–3, 165). Underpinning this position is a commitment to pluralism and diversity, which was enshrined in public service broadcasting systems, particularly in western Europe, and in which 'serious' journalism was a core characteristic (Williams, 2001: 12–13). Given that investigative journalism was seen as being highly dependent on a commitment to the free-flow of ideas, liberalisation and deregulation of the media from the 1970s was taken as either an opportunity or a threat (see Holland, 2001).

The most persistent critique of western liberal democracies' performance as exemplified by the state of investigative journalism has drawn heavily on political economy theory. Crudely, the idea that 'freedom of the press is guaranteed only to those who own one' (Liebling, 1961) was taken as an indication of the ability of the market to subvert the intent of investigative journalism (Chambers, 2001a: 89). More than that, marketisation resulted in the commodification of citizenship, in which rights were considered to be objects of private consumption, diminishing the role of the public sphere as a 'neutral' space in which to pursue 'reason and truth' – the stock-in-trade of investigative journalism (Chambers, 2001b: 109). Confronted by this situation, citizens seemed to respond not by demanding a return to the 'principles of serving the public through committed expository reporting' (Chambers, 2001b: 121), but by expressing hostility to the practicalities of 'a free press'. This left many wondering 'how . . . citizens reached a point where they, evidently out of profound frustration and distrust of the media, reject a basic premise on which [a democratic] nation was formed' (Greenwald and Bernt, 2000: 3).

Socio-economic theories

Political economy has played a key role in the socio-economic theorising of investigative journalism. While on the one hand, it was argued that marketisation resulted in a shift in media revenue raising from advertising to sales and in hyper-competition through mass appeal (Chambers, 2001b: 110), on the other hand, it was equally contended that advertising held too much sway and competition among the media 'dwindled' as a consequence of the concentration of ownership (Daniel, 2000: 12). In both instances, however, it was believed that the result was a decline in investigative journalism. The lack of a clear consensus on the political economy causes of any diminution in the quantity or quality of investigative journalism has led scholars to consider other factors, given that in the end the argument seemed to progress no further than the essential Marxist position that 'whoever owns or controls the media can choose, or set limits to, what they do' (McQuail, 2005: 79).

A focus on content can unpack issues of the social function of the media in conveying ideas and values, in forming public opinion and in creating the potential for change. A persistent theme in scholarly work on investigative journalism has been that of promoting an 'open society' by exposing malfeasance and enlightening the public through publication or broadcast with the objective of stimulating corrective and progressive change (Armao, 2000: 43; Boyd, 2001: 29; de Burgh, 2000: 9; Greenwald and Bernt, 2000: 4; Leigh, 2000). Journalists as a whole adopted this agenda, seeing themselves as 'watchdogs' and as members of the Fourth Estate 'watching, questioning, analysing and informing' (Haxton, 2002: 33; Schultz, 1998: 6). After interviewing investigative journalists in America, Ettema and Glasser (1998: 7) concluded that practitioners believed they were charged with reflecting back to the public its own morality and lapses from it, and did so through the adoption of a specific narrative style which emphasised the polar opposites of good and evil. Ettema and Glasser characterised this as 'an exercise in public conscience despite itself' as the limited journalistic repertoire failed ultimately to carry the public with it (p. 200). While examples such as the Watergate investigation and Edward R. Murrow's challenging of Senator Joseph McCarthy were lauded for building consensuses around a shared set of values (Jensen, 2000: 135, 250–51), Ettema and Glasser (1998: 84) found that the investigative journalism style militated against mutual understanding. Thus, investigative journalism could be seen functionally as both mobilising and integrating *and* disabling and divisive (Bromley, 2005: 318–19), bringing into question assumptions about its role in processes of democracy, especially in the so-called developing world (Waisbord, 2000: 250). Indeed, it was the contention of Protess *et al.* (1991: 249–54) that much investigative journalism was pre-determined through prior complicity with policy-makers rather than in collaboration with the public.

This reminds us that texts are to some extent the outcomes of production, and much social theory has been directed at the organisational, routine and personal dimensions of journalism as sets of practices located within specific institutional settings and which form influential social systems (for a brief summary, see Tumber, 1999: xvi). The decline of investigative journalism can be cast as a corollary of 'the [broader] decline of journalistic authority' already alluded to (Hardt, 2000: 209). The challenges for investigative journalists are seen as transcending the historical task of promoting democracy to 'reviving the Fourth Estate' itself (Schultz, 1998). Many view investigative journalism as the apotheosis of journalistic practice in affording its practitioners freedom (Malarek, 1998: 45). It is regarded as offering a site where journalists can demonstrate their commitment to freedom, justice and truth and prove their courage (Pilger, 2004: xvii). In order to establish investigative journalism as a social practice, it was necessary to preserve and nurture it by permitting its practitioners to 'apply and live the virtues while carrying out the practice' (Aucoin, 2005: 204–5). That has been achieved, if at all, not through the media as institutions but by voluntary collectivism in organisations such as Investigative Reporters and Editors (IRE) (Aucoin, 2005: 214–15). The number of such entities has grown significantly since IRE was formed in 1975, and has reached beyond the west to Latin America, Asia, and Eastern and Central Europe, with individual investigative journalists linked through an international directory and collaborating through the International Consortium of Investigative Journalists (see http://www.globalinvestigativejournalism.org/resources/organizations.html for a comprehensive list; also http://www.publicintegrity.org/icij/). These developments point to a resurgence of autonomy from organisational, routine and perhaps even personal constraints.

Professionalism, which as a concept connects administrative, normative and socio-economic approaches, has been central to analyses of investigative journalism as a more or less autonomous practice, underscoring the importance of ethics, analytical capacity, knowledge and understanding of a wide range of topics and areas, intelligence and interpretative ability which are developed increasingly in higher education, and bestow the 'authority and influence' which is characteristic of a professional and which, in Australia at least, is seen as providing influential status (Pearson, 2002: 323; Waterford, 2002: 43–4). Others have questioned the appropriateness of the application of professionalism, and characterised journalists as grey- rather than white-collar workers. Investigative journalism allows some to hide behind the veil of professionalism (Hirst, 2001). Addressing journalism more generally, Zelizer (1992: 9–10) argued that it constituted an 'interpretive community' which 'authenticates itself through narratives and collective memories' which level out distinctions of status, and construe journalism as a shared cultural experience.

Cultural theories

Schudson (1995: 142–9), too, proposed that investigative journalism should be approached as a cultural phenomenon. Watergate specifically symbolised the assumed importance of investigative journalism to belief in a healthy liberal democracy through the intersect of a popular myth (David and Goliath) and a journalistic myth ('speaking truth unto power'). Culturalist approaches put a greater emphasis on the rituals of production, and account more fully for reception, in assembling the symbolic reproduction of reality (Carey, cit. in McQuail, 2005: 112). Investigative journalism was classified as ideological work, in which 'a shared culture is created, modified and transformed' (Carey, 1995: 366), rather than being seen as independent, objective, clinical practice (Faure, 2005: 156). A culturalist approach challenged the idea of investigative journalism as a mobilising force (Protess *et al.*, 1991: 12), and suggested that it worked within existing cultural paradigms to co-create meaning – whether of political scandal, corporate corruption, or celebrity misbehaviour – dependent on the extent to which 'public interest and human rights' were integral to cultural understanding (Faure, 2005: 166; Raphael *et al.*, 2004: 167–8). Investigative journalism, then, was a form of 'self-knowledge' (Yau *et al.*, 2006: 22).

Insofar as investigative journalism's practices and texts were imbricated with their reception, changes in both quantity and quality were implicated with a range of contextual cultural factors – the 'crisis of democracy', a cynical audience, the 'promotional culture', distrust of institutions, democratisation of knowledge. Rather than acting to reveal 'outrageous civic vice' (Ettema and Glasser, 1998: 7) investigative journalism was a participant in the power play around the 'scandal' in which it traded. In these conditions, evidence, 'facts' were replaced by a ritual of allegation, speculation and counter-allegation (Tumber, 2001: 98–9, 107, 109). This coincided with a rising tension between the presentation of journalism as a consumer good 'meant to be referred to, not read' – a display of 'bits of information' as if in a shop window – and a social scientific turn to generalise from specifics, to abstract, to interpret and to discern deeper patterns and themes (Barnhurst and Mutz, 1997: 47–51).

Furthermore, it was commonplace that all forms of 'serious' journalism addressing politics, business, economics, etc., were particularly heavily gendered, even within a 'laddish occupational mythology' (Aldridge, 1998: 122; McQuail, 2005: 122). As journalism was increasingly feminised, myth confronted reality (Aldridge, 1998: 123). Yet access to the lionisation of elite categories of journalist, including investigative journalists, was largely denied to women.★ Cultural theorising implied, then, that investigative journalism

---

★ There were notable exceptions. In 2006 Anna Politkovskaya, a Russian investigative journalist, later murdered, was named as one of the International Press Institute's world press freedom heroes (IFEX, 2006).

was – or ought to be – more affective than effective, and more show than substance.

Socio-technological

Digitisation held out the promise of 'a new frontier' to investigative journalism, revitalising the primacy of ideas, revelation and mobilisation over the participation in scandal and display (DeFleur, 1997: 2, 5, 18). Computers provided investigative journalists with the wherewithal to monitor government – 'their traditional role as watchdogs' (DeFleur, 1997: 22–3). By the late 1990s computer-assisted investigative reporting was more rather than less routine in many newsrooms, accelerated by the rapid digitisation of official records (DeFleur, 1997: 85–9). Nevertheless, from the perspective of a growing body of those who professed to be most committed to journalism's traditional professionalism, the new multimedia environment had fostered a 'culture of news' that was antithetical to investigative journalism (Kovach and Rosenstiel, 1999: 1). It was proposed that this had five characteristics, arising directly from a set of causal factors, and resulting in the degeneration of journalism:

1 24/7 multi-platform news competition produced a 'never-ending' news cycle which demanded instant content, and which in turn led to less competent journalism done in a hurry.
2 A greater demand for news benefited the public relations business, as suppliers, and resulted in a shift in their power relations with journalists, with spin doctors gaining the upper hand.
3 Consumer preferences were met by more specialised and targeted news outlets with little in common, including the 'professional standards and ethics' by which their journalists operated.
4 The need to fill the news-hole promoted an 'argument culture' based on commenting on the news, chat and punditry rather than reporting, and undermining the need to verify information.
5 In a highly-competitive environment news providers strove to grab the public's attention and over-relied on 'blockbusters', a form of 'cheap and easy' journalism which stripped resources from more difficult, and less sensational, reporting tasks (Kovach and Rosenstiel, 1999: 6–8).

The same authors proposed a nine-point programme of principles, which represented a consensual response elicited through more than 100 interviews with journalists, as a counter to these tendencies. Based on the notion that 'the purpose of journalism is to provide people with the information they need to be free and self-governing', they embraced many of the core tenets of investigative journalism: a first obligation to the truth; a first loyalty to citizens; an essential discipline of verification; monitoring power and giving voice to the voiceless (Kovach and Rosenstiel, 2001: 12–13). Journalists, who asserted a 'pure' form of journalism which relied on 'truth, independence and clarity', now found themselves implicated in 'a whole entertainment-information industry' facilitated by digital platforms which carried all genres of content in seamlessly and in non-linear form (Lawe Davies, 1999: 54–7).

Moreover, it was evident that digitisation enabled more information to flow and be stored, more incessantly and more interactively, and that more people were creating (as well as receiving) this information, and doing so seamlessly and simultaneously. The era of 'we media' seemed to have arrived (Bowman and Willis, 2003). The most comprehensive way of explaining this revolved around a notion of produsage – 'the collaborative and continuous building and extending of existing content in pursuit of further improvement' in which producers and users were indistinguishable (Bruns, 2005b). 'We media' were characterised as places where audiences shaped news and information in 'a new media ecosystem' in which software was used to create original material to be made available, amended, corrected, extended, annotated, amplified, discussed and re-entered into the system for the cycle to begin over again. 'The interaction of these elements advances the state of technology, community and knowledge' (Bowman and Willis, 2003: 13; Lih, 2004: 26). The authoritative publisher or broadcaster who controlled once-and-for-all access was being replaced by an open reiterative process: gatewatching – keeping an active eye on the world and how it was reported – was supplanting the more traditional role of gatekeeping – deciding what should be made available to passive recipients – traditionally practised by investigative journalists and their editors (Bruns, 2005a). The foundation of these forms of citizen journalism was individualised, two-way and peer-to-peer communication, rather than the top-down mass-based flows associated with traditional media (Thompson, 2003: 1–2) which came to resemble a kind of 'first person news network', offering the citizen 'take' on events including the death of Princess Diana, the 9/11 terrorist attacks and the 2003 invasion of Iraq (Allan, 2006: 27, 32–3, 61).

More than technology was at work, however, and media organisations struggled to come to terms with the 'supervening social necessity', the dynamic general social environment which dictated whether a technology was taken up, when, how, by whom and for what purpose (Winston, 1998: 5–7). The use of digital technologies (computers, mobile phones, MP3 players) to facilitate social networking led media to contemplate reconstructing themselves as 'social media' to meet the social requirements of citizens (Kiss, 2007). This suggested that digitised, web-based platforms were not just 'sophisticated, interactive variants of the older media' (Knight, 2000: 2), and that investigative journalism needed to adopt to accommodate new social realities. Yet there was little consensus on how (McQuaid, 2006), or what 'the people's journalism' might look like (Tumber, 2001: 108).

Conclusion

Investigative journalism remains relatively under-theorised, and the majority of theories have been developed from and applied in broader fields of communication, cultural and media studies. Surprisingly, normative assumptions continue to provide the foundation for much theorising about investigative journalism. On the whole, investigative journalism is seen as 'a good thing', central to the idea of 'the press', and even if flawed in practice, an essential component of flourishing liberal democratic systems. In short, such worlds would be worse off without it, and political economy theorists in particular have been exercised by the prospect of investigative journalism being squeezed from the media by market factors such as commercialisation and hyper-competition. On the other hand, the same critics have been sceptical about the digitally-enabled scope and scale of open source citizen journalism (for an example, see http://www.dailykos.com/story/2005/2/16/181428/870). This ambivalence was also evident in responses to media liberalisation and deregulation which, at one and the same time, threatened to starve investigative journalism of resources, and to provide additional opportunities for freer and more channels of expression, both in the cause of market forces.

This position was based primarily on the concept of investigative journalism as a consensus-building and mobilising force. Investigative journalism as a social practice was dependent on its practitioners building internal competence and external confidence. While much rhetoric was constructed around this idea – the investigative journalist as 'hero' – doubts have been cast on the efficacy of either professionalism or investigative journalism texts in either establishing claims to 'clinical' status or in effecting public responses. Nevertheless, the burgeoning of citizen journalism has been far from welcomed as a way of democratising investigative journalism. Of the theoretical approaches surveyed (necessarily in truncated form) here, only cultural theory accepted that investigative journalism, as normatively construed, may be in need of revision; that the substance of investigative journalism may be less important than its form, and that investigative journalism no longer bears meaning (if it ever did) as 'watchdog' oversight of the military-industrial complex but rather as a participant in the working-out of morality through the display of celebrity behaviour (de Burgh, 2005: 8).

Bibliography

Aldridge, M. (1998) 'The tentative hell-raisers: identity and mythology in contemporary UK press journalism', *Media, Culture & Society*, 20 (1), 109–27.

Allan, S. (2006) *Online News*. Maidenhead, Berks: Open University Press.

Andrews, L. (1962) *Problems of an Editor: A Study in Newspaper Trends*. London: Oxford University Press.

Armao, R. (2000) 'The history of investigative reporting', in M. Greenwald and J. Bernt (eds) *The Big Chill: Investigative Reporting in the Current Media Environment*. Ames: Iowa State University Press, 35–49.

Aucoin, J.L. (2005) *The Evolution of American Investigative Journalism*. Columbia: University of Missouri Press.

Bernstein, C. and Woodward, B. (1974) *All the President's Men*. New York: Simon and Schuster.

Barnhurst, K. and Mutz, D. (1997) 'American journalism and the decline of event-centred reporting', *Journal of Communication* (Autumn), 27–52.

Bowman, S. and Willis, C. (2003) *We Media. How Audiences are Shaping the Future of News and Information*, Reston VA: The Media Center at the American Press Institute.

Boyd, A. (2001) *Broadcast Journalism: Techniques of Radio and Television News*, 5th edn. Oxford: Focal Press.

Brennen, B.S. (2003) 'Sweat not melodrama: reading the structure of feeling in *All the President's Men*', *Journalism: Theory, Practice and Criticism* 4 (1), 113–31.

Bromley, M. (2005) 'Subterfuge as public service: investigative journalism as idealized journalism', in S. Allan (ed.) *Journalism: Critical Issues*. Maidenhead, Berks: Open University Press, 313–27.

Bruns, A. (2005a) *Gatewatching: Collaborative Online News Production*. New York: Peter Lang.

Bruns, A. (2005b) 'Some exploratory notes on produsers and produsage', *surblog*. Posted at http://snurb.info/index.php?q=node/329: accessed 15 June 2007.

de Burgh, H. (ed.) (2000) *Investigative Journalism: Context and Practice*. London: Routledge.

de Burgh, H. (2005) 'Introduction: journalism and the new cultural paradigm', in H. de Burgh (ed.) *Making Journalists*. London: Routledge, 1–21.

Carey, J.W. (1995) 'Mass communications and cultural studies', in O. Boyd-Barrett and C. Newbold (eds) *Approaches to Media: A Reader*. London: Arnold, 365–73.

Chambers, D. (2001a) 'Critical approaches to the media: the changing context for investigative journalism', in H. de Burgh (ed.) *Investigative Journalism: Context and Practice*. London: Routledge, 89–107.

Chambers, D. (2001b) 'Globalising media agendas: the production of journalism', in H. de Burgh (ed.) *Investigative Journalism: Context and Practice*. London: Routledge, 108–25.

Chelysheva, O. (2007) 'The slow, painful death of journalism in Russia', *Independent* (5 February). Posted at http://comment.independent.co.uk/commentators/article2237670.ece: accessed 9 July 2007.

Clarkson, W. (1990) *Dog Eat Dog: Confessions of a Tabloid Journalist*. London: Fourth Estate.

Commission on Freedom of the Press (1947) *A Free and Responsible Press*. Chicago: University of Chicago Press.

Conley, D. and Lamble, S. (2006) *The Daily Miracle: An Introduction to Journalism*, 3rd edn. South Melbourne: Oxford University Press.

Daniel, D.K. (2000) 'Best of times and worst of times: investigative reporting in post-Watergate America', in M. Greenwald and J. Bernt (eds) (2000) *The Big Chill: Investigative Reporting in the Current Media Environment*. Ames: Iowa State University Press, 11–33.

DeFleur, M. (1997) *Computer Assisted Investigative Reporting: Development and Methodology*. Mahwah, NJ: Lawrence Erlbaum.

Doig, A. (1997) 'The decline of investigatory journalism', in M. Bromley and T. O'Malley (eds) *A Journalism Reader*. London: Routledge, 189–213.

Dragin, B. (2001) 'Return of the muckraker', *San Francisco Chronicle* (13 August). Posted at http://www.commondreams.org/views01/0813–04.htm: accessed 12 July 2007.

Ettema, J.S. and Glasser, T.L. (1998) *Custodians of Conscience: Investigative Journalism and Public Virtue*. New York: Columbia University Press.

Ettema, J.S., Whitney, D.C. and Wackman, D.B. (1997) 'Professional mass communicators', in D. Berkowitz (ed.) *Social Meanings of News*. London: Sage, 31–50.

Evans, H. (1994 edn) *Good Times, Bad Times*. London: Phoenix.

Faure, C. (2005) 'Investigative journalism as a democratic practice: a *Mail & Guardian* case study (2002–3)', *Communicare* 24 (1), 154–70.

Foot, P. (1999) 'The slow death of investigative journalism', in S. Glover (ed.) *The Penguin Book of Journalism: Secrets of the Press*. London: Penguin, 79–89.

Forbes, D. (2005) *A Watchdog's Guide to Investigative Reporting*. Johannesburg: Konrad Adenauer Stiftung.

Greenwald, M. and Bernt, J. (eds) (2000) *The Big Chill: Investigative Reporting in the Current Media Environment*. Ames: Iowa State University Press.

Griffiths, D. (ed.) (1992) *The Encyclopedia of the British Press, 1492–1992*. London: Macmillan.

Halloran, J. (1974) *Mass Media and Society – The Challenge of Research*. Leicester University Press: Leicester.

Hanna, M. (2005) 'Investigative journalism', in B. Franklin, M. Hamer, M. Hanna, M. Kinsey and J.E. Richardson, *Key Concepts in Journalism Studies*. London: Sage, 122–4.

Hardt, H. (2000) 'Conflicts of interest: newsworkers, media and patronage journalism', in H. Tumber (ed.) *Media Power, Professionals and Policies*. London: Routledge, 209–24.

Haxton, N. (2002) 'The death of investigative journalism', in S. Tanner (ed.) *Journalism: Investigation and Research*. Frenchs Forest, NSW: Longman, 20–36.

Hirst, M. (2001) 'Journalism in Australia: hard yakka?', in S. Tapsall and C. Varley (eds) *Journalism: Theory in Practice*. South Melbourne: Oxford University Press, 55–70.

Holland, P. (2001) 'Authority and authenticity: redefining television current affairs', in M. Bromley (ed.) *No News is Bad News: Radio, Television and the Public*. Harlow: Longman, 80–95.

Hume, E. (1998) 'The weight of Watergate', in N.J. Woodhull and R.W. Snyder (eds) *Defining Moments in Journalism*. London: Transaction, 53–7.

IFEX (2006) 'IPI names murdered Russian journalist Anna Politkovskaya World Press Freedom Hero' (7 December). Press release posted at http://canada.ifex.org: accessed 2 July 2007.

Jensen, C. (2000) *Stories that Changed America: Muckrakers of the 20th Century*. New York: Seven Stories Press.

Kiss, J. (2007) 'CNET, journalists and the whole social net thing', *Guardian Unlimited* (17 January). Posted at http://blogs.guardian.co.uk/organgrinder: accessed 18 January 2007.

Knight, A. (2000) 'Online investigative journalism', *ejournalism* at http://www.ejournalism.au.com/ejournalist/inv.pdf: accessed 2 July 2007.

Knightley, P. (1998) 'The inside story of Philby's exposure', *British Journalism Review*, 9 (2), 35–40.

Knightley, P. (2005) 'Why we still need serious journalism', speech to the fourth members' meeting of the International Consortium of Investigative Journalists, London. Repro. in *New Matilda* (17 August) at www.newmatilda.com: accessed 1 July 2007.

Kovach, B. and Rosenstiel, T. (1999) *Warp Speed: America in the Age of Mixed Media.* New York: The Century Foundation Press.

Kovach, B. and Rosenstiel, T. (2001) *The Elements of Journalism: What Newspeople Should Know and the Public Should Expect.* New York: Crown.

Lambeth, E.B. (1992) *Committed Journalism: An Ethic for the Profession*, 2nd edn. Bloomington: Indiana University Press.

Lawe Davies, C. (1999) 'Journalism, corporatism, democracy', *Media International Australia*, 90, 53–64.

Leapman, M. (1993) 'The misanthropic media gurus', *British Journalism Review*, 4 (3), 54–5.

Leigh, D. (2000) 'Global disclosure', *MediaGuardian* (31 January). Posted at www.media.guardian.co.uk/mediaguardian/story/0,7558,358614,00.html: accessed 11 September 2001.

Liebling, A.J. (1961) *The Press.* New York: Ballantine.

Lih, A. (2004) 'The foundations of participatory journalism and the Wikipedia project'. Paper presented to the Association of Education in Journalism and Mass Communication conference, Toronto (7 August).

Linklater, M. (1993) 'An insight into Insight' *British Journalism Review*, 4 (2), 17–20.

McNair, B. (1998) *The Sociology of Journalism.* London: Arnold.

McQuade, J. (2006) 'Charles Lewis on the future of investigative journalism on the web', *newassignment.net* (20 November). Posted at http://www.newassignment.net/blog/john_mcquaid: accessed 2 July 2007.

McQuail, D. (2005) *McQuail's Mass Communication Theory*, 5th edn. London: Sage.

Malarek, V. (1998) 'What it takes to be an investigative reporter', in D. Logan (ed.) *Journalism in the New Millennium.* Vancouver: Sing Tao School of Journalism, 44–56.

Milner, A. (1994) *Cultural Theory: An Introduction.* London: UCL Press.

Neil, A. (1996) *Full Disclosure.* London: Macmillan.

Northmore, D. (1996) *Lifting the Lid: A Guide to Investigative Research.* London: Cassell.

Page, C. (2006) Journalists in the movies, *NewsHour*, PBS, 4 October 2006. Transcript posted at http://www.pbs.org/newshour/bb/entertainment/july-dec06/journalists_10–04.html: accessed 12 December 2007.

Pearson, M. (2002) 'The legal process', in S. Tanner (ed.) *Journalism Investigation & Research.* Frenchs Forest, NSW: Longman, 316–26.

Pierce Jones, V. (1988) *Saint or Sensationalist? The Story of W.T. Stead.* West Sussex: Gooday.

Pilger, J. (ed.) (2004) *Tell Me No Lies: Investigative Journalism and its Triumphs.* London: Jonathan Cape.

Protess, D., Lomax Cook, F., Gordon, M. and Ettema, J. (1991) *The Journalism of Outrage: Investigative Reporting and Agenda Building in America.* New York: Guilford.

Rampton, S. and Stauber, J. (2003) *Weapons of Mass Deception: The Uses of Propaganda in Bush's War on Iraq.* New York: Tarcher/Penguin.

Raphael, C., Tokunaga, L. and Wai, C. (2004) 'Who is the real target? Media response to controversial investigative reporting on corporations', *Journalism Studies*, 5 (2), 165–78.

Schudson, M. (1995) *The Power of News.* Cambridge, MA: Harvard University Press.

Schultz, J. (1998) *Reviving the Fourth Estate: Democracy, Accountability and the Media*. Melbourne: Cambridge University Press.

Serrin, W. and Serrin, J. (eds) (2002) *Muckraking! The Journalism that Changed Amercia*. New York: New Press.

Smythe, D.W. and Van Dihn, T. (1983) 'On critical and administrative research: a new critical analysis', *Journal of Communication* (Summer), 117–27.

Spark, D. (1999) *Investigative Reporting: A Study in Technique*. Oxford: Focal Press.

Stevenson, N. (1995) *Understanding Media Cultures: Social Theory and Mass Communication*. London: Sage.

Thompson, G. (2003) 'Introduction', *Transformations*, 7 (September). Posted at http://transformations.cqu.edu.au/journal/issue_07/article_02.shtml: accessed 21 May 2007.

Thompson, P. and Macklin, R. (2004) *The Man Who Died Twice: The Life and Adventures of Morrison of Peking*. Crows Nest, NSW: Allen & Unwin.

Tumber, H. (ed.) (1999) *News: A Reader*. Oxford: Oxford University Press.

Tumber, H. (2001) 'Democracy in the information age: the role of the Fourth Estate in cyberspace', *Information, Communication & Society*, 4 (1), 95–112.

Tumber, H. and Bromley, M. (1998) 'Virtual soundbites: political communication in cyberspace', *Media Culture and Society*, 20 (1), 159–67.

Ullmann, J. (1995) *Investigative Reporting: Advanced Methods and Techniques*. New York: St Martin's Press.

Ullmann, J. and Colbert, J. (1991) *The Reporter's Handbook: An Investigator's Guide to Documents and Techniques*, 2nd edn. New York: St Martin's Press.

Van Eijk, D. (ed.) (2005) *Investigative Journalism in Europe*. Amsterdam: Vereniging van Onderzoeksjournalisten.

Waisbord, S. (2000) *Watchdog Journalism in South America: News, Accountability and Democracy*. New York: Columbia University Press.

Ward, I. (2007) 'Mapping the Australian PR state', in S. Young (ed.) *Government Communication in Australia*. Port Melbourne: Cambridge University Press, 3–18.

Waterford, J. (2002) 'The editor's position', in S. Tanner (ed.) *Journalism Investigation & Research*. Frenchs Forest, NSW: Longman, 37–47.

Wiener, J.H. (1996) 'The Americanization of the British press, 1830–1914', in M. Harris and T. O'Malley (eds) *Studies in Newspaper and Periodical History: 1995 Annual*. Westport, CT: Greenwood, 61–74.

Williams, K. (2001) 'Demise or renewal? The dilemma of public service television in western Europe', in M. Bromley (ed.) *No News is Bad News: Radio, Television and the Public*. Harlow, Essex: Longman, 9–27.

Williams, K. (2003) *Understanding Media Theory*. London: Hodder Arnold.

Winston, B. (1998) *Media Technology and Society. A History: From the Telegraph to the Internet*. London: Routledge.

Woodress, J. (1987) *Willa Cather: A Literary Life*. Lincoln, NE: University of Nebraska Press.

Yau Fai Ho, D., Tin Hung Ho, R. and Siu Man Ng (2006) 'Investigative research as knowledge-generation method: discovering and uncovering', *Journal for the Theory of Social Behaviour*, 36 (1), 17–38.

Zelizer, B. (1992) *Covering the Body: The Kennedy Assassination, the Media and the Shaping of Collective Memory*. Chicago: University of Chicago Press.

Zelizer, B. (2004) *Taking Journalism Seriously: News and the Academy*. London: Sage.

Part II

CASES

11

FROM SHADOW BOXING TO
GHOST PLANE

English journalism and the War on Terror

Paul Lashmar

> In my career as a journalist, there has never been a war on terror but a
> war of terror.
>
> John Pilger.[1]

> In our time, political speech and writing are largely the defense of
> the indefensible. . . . This political language has to consist largely of
> euphemism, question-begging and sheer cloudy vagueness. Defence-
> less villages are bombed from the air, the inhabitants driven out into
> the countryside, the cattle machine-gunned, the huts set on fire with
> incendiary bullets: this is called pacification. Millions of peasants are
> robbed of their farms and sent trudging along roads with no more
> than they can carry: this is called transfer of population or rectifica-
> tion of frontiers. People are imprisoned for years without trial, or
> shot in the back of the neck . . . this is called elimination of unreliable
> elements. Such phraseology is needed if one wants to name things
> without calling up mental pictures of them.
>
> George Orwell, 'Politics and the English Language', 1946

Rendition

Arguably the finest example of investigative journalism during the 'war on
terror' has been the exposure of the Central Intelligence Agency's 'extraordinary
rendition' programme. Probing journalists, whose researches were encapsulated
in British journalist Stephen Grey's book *Ghost Plane* in 2006, have painstakingly identified over 1000 CIA 'ghost flights' criss-crossing the globe since
2001.[2] Many of these flights were for 'extraordinary rendition' where terror
suspects were secretly, without the suspect's agreement, taken by force from
one country to another and in some cases kidnapped.

Rendition flights have not been used to move suspects from war zones like
Afghanistan or Iraq to the United States where they might be charged and

tried. The receiving nation was not the US but a third country where the security services were sympathetic to the US and cooperative with the CIA. These third-party states are alleged to include Egypt, Jordan, Syria, Morocco and Uzbekistan. Suspects were then incarcerated, interrogated, and in many cases tortured to extract their alleged knowledge of al Qaeda. Some of the suspects have died in custody. It is estimated that at least one hundred 'suspects' have been 'rendered'.

Rendition is exactly the kind of practice that journalists exist to expose because it is extrajudicial, i.e. those operating rendition seek to avoid the normal processes of habeas corpus and trial, and nation states are abusing fundamental human rights.

As Bob Baer, a former CIA operative in the Middle East, has commented: 'If you want a serious interrogation you send a prisoner to Jordan. If you want them to be tortured you send them to Syria. If you want someone to disappear . . . you send them to Egypt.'[3]

The best documented and widely publicised case of extraordinary rendition is that of an Egyptian refugee in Italy named Osama Nasr, known more widely as Abu Omar.[4] Council of Europe investigator, Dick Marty, later described the abduction of Abu Omar as a 'perfect example of extraordinary rendition'.[5]

In 2003 Abu Omar was an Imam who had been granted asylum and was living in Italy. The Egyptians believed he belonged to al-Gama'a al-Islamiyya, an organisation they had designated as illegal as its aims are said to include the overthrow of the democratically elected Egyptian government. It is considered a terrorist organisation by the United States and European Union. Abu Omar was suspected by the US of plotting terrorist acts.

On 17 February 2003 Abu Omar was walking along the street in Milan on his way to noon prayers at the local mosque. As he strolled along the Via Guerzoni, he was kidnapped by a CIA snatch team and bundled into a car. Abu Omar was taken to the air base at Aviano. Later that day he was flown in a US Air Force jet to Ramstein airbase in Germany and there put on a CIA-hired aircraft and flown on to Egypt.

The CIA plane landed at Cairo and Abu Omar was put into the hands of Egyptian intelligence (the Mukhabarat). Abu Omar claimed he was tortured both by them and by State Security, Egypt's feared secret police. He was kept locked up for many months and, he says, torture ranged from hanging him upside down and applying electric shocks to genitals to putting him in a room where loud noise was played, damaging his hearing. He was interrogated as to whether he was an al Qaeda militant. Then after thirteen months he was suddenly released and told to keep his mouth shut. An Egyptian court had ruled his imprisonment was 'unfounded'.[6]

What his CIA abductors had not reckoned with was that independent Italian prosecutors would not ignore these events. Prompted and assisted by journalists from a range of countries they began an inquiry. As a result we now know that a group of Italian secret service officials colluded with the CIA in the kidnap of Abu Omar.[7] Twenty two European arrest warrants were issued in December 2005 and Italian security service (SISM) officers were among those arrested. The Italian judge also issued arrest warrants for four Americans, three CIA agents and a US Lieutenant Colonel who had been based at Aviano airport.

The start of the trial was set for June 8 2007, although it was adjourned until October 2007, pending an upcoming ruling by Italy's Constitutional Court regarding the possible violation of state secrecy laws by Milan prosecutors who used phone taps on Italian agents during their investigation.[8] Two other Italian suspects reached plea bargains.[9]

The Italian legal authorities have asked the United States for the extradition of a CIA operative involved with the kidnapping. While it is almost inconceivable that the United States will concede these extraditions, the request has caused the White House no little embarrassment. His lawyer says Abu Omar is now living in Egypt and has agreed to return to Italy to give evidence in the abduction trial.

Abu Omar's is only one of many cases of rendition, the details of which have been revealed as a result of painstaking forensic work by journalists.[10] Yet the United States continues to deny that it was engaged in rendition. Secretary of State Condoleezza Rice stated in an April 2006 radio interview that the United States does not transfer people to places where they know they will be tortured.[11]

The exposure of the CIA's extraordinary rendition programme and the collusion of other Governments around the world in this illegal and immoral practice has been one of the most successful episodes of investigative journalism in covering the 'war on terror' and its excesses.[12]

As *Ghost Plane* author Stephen Grey, whose work on rendition has been pre-eminent, says:

> The outlines of the CIA's rendition programme have emerged not from any single piece of reporting by a journalist or any single disclosure by a public official. Instead, details have come to light in a piecemeal fashion. Beat reporters like me who have followed this story have worked co-operatively – not in concert but by picking up pieces of the jigsaw puzzle disclosed by others, and then adding new pieces to the picture of what we know so far. Much more remains to be discovered.[13]
>
> (Grey, 2006)

Indeed the question remains as whether the CIA had a secret network of 'black' prisons in European and other countries, where suspects where held and tortured.

What is significant about the rendition story is that investigative journalists from around the world have cooperated in a way that has no precedent. For the reporting of the war on terror has shown that reports of the death of investigative journalism are premature. Good investigative journalism has been at the forefront of revealing both the iniquities of terrorism and also the parallel illegalities of the war on terror. But separating investigative journalism from other reporting, given the intense scrutiny of the war on terror, can be difficult. As we shall see, not all reporting of this dark and depressing period has been inspired.

There has been much discussion about an exact definition of investigative journalism. Elsewhere in this book Gavin MacFadyen identifies research as the one key essence that distinguishes investigative journalism from other reporting. Another vital ingredient is that this research should result in a highly accurate piece of journalism, which usually contains information that someone, typically in a position of power, does not want public. It should stand the test of time and be in the public interest.

What we can already say is that the landmark journalism on the rendition story was based on impressive research. The journalists involved went to great lengths to find and contact eyewitnesses, sources, participants, victims and experts. They obtained documents that were classified.

Stephen Grey made great use of thousands of flight records and was astonished that he could eventually obtain information on the exact movements of CIA planes.[14] He obtained these both from his own confidential source with access to European air traffic records but also a worldwide network of plane-spotters and information released to subscription aviation databases by the US Federal Aviation Administration. He also made sophisticated use of the relatively new art of computer-aided journalism. He used a specialist computer programme to analyse the raw data and separate from the millions of routine aircraft movements the flights flown by CIA front companies to transport 'suspects' illegally.

While rendition is a clear example of good investigative reporting, it is much harder to pick other examples in the complex and crowded media coverage of the war on terror in all its forms. Defining and separating investigative journalism from other reporting may appear on the surface to have the value of the arcane theological exercise of deciding how many angels can dance on the head of a pin. But the war on terror has produced so much poor and hasty reporting, and worse, disguised propaganda, that there is now a need for reflection on practices of contemporary journalism. In too many cases media organisations and journalists need to account for their past failings before the media can regain public trust in their reporting.

Covering the war on terror has been among the most difficult and demanding jobs in journalism in recent history. Domestically, the probing journalist is up against the wilderness of mirrors created by the intelligence agencies and politicians. Terrorists are by their very nature secretive and their hinterlands, whether at home or abroad, are potentially dangerous places to operate. Covering

Afghanistan, Iraq and the battlefields of this war has been more dangerous for journalists than any war before.

War on terror

The terror attacks of 11 September 2001 were a watershed, not least for the media. Before the attacks news organisations were hardly curious about the Muslim world. That changed instantly after 9/11 and the interest became instant and intense, with any subsequent lack of concentration refocused by another terror attack or political or military excess.

With hindsight, the warning signs had been there but few in the media wanted to see them, confirming again the conformism of many media organisations in the West. Prior to 9/11 there had been an escalation of terror attacks aimed at Western targets, emanating from fundamentalist terror groups coalescing around the leadership of former Saudi citizen and former mujahedeen Osama bin Laden. These included the attacks on United States embassies in East Africa and the sea-borne attack on the USS *Cole* off Yemen. There had been some reporting and some investigative journalism of these developments but certainly it was generally perceived in the UK media as far from centre stage news.

With the hijacked airliners caught on video as they ploughed into the World Trade Center, the drama and impact of the attacks and 2,950 deaths on 11 September 2001 really justify use of the expression 'new paradigm'. The world was suddenly a very different place. Global attention fixed on a few acres of smouldering earth and rubble in the centre of Manhattan. The search, by governments and media alike, for the perpetrators of this unparalleled act of terror, began instantly. All knew that America would respond with force; the only question was how that revenge would be framed. Within weeks in his address to a joint session of Congress following the attacks on September 11, US President George W. Bush defined a 'war on terror':

> Our war on terror begins with al Qaeda, but it does not end there. It will not end until every terrorist group of global reach has been found, stopped and defeated.[15]

> (Bush, 2001)

In retrospect we can see the tone of reporting after 9/11 was set in reaction to the horror of the event which muted objective reporting. There was some critical reporting on whether the United States should have been better prepared and whether early warning of the attacks had been ignored by the US authorities. But it was the exception rather than the rule.

Sir Harold Evans, the former *Sunday Times* Editor and New York resident, would later point to a string of failures by the American press, most especially in the months prior to 9/11. He was scathing about the fact that 'not a single major newspaper' took seriously enough the February 2001 report by Senators Rudman and Hart which gave warnings about the likelihood of a terrorist attack.

He conceded that following 9/11 a wave of patriotism in the US made criticism and dissent much harder. He said: 'I felt rage myself. I was in New York'. But it required the press to stand back and take stock rather than be caught up in the emotion.[16]

There can be few events in history that have attracted as much media coverage as 9/11 and the events stemming from it. How much of that coverage was objective and could be described as investigative is more complicated. Investigative journalism usually thrives in places where there is little or no serious reporting. After 9/11 every decent journalist wanted to be engaged in what was clearly to be the most important story of the decade.

US journalists became preoccupied with a domestic story, the discovery of anthrax in various government buildings. For months reports suggested a range of suspects from Iraqis to al Qaeda.[17]

In the wake of 9/11 various conspiracy theories emerged, mostly suggesting that the US government covertly organised the attacks. Some conspiracy theorists have claimed that the collapse of the World Trade Center was the result of a controlled demolition. Some also contend that a commercial airliner did not crash into the Pentagon, and that United Airlines Flight 93 was shot down. Few of these claims, however, were taken seriously by mainstream journalists and were largely confined to the alternative media. Over time none of these theories have yet been shown to be compelling.[18] As wise minds are wont to observe: If you can't trust your own media to tell you the truth you are more likely to believe in conspiracies.

Many western journalists looked to the Muslim world, trying to establish the extent of the al Qaeda network and threat. In the atmosphere of shock and revenge the media were often uncritical if not outright supportive of the American-led invasion of Afghanistan in the same month and the removal of al Qaeda's mentors, the Taliban, from government.

In the UK, investigative activity concentrated on the links between the 9/11 plotters and their relationship with Britain. When a British national and a convert to Islam, Richard Reid, was arrested in December 2001 on a transatlantic flight after having attempted to set off a bomb in his shoe, the focus for the UK media began to shift to the threat within the UK.[19]

The world was taking on a new, more sinister shape, not least for inquiring journalists. 'In the year since the September 11 attacks on the United States, the world has become a more uncertain place', said Aidan White of the International Federation of Journalists at the end of 2002. 'The declaration of "a war on terrorism" by the United States and its international coalition has created a dangerous situation in which journalists have become victims as well as key actors in reporting events.'[20]

Following what then appeared to be the efficient and effective regime change in Afghanistan, the US and UK governments brought the repressive dictatorship of Saddam Hussein under intense scrutiny and criticism. There was a feeling that the West had failed to tackle Saddam Hussein effectively at the end of the first Gulf War. But more pressing were the links to be made between Saddam and bin Laden that would justify an invasion.[21]

From late 2001 we see the campaign by those governments to persuade their public and world opinion that Saddam Hussein had links with al Qaeda and that he was developing Weapons of Mass Destruction (WMD) that threatened US, UK and Western interests. These government claims were largely supported by media. While no one doubted the barbarity of Saddam's regime, many journalists took the extra step and accepted the neo-conservative perspective of Iraq as the dominant global threat.

Observers worried about the media's coverage after 9/11. Aidan White's report for the International Federation of Journalists observed that media reporting in the UK tended to follow the political direction of the Government and was very pro American: after September 11 this tendency overrode everything else. Reporting the war aims of the coalition was uncritical and for a month or two dissenting voices were bitterly attacked.

> However, it must be stated that there has been some excellent coverage, and not just in the obvious paper, the *Guardian*, the leading liberal paper. In particular the *Daily Mirror*, the second highest circulating national paper, which had been totally 'Blairite', converted itself to a critical position in March 2002 and has run some critical coverage, which has been widely welcomed among journalists.[22]
>
> (White, 2002)

White made a prescient comment:

> But the media need to resist the pressure of politicians who are willing to sacrifice civil liberties and press freedom to win their propaganda battles. The priority must always be the right to publish words and images – however unpalatable – that help people better understand the roots of the conflict.
>
> (ibid.: 2)

Columnist George Monbiot later commented that the government position found support in surprising places. The *Observer*, he pointed out, published five articles claiming that there were 'direct Iraqi links with the US hijackers' who carried out the 9/11 attacks.[23] One of them suggested that 'Iraqi training, intelligence and logistics were hidden behind Islamist façade'. Iraq, it claimed 'ran a terrorist camp for foreign Islamists, where it taught them how to hijack planes with boxcutters'.[24]

The worst offender, Monbiot claimed, was the *Sunday Telegraph* with a range of articles. For example, in September 2001, it opined that 'the Iraqi leader had been providing al-Qaeda . . . with funding, logistical back-up and advanced weapons training. His operations reached a "frantic pace" in the past few months.'[25]

Brutality – warning bells unheeded

As in all wars, at the sharp end the military often did not behave in keeping with the high moral tone struck by their political leaders. In December 2002 came the first of what would become a long stream of allegations of brutality by allied forces towards prisoners in the war on terror. A *Washington Post* article by Dana Priest and Barton Gellman exposed the abuse of al Qaeda and Taliban prisoners, detailing a 'brass-knuckled quest for information' that includes 'stress and duress techniques.'

> 'Americans with direct knowledge and others who have witnessed the treatment', the Post reported, said that 'captives are often "softened up" by MPs and US Army Special forces troops who beat them up and then confine them in tiny rooms'. The paper also made an early mention of the practice of 'extraordinary renditions' – shipping prisoners to countries where they can be tortured more freely. One official who was 'directly involved' explained: 'We don't kick the [expletive] out of them. We send them to other countries so they can kick the [expletive] out of them.[26]
>
> (Priest and Gellman, 2002)

Little attention was paid to this story of brutality with its hint of the shape of things to come. In late 2002 the media's reporting focused on the increasing tension between the international team of weapons inspectors and the US Government.

Leading campaigning journalist John Pilger was already alarmed:

> The attempts by journalists in the US and Britain, acting as channels for American intelligence, to connect Iraq to 11 September have also failed. The 'Iraq connection' with anthrax has been shown to be rubbish; the culprit is almost certainly American. The rumour that an Iraqi intelligence official met Mohammed Atta, the 11 September hijacker, in Prague was exposed by Czech police as false. Yet press 'investigations' that hint, beckon, erect a straw man or two, then draw back, while giving the reader the overall impression that Iraq requires a pasting, have become a kind of currency. One reporter added his 'personal view' that 'the use of force is both right and sensible'.[27]
>
> (Pilger, 2002)

In September the UK government published a dossier, based on material from British intelligence, making the case that Saddam and Iraq had weapons of mass destruction. It had a foreword by then British Prime Minister Tony Blair which said:

> The document discloses that his military planning allows for some of the WMD to be ready within 45 minutes of an order to use them.[28]

> (Blair, 2003)

On 24 September 2002 Prime Minister Tony Blair told MPs the intelligence revealed that Saddam Hussein 'has existing and active military plans for the use of chemical and biological weapons, which could be activated within 45 minutes, including against his own Shia population'.[29] The *Evening Standard* carried the headline '45 minutes from attack'. The *Sun* carried the headline 'Brits 45 mins from doom' about the threat to troops in Cyprus.

In early February, televised briefings by US Secretary for State Colin Powell at the UN detailed 'evidence' of weapons of mass destruction within Iraq which were largely accepted by the media. Powell pointed to blown-up aerial spy pictures purporting to show Saddam's mobile biological warfare production facilities.

Powell drew on the British Government's second dossier on Iraq published in February 2003.[30] It is worth noting that a week later the Government's dossier was exposed by Glen Rangwala, a Cambridge academic and writer who has excellent investigative skills, to have been an extensive piece of plagiarism, mostly of old material. The Cabinet Office authors had lazily lifted material from three different sources on the internet, most extensively from a postgraduate at the Monterey Institute. This 'cut and paste' document was given the lasting sobriquet the 'dodgy dossier'.[31]

As part of their case both the British and American governments made much of the earlier arrest of an alleged terrorist cell claimed to be planning a lethal ricin poison[32] attack in Britain. After the arrest of six men in 2002 in what was known as the 'ricin plot', the *Sun* claimed: 'The men are thought to be linked to fanatical Algerian Islamic groups which are part of Osama bin Laden's al Qaeda network.'[33]

Prime Minister Blair, David Blunkett, then minister responsible for internal security, and British senior police officers, emphasised that the plot was a threat from what they called a new and highly dangerous kind of terrorist. To back up their case for war, politicians suggested there was a clear link between Saddam Hussein, al Qaeda, and terrorists planning chemical or biological attacks on targets in the west, including London.

The ricin claims were used most strikingly by Colin Powell, the US Secretary of State, in his UN speech. Insisting 'every statement I make today is backed up by sources, solid sources', Powell spoke of a 'sinister nexus between Iraq and the al Qaeda terrorist network'. (These British and American claims were to look very different after the court case in 2005.[34])

So it was these government presentations that set the tone for the launch of the second Gulf War. On 7 March 2003 Hans Blix, who had been recalled by Kofi Annan to head the United Nations Monitoring, Verification and Inspection Commission, told the Security Council that a series of searches had found no evidence of mobile biological production facilities in Iraq. This received little media coverage.

On 20 March American missiles bombed Baghdad, marking the start of a US-led war to topple Saddam Hussein. In the following days US and British ground troops entered Iraq from the south.

By 9 April US forces had advanced into central Baghdad. Saddam Hussein's hold on the city was broken. On 1 May 2003 George W. Bush landed on the aircraft carrier *Abraham Lincoln*. A huge poster hung from the ship's bridge proclaiming 'Mission accomplished'. In the subsequent press conference to the world the US President declared that 'major combat operations in Iraq have ended'. 'The Battle for Iraq,' he added, 'is one victory in a war on terror that began on September the 11th 2001 and still goes on.'[35]

The Hutton inquiry

Reporting in Britain in the immediate post invasion period was greatly influenced by a confrontation between the BBC and the government. On 29 May 2003 BBC Radio 4's *Today* programme defence correspondent Andrew Gilligan said in a early morning two-way interview that he had a senior source, who had said the 45-minute claim was the 'classic example' of how the dossier was 'sexed up'.[36]

Regarded as a talented investigator with the ability to conduct deep research, Gilligan had been probing the government's case for war. The Prime Minister's Office especially objected when the BBC reporter said that the Prime Minister's Office 'probably knew' the claim was wrong when it was put in the dossier.

It was the Prime Minister's Head of Communications (and right-hand man), Alistair Campbell, who took Gilligan's allegations most personally. Campbell was, to use that colourful cliché, 'incandescent with rage'. On the 6 June he sent a four-page denunciation of Gilligan's reporting to BBC Director of News Richard Sambrook.

Campbell's letter ends with:

> On the word of a single, uncorroborated source, you have allowed one reporter to drive the BBC's coverage. We are left wondering why you have the guidelines at all, given they are so persistently breached without any comeback whatsoever.
>
> (Campbell, 2003)

Over the next few weeks a battle of wills raged. The Prime Minister's Office demanded an apology and the BBC refused to give it. The strength of reaction from the Prime Minister's Office against the BBC over this broadcast was compelling. It influenced not only BBC correspondents but other journalists' views on the claims for the existence of WMD. The Foreign Office and other government departments continued to brief that there were WMD in Iraq and this remained the overriding priority for war.

But then the drama cranked up when, on 17 July, the apparent source of Gilligan's claim, government scientist David Kelly, was found dead. By most accounts he had committed suicide, following his treatment by Parliamentary investigators and by his civil service colleagues. Prime Minister Blair quickly proposed an independent judicial inquiry 'urgently to conduct an investigation into the circumstances surrounding the death of Dr Kelly'.

To conduct the inquiry Blair chose Lord Hutton, a senior judge. A key witness was John Scarlett, the head of the leading branch of British intelligence services, MI6, who defended the controversial 45-minute claim at the inquiry, calling it 'well-sourced intelligence' but saying it concerned munitions, mortar shells or similar weapons, not missile warheads.

When he reported in January 2004 Lord Hutton was very critical of the BBC's journalism and management of news.[37] Among the inquiry's conclusions were:

- the BBC claim that Downing Street 'sexed-up' the dossier on Iraqi weapons was 'unfounded'.
- Reporter Andrew Gilligan was wrong to claim Number 10 inserted intelligence knowing it was suspect.

Lord Hutton went further, calling BBC editorial procedures that allowed the report to be broadcast 'defective'. Worse for the Corporation, he criticised both managers and governors for not investigating the government's complaints quickly and fully. After Lord Hutton reported, Alistair Campbell made his feelings clear: 'If the Government faced the level of criticism . . . which today Lord Hutton has directed to [*sic*] the BBC, there would clearly have been resignations by now. Several resignations at several levels. Today the stain on the integrity of the prime minister and the government has been removed.'[38]

Despite initial resistance, within days both the Chairman of the BBC Governors Gavin Davies and the BBC Director General Greg Dyke resigned. Andrew Gilligan departed too. What did surprise many observers was not Lord Hutton's criticism of the BBC but his reticence to criticise the way the government had operated, especially over the writing of the Iraq dossier.[39] The Hutton inquiry served, at the very least, to distract the media from events in the Middle East and Iraq in particular. There was for time a dampening of the media's spirit of inquiry into the circumstances around the invasion of Iraq.

The Hutton affair left the BBC vulnerable. Many felt the humbled organisation was avoiding any further confrontation with the government. It was open season for attacks on the BBC for lacking patriotism. It is notable that the rest of the media were harshly critical of the BBC's failing, yet in most cases their own reporting standards, especially in newspapers, would not have withstood the same intense scrutiny.

Over the next few months the BBC came under attack by politicians and some of the media for its alleged anti-war coverage. The perfidy of these attacks was demonstrated by a later Cardiff University report that showed that the BBC 'displayed the most "pro-war" agenda of any broadcaster'.[40]

The BBC has also been criticised for being too pro-government. One target was the BBC's flagship current affairs programme, *Panorama*, whose investigation had provided support for the government's position prior to the Iraq invasion. In the *Australian Financial Review*, Brian Toohey, his country's most distinguished investigative journalist, reminded readers that *Panorama* on 23 September 2002 claimed to have 'hard evidence' about Iraq's weapons of mass destruction. 'It did no such thing', wrote Toohey. 'Instead, it presented a load of nonsense which bolstered the case for subsequent invasion.' One of the programme's prime sources was an Iraqi, Adnan Seead al-Haideri, whom it described as 'credible'. He claimed that a secret biological weapons laboratory existed under a major hospital in Baghdad.[41]

The programme's reporter Jane Corbin summed up: 'So the new weapons and technology have been hidden away in heavily populated areas, even under a hospital in Baghdad according to Haideri. Beneath Saddam's many presidential palaces too, and weapons are constantly on the move to outwit the vigilant spy planes.'

'Haideri's most harrowing account comes from people forced to work inside the secret weapons programme. They've told him Saddam's ordered the testing of chemical weapons on prisoners.'[42]

John Pilger commented: 'That edition of *Panorama* was not untypical of the BBC's coverage of the build-up to the invasion, and the "war on terror", or indeed any war fought or supported by the British establishment in living memory.'[43] Pilger also cites a Cardiff University report stating that 90 per cent of the BBC's references to weapons of mass destruction suggested that Saddam Hussein actually possessed them.[44]

In the New Year of 2004 *Panorama* transmitted a programme on the Hutton Inquiry that was critical of their former colleague, Andrew Gilligan. Reporter John Ware concluded: 'The BBC still insists it got its story largely right – despite some flawed reporting.'[45]

The same team some weeks later went on to analyse the intelligence failure that had led to the Iraq war. At the end of the programme, reporter John Ware said:

> The war has been over for 15 months. Iraqis have been liberated from a tyrant. But the military objective was to disarm him of his weapons of mass destruction. No weapons have yet been found. The cost has

been countless injured and perhaps 11,000 dead. But already a key bit of the case for war has officially been withdrawn by MI6. We've been told by a reliable intelligence source whose identity we have to protect, that MI6 no longer trusts its report that underpinned the dossier's claim that 'Iraq has continued to produce chemical and biological agents'.[46]

(Ware, 2004)

To this day seasoned reporters from across the media consider that the BBC and C4 current affairs departments lost their nerve in the wake of the Hutton inquiry. Some say the BBC would not tackle controversial subjects. Some insiders say this lasted a year after Hutton, others say longer.

There is broad view that both organisations failed to deliver as broad a range of challenging programmes on the war on terror that you might have expected. Executives of both organisations I have spoken to deny such claims. BBC Journalists are categorical that the BBC avoided controversial items on Iraq in the months after Hutton. BBC editors now deny lack of post-Hutton journalistic vigour. But BBC journalists often disagree. One told me that his editors: 'genuinely seem to have convinced themselves like a bunch of UFO alien abductees'.

The truth will out

The tide was turning; the government and intelligence service's credibility further plummeted after the failure to find any WMD in Iraq. By September 2004 Foreign Secretary Jack Straw was also forced to admit to Parliament that MI6 had withdrawn the 45 minute claim.

Meanwhile in the United States the justifications for the invasion were also being unpicked.[47] The United States also had it own scandal, a complicated affair centring around the *New York Times* reporter Judith Miller, who had been at the forefront of reporting the existence of WMD in Iraq. It later turned out that her sources consisted of officials close to the neo-conservatives at the heart of the Bush administration and also the Chalabi camp of exiled Iraqis, now discredited for providing unreliable intelligence from within Iraq.[48]

Meanwhile British public attention was dramatically drawn to more domestic aspects of terrorism. After 9/11 there was little doubt that the UK was a target for al Qaeda-inspired terrorism. There was clear and increasing danger from bin Laden's supporters looking to attack high-profile targets in the UK.

Initially the concern was that attacks would be conducted by non-indigenous Muslims. MI5 sought potential terror plots among those who were citizens of the Middle East and North Africa, while not discounting the odd indigenous maverick in the shoe bomber mould.

Following the raid on the Finsbury Park mosque in January 2001, the

Evening Standard reported: 'Scotland Yard is now liaising with French and American intelligence agencies in connection with recent arrests. Other North African countries are also believed to be involved in the terror conspiracy. Members of the Libyan Islamic Fighting Group as well as Tunisians with links to extremist groups are believed to be under investigation.'[49]

But as plot after plot was detected attention moved to British-born terror suspects. Britain's involvement with the Iraq invasion and its perceived anti-Islamic stance clearly provoked some young indigenous Muslims to align themselves with al Qaeda.

The result was the 7/7[50] and 21/7[51] attacks of 2005 which appeared to be organised entirely by 'home grown' Muslims.[52] The Prime Minister and his cabinet maintained that his alliance with the US and the invasion of Iraq had played no part in the radicalisation of British-born Muslims. To their credit much of the media has never accepted this perverse political logic.

Meanwhile back in Iraq . . .

Reports from Iraq after the invasion were producing a string of stories alleging brutality by British troops during and after the invasion period. Many troops were later to face court martial. But attention was beginning to focus on US internment camps. The key camp was Abu Ghraib, also known as the Baghdad Correctional Facility, which housed prisoners suspected of Baathist and al Qaeda connections and was staffed by US military intelligence units, notably the 372nd Military Police Company.

In the one of the first reports the *Associated Press* said that detainees in Iraq were being subjected to torture and inhumane living conditions and told of an instance where a prisoner was shot and killed. The article reported the story of one prisoner, Saaed Naif, who said he saw another prisoner 'shot dead at Abu Ghraib when he approached the razor wire'. Many former prisoners of the detainment centers agreed that some of the worst atrocities at the prisons were the guards' treatment of the women, sick, and disabled.[53]

The full horror of Abu Ghraib was to be told by Seymour Hersh in the *New Yorker* magazine.[54] As journalist Nick Davies points out, Seymour Hersh's investigative reporting on the war on terror has been exemplary, not least on Abu Ghraib:

> Generally, Seymour Hersh has been there way out in front of just everybody and although CBS ran the Abu Ghraib pictures before him, its clear they were dithering and eventually put them out only because they heard that he was about to run them in the New Yorker.[55]
>
> (Davies, 2007)

The photographs of Lynndie England, Charles Graner and other American military personnel degrading Iraqi detainees, in so casual yet so debasing a way, caused immeasurable worldwide damage to the United States' claims to morality of purpose in Iraq. In its pursuit of a war on terror the Bush Administration has been accused of acting in violation of international law, human rights, and the US Constitution in its execution of the campaign, particularly with regard to the internment of prisoners of war (or 'illegal combatants') in its military prison at Guantánamo Bay, Cuba.

In Iraq the situation after the invasion gradually deteriorated. Investigations by the media show that neither the US or UK had thought through their post-invasion strategy. The main beneficiaries were corrupt Iraqis in positions of power and the Western private security companies who were paid hundreds of millions of dollars to protect key installations and personnel.[56]

The insurgency grew in strength and increasingly Iraq was referred to as suffering a Civil War. The media received no special treatment or quarter. Most news organisations were forced to remain in a specially protected 'Green Zone' in Baghdad for fear of kidnapping, torture and murder.

Reporting in Iraq has on the occasion shown again the difficulties of separating out investigative reporting from other good reporting. There has been some exceptional revealing and courageous reporting from foreign correspondents on the ground.

As Noam Chomsky commented:

> The scale of the catastrophe in Iraq is so extreme that it can barely be reported. Journalists are largely confined to the heavily fortified Green Zone in Baghdad, or else travel under heavy guard. There are a few regular exceptions in the mainstream press, such as Robert Fisk and Patrick Cockburn, who face extreme hazards, and there are occasional indications of Iraqi opinion.[57]
>
> (Chomsky, 2006)

Reporters have taken tremendous personal risk to deliver detailed and disturbing reports on the failure of the US-led alliance to transform Iraq into a peaceful democratic society. These reporters are seen as foreign correspondents but their work is heavily researched and accurate.

Head of current affairs at C4, Dorothy Byrne, says:

> Our key pieces on Iraq have tended not to be investigations (although we have made good films like *Iraq's Missing Billions*) but reportage and analysis. It has been so difficult to show what is really happening in Iraq that this form of current affairs – working with Iraqis to show the truth on the ground – has been important and influential. Politicians have tried to claim that there was not civil war and finding ways to get out there and show people just how normal civil society was falling apart has been key.[58]
>
> (Byrne, 2007)

Investigations

For this chapter I conducted a straw poll of some of the UK's investigative reporters and editors. The question I asked was: 'What do you think is the most important contribution investigative journalism has brought to the Iraq War and the war on terror coverage in the last couple of years?' I asked them to look from a primarily a UK perspective.

A number of stories were repeatedly cited. Top of that list by far was the coverage of 'extraordinary rendition'. There was also general agreement that former *Sunday Times* journalist Stephen Grey has undertaken outstanding work on rendition. The approach to the rendition story has moved the practice of investigative journalism a step forward, in a variety of ways including innovative use of computer-aided journalism and cooperation by journalists in many different countries. Stephen Grey has shown how an effective freelance investigative journalist can work across the media and national boundaries. It shows that journalists can improvise a global response to stories that transcend any one country.

Another important story that was acclaimed in the straw poll was former *Daily Telegraph* defence correspondent Michael Smith's 'Downing Street memo' story.[59] This was the leak of a document clearly from a highly placed source revealing that Tony Blair was intent on an invasion of Iraq much earlier than he had admitted. But this story raises an interesting point. Using Gavin MacFadyen's criteria of research, this story is a leak and is difficult to see it as investigative reporting. An excellent example of leak-based journalism and a great piece of journalism but not an investigation.

The importance of this and other documents leaked from Whitehall was summed up later by the *Guardian*'s security editor, Richard Norton-Taylor:

> The full extent of Tony Blair's mendacity over the invasion of Iraq has been emphatically revealed in classified Downing Street documents leaked since the invasion. They make up a devastating indictment of the way we were led into an adventure with the US whose bloody consequences show no sign of relenting.[60]
>
> (Norton-Taylor, 2007)

Other UK stories suggested include:

* The exposure as false of the claim that Saddam Hussein had sought 'yellowcake' unrefined uranium ore from Niger as part of a nuclear weapon development programme. *The Independent on Sunday*'s coverage has been influential.[61]
* Revealing the Attorney General's advice on the Iraqi invasion, a story which Channel 4 News excelled at. C4 News obtained a leak of the vital advice to then Prime Minister Tony Blair on which the nation had

gone to war. The leak revealed the Attorney General's original advice was full of caveats that were stripped out of the summary he gave to Parliament.

- BBC2's nightly current affairs programme *Newsnight* has produced some illuminating reports, not least that suicide bomber Mohammed Siddique Khan was under surveillance by the security services a year before the 7/7 suicide attacks.[62]

- Reporting of troop shortages, kit shortages and failure to provide 'hard skinned' transport for military operations in both Afghanistan and Iraq.[63]

- The exposure of the rescue of female US soldier Private Jessica Lynch during the Iraq invasion as false and a US military PR exercise.[64]

Alex Thomson of C4 News believes that media coverage of military operations has highlighted political failures: 'In Afghanistan the persistent inquiry into general overstretch and under-supply of critical equipment in both Afghanistan firstly and Iraq too has been very effective in calling the government to account and I suspect – created the climate of unsackability which allows people like Dannant [the British General in command – ed.] to say what they said.'[65, 66]

Much coverage of the US government's Guantanamo Bay detention camp on Cuba has been driven by British journalists, including David Rose at the *Observer*, although some US colleagues have undertaken fine investigations.[67]

Stories by US journalists, which should particularly be taken into account, include:

The exposure of the Bush administration exaggeration and misuse of intelligence provided by the informant 'Curveball', an Iraqi defector was written by Bog Drogin and John Goetz in the *Los Angeles Times*.[68] The investigation revealed that the source claiming to have seen mobile bio-weapons labs was the brother of one of the senior aides to Ahmed Chalabi, the leader of the Iraqi National Congress, who boasted how the erroneous information provided by his group achieved his long-cherished goal of toppling Saddam.

Curveball was an asset of German intelligence and was never directly interviewed by US officials. The Pentagon and the Central Intelligence Agency did not even know exactly who he was, the *LA Times* reported.[69] This first-hand intelligence source on Saddam Hussein's alleged mobile bio-weapons labs was a politically motivated Iraqi defector now dismissed as an 'out-and-out fabricator'. The mobile labs, since exposed by weapons inspectors as hydrogen production facilities at best and phantoms at worst, were one of the centrepieces of the US Secretary of State Colin Powell's pre-war address to the United Nations.

Discussion

There are many questions about the reporting of the 'war on terror'. Could the British media have warned the public before the Iraq invasion that there were no WMD? In the face of such relentless government claims that WMD existed it was hard to challenge. Perhaps the best response on WMD comes from Hans Blix, the UN Weapons Inspector who was later vilified by the US for not finding WMD. 'In the autumn of 2002 I still thought there were Weapons of Mass Destruction'. As he pointed out it is hard to prove a negative. But he went on to say: 'It is extraordinary that the intelligence services of the World's most advanced nations made such a major error.'[70]

It is clear that reporting of the war on terror has not always been of the highest standard, sometimes it was plain wrong and sometimes it hid behind the coattails of unidentified sources.

Perhaps the most controversial piece of investigative reporting in the UK was Andrew Gilligan's famous report. Many reporters believe that Gilligan's methods were not always proper or professional and he put the source in danger of exposure. Hutton came down hard on the fact that Gilligan had relied heavily on one source. But many experienced investigative reporters feel that while the two source rule should apply generally, when it comes to covering intelligence an exception can be made by experienced reporters. To have one high-level intelligence source is no small achievement. Other reporters were also getting worried source reports from within the intelligence service on the same grounds.[71] If the hurdle was set at two sources it would dramatically restrict coverage of this important subject of the intelligence services. If we have learnt anything from war on terror it is that intelligence services are politically influenced and capable of making major errors. They, almost more than any other organisation, need the scrutiny of the investigative reporter to make sure they do not abuse their exclusive powers.

No better can this be demonstrated than by the difficulty journalists have in establishing whether MI5 knew of links between the terror cell that were caught making a fertiliser bomb and the 7/7 suicide bombers. MI5's briefed in late 2005 that Mohammed Siddique Khan, the leader of the 7/7 bombers had been identified months before the suicide bombings only on the 'periphery' of the fertiliser bomb cell.[72] It now looks like the Police and MI5 had many more leads on Khan than they admitted. This leaves the question – are they hiding other key facts. Should MI5 have prevented 7/7?

As Gilligan pointed out there are many stories that we simply have not been able to investigate. 'What has happened on Diego Garcia?' he asks.[73] The British protectorate of Diego Garcia in the Indian Ocean is a secret base and journalists have no access. It also has an air base and military facilities. It has been associated with the rendition operations. But no one has been able to establish what the base has been used for and whether terror suspects have been held there.

Four years on, how does Gilligan's story, perhaps the best-remembered piece of journalism so far in the war on terror, stand the test of time? Now, few would seriously contest his central point that the government's dossier claiming Iraq had WMD was 'sexed up'. As Gilligan pointed out in an interview for this chapter, the government in their initial counterattack claimed to be angry because he accused it of lying. This he points out he never did. The obvious implication is that the attack on Gilligan was a device to frighten the BBC and curtail criticism. It may have worked.

And that bring us onto a key point. One overarching observation has to be made about the media reporting of the war on terror. Even if you have high quality and consistent reporting, investigative or otherwise, that shows that a government has misled the public and made errors of judgement on a truly epic scale, if the executive has an overwhelming electoral majority it can withstand such criticism.

In the UK, if the quality of reporting has been varied over the last six years, good journalists including investigative journalists made a compelling case that Prime Minister Blair and his successors in government have committed a most serious foreign policy disaster. Reporters have shown conclusively that Blair and his cabinet were either fools or knaves in the way we were enrolled into the war on terror. Even now it is hard to discern whether Blair did or did not believe that there were WMD in Iraq. Yet the Labour Government remains in power, Tony Blair has chosen his own time to retire. You could equally say the same for President Bush in the United States. Here we have sobering examples of the limitations on the power of the media at a point when it was most necessary.

Notes

1 On 14 April 2006, the Heyman Center for the Humanities at Columbia University in New York brought together John Pilger, Seymour Hersh, Robert Fisk and Charles Glass for a discussion entitled 'Breaking the Silence: War, Lies and Empire'.

2 Grey, S. (2006) *Ghost Plane: The Inside Story of the CIA's Secret Rendition Programme*. London: Hurst & Company, p. vii.

3 Grey, S. (2004) 'US accused of "torture flights" ', *Sunday Times*, London, 14 November 2004.

4 Full given name: Hassan Mustafa Osama Nasr, born 18 March 1963.

5 Willey, D. (2007) 'Italy secrets Threaten CIA trial', BBC *News*, 8 June 2007.

6 Nasrawi, S. (2007) 'Egyptian kidnap victim "was tortured" ', *Independent News*, 13 February 2007.

7 *Ghost Plane*, pp. 170–90.

8 (2007) 'CIA trial in Italy delayed to October', *The Middle East Times*, 24 June 2007.

9 (2007) (AP Story) 'Italy indicts 31 linked to CIA rendition case', *International Herald Tribune*, 16 February 2007.

10 *Ghost Plane*, pp. 170–90.

11 Naughtie, J. (2006) Interview of Secretary Rice With British Foreign Secretary Jack Straw. BBC Radio 4's *Today* Programme, 1 April 2006.

12 European government including the British have been suspected of discretely assisting the CIA by allowing the flights to use their airports.

13 *Ghost Plane*, p. vii.

14 Grey, S. (2007) email to Paul Lashmar, 19 September 2007.

15 'President Declares Freedom at War with Fear' http://www.whitehouse.gov/news/releases/2001/09/print/20010920–8.html

16 Evans, Sir H. (2006) 'Journalism under pressure', reporting terrorism speech by Sir Harold Evans, IPI world congress, Edinburgh.

17 Six years on the culprit has never been conclusively identified.

18 Some of the wilder conspiracy theories grew out of legitimate reporting. For instance just after 9/11 Greg Palast and Meirion Jones of BBC2's *Newsnight* programme were handed a secret FBI report showing that they'd been investigating the Bin Laden family but had been taken off the case both under Clinton and Bush. The agents were furious. What particularly annoyed the agents was that the Bin Ladens had been flown out of the US without proper questioning as soon as the 'no-fly' ban had been lifted. The story got coverage in the UK but didn't suit the legend that was being created in the US at the time. Later the conspiracy theorists got hold of it and their version is that the Bin Ladens were flown out during the 'no-fly' ban which of course is unlikely.

19 According to al Qaeda operative Mohammed Mansour Jabarah (who was captured and interrogated in Oman in 2003), Reid was a member of al-Qaeda and had been sent on the bombing mission by Khaled Shaikh Mohammed, a senior member of the organisation.

20 White, A. (2002) 'Journalism and the War on Terrorism: Final Report of the Aftermath of September 11 and the implications for Journalism and Civil Liberties', *International Federation of Journalists*, p. 2, 3 September 2002.

21 When did the 'War against terror' become a campaign against Saddam Hussein rather than Osama bin Laden? Less than a month after the September 2001 attacks on the World Trade Centre and the Pentagon, some hawkish members of the US administration were stressing a connection with Iraq, but the shift did not become clear until George Bush's State of the Union address in January 2002, when the 'axis of evil' was unveiled. Suddenly Baghdad was in the frame, and al Qaeda took a temporary back seat. For some months the name of Bin Laden was hardly referred to by President Bush. He name-checked al Qaeda in the 2003 State of the Union speech but its leader was not mentioned. Instead Washington has acted as though the link between Iraq and terrorism were self-evident.

22 White, A. (2002) 'Journalism and the War on Terrorism', Final Report of the Aftermath of September 11 and the implications for Journalism and Civil Liberties, *International Federation of Journalists*. Published on September 3, 2002.

23 Rose, D. and Vulliamy, E. (2001) 'US hawks accuse Iraq over anthrax', *Observer*, 14 October 2001; Rose, D. (2001) 'The Iraqi connection', *Observer*, 11 November 2001; Rose, D. (2001) 'The case for tough action against Iraq', *Observer*, 2 December 2001; Rose, D. (2002) 'A blind spot called Iraq', *Observer*, 13 January 2002; Rose, D. (2003) 'Spain links suspect in 9/11 plot to Baghdad', *Observer*, 16 March 2003.

24 Monbiot, G. (2004) 'The Lies of the Press' on Monboit.com. 20 July 2004.

25 Berry, J., Sherwell, P. and Wastell, D. (2001) 'Army alert by Saddam points to Iraqi role', *Sunday Telegraph*, 23 September 2001.

26 Priest, D. and Gellman, B. (2002) 'US Decries Abuse but Defends Interrogations', *Washington Post*, 26 December 2002, p. A01.

27 Pilger, J. (2002) 'The Media and Iraq: A compliant press is preparing the ground for an all-out attack on Iraq', 21 March 2002, www.johnpilger.com/page.asp?partid=395

28 'Iraq – Its infrastructure of Concealment, Deception and Intimidation' (or Iraq Dossier for short) was a 2003 briefing document for Labour government use. It was issued to journalists on 3 February by Alastair Campbell, then Tony Blair's Director of Communications and Strategy, and concerned Iraq and weapons of mass destruction; published 30 January 2003.

29 BBC (2004) TimeLine: The 45-minute claim, BBC *News*, 13 October 2004.

30 'Iraq: its infrastructure of concealment, deception and intimidation'. http://www.pm.gov.uk/output/Page1470.asp

31 Channel 4 *News*, 6 Feb 2003.

32 Ricin is a very toxic poison extracted from the castor bean, if inhaled, injected, or ingested, acting as a toxin by the inhibition of protein synthesis. There is no known antidote.

33 Sullivan, M. (2003) 'Factory of Death', *Sun*, 8 January 2003.

34 The 'ricin plot' proved to be an embarrassment for the security services. As tests later showed there was no ricin. Only one person was found guilty, an Algerian who fatally stabbed a police officer during his arrest. Several other Algerians were acquitted. Supposed al Qaeda terror manuals had been lifted in large part from survivalist manuals openly published in the US. The best account of the fiasco was written by investigative journalist Duncan Campbell who gave evidence for the defence. See Campbell, D. (2005) 'The ricin ring that never was', *Guardian*, 14 April 2005.

35 BBC (2003) Bush declares victory in Iraq, BBC *News online*, 02 May 2003.

36 We now know the source to have been David Kelly, a leading British WMD expert and former arms inspector. A transcript of the Gilligan broadcast can be found at: http://news.bbc.co.uk/1/shared/spl/hi/uk/03/hutton_inquiry/hutton_report/html/chapter02.stm#a9

37 The report can be found at the Hutton Inquiry website: http://www.the-hutton-inquiry.org.uk/

38 Wells, M., White, M. and Wintour, P. (2004) 'Crisis cuts through the BBC', *Guardian*, 29 January 2004.

39 Hutton's absolution of the British Government was a genuine surprise even to ministers who could not believe their good luck. Whitehall experts said they had expected a 'massively destructive week for the establishment'. Most were convinced the judge would spread the blame across the field, though criticising Gilligan more than most. Ministers and officials were exonerated from any wrongdoing, or as Hutton put it, from anything 'dishonourable or underhand or duplicitous'.

40 Wells, M. (2003) 'Study deals a blow to claims of anti-war bias in BBC news', *Guardian*, 4 July 2003.

41 Toohey, B. (2004) *Australian Financial Review*, 31 January 2004.

42 http://news.bbc.co.uk/hi/english/static/audio_video/programmes/panorama/transcripts/23_09_02.txt

43 Pilger, J. (2004) 'John Pilger argues that Gilligan was an exception', *New Statesman*, 09 February 2004.

44 Lewis. J., Brookes, R., Mosedell, N. and Threadgold, T (2006) *Shoot First and Ask Questions Later: Media Coverage of the 2003 Iraq War*, New York: Peter Lang. One of the report's authors, Justin Lewis says; 'Pilger's quote gets the spirit but loses the detail. The actual figure is 89 per cent, and refers to all British broadcasters, not just the BBC (whose record here is better than the others, the worst offenders being Sky).

45 BBC1 (2004) 'A fight to the death', *Panorama* Special, 21 January 2004.

46 BBC1 (2004) 'A failure of intelligence?', *Panorama*, 11 July 04.

47 The task of challenging the Saddam/Al Qaeda link first fell to the leading US investigative reporter Seymour Hersh, whose track record goes back to revealing

the My Lai massacre in 1969. Hersh reported in *The New Yorker*, in October 2003: '. . . it was understood by many in the White House that the President had decided, in his own mind, to go to war'. Hersh added, 'The undeclared decision had a devastating impact on the continuing struggle against terrorism. The Bush Administration took many intelligence operations that had been aimed at Al Qaeda and other terrorist groups around the world and redirected them to the Persian Gulf. Linguists and special operatives were abruptly reassigned, and several ongoing antiterrorism intelligence programs were curtailed'. Then Hersh focused on the role of Iraqi leader in exile, Ahmed Chalabi, who was subsequently revealed as an arch manipulator and purveyor of skewed intelligence. 'Chalabi's defector reports [are] now flowing from the Pentagon directly to the Vice-President's office, and then on to the President, with little prior evaluation by intelligence professionals.' The piece quoted Greg Thielmann, top intelligence official for the State Department, as saying, 'There was considerable scepticism throughout the intelligence community about the reliability of Chalabi's sources, but the defector reports were coming all the time. Knock one down and another comes along. Meanwhile the garbage keeps getting shoved to the President'.

48 Judith Miller was based in Washington DC and close to leading Government officials. She became well known through her involvement in two stories. Firstly about Iraq's alleged Weapons of Mass Destruction (WMD) Programme. Secondly for her involvement in the Plame Affair. Miller announced her retirement from the *New York Times* on November 9, 2005. In July of 2005, Miller was jailed for contempt of court for refusing to testify before a federal grand jury investigating a leak naming Valerie Plame as a covert CIA agent. Miller did not write about Plame, but was said to be in possession of evidence relevant to the leak investigation. After her release on September 29 2005, Miller agreed to testify to the grand jury the identity of her source, Lewis Libby, Vice President Dick Cheney's chief of staff. Miller and Bill Keller, executive editor of the *New York Times*, have not disclosed to the *New York Times* Miller's role in covering the Plame story. Miller now works at the *Los Angeles Times*.

49 Davenport, J. and Dovkants, K. (2003) 'Mosque Linked to Key Terror Network', *Evening Standard*, 21 January 2003.

50 The 7 July 2005 London bombings were a series of coordinated terrorist bomb blasts that hit London's public transport system during the morning rush hour. At 8:50 a.m., three bombs exploded within 50 seconds of each other on three London Underground trains. A fourth bomb exploded on a bus nearly an hour later at 9:47 a.m. in Tavistock Square. The bombings killed 52 commuters and the four suicide bombers, and injured 700.

51 On 21 July 2005, a second series of four explosions took place on the London Underground and a London bus. The detonators of all four bombs exploded, but none of the main explosive charges detonated, and there were no casualties. All suspected bombers from this failed attack escaped from the scenes but were later arrested. A number of men have been tried.

52 The suicide bombers are not around to tell their side of 7/7. At the time of writing a number of men were standing trial for the 21/7 incident and are innocent unless proven guilty by the jury.

53 *Associated Press*, 11 March 2003.

54 Hersh, S. (2004) *New Yorker* magazine, May 2004.

55 Davies, N. (2007) email to Paul Lashmar, 28 January 2007.

56 ITV (2004) 'Secrets of the Iraq War', TV documentary by Films of Record for ITV, producer Ed Harriman, 1 hour, January 2004.

57 Chomsky, N. (2006) *Failed States*. London: Penguin, p. 52.

58 Byrne, D. (2007) email to Paul Lashmar, February 2007.
59 Smith, M. (2005) 'Blair hit by new leak of secret war plan', *Sunday Times*, 1 May 2005, p. 1.
60 Norton-Taylor, R. (2007) 'Memo to Mendacity: Blair subverted the truth to take us to war', Comment section, *Guardian*, 17 April 2007.
61 Whitaker, R. and Buncombe, A. (2007) 'How an article in the "IoS" led to the conviction of Lewis "Scooter" Libby', *Independent on Sunday*, 11 February 2007.
62 BBC2 (2005) 7 July bomber 'filmed in 2004', *Newsnight*, reporter Richard Watson, 25 October 2005, http://news.bbc.co.uk/1/hi/programmes/newsnight/uk_terror_threat/default.stm
63 Shipman, T. (2002) 'Fighting forces hit by shortfalls in Equipment and medical care; Scandal of our khaki heroes in tattered trousers', *Sunday Express*, 5 April 2002, p. 4; Hickley, M. (2003) 'They've got the courage, Mr Blair, but have given them the equipment?' *Daily Mail*, 22 January 2003, pp. 1, 5.
64 BBC2 (2003) *War Spin*, presented by John Kampfner and produced by Sandy Smith, 18 May 2003.
65 Lt Gen. Sir Richard Dannant, the Commander of the Allied Rapid Reaction Corp from 2003.
66 Thomson, Alex (2007) email to Paul Lashmar, 29 January 2007.
67 Guantanamo Bay detainment camp is a joint military prison and interrogation camp under the leadership of Joint Task Force Guantanamo since 2002.[1] The prison, established at Guantanamo Bay Naval Base, holds people suspected by the executive branch of the US government of being al Qaeda and Taliban operatives, as well as those no longer considered suspects who are being held pending relocation elsewhere. The detainment areas consist of three camps in the base: Camp Delta (which includes Camp Echo), Camp Iguana, and the now-closed Camp X-Ray. The facility is often referred to as Guantanamo, Gitmo (derived from the abbreviation 'GTMO'), or Camp X-Ray.
68 Drogin, B. and Goetz, J. (2005) 'The Curveball Saga', *Los Angeles Times*, 20–21 November 2005.
69 'The Curveball Saga' (2005).
70 BBC (2007) *On the Ropes*, BBC Radio 4, 24 April 2007.
71 Lashmar, P. and Whitaker, R. (2003) 'On the brink of war: The spies' revolt MI6 and CIA: the new enemy within', *Independent on Sunday*, 9 February 2003.
72 The author of this chapter experienced misleading information from official sources on the knowledge of Khan.
73 Gilligan, A. (2007) telephone interview by Paul Lashmar.

Bibliography

Burke, J. (2005) *Al-Qaeda: The True Story of Radical Islam*, 2nd edn (revised). London: Penguin Books.

Drogin, B. (2007) *Curveball: Spies, Lies, and the Man Behind Them – The Real Reason America Went to War in Iraq*. London: Ebury Press.

Cockburn, P. (2007) *The Occupation: War and Resistance in Iraq*, 1st edn. London: Verso.

Davies, N. (2008) *Flat Earth News: An Award-winning Reporter Exposes Falsehood, Distortion and Propaganda in the Global Media*. London: Chatto and Windus.

Grey, S. (2006) *Ghost Plane: The Inside Story of the CIA's Secret Rendition Programme*. London: Hurst & Company.

Fisk, R. (2006) *The Great War for Civilisation: The Conquest of the Middle East*. London: Harper Perennial.

Glees, A. and Davies, P. H. J. (2004) *Spinning the Spies: Intelligence, Open Government and the Hutton Inquiry*. London: Social Affairs Unit.

Rogers, S. and *Guardian* reporters (2004) *The Hutton Inquiry and Its Impact*. London: Politico's Publishing.

Hersh, S. (2005) *Chain of Command*. London: Penguin Books.

Husain, E. (2007) *The Islamist: Why I Joined Radical Islam in Britain, What I Saw Inside and Why I Left*. London: Penguin Books.

Stafford Smith, C. (2007) *Bad Men: Guantanamo Bay And The Secret Prisons*. London: Weidenfeld & Nicolson.

12

HIGH POLITICS AND
LOW BEHAVIOUR
Sunday Times Insight

Hugo de Burgh

Insight and British public life

Insight is a news-gathering and analysis operation of the *Sunday Times* parallel to and separate from the departments of Home News and Foreign News and, like them, answering to the Managing Editor of News. Insight has no dedicated space and no requirement to produce a story each week; its manpower has usually been around five experienced journalists, many of whom have written books based upon their investigative work (some are listed at the end of the chapter).

Insight is the by-line most associated with investigative journalism in the UK press, although there have been other teams and units in other newspapers which have competed with it, particularly, in recent years, the *Guardian*. Insight first appeared on 17 February 1963. At the time advertisers were growing in number and in their demands; more space for advertisements was resulting in expanded space for editorial copy, and there was space to allow journalists to write at length. The first major story covered as a result of these developments was a 6000 word piece on UK government minister John Profumo, accused of lying to the House of Commons over his association with a potential spy published on 9 September 1963. What was unusual about the piece at the time were first its narrative presentation, and second the 'close attention to detail which was to become an identifying feature of Insight' (NICAD, 1997). Then came the Rachman exposure, an account of the rise of a Polish immigrant whose name has now entered the language to mean a grasping, unscrupulous, slum landlord. In October [1963] Insight published a story headed 'Backstage at Blackpool: hour by hour in the fight for power'. The story told the problems within the Conservative Party after the Prime Minister, Harold Macmillan fell ill just before the party conference (NICAD, 1997).

The 1970s are widely regarded as the great days of UK investigative journalism, and where this is so it is because of Insight. 'Insight was the role

215

model of the period, with huge investigations, plenty of time, large budgets and a strongly supportive editorial approach' (Doig, 1992: 46). There was always a strong sense of purpose and idealism, infused above all by the *Sunday Times* editor Harold Evans. Under him Insight's main achievements of many, were the thalidomide and the DC-10 air disaster stories, both described elsewhere in this book, as well as the Philby Spy Scandal (see Knightley, 1997, 1998). Careful groundwork was expected: The idea was that you became as expert on the subject, whatever it was, as those involved in it, so that when the time came to confront Mr Big, or to explain why his technicians had inserted a faulty bolt in the flange bracket, you not only knew as much about the business as he did, but you could probably sell his phony insurance policy or build his bridge as well, if not better, than he had done (Linklater, 1993: 19).

By the late 1980s, the combination of new proprietor Rupert Murdoch's change of style at the *Sunday Times* and the willingness of television executives to spend money on investigations meant that the best investigative journalism was appearing on television. Knightley (1999) believes that newspapers' loss of enthusiasm for investigative journalism came about because, first, before new technology, the salaries element of the total costs of production of newspapers was very small – he says 11 per cent; however, once new technology came in, salaries came to a much larger percentage of total production costs and were seen as ripe for cutting. Second, he says that new technology made it possible to see instantly the productivity, in terms of words per pound spent on salary and overheads, of any particular journalist. Since investigative journalists had typically produced much less copy, they were vulnerable. 'Efficiency was judged by quantity published in the newspaper. Investigative journalists who don't get their story into the paper for a year don't look very cost effective' (Knightley, 1999).

Television salaries and benefits were famously very good in the late 1970s and early 1980s, and this may have contributed to the strength of investigative journalism, as well as the glamour of an industry still in its discovery stage and attracting top talent. However, Linklater believes that economics was less significant in the change of tone at the *Sunday Times* than ideology, since, after all, the company owning the *Sunday Times* is enormously wealthy (Linklater, 1993).

Former Insight people believe that by the late 1980s there was little sympathy for the craftsmanship of the 1970s, and Linklater mentions in evidence for this lack of sympathy the three-year investigation of a tycoon's financial affairs by the distinguished financial journalist Charles Raw, which he describes as 'one of the most brilliant pieces of financial investigation I have ever seen', that was spiked by Murdoch (Linklater, 1993: 20). Although claimed by Andrew Neil (Neil, 1996: ch. 12) as one of Insight's 1980s successes, there are question marks over the story of 'Arthur Scargill's Libyan Connection', which declared that the senior employee of the National Union of Mineworkers was seeking financial help for the then strike from the most reviled regime in the world. Although the trip certainly took place and was a spectacular own goal for the miners' union, the man who undertook it was later found to be in the camp of the Union's enemies; the story ideally suited the UK government at the time and it has been suggested that the British intelligence services had a hand in ensuring that Insight got the details of the story (Milne, 1995: 148–56).

When in 1986 a rail crash took place in Clapham, South London, Insight reporters claim that they were the first to find the culprit, a technician who had failed to insulate wires; however the editor would not publish the identification of the culprit as he believed this would constitute an 'unfair, vindictive attack on an individual' (Leppard, 1997). Another 1986 success for Insight was the revelation, made on 5 October 1986, that Israel had secretly developed a military nuclear capability and that it was of an unimaginable extent and advancement. The story fell into the lap of Insight because other newspapers failed to see its significance, or failed to find the informant, Mordechai Vanunu, credible. Vanunu was only too genuine and had photographs taken within the nuclear installations that were even more so, as Insight reporter Peter Hounam realised and as was confirmed to him by the experts he employed. Two matters diminished the glory; first, the *Daily Mirror*, whose proprietor and Foreign Editor were both involved in different ways with the Israeli security services, according to Hersh (1991: 307–15), published a spoiler shortly before in which they rubbished Vanunu and diminished his revelations; second, the *Sunday Times* failed to hold onto their informant, Vanunu, whom they allowed to become so lonely as to fall for a secret service honey trap that led to his being kidnapped and taken home for trial. Finally, in the 1980s, Insight ran a series of articles called 'The Water Rats' exposing 'the top industrialists poisoning Britain's rivers' for a lengthy period in 1989. Stories in the 1990s included Asil Nadir and the Polly Peck Scandal (share manipulation by a colourful businessman), offshore trust tax loopholes and how National Car Parks waged a commando-style industrial espionage war against its rival. A fraudulent story, claiming that the then leader of the Labour Party Michael Foot had been the agent of a foreign government, led to the aggrieved party winning damages from the *Sunday Times*.

Insight is after 'the big story, not dodgy insurance salesmen or councillors or medical reps bribing doctors' (Leppard, 1997) and the target must be above a 'certain threshold', people near the centre of power, whether civil servants or politicians, who are wrong-doers. Insight will eschew the story of a minister's dishonestly conducted affair, but might investigate how others set the minister up, as they did in the case of a disgraced Conservative minister, David Mellor, when his mistress sold recordings of his intimate conversations to the *People* in 1992; in 1993 when other newspapers revealed the existence of the 'Squidgygate' tapes, providing evidence of Princess Diana's extramarital affections, Insight's story dealt with the manner in which the tapes had been obtained because of what this revealed about public agencies.

In 1995 Insight set up an elaborate sting in order to trap corrupt members of parliament. A company was set up which purported to be looking for MPs prepared to ask questions about pharmaceuticals, and the newspaper was later to be accused of entrapment for so doing. At the same time the *Guardian* was carrying out its own investigations in this area, which became the 'Cash for Questions' scandal (see Chapters 1 and 3).

In recent interviews the Insight editor has claimed that Insight has found 'the stakes raised by the (British) government's establishment of a Rapid Rebuttal Unit, and by its PROs' vitriolic abuse and intimidation whenever reporters appear to be near a story' (Leppard, 1997). Specifically Insight claims to have been warned off examining the business connections of the husband of a minister; these connections became pertinent to central issues of corruption and undue influence when the *Financial Times* and *Sunday Telegraph* revealed how the Prime Minister had allowed himself to be addressed on policy matters by their wealthy associates (Leppard, 1997).

Despite these warnings, Insight has continued its close interest in the government's appointments, examining the responsibilities of millionaire minister Lord Sainsbury of Turville; the Sainsbury family are major benefactors of the Labour Party and, as shareholders of a massive supermarket and banking operation, stand to be affected by planning decisions to be taken by the Deputy Prime Minister in his executive capacity. In the late 1990s concern about genetically modified foods surfaced in Britain, and it became a matter of controversy that the same Lord Sainsbury had had connections with the genetically modified food lobby in the recent past. In such a climate, everyone who visits the Prime Minister or who is appointed by him is of potential interest, as of course are those companies that donate to the governing party. Leppard (1997) believes that he will in time establish that some of these are foreign defence companies, acting via lobbyists; were this proved so it would be ironic, given the capital made by Labour when in opposition out of the connections of the Conservatives with arms companies, and out of the 'Arms to Iraq' affair, to which we turn later in the chapter. Before we do so, however, it is appropriate to consider the context within which this kind of investigative journalism is deemed important.

Public opinion, public policies and journalists

Journalists have ambivalent relationships with high politics. Former *Sunday Times* editor Andrew Neil describes in his memoirs how he would chat to Prime Minister Major on the telephone (Neil, 1996); the place settings at one of John Major's dinner parties gives an indication of the intimacy that is possible (Tunstall, 1996); national journalists go to the homes of ambitious politicians as well as meeting them regularly at Westminster or the many other meeting points for the political elite. Yet the journalists are always on the look out for the weak point, the revelation, the scandal; the greatest fame attaches to those who can bring down a national politician.[1] For many journalists, as doubtless for many observers, Watergate (see Chapter 3) is the quintessential investigative journalism. This is partly on account of its methods, partly on account of its execution, which 'encapsulated and exemplified all of the difficulties and challenges' (Leppard, 1997), involving source development, triangulation, tensions with editors and tremendous political risks, and partly on account of its influence on journalism everywhere. Most of all, however, it is quintessential because of its target. For Insight in particular, investigative journalism today is about national policy and national policy-makers. Its reporters want to know that policy is being made for the right reasons and that policy-makers are behaving in accordance with the principles they profess.

Hence the classic status of Watergate, which demonstrated misdemeanours and derelictions out of keeping with society's expectations of the executive. Hence also the significance to journalists of British equivalents. In the 1970s the UK had the Profumo affair and Poulson, because it implicated a prime minister in waiting; in the 1980s, while the USA was attending to the Iran-Contra story, which undermined the Reagan administration – a premonition of the forthcoming British arms scandal – Rinkagate was the big UK story, in which a senior politician was investigated for incitement to murder. In the 1990s, the two biggest British investigations of the conduct of people in high places, 'Cash for Questions' and 'Arms to Iraq', were significant for similar reasons.

The importance ascribed to such investigations is based on a number of premises. One is the theory of journalism's social responsibility, upon which we have already touched. Another is the assumption that public persons are accountable to public opinion for aspects of their lives once deemed private; another, the theory that public policy should defer to public opinion. That it is not possible to make public policy without carrying public opinion is now probably well established in the folklore of high politics, at least since the Poll Tax fiasco when Prime Minister Thatcher was forced by hostile public opinion to withdraw an important element of her tax reforms; thus governments increasingly try to persuade people of their policies. The effort and money government now puts into the manipulation of public opinion is enormous (Franklin, 1994). The connection between the public and those seeking to make or to influence public policy via public opinion is made by the media. The media can set the agenda of debate by highlighting some matters more than others (Iyengar et al., 1984); they can 'gatekeep' or exclude some matters; they can prioritise or hype (Cohen, 1972; Edelman, 1988); they can popularise the concerns of elite groups (Mayer, 1991). Public policy is sometimes made in immediate response to public opinion as mediated by the media; for example, recent British legislation on handguns, dangerous dogs and terrorism is widely regarded as a manifestation less of legislative forethought than of public opinion as represented by the media. By contrast, public opinion is insufficient when the political elite, presumably in cahoots with the mediators, sets its face against a policy; the obvious examples in the UK are capital punishment and privacy. The 'establishment model' of policy-making (Parsons, 1995: 110–22) suggests that a major institution needs to take up an issue for it to become sufficiently important to change public policy. Outsiders have two main choices in trying to influence public policy; the backdoor, lobbying mode, which is increasingly systematised and used by many professional and trade organisations, plus individual companies and countries (Jordan, 1990), and the public mode. When campaigners for lead-free petrol came to the conclusion in 1981 that their lobbying had failed against more powerful resistance from counter-lobbies, they decided to go for a public campaign (Wilson, 1984), bearing in mind the successes of such high-profile campaigns as those on housing (Shelter), family benefits (Child Poverty Action Group) and recycling (Friends of the Earth). They called it CLEAR (Campaign for Lead Free Air).

The CLEAR campaign forced the government of the day to change public policy by mobilising public opinion. Factors included the quality of CLEAR's argument and of its presentation, together with the acceptability of its scientific testimonials; it was also executed in a carefully planned and efficient manner. Arguably the most important factor, however, was the targeting of journalists who were leaders and opinion-formers, not only by virtue of their jobs but because of the respect they commanded in their profession. CLEAR's approach accorded with theories of the processes by which the media influences public opinion. The *pluralist* conception (the media is a marketplace of ideas making free debate possible) is largely discredited, as is the *hypodermic* model (the media injects, and we believe); it is widely agreed that the media set agendas, gatekeep, in that they can include or exclude issues from debate, and, in Mayer's 'reflection and reinforcement model' (Mayer, 1981), that they reflect concerns of knowledgeable minorities and then blow them up into public issues. The role of media owners and of advertisers in this process may be considerable, but is more difficult to pin down. What is the evidence that the media have a significant influence in the formation of public opinion? Studies exist which demonstrate how, in the USA, the media influenced public opinion of the Vietnam War, particularly in de-romanticising it, and therefore influenced public policy towards that war, although many disbelieve the studies. Important attitude changes, for example the increasing acceptance of homosexuality in the UK after the liberal legislation of the 1960s, may be attributable to media treatment, but the dynamics of this have yet to be explored. There have been periods in UK public life when the media have been thought to have set the public agenda, notably in the 1960s with the issue of police corruption. Iyengar *et al.*'s study demonstrated the influence of media coverage on US Presidential policy in the 1980s. In the UK there are claims as to the influence of the media upon the presentation of legislation to Parliament, and in the 1990s the National Commission on Standards in Public Life and the Scott Report came about as a consequence of the media's direct influence upon public affairs.

That journalists themselves might have strong opinions that should be listened to was an idea that, grudgingly, the political classes came to accept in the middle of the nineteenth century. Journalism was the Fourth Estate – after the monarchy (or the spiritual peers), the Lords and the Commons – because it represented the views of large numbers of people in a manner other than by election or by interests, and could influence those people. That journalists might have better information than political decision makers and business people (Desmond, 1978: 320ff) was another idea that began to catch on as foreign correspondence developed. But that journalists had a social obligation to criticise, expose and exhort was a development to which those in authority did not take kindly – it suggested that journalists had a kind of moral authority perhaps superior to that of anyone else. From observers and informants they became brokers of information, and then the determinants of what constitutes significance, and the creators of the agenda. Their power came from their signalising role and also from their access to readers, an access which politicians needed; they were sometimes trusted by their readers because of their supposed impartiality, or at least clear-mindedness; they could deny such access to those in authority or those with whom they disagreed. These were the foundations which made it possible for journalists to use their various tools, sometimes in combination: investigation and exposure would be one way; moral censure another; analysis, argument and criticism a third.

In these ways it may be said that the journalist is important in creating the relationship between public opinion and policy-maker. The manner in which s/he reacts to pressure from interest groups, government or politicians probably determines which policy ideas conquer public opinion and which do not. Furthermore, the vigilance with which journalists scrutinise the doings of politicians determines how effective they can be at promoting or executing their policies; the last Conservative government can be argued to have been disabled by the revelations of journalists in the 'Cash for Questions' and 'Arms to Iraq' stories, examples of journalists taking the initiative rather than responding to events or simply mediating facts.

The 'Arms To Iraq' affair

This matter spread throughout UK public life, and to a much lesser extent also touched upon the EU and USA for at least 17 years. Because of its alleged influence upon the decline and, in 1997, the defeat of the Conservative government of John Major, its detail may have become confounded in lay minds with the 'Cash for Questions' affair; some Conservative supporters may simply think of it as one of those weapons with which hostile journalists sought to beat the government and bring nearer the possibility of a victory for Mr Blair.

Although there were doubtless many who wanted to exploit the affair to discredit the government, it is much more than that. Not only did the affair reveal moral muddle and incompetence within the public administration; it also found ministers attempting to prevent the revelation of truth. It dealt with an area of life – arms sales – of concern to many people, either because their livelihoods depend upon them or because they find the trade repugnant.

'The Arms to Iraq' affair: glossary

DTI: Department of Trade and Industry
ELp: Export Licences permits
HMCE: Her Majesty's Customs and Excise (the organisation that polices imports and exports)
HMG: Her Majesty's Government
MI5: Military Intelligence 5 (the UK secret service)

'The Arms to Iraq' affair: time line

1980:   Iran–Iraq War starts
1984:   HMG decides not to take sides in the war and bans sales of arms
1985:   October – Geoffrey Howe, Foreign Secretary, announces Guidelines
1987:   November – MI5 records the fact that UK machinery is being used to make weapons
1988:   January – DTI tells Matrix Churchill (an arms-making company) that its Export Licences have been frozen
1988:   February – Matrix Churchill receives Export Licences for machine tools used to make shells
1988:   August – Ceasefire between Iran and Iraq
1988:   December – Guidelines on exports to Iraq relaxed
1989:   February – DTI Approval for further Matrix Churchill exports
1989:   November – DTI Approval for further Matrix Churchill exports
1990:   April – Parts for an Iraqi 'supergun' seized by HMCE
1990:   June – HMCE raids Matrix Churchill
1990:   July – DTI Approval for further Matrix Churchill exports
1990:   August – Iraqi invasion of Kuwait
1990:   October – Arrest of directors of Matrix Churchill
1991:   January – Gulf War
1992:   February – Directors of Ordtech Ltd convicted of illegal exporting of arms-related equipment to Iraq
1992:   June–September – Signing of Public Interest Immunity Certificates by ministers which would prevent the disclosure of information that would have assisted the Matrix Churchill defence
1992:   November – Matrix Churchill trial starts, and collapses (because of admission by Minister Clark); Prime Minister John Major appoints Judge Sir Richard Scott to conduct an Inquiry on ministers' role
1993:   May – Scott Inquiry begins

1996: February – Scott Report published, concluding that Parliament was misled

(with acknowledgments to the *Sunday Times*, 18 February 1996)

In essence the story is as follows. In 1980 war broke out between Iran and Iraq. Neither regime was very attractive to the West, Iran's leaders having declared their extreme hostility to the West and equated that hostility with the very raison d'être of their theocracy; Iraq was ruled by a racist, totalitarian and utterly brutal Arab government. Western governments perceived Iraq as less of a threat, and were therefore less hostile to her and her supreme leader, Saddam Hussein.

The Western media were able to publish extensive detail on the war; two items in particular stuck in the popular imagination. One was that the Iranians were sending hordes of boys as young as 8, virtually untrained and armed with little more than faith, to attack and be slaughtered; the other was that the Iraqis were using chemical weapons upon these children, and upon minority Kurdish inhabitants of Iraq with horrible consequences. People were killed, maimed, disfigured and died in great agony. Iraq was doing, it was remarked at the time, what even Adolf Hitler feared to do on the battlefield (Sweeney, 1993).

The UK government decided, in the light of this, to ban sales of arms to either side. However, some manufacturers, including a company called Matrix Churchill, whose ultimate owner was the Iraqi government, continued to export. Export licenses were issued to Matrix Churchill by the DTI; yet, in June 1990 Matrix Churchill was raided by HMCE under suspicion of exporting illegally. On the face of it this was an example of lack of coordination by the administration: the DTI was permitting what HMCE was forbidding. If it was indeed government policy that there be no arms sales, then the DTI was wrong. If, on the other hand, the policy had been relaxed, then HMCE was wrong.

However, the situation was not so clear cut. The Gulf crisis blew up with Iraq's invasion of Kuwait in August 1990, and it was evident that the UK might soon be involved in a war with Iraq, which indeed did break out on 16 January 1991. Furthermore, the information that had enabled HMCE to raid Matrix Churchill had come from within Matrix Churchill, whose directors not only believed that they had been encouraged by the DTI to continue their sales, but who also contained among them at least two agents of MI5. When the directors of Matrix Churchill were arrested and charged with breaking the export ban in October 1990, it is not surprising that they were peeved.

Thus the affair became not merely one of how companies flouted government policy or even of how government agencies encouraged them to do so, but of how UK agents were being sacrificed to hide the hypocrisy of the government. The story took a further twist when, in 1992, ministers attempted to prevent a proper self-defence by the Matrix Churchill directors through their action in signing Public Immunity Certificates, which are orders preventing the disclosure of apposite documents on the grounds of national security.

The 'Arms To Iraq' affair and journalists

The story developed in nine stages:

1   reporting, often critical, of the arms trade
2   suspicions that Western firms were involved in the arming of Iran and Iraq
3   evidence that British companies had breached the guidelines
4   evidence that parts of government knew this was happening
5   evidence that ministers had encouraged this
6   evidence that ministers had tried to prevent the truth coming out
7   media revelations resulting in a public inquiry
8   the public inquiry analysed for its lessons
9   the influence of the affair upon public opinion.

Various newspaper journalists had been involved in different aspects of the story up to December 1990 when the *Sunday Times* brought the story up to stage 5 with its Insight article 'Minister helped British firms to arm Saddam's soldiers':

> Straddling the metalled highway that runs south out of Baghdad towards the Kuwaiti border lies the Taji industrial plant, a sprawling complex that is the centre of the Iraqi arms industry. Behind two huge ornamental gates, past the fortified guardhouse, thousands of production workers are feeding President Saddam Hussein's burgeoning war machine.
>
> Inside shed C, one of the largest of the work areas, stand row upon row of computer-controlled lathes programmed to making the casings, fins and nose cones of mortar shells. The lathes were supplied by two leading British companies. In shed D, more British equipment stands ready for plating shells and missile parts. Only a few miles to the west, at Al-Iskandariya, is the Hutteen factory complex where British-made machines are mass-producing shells and ammunition. It is the same at the Badr and Qaqa establishments to the west of Baghdad, on the road to Ramadi, where Farzad Bazoft, the British journalist, tried to take soil samples and photographs before he was arrested, then hanged as a spy last March . . . The *Sunday Times* Insight team has investigated how this British equipment came to be in Iraq and discovered that a government minister allowed firms to break the spirit of the government's arms embargo forbidding the export of military goods to Iraq.
>
> (*Sunday Times*, 2 December 1990)

How had the *Sunday Times* arrived at this? According to Leppard, once the Gulf War had begun in late 1990 'with fears of a nuclear war between Israel and Iraq, the whole news agenda shifted to the Middle East' (Leppard, 1997). UK-based journalists, unable to compete in the coverage from the Middle East, sought a domestic angle and decided to look at the trade which had allowed Saddam to build up such a mighty military force. Was government involved in allowing that trade to take place? Insight trawled the trade press for companies selling machine tools to Iraq and made a short list, always aware that sanctions-busting by a few companies would not be a significant story, whereas government complicity would be. Leppard had a list of six companies to telephone and by chance called the Matrix Churchill Managing Director Paul Henderson '45 minutes after he had been sacked' and was in the mood to talk. He offered Leppard the memo of a meeting with minister Alan Clark advising him to keep on with his business in defiance of sanctions. What followed Leppard's good fortune is best described in the words of the Scott Report:

> 2 December 1990: The *Sunday Times* 'Insight' article entitled 'Minister helped British firms to arm Saddam' was published. The main thrust of the article was that Mr Alan Clark, while Minister for Trade, had encouraged machine tool manufacturers, when applying for licences to export to Iraq machine tools intended for the manufacture of munitions, to cloud the truth and stress the civil manufacturing potential of the machines in order to facilitate the grant of export licences. One effect of the article was to highlight the political implications of the Matrix Churchill investigation and a future prosecution.
>
> (Scott, 1996: 1098, see also p. 1156)

> Another effect was that on the morning of 3 December 1990 a meeting at the Cabinet Office was attended by a number of very senior officials . . . The purpose of the meeting was to discuss the *Sunday Times* article and the answer that might be given by the Prime Minister (to a letter on this subject).
>
> (Scott, 1996: 1161)

Later that day 'Mr Clark met the Prime Minister, Mr John Major, to discuss the *Sunday Times* article' (Scott, 1996: 1098). A later effect was that at the *Sunday Times* Christmas party minister Alan Clark threatened editor Andrew Neil that he'd 'have his balls' and sue the *Sunday Times* (Leppard, 1997). The story then took off, especially when Insight established the extraordinary contradiction that HMCE was bringing Matrix Churchill to court but that MI5, another arm of government, was using the company for intelligence-gathering.

'Arms to Iraq' has been denigrated as a journalistic investigation by other journalists, first on the grounds that it 'was just an ordinary news story, not an investigation in the true sense' (Knightley, 1999) and secondly on the grounds that:

> The role of journalists and their respective media institutions in that case, as in the case of the numerous fraud trials of the time, was to observe merely the proceedings from the sidelines and provide a detailed 'analysis by post mortem'.
>
> (Northmore, 1994: 319)

If all investigations are to be measured for their length and complexity by the standards of the thalidomide and DC-10 stories, then 'Arms to Iraq' cannot compare. Yet, despite Northmore there was investigation, even if it did not require the kind of investment made, unnecessarily if we are to agree with Bruce Page (Page, 1998), by the *Sunday Times* in the thalidomide story. In his essay Northmore offers a useful list of suggestions as to what sources investigative journalists might have used to get to the Matrix Churchill story earlier (Northmore, 1994: 330–31); in fact some of these sources were used, but the story was not an editorial high priority until, first, war with Iraq seemed likely, and second, the *Sunday Times* managed to establish the role of minister Alan Clark.

Insight continued to publish on the story after that exposure, but it can be argued that little more original investigation came from its reporters, who relied upon the court cases and the Scott Inquiry to disclose new facts. Equally it should be said that Insight had done its bit, ensuring that the government could not hide its role.

From a humanitarian and moral viewpoint the story always mattered, but it was not significant in terms of public policy and political leadership until the December 1990 article. Once that article had made the vital link, all the other factors joined to make 'Arms to Iraq' an important investigation because of:

1   the consequences of Western companies' success in supplying Iraq, i.e. the wars against Iran, Kuwait and finally the Allied Coalition;
2   the awfulness of the direct results of that supply upon defenceless populations, including minorities within Iraq;
3   the fact that ministers had broken their own rules and connived at the continuance of a trade which they condemned in public.

What made the story an achievement of investigative journalists was that, in large measure as a result of their efforts, government was not able to hide the chaos and corruption, but was obliged to set up an inquiry which then consolidated their case. Contradictions in public policy were revealed, and the resulting revelations probably contributed to the further discrediting and ultimate electoral defeat of the then government.

Note

1 Peter Oborne (1999) interprets the change in relationship between journalists and politicians since the 1970s as the rise of a new 'media class', and describes the features in Chapter 7.

Bibliography

Booker, C. (1994) *The Mad Officials*. London: Constable.

Cohen, S. (1972) *Folk Devils and Moral Panics*. London: Paladin.

Desmond, R. (1978) *The Information Process: World News Reporting to the Twentieth Century*. Iowa: University of Iowa Press.

Doig, A. (1992) Retreat of the investigators. *British Journalism Review*, 3 (4).

Eddy, P. (1976) *Destination Disaster*. London: Granada.

Edelman, M. (1988) *Constructing the Political Spectacle*. Chicago: Chicago University Press.

Franklin, B. (1994) *Packaging Politics*. London: Edward Arnold.

Gibbons, T. (1998) *Regulating the Media*. London: Sweet and Maxwell.

Henderson, P. (1993) *The Unlikely Spy*. London: Bloomsbury.

Hersh, S. (1991) *The Samson Option: Israel, America and the Bomb*. London: Faber and Faber.

Home Office (1998) *MI5: The Security Service*. London: HMSO.

Iyengar, S., Kinder, D. R., Peters, M. D. and Krosnick, J. A. (1984) The evening news and the Presidential evaluations. *Journal of Personality and Social Psychology*, 46: 778–87.

Jordan, G. (1990) *The Commercial Lobbyists: Politics for Profit in Britain*. Aberdeen: Aberdeen University Press.

Knightley, P. (1997) *A Hack's Progress*. London: Jonathan Cape.

Knightley, P. (1998) The inside story of Philby's exposure. *British Journalism Review*, 9 (2).

Knightley, P. (1999) Interview with Hugo de Burgh, 22 May 1999.

Leigh, D. (1980) *The Frontiers of Secrecy: Closed Government in Britain*. London: Junction.

Leppard, D. (1997) The Watergate model in UK journalism. Talk to students on the MA Investigative Journalism course at Nottingham Trent University, 27 November 1997.

Linklater, M. (1993) An insight into Insight. *British Journalism Review*, 4 (2).

Mayer, R. (1981) Gone yesterday, here today: consumer issues in the agenda setting process. *Journal of Social Issues*, 47: 21–39.

Milne, S. (1995) *The Enemy Within*. London: Pan.

Neil, A. (1996) *Full Disclosure*. London: Weidenfeld and Nicolson.

NICAD (1997) Briefing from News International Corporate Affairs Department, 10 September 1997.

Northmore, D. (1994) Probe shock: investigative journalism. In R. Keeble *The Newspapers Handbook*. London: Routledge.

Norton-Taylor, R. (1985) *The Ponting Affair*. London: Cecil Woolf.

Oborne, P. (1999) *Alastair Campbell: New Labour and the Rise of the Media Class*. London: Aurum.

Page, B. (1998) A defence of 'low' journalism. *British Journalism Review*, 9 (1).

Parsons, W. (1995) *Public Policy*. Aldershot: Edward Elgar.

Scott, Sir R. (1996) *Report of the Inquiry into the Export of Defence Equipment and Dual-Use of Goods to Iraq and Related Prosecutions* (The Scott Report). London: HMSO.

Sweeney, J. (1993) *Trading with the Enemy: Britain's Arming of Iraq*. London: Pan.

Tunstall, J. (1996) *Newspaper Power: The National Press in Britain*. Oxford: Oxford University Press.

Wilson, D. (1993) *Campaigning: The A–Z of Public Advocacy*. London: Hawksmere.

Further reading

Parsons, W. (1995) *Public Policy*. Aldershot: Edward Elgar.

Sweeney, J. (1993) *Trading with the Enemy: Britain's Arming of Iraq*. London: Pan.

13

INVESTIGATING CORPORATE CORRUPTION

An example from BBC's *File on Four*

Hugo de Burgh

The medium of radio in the UK

The BBC was founded in 1922 as a national, publicly regulated corporation. It was founded in this manner because the unregulated US radio sphere was seen as chaotic (Franklin, 1997: 117) and a negative model. One of the most important influences upon the development of BBC radio, which itself influenced the institutions created for television after the Second World War, was the personality of the first Director General, Lord Reith, who exemplified many of the values admired by his generation.

Lord Reith believed that the medium should 'inform, educate and entertain'. By this he meant that its principal responsibilities included the provision of impartial information upon which citizens could base their decisions; the expression of a national consensus in matters of morality and taste, a consensus guided by his own Presbyterian instincts; that quality of output should always take precedence over profit. The institutions were created through a number of measures, of which the most important were the Acts based on the Crawford reports, which made Reith's vision possible to implement. Independence from the politicians was assured by the creation of an independent board of directors whose main function was to defend the BBC from political pressures; public funding was provided in ten year tranches so that the BBC was not required to raise money in the market.

As a result of these arrangements Lord Reith was able, in 1926, successfully to resist calls by politicians to take the side of the government of the day over the General Strike; this was a propitious moment in the development of the BBC, since it defined its position. This event, together with its metamorphosis into a 'national institution' to which everybody listened during the crisis years of the 1930s and the Second World War, enabled it to emerge from that war as a national institution of authority and influence, respected at home as abroad for its high standards of reporting and production.

Competition from television and technological developments menaced the Corporation in the 1960s, as did social and cultural evolution. It was the period of the establishment of commercially produced popular music, of the expansion of advertising and of that expansion's impact upon the media, and of the start of modern consumerism. In 1967 the Pilkington Committee recommended the introduction of local radio, and in the same year the BBC set up Radio 1 in acknowledgement that the existing services catered only inadequately to varieties of taste.

In 1972 the Sound Broadcasting Act established Independent Local Radio, which expanded hugely under the free enterprise impetus of the Thatcher government from 1979. These commercial stations were intended to be profit-making; their owners were not necessarily imbued with the public service ideal. Their views on the media were expressed in the 1990 Broadcasting Act which changed British radio broadcasting dramatically by not requiring the new radio stations to educate or inform, by limiting the involvement of the government in the monitoring of quality and by selling the right to broadcast to the highest cash bidder.

In 1992 the first British whole-nation commercial channels went on air; there are now three (1992 Classic FM, 1993 Virgin, 1995 Talk Radio). A BBC response to this was to launch BBC Radio 5. The 1996 Broadcasting Act stabilised this situation and also permitted more cross-ownership; however it did confirm the BBC's special status for the moment.

Faced with competition from commercial channels, the BBC is criticised for becoming much more populist in order to compete with them. The reforms undertaken in the 1990s in order to try to make the BBC more competitive are widely believed to be to the detriment of radio, cutting investment in radio, forcing newsrooms to go bimedia. The paring down of established schedules and diminishing of highbrow content do not appear to have solved the perceived problem of the BBC which, according to figures in late 1998, has lost audiences at an even faster rate (Hellen, 1998).

File on Four

There are two principal vehicles for investigation on BBC radio, *File on Four* and *Face the Facts*. The *Face the Facts* team also inputs into news. Other BBC programmes with a tradition of investigative work are *You and Yours, The Food Programme, Farming Today, The Today Programme, World at One* and *World this Weekend*. As yet there are few if any outlets for investigation on commercial radio in the UK, which is a pity since radio has many advantages over television in this field; people are more likely to talk when not expected to be in vision than when in front of a camera and issues of identification are much easier to deal with.

The two BBC series are complementary. *Face the Facts* is a popular, 'getting wrongs put right' programme whereas *File on Four* attempts the stories with wider ramifications and issues of policy behind them. *File on Four* was first transmitted in October 1977. It is transmitted for 40 minutes weekly and has an audience of one million per week for its two broadcasts, an audience which is more male than female, whose members are in their 30s and 40s and who are dedicated Radio 4 listeners. It is produced in four weeks, butted up to transmission. The production team consists of the series editor and aide, the producer, responsible for structure, and the reporter who does the writing and interviewing. The reporter takes responsibility and must have the authority to convince the listener of the significance of his case and individual arguments, as well as the communication skills to make significant or interesting 'sometimes quite dreary bits of fact' (Heggie, 1997). At the time of writing the Editorial team were very pessimistic about the future of their programme because of BBC budget cuts; already they found it almost impossible to mount a long investigation, for financial reasons.[1] Facts that have been investigated include the lack of controls on locum doctors, the poor conditions and lack of legal protection for child labourers, the regulatory framework for small airlines, corruption in Palestine under Yasser Arafat, the morale of the Russian army, hormone disruption chemicals, phoenix directors (those who reappear with new companies after the destruction of the old) and the exploitation of the citizens of poor countries for medical research. In 2002 a special web tribute was produced to mark *File on Four*'s 25th anniversary, and many of its most significant investigations to date are described therein. In 2003, the programme won the Sony Gold Award for an investigation into cot deaths which helped to quash a conviction.

File on Four also won an international George Peabody Award for excellence in media. One of the winners of the 62nd annual awards, a *File on Four* programme was described as 'an in-depth examination that revealed how nations illicitly procured "dual use" materials for the development of nuclear weapons'.[2]

The editor 'never employs specialists' but takes pride when his programmes are admired by experts in the field with which they have made themselves familiar. For example *File on Four* has been awarded both Gold and Silver awards of the Medical Journalism Association (Ross, 1999). According to David Heggie, one of the producers of *File on Four*, the programme is investigative in every sense. It finds its own stories – there is 'nothing that comes off diary'; it has an utterly different agenda from news; it is long-form programming with the implications this has for the nature of the subject and the kinds of treatment. The subjects have major policy implications and matter to large numbers of people; therefore once embarked upon, a subject has to be treated thoroughly so that no listener can imagine that the programme is dressing up a 'cheap scandal' as something more significant. The editor, David Ross, is very clinical early on as to what the core of the subject is and starts by writing the billing: 'We are ostentatious about dotting Is and crossing Ts and only make claims that we can substantiate; moreover we believe that the plural of fact is not data and that facts in themselves are not truth'. *File on Four*'s team believes that its reputation depends upon its evidence: 'there is no rhetoric except that coming from other people' and it does not campaign, 'campaigning is for others. We produce the facts' (Heggie, 1997).

This characterisation is endorsed by editor David Ross, who talks of *File on Four* as being not investigative journalism but 'evidential reportage': the 'reportage' is in the getting away from the daily debate and trying to look at the effects of policy and decisions on how people actually live, the 'evidential' is looking for evidence first hand. It is the level and quality of detail that marks out *File on Four*. What is the difference between evidential and analytical? 'Not wheeling in the experts but getting out and seeing what's going on' (Ross, 1999). It is programmes dealing with aspects of business that he mentions when asked to illustrate his method, and in particular business interfacing with the public sector. In 1996 his team looked at the background of US companies coming into the UK power market (*FoF*, 30 January 1996). 'We found that you need very strong regulation if you are to deal effectively with these power companies. We questioned the effectiveness of the regulatory mechanisms' (Ross, 1999). Similar lessons were learned from an investigation of the outsourcing of public service computer contracts by the Department of Social Security and Immigration Service; here were 'massive contracts and things not going right' (*FoF*, 2 March 1999).

The same theme has run through several investigations into fraud in the European Commission since January 1998, well before the European Parliament publicised such fraud in early 1999. Through his contacts in Brussels reporter Richard Watson opened up the scale of the fraud by revealing that over 200 agriculture projects were under investigation. One of those he exposed was a project where the recipient company in Ireland received hundreds of thousands of pounds for work done in Sicily costing minimal amounts (*FoF*, 6 January 1998).

Business issues and investigative journalists

Government is a clear target, businesses less so. There are thousands of businesses carrying on unimaginably varied activities. Whereas we are all affected by public administration, for an investigation into business to be appealing to an audience, and therefore worth doing, a journalist must feel confident either that its name is sufficiently known, or its activities sufficiently heinous, for impact to be possible. The kind of activities that investigative journalists in the UK have found their public to be interested in include the production of goods that harm substantial numbers of people; apparent price-fixing, so that consumers are short-changed; faulty manufacturing and safety procedures which result in death; dishonest use of investment funds; tax evasion by the rich; anti-competitive practices by well-known companies and, at least in the case of one well-known company with a following of popular shareholders, the cheating of its owners; the failures of professional regulation. Opportunities are provided for the investigative journalist by the fact that regulatory bodies and professional codes exist, in some cases as a result of revelations by earlier journalists. They provide the touchstone against which business may be judged, rather than against mere abstract moral laws of behaviour. There are the consumer protection watchdogs and the industry watchdogs such as the Gas Users' Council. In the UK the Financial Services Acts spawned several regulatory bodies for the investment industries and there is the Monopolies Commission. The Companies Acts provide the basic rules of operation. These are the structures which police business – apart from the general laws – and even a cursory knowledge of them opens the eyes of the investigative journalist to opportunities.

One common fact emerges from the examination of some of the best-known cases of business malpractice that have been investigated. It is that companies often create their own moralities, forgetting their responsibilities to the larger society; this is potentially dangerous when their actions can affect so many people, and particularly so when they are insulated from the consequences of what they do either because the regulations are inadequate, perhaps because nobody in the public domain really understands what they do, or because, being trans-national, they can be made subject to no national laws, or because law itself allows them to create structures which ensure that blame can be isolated or deflected from the principals. Eddy makes this point very well, in his summing up of the DC10 investigation (Eddy, 1976), when he quotes Cavour saying, 'if what we did were not done for Italy, what criminals we would be'.

In an attempt to undermine the socially negative aspects of these cultures, a UK pressure group, Public Concern at Work, has promoted the Public Interest Disclosure Bill (1998) which came into force in 1999. In effect, it supports whistle-blowers, giving them protection for revealing their employers' malfeasance.

Doubtless there are many scandals awaiting exposition; Walter Ingo's *Secret Money* (1985) hints at the opportunities for the investigative journalists in tracking tax avoidance by multinationals; Anthony Sampson's series of books on multinational arms dealers, computer companies, oil moguls and bankers tells us of their awesome power to circumvent regulation; Davis' *The Corporate Alchemists* (1984) suggests ways in which the unchecked power of the chemical industries needs to be exposed.

In the following brief sketch of the extent of the investigation of business, I exclude those stories where the emphasis has been on the relationship of business to public administration (political party funding, for example) or to political policy (breaking of embargoes, selling of military or police equipment or services). Moreover, the most prominent of the recent business stories are mentioned in Chapter 4.

There are two outstanding stories that have investigated how it was possible for products which have either killed or maimed large numbers of people to be manufactured and distributed. First, the thalidomide story is well described in several books, succinctly by Evans (1983) and in more detail by Rosen (1979), and the *Sunday Times* Insight (1973 and 1979); it is briefly summarised in Chapter 3.

The other major manufacturing story also comes from the 1970s: the worst air crash the world had then seen occurred just outside Paris on a fine Sunday. Ten minutes after taking off for London from Orly Airport, at 12.30 pm on 3 March 1974, a DC-10 airliner operated by Turkish Airlines plunged 11,500 feet into the Forest of Ermenonville at 497 miles per hour. There were 346 victims. They died violently because the DC-10 had a lie in it.

> It took two years to trace that lie, and with it the disaster that should never have happened. It brought us into conflict in a California court with McDonnell Douglas which built the doomed DC-10, their Ship 29, and it raised the question, as did the thalidomide tragedy, of how far the press should go on behalf of the citizen in challenging corporate power. It was piquant that in this contest with McDonnell Douglas they quoted the thalidomide campaign as an example of our irresponsibility.
>
> (Evans, 1983: 26)

In essence, the *Sunday Times* discovered that a known fault had not been corrected; its implications had been clear for two years, yet no action had been taken and that therefore many travellers' lives were at risk. The investigation, which required that the journalists become experts in the subject in hand to a remarkable degree (Eddy, 1976: 302ff), and without which the important facts of the case might never have come to light, indicted the civil aviation industry for its procedures, the failure of the agency responsible for the public control of safety standards and the commercial and political pressures upon the manufacturers to which it accorded much of the blame.

Price-fixing is a perennial issue, presumably because editors know that it riles their audiences. In 1998 there was a series of exposures in several media of the fact that British consumers pay more for their supermarket food than those on the continent of Europe; in 1991 the *Sunday Times* had already shown that mark-ups by British supermarkets, at 60 per cent, were much higher than in the US or Germany (Neil, 1996: 335). Bank charges are a similar staple. At the time of going to press the British government claims to be taking serious action to deal with these issues identified by journalists. One impressive group of investigations into price-fixing, covered by television and several newspapers, concerned the by now well-known fact that UK consumers pay vastly more for cars than their continental counterparts. At least one television programme (BBC *Panorama*, 1998) exposed the unethical practices that achieve this, and the way in which a coalition of manufacturers and dealers had ensured that it was virtually impossible for British consumers to buy right-hand drive cars on the Continent; it also demonstrated how the second-hand car market was being rigged to support the excess profits being made in the new. As an example of how millions of people's incomes and necessities are affected by business malpractice, this could hardly be bettered. There have been many after the fact investigations of investment malpractice. The 1960s saw the introduction of a number of invest and save schemes including that of IOS, Investors Overseas Services, run by a Bernard Caulfield; his operations were the subject of extensive journalistic investigation by Insight, described in Raw (1971), who went on to cover the Slater Walker financial scam, written up in Raw (1977). In June 1988 the Barlow Clowes scandal broke, 'an immense deception carried out with almost farcical ease by one man against major financial institutions, government departments and over sixteen thousand private investors' (Lever, 1992). It illustrated well the failure of auditors to identify problems, the limitations of legal regulation and, probably, the lack of competent journalists in this important field. The earliest example of the investigation of tax evasion of which I am aware is the series of articles by Philip Knightley on 'The Gilded Tax Dodgers' in the *Sunday Times* during 1980. Knightley later went on to write up the story of the family that had made tax avoidance a core principle of its business since the First World War in his *The Vesteys*, providing a beginners' guide to methods which, it may be speculated, have since become widely applied. In 1988 the *Sunday Times* reported that the Kuwait Investment Office, despite having a £15 billion portfolio of British shares, 'did not pay a penny of tax' (Neil, 1996: 329); in 1990 Insight also exposed how the 1981 British Finance Act had made possible large-scale tax avoidance through offshore trusts (ibid.: 330). More recently there have been stabs at understanding how Rupert Murdoch's business empire has succeeded in paying very little tax.

Anti-competitive practices are probably only of general interest when the companies involved are well known and the story has a touch of the thriller about it. The latter was so when National Car Parks, Europe's biggest, was exposed as having 'conducted an industrial spying campaign against (its rival) Europarks' (*Sunday Times*, 5 August 1990). Better known is the 'dirty tricks campaign' mounted by British Airways against its rival, Virgin, also exposed in the *Sunday Times*. The investigation became really popular when agents of British Airways were caught trying to steal the household refuse of the *Sunday Times*'s business editor.

The most notorious examples of management abuse of shareholder funds are those of Guinness – which resulted in the imprisonment of the Chief Executive of that world-class company – Polly Peck and BCCI. Insight found that Polly Peck's managers were buying their own shares in order to lift their price, and using the company's own money in order to do so. This investigation was made more intriguing by the fact that Polly Peck's founder, Asil Nadir, fled bail and took refuge beyond British law by his associations with politicians and donations to the Conservative Party and by the extraordinary saga of contacts between the exiled entrepreneur and the British government.

The Bank of Credit and Commerce International (BCCI) was being investigated by journalists in 1990, well before its collapse a year later. Essentially, the BCCI story is that of a bank set up to cheat the gullible; millions of devout Muslims or others with a Muslim connection put their money into BCCI because they believed it would be run on Islamic lines by their coreligionists. In reality the bosses siphoned off much of the money either for themselves and their families, or for their pet political or charitable projects, as in the case of *South* magazine. Much information about what was going on had been available for a long time beforehand, had anyone read the accounts of BCCI and its subsidiaries. One of the journalists who worked on the story, Nick Fielding, makes a number of points relevant to investigations in this area. He believes that the regulators (the Serious Fraud Office) in the UK need to be much more proactive in gathering intelligence on potential fraud; that liquidators are a source of important information that is rarely exploited by journalists because it is not published; that qualifications on company accounts need to be highlighted publicly for them to be accessed by journalists in the UK (Fielding, 1993).

Finally, employee exploitation is also a staple of UK media investigations. One that aroused considerable interest was 'Pesticides in Kenya' (1996), which had more audience response than any *File on Four* for the previous few years, suggesting that its listeners are not parochial if the topic is made relevant and addresses existing concerns. 'Pesticides in Kenya' aroused much wrath among listeners; for different reasons it did so too in Kenya, with Kenya Radio denouncing the *File on Four* team as spies (Heggie, 1997).

The original intention of the team was to make a programme about pesticides in the UK but *File on Four* failed to find any adequate evidence of malpractice. By that time *File on Four* was in contact with the Pesticides Action Network which suggested Equador. While examining Equador they came across two researchers, one of whom was a Kenyan with convincing evidence of medical problems caused to agricultural workers through pesticide handling and the other a postgraduate student who had studied pesticide labelling in Kenya. *File on Four* was able to build upon both of these.

The kernel of the story then became the impact upon poorer countries of Western market demands. Its achievements included the fact that the journalists managed to provide incontrovertible evidence of what had first aroused their investigative urges; that they were able to bring together information with which to confront the authorities; that they showed that the large transnational corporation Del Monte imported banned chemicals.

Example: insolvency practitioners

'Insolvency Practitioners' is a *File on Four* that deals with the failure of professional regulation – regarded in legal and social theory as an important bulwark of society. There are 2000 insolvency practitioners in the UK, working mainly for the banks who lend out money to businesses, and regulated by their own professional body working closely with other professional bodies such as the accountancy regulator. When lenders or creditors are concerned about the future of their investments in a company, they call in insolvency practitioners to examine the best method of protecting their investment. The law gives insolvency practitioners great discretion, yet the rules that bind them are, according to the programme 'few, vague and not always enforced'. In other words, it is widely believed that insolvency practitioners act more in their own interests than in the interests of their clients, let alone those whom they are investigating. Since they stand to gain, it is argued, from declaring a company insolvent and disposing of its assets, they will always prefer this option to any other. This is hard on the companies which, sometimes through no fault of their directors, have difficulties that may often be remediable; furthermore it is damaging to society and to the economy if businesses are closed unjustly and unnecessarily.

The treatment

The programme starts with an image that – this being radio – has to be described to us. It is of a Mr Barrie Chapman standing before the house he used to own as we are told that it was taken from him when his 100-year-old business was closed down unnecessarily. It then goes on to state the case of the programme very succinctly, first in the words of the reporter, Jolyon Jenkins, who says, 'most people involved in insolvency are losers, but one player always wins – the insolvency practitioner'. Whereupon another voice is heard (that of Prem Sikka, who will be introduced later) giving the rationale for the programme:

> you will find that these insolvency practitioners do not owe a duty of care either to unsecured creditors or shareholders or employees. What we need is more public scrutiny because what is at stake is not only the particular fortunes of a company, but the fortunes of our economy.

All of this has happened within 30 seconds and precedes the signature tune that leads us into the programme proper. In the traditional way the programme will tell stories that illustrate the points and provide evidence in the form of verifiable facts and testimony. Thus, having heard the case stated at the outset, we will then listen to it being built up and be able to decide whether the investigation has proved it.

In this particular story, we could divine that illustrations from victims of the insolvency practitioners' procedures would follow, providing evidence of specific cases. These cases would be generalised with reference to data on the number of cases taken on by insolvency practitioners and the 'destruction rate'; it is possible that further statistical colour might be found by trawling government agencies' publications. Insolvency practitioners themselves, here set up as the villains, would be asked to comment, individually in the matter of the particular illustrative cases used, and as a body through their professional association on the general charges. Such might be anticipated. How does the programme actually deal with the story?

Illustration A

Farm noises tell us that we are in the countryside and Jolyon explains where we are and that we are with a farmer, Thriepland, whose farm used to be a 'multimillion pound business until Mr Thriepland got embroiled in the curious world of the insolvency practitioner'. Thriepland shows us around the buildings in which he used to produce cheese and the reporter explains that when the price of cheese fell he went to his bank for advice. The bank appointed an investigating accountant, KPMG Peat Marwick, to assess Thriepland's business.

Thriepland gives his comment on what then occurred. A very young man was sent by KPMG to assess the value of Thriepland's stock, whose value he decided – seemingly arbitrarily and without any experience or knowledge of the industry he was assessing – to halve. The one day report by the youth cost £3,000 and was charged to Thriepland. As a result of that report the bank thought the business was failing and appointed an insolvency practitioner to take control of the business and sell off any assets.

Mr Thriepland refused to cooperate and obtained another valuation backing his contention that the business could survive. A wrangle took place over many months of meetings. Thriepland was lucky in that he had excellent contacts, including a banker and a senior lawyer who represented him without charge; the bank was represented by KPMG who then charged him. Thriepland won in the sense that he forced the bank to back down over declaring him insolvent but the case was costly and he was obliged to sell off his cheese-making operation. Furious at his treatment, he tried to sue KPMG upon the assumption that they had failed in their 'duty of care' to him but found that, legally, they owed him no duty of care, so he had no grounds for complaint.

Illustration B

This time we hear the sounds of the demolition of buildings formerly belonging to the Bass Group, another long-established company, this time in packaging and timber. Again the Bank had commissioned a report when the company wanted extended terms; again the report was done speedily by a firm of accountants, Ernst and Young. This firm recommended that the Group be handed to administrators to manage, which it was. The 'even more lucrative task of carrying out their own recommendations', says reporter Jolyon Jenkins, was awarded to Ernst and Young.

There then follows an interview with a senior executive of Bass who believes that the interpretation of the accounts by Ernst and Young was quite simply wrong and that the company was making a profit. The reporter goes on to describe the efforts by the board of the company to obtain a third opinion from a business academic; the academic found it extraordinary that the company he investigated and saw as basically successful and with good potential in its new products should be 'presented as a dead duck'. The academic also pointed out that assets of the Bass Group were undervalued by Ernst and Young. A building valued by Bass at £300,000 was revalued by Ernst and Young at a mere £170,000 and its sale obliged; yet a few months later it was going for £360,000.

After five months of administration by Ernst and Young, the Bass Group ceased trading and administrators gave way to liquidators. The liquidators were Ernst and Young. They sold off the assets and raised enough money for 'nearly all' the debts owed to the creditors to be paid back. 'Not bad' as the reporter says 'for an allegedly insolvent company', especially as about £1 million was paid out in fees, a good deal of it to Ernst and Young. This very strong case against the system is now given a further twist. Former directors of Bass Group want to complain formally, yet the evidence they require to back their case lies in the Group's books which are held by Ernst and Young and to which they, being no longer directors, have no access. This predicament is put by the reporter to the Head of Professional Ethics at the Institute of Chartered Accountants, the professional body that regulates Ernst and Young, but he receives no support for his suggestion that the directors should be provided with the information necessary.

The moral that the reporter takes from this story is that investigating accountants should not be allowed to recommend receivership and then become the receiver. He finds that specialists in this area have been arguing for the dual role to be banned. Prem Sikka, a university Reader in Accounting and Finance, believes that businesses are less likely to be recommended for liquidation if investigating accountants have nothing to gain from doing so. At this point the reporter, as we predicted, produces such statistical evidence as he has. He claims that in general there is 'striking statistical evidence that banning insolvency practitioners from acting as receivers for companies they've investigated would mean more companies surviving' and cites the Royal Bank of Scotland as having decided not to commission insolvency practitioners to do both jobs. However, the accountants themselves are very keen that the Royal Bank's example not be followed, and this is stated by the professional body's spokesman who believes that his members are scrupulous about all the various threats to their objectivity.

Having failed to get any agreement on his point from the 'villains', the reporter then proceeds to undermine the case that accountants do bind themselves by rules of impartiality. One such professional rule is that there should be no close connection between the accountant selling off the assets of a bankrupt company and those to whom the assets are sold. Jenkins gives the example of a Nottingham printing company. According to him, not only did the receivers, accountancy firm Grant Thornton, refuse a higher offer for the business than they subsequently accepted, but Grant Thornton's manager for the receivership was the main person to buy it, and was apparently improving it before he actually became its main owner. This is definitely unethical and against the profession's rules. The reporter returns to the professional body. Such action as described is unethical, he establishes, and would be subject to complaint and disciplinary action. Yet nothing has been done.

Having verified his point that the regulatory bodies cannot be relied upon to 'police the system with small companies', the programme moves on to a bigger field, showing that similar, or worse, behaviour can take place at capital or national level. Corporate Communications, a major public relations company, went into receivership, in other words was bankrupt and had its management taken over by accountants supposedly acting in the interests of the creditors. This happened, it was alleged, at least partly due to the greed of the executive directors who took far too much out of the company; yet when the accountants were called in they promptly sold the assets back to those directors, conveniently excluding some major shareholders. The old company, the shareholders not in on the plot and its creditors were thus put out of the way. Cork Gully, the insolvency arm of accountancy firm Coopers and Lybrand, managed the whole affair so fast that the shareholders and creditors had no time to challenge the process yet, according to the programme, were left with no money because the asset sale had not raised enough.

Here we come to some sleuthing by the programme that reveals that the trick was premeditated. The researchers discovered that:

1   the receivers had been consulted before they had even been appointed, and the whole process had been planned in advance;
2   the claims that speed was essential if the business was to be saved and that there was no other buyer for one particularly sensitive part of the business cannot be substantiated and were probably false;
3   a rule of the Society of Practitioners of Insolvency was broken in that Coopers & Lybrand was both a consultant to the company well before liquidation and then its receiver.

The programme has documentary and testimonial evidence to support these allegations. It then goes to the Society and asks in general terms whether the kind of things described above would be against the rules and is informed that they are. However, its expert witness, Prem Sikka, warns that self-regulation does not work, pointing out that regulatory bodies made up of committees, many of whose members represent firms making hundreds of millions of pounds from these practices, are not very disposed to control them.

Jenkins has the last word:

Last year, 5000 companies went into receivership. The insolvency practitioners who took them over had virtually unlimited and unchallengeable powers to dispose of them as they saw fit. But our cases show that what they do is not always in the best interests of the company. The accountants have not yet been called to account.

Discussion

The world of insolvency is full of arcane terms and business jargon and the programme very effectively deals with this by first giving a helicopter view of what the theme is and going on to very simple and concrete examples. It is everywhere clear, at least in part because the stories are well told, with disciplined testimonials. Expertise is only used to clarify or to offer comment where comment by the reporter would be out of order.

To undertake this programme for television would have been extremely expensive; for it to have been written as a newspaper feature would have demanded such space as to tax the concentration of all but the most dedicated readers. Yet it is entertaining as well as informative as radio, suggesting that radio is an excellent medium for investigative journalism, something that has not been fully exploited.

As to the content, the remarkable implications, in particular of the Corporate Communications case, were not fully spelt out: if it is illegal to privilege some creditors of a liquidating company over others and if directors' liabilities and responsibilities of good governance mean anything, how was it that Corporate Communications' original directors and their advisers were not prosecuted? The way in which this aspect was dealt with was not as decisive as the earlier parts of the programme.

Nevertheless this programme is a classic example of dealing with a business story in investigative journalism because it satisfies the conditions of a good investigation and a good human interest story. It identifies cases that represent issues with far-reaching implications; challenges villain with victim; clarifies complex issues by going to the root of the matter; uses whatever techniques are required to gain that access or information that provide the appropriate evidence. These are necessary conditions of investigative journalism.

Notes

1 O'Halloran, J. (2007) *File on Four*, interviewed by Katie Byrne.
2 http://news.bbc.co.uk/go/pr/fr/-/1/hi/programmes/file_on_4/4223419.stm

Bibliography

BBC (1996) 'Pesticides in Kenya', *File on Four*. Manchester: BBC.
BBC (1997) 'Insolvency Practitioners', *File on Four*. Manchester: BBC.
BBC (1998) 'The Car Cartel', *Panorama*. London: BBC.

Crook, T. (1998) *International Radio Journalism*. London: Routledge.

Davis, L. (1984) *The Corporate Alchemists*. London: Temple Smith.

Eddy, P. (1976) *Destination Disaster*. London: Granada.

Evans, H. (1983) *Good Times, Bad Times*. London: Phoenix.

Fielding, N. (1993) Investigating BCCI: a journalist's experience. *Crime, Law and Social Change*, 20 (4): 311.

Heggie, D. (1997) 'File on Four' Talk given to students on the MA Investigative Journalism course at Nottingham Trent University, 23 November 1997.

Hellen, N. (1998) Boyle to go in Radio 4 disaster. *Sunday Times*, 1 November 1998: 9.

Ingo, W. (1985) *Secret Money*. London: George Allen.

Jordan, G. (1990) *The Commercial Lobbyists: Politics for Profit in Britain*. Aberdeen: Aberdeen University Press: 13–46.

Knightley, P. (1980) The gilded tax dodgers. *Sunday Times*, Oct–Nov 1980.

Knightley, P. (1993) *The Rise and Fall of the House of Vestey. The True Story of How Britain's Richest Family Beat the Taxman – and Came to Grief*. London: Warner.

Lever, L. (1992) *The Barlow Clowes Affair*. London: Macmillan/Channel 4.

Neil, A. (1996) *Full Disclosure*. London: Macmillan.

Raw, C. (1971) *Do You Sincerely Want to be Rich?* London: André Deutsch.

Raw, C. (1977) *Slater Walker*. London: André Deutsch.

Rosen, M. (1979) *The Sunday Times Thalidomide Case: Contempt of Court and the Freedom of the Press*. London: Writers and Scholars Educational Trust. For the British Institute of Human Rights.

Ross, D. (1999) Interview with Hugo de Burgh, BBC Manchester, 24 March 1999.

Sampson, A. (1973) *Sovereign State: The Secret History of ITT*. London: Hodder and Stoughton.

Sampson, A. (1978) *The Arms Bazaar*. Sevenoaks: Coronet.

Sampson, A. (1981) *The Money Lenders*. London: Hodder and Stoughton.

Sampson, A. (1993) *The Seven Sisters: The Great Oil Companies and the World They Made*, 3rd edn. London: Coronet.

Stephens, M. (1997) *A History of News*. Fort Worth, TX: Harcourt Brace.

Sunday Times (Insight Team) (1973) *The Thalidomide Children and the Law*. London: André Deutsch.

Sunday Times (Insight Team) (1979) *Suffer the Children: The Story of Thalidomide*. London: André Deutsch.

Further reading

Crook, T. (1998) *International Radio Journalism*. London: Routledge.

Franklin, B. (1997) *Newszak and News Media*. London: Edward Arnold.

14

PANORAMA – INVESTIGATIVE TV?

Ivor Gaber

Introduction

Panorama – to quote the BBC's own website – is "the world's longest-running investigative TV show".[1] The question this chapter addresses is, was it ever, and is it today?

The programme, often referred to as the BBC's 'flagship' current affairs programme, was first broadcast on 11 November 1953 and it began life somewhat uncertainly. Stephen Bonarjee, who was one of the programme's first producers, described it as: 'the most disastrous single production with which I have ever been associated. Literally everything went wrong. The overall memoir is of this terrible shambles'.[2] The programme's attempt to combine jokey items with serious current affairs analysis backfired badly, not helped by a series of technical mishaps. The fledgling 'flagship' was hastily removed from air, but a few weeks later reappeared and has been sailing on ever since, more or less continuously, if not serenely. More than half a century on, *Panorama* is now a British broadcasting institution. For a television programme to have appeared, more or less regularly, for 55 years is, given the transient nature of television, a quite spectacular record, for which the BBC can be justifiably proud.

The programme has traditionally claimed for itself the title of Britain's pre-eminent current affairs television programme, a claim that has always been contested. For most of the past half century ITV's *World in Action* and *This Week* could both make convincing arguments as to why they could equally assert their rights to make a similar assertion, and then, since the establishment of Channel Four, that channel's weekly *Dispatches* has been the new kid on the blog disputing the champion's crown. Today it is more likely that BBC2's daily *Newsnight* or *Channel Four News* would be regarded as the principal site of television current affairs and perhaps that has been one of *Panorama's* problems as it has struggled to find a new role for itself in the changed broadcasting environment of the digital age. However, whether it is now, or was ever, the nation's premier current affairs outlet is a debate to which there can be no conclusion, but what is clear is that in making the claim in the past, *Panorama* would never have made it on the basis of its record as an 'investigative' programme, as it does now.

The programme's strapline as 'The world's longest running investigative TV show', bears some consideration. First, there's a touch of hubris about the claim – is it provable? *Panorama* is certainly older than one of its main international comparators – CBS's *60 Minutes,* which was first broadcast in 1967; but there might well be, in some other part of the broadcasting ecology, another current affairs programme that pre-dates *Panorama*. And it's also, from a promotional point of view, a slightly odd claim to make; not unlike British Airways, for example, promoting itself as 'the world's oldest airline' – not a slogan likely to win too many awards in the world of advertising.

Then there's the use of that word 'show', which is somehow indicative of a new style and philosophy – one that's more about 'impact' than content. Most television journalists tend to talk about their 'programme', not their 'show' – a term more commonly associated with light entertainment rather than current affairs. However, it is the claim that, *Panorama* is, in essence, an 'investigative' programme that gives rise to the most serious questions and these are addressed in this chapter.

Whether or not *Panorama* is now an investigative programme is a matter of judgement; what is not, is the fact that for most of the programme's history, it saw itself as carrying out a very different mission. It was a mission characterised by the programme's unofficial biographer, Richard Lindley (who worked on *Panorama* for 15 years) as: '. . . to explore and explain the world we live in, week in, week out'.[3] This it did through straight reportage, analysis and landmark interviews. It is significant that in Lindley's 404 page book, the words 'investigative journalism' occur just three times. One of the references is to a 1979 incident when a *Panorama* team filmed an IRA roadblock at Carrickmore in Northern Ireland – a sequence that, whilst it never made it onto air, did succeed in deeply offending the then Prime Minister, Margaret Thatcher, and led to the temporary sacking of the then programme editor. The other two references to investigative journalism are to a programme, a few years later, called 'Maggie's Militant Tendency', an attempt to link some of Mrs Thatcher's right-wing supporters in Parliament to past neo-nazi political activity. It caused another political storm, and also to an expensive out-of-court libel settlement for the BBC, described by Lindley as 'an extraordinary humiliation'[4]. The political and legal storms that followed these programmes clearly shook *Panorama*'s confidence in its ability to make investigative programming for many years to come.

So it is worth bearing in mind that, whatever castigations, in terms of the inadequacy of its investigative programming, might be applied to today's *Panorama*, for most of its existence investigations were seen as a relatively minor part of its overall offering.

The 'new' *Panorama*

In recent years *Panorama* has been seen to be in the television doldrums, being consigned to a slot late on Sunday nights which attracted ever smaller audiences. However, it was re-launched in January 2007 to great fanfare, modestly described by its new presenter, Jeremy Vine, as 'the biggest media event of 2007'.[5] In its new incarnation *Panorama* lost 10 minutes of air-time (down from 40 to 30 minutes) but it gained in terms of the regularity of its appearance and a move from a Sunday to a Monday evening slot. As to audiences, it has attracted a younger profile and it has added around 400,000 to take its average to around 3 million viewers, not sensational, but, in a multi-channel environment, quite a respectable performance. However, an analysis of the programmes broadcast in 2007 raises questions about the extent to which it has lived up to its claim to be an 'investigative show'.

Making judgements about what is, or isn't, 'investigative journalism' is bound to be subjective. The Cambridge Dictionary defines investigative journalism as 'the activity of news reporters trying to discover information which is of public interest but which someone might be keeping hidden'. It's as good a starting point as any. The key phrase in this definition is 'public interest' – a concept that, in the context of investigative journalism, was addressed by Lord Wilberforce, in a judgement in a case involving Granada TV's *World in Action*, which was being sued by British Steel. They were challenging the programme's right to broadcast information contained in confidential documents which had been given to the programme by a British Steel 'mole'. In finding in favour of Granada, who argued that the documents revealed issues of 'public interest' Wilberforce observed: '... there is a wide difference between what is interesting to the public and is what in the public interest to make known.'[6]

Using this as a touchstone, it is possible to classify *Panorama* programmes into 'substantive investigations' i.e. those in the public interest, and 'populist' i.e. those that are interesting to the public. For this research the programmes were divided into four categories, as follows:

- 'Substantive Investigations'– defined as a programme that involves either revelatory investigation into a matter of public importance that has not yet entered the public domain; or an investigation into a current issue that throws significant new light onto the subject. Examples of such *Panorama* programmes in 2007 included investigations into the London bombers, the Saudi arms scandal, people traffickers and the shortage of midwives in the health service.
- 'Populist Investigations' – defined as programmes that might utilise the techniques of investigative journalism, and involve significant revelation, but whose subject matter raises no substantive issues of public policy. Examples of these on *Panorama* in 2007 included programmes about

Scientology, Bob Woolmer's 'murder', dog-fighting and a British woman married to a Mafia boss.

- 'News Backgrounders' – defined as programmes that look at a current issue and provide additional information that, whilst enlightening, cannot be judged to be significantly new so as to add substantially to public understanding. Examples included programmes about the sub-prime crisis, Barak Obama, Alan Johnson's kidnapping and British forces in Afghanistan and Iraq.
- 'Self-referential' – the occasional reprise of recent *Panorama* hits.

In 2007, 51 *Panorama* programmes were broadcast. (It's worth pointing out that this regularity of appearance is in marked contrast to the recent past which saw 36 programmes broadcast in 2006 and just 32 the preceding year.) Using the above categories, the research identified the following:

Panorama 2007

Substantive investigations	14
Populist investigations	8
News backgrounders	28
Self-referential	1
TOTAL	51

Substantive investigations (14)

January 15: 'IVF undercover'
Police officers have made unannounced visits to two clinics run by Britain's most successful test-tube baby doctor.

January 29: 'Secrets of the drug trials'
Secret emails reveal that the UK's biggest drug company distorted trial results of an anti-depressant, covering up a link with suicide in teenagers.

February 12: 'Please look after mum'
Older people were put at risk in two substandard nursing homes, according to the regulator for homes in England. A whistleblower describes the 'mental torture' of residents by staff to *Panorama*.

March 13: 'A good kicking'
Panorama reveals that British soldiers suspected of torturing Iraqi civilian detainees were not brought to justice.

April 23: 'TV's Dirty Secrets'
GMTV suspends phone-ins after a BBC investigation finds callers have been defrauded out of millions of pounds.

April 30: 'Did MI5 miss the London bomber?'
Panorama's Peter Taylor reveals the truth behind what MI5 really knew about two of the 2005 London bombers – and asks if they could be stopped.

May 03: 'Midwives Undercover'
Undercover *Panorama* reporter, Hayley Cutts, reveals the acute problems she found on maternity wards.

June 04: 'On a Wing and a Prayer'
An RAF whistleblower has told BBC *Panorama* about deep concerns among servicemen concerning the state of the UK's fleet of Nimrod spy planes.

June 11: 'Princes, Planes and Pay-offs'
Reporter Jane Corbin tells how *Panorama* finally uncovered the story behind the al-Yamamah arms deal with Saudi Arabia.

September 10: 'Destination Europe'
Panorama reports on the hazardous journey of 27 migrants trying to get to Europe from Africa and discovers how criminal gangs are cashing in on people trafficking.

October 22: 'Fifa and Coe'
Panorama's Andrew Jennings investigates new allegations against Fifa officials and asks if Fifa ethics chief Seb Coe can expect 'fair play' from the rulers of the beautiful game.

October 29: 'Jill Dando: The Jury's Out'
An investigation into the conviction of Barry George for the murder of Jill Dando has cast doubt on the evidence central to the prosecution. Raphael Rowe reports.

November 12: 'What Next for Craig?'
Reporter, Shelley Jofre reveals that new research shows giving children drugs for ADHD works no better than doing nothing in the long-term.

December 03: 'Cheryl and Eric Please Look After Dad'
Panorama reveals that anti-psychotic drugs frequently prescribed to treat dementia patients could shorten lives and, if used over long periods, don't work.

Populist investigations (8)

April 02: 'Death in Corfu'
Safety checks at a hotel bungalow where two children died were 'not made by a gas expert', BBC *Panorama* learns.

May 10: 'Murder at the World Cup'
Since the transmission of this programme, Jamaican police have attributed the death of Bob Woolmer to natural causes.

May 14: 'Scientology and Me'
The battleground is YouTube and Scientology's weapon is a clip of *Panorama* reporter John Sweeney losing it.

May 21: ;Wi-Fi: a warning signal'
As more than half of Britain's schools embrace Wi-Fi, *Panorama* investigates whether the new technology poses any potential health risks.

May 28: 'Married to the Mob'
John Ware meets Ann Hathaway, wife of one of Sicily's most powerful Mafiosi as she prepares to return to her native North-West to start a new life.

June 18: 'Is TV Bad for My Kids?'
We took TV's computer and games consoles away from 7 and 8 year olds for two weeks.

July 30: 'Children's Fight Club'
Police chiefs urge websites to remove violent video footage of children fighting, following a BBC probe.

August 30: 'Dog-Fighting Undercover'
For 18 months a *Panorama* undercover team has been operating alongside hardcore dog-fighting gangs in the UK and Europe, capturing on camera the savagery of organised dog-fights.

News backgrounders (28)

January 22: 'How to poison a spy'
The Kremlin has angrily branded Alexander Litvinenko's widow Marina a 'liar' following comments she has made in her interview for *Panorama*.

February 5: 'Should I fight back?'
A Home Office minister has suggested people 'distract' potential criminals while waiting for police to arrive and intervene. Tony McNulty MP agreed that jumping up and down could help.

February 19: 'For Queen and Country'
The armed forces minister has said the government should have acted sooner to deal with the backlog of inquests for soldiers killed in Iraq.

February 26: GBH on the NHS'
Violence and abuse against staff costs the NHS more than £100m a year in extra security, absenteeism, training of staff and legal bills.

March 05: 'Go Green or Else!'
We are told climate change is the biggest threat facing the world but is there anything the average family can do about it? The Rowlatts 'went green' for an entire year.

March 12: 'Murder in slow motion'
The UK is 15 years behind the US in preventing attacks and murders by stalkers, BBC's *Panorama* is told.

March 26: 'Soldiers on the run'
AWOL soldiers tell BBC *Panorama* the army fails to help them cope with the traumas of serving in Iraq.

April 16: 'Life Behind Bars'
Panorama investigates the reality of life behind bars in one of the UK's increasing number of private prisons.

May 07: 'White Fright'
Panorama investigates the growing segregation between Muslim Asians and whites in UK towns and cities.

July 02: 'Missing Children'
A couple, who had three children taken into care after allegations of abuse, have been cleared of the charges and allowed to keep their fourth child.

July 09: Heroes of 21/7'
People who tackled the bombers on 21 July speak to *Panorama* about their heroic actions.

July 10: 'Tagging Undercover'
Does the tagging of offenders work? *Panorama* featured the cases of three
offenders convicted of murder or manslaughter while on a tag.

June 25: 'Trust Me, I'm Gordon – Not Tony'
As Gordon Brown asks for the nation's trust, John Ware examines the next
prime minister's record on the truth.

July 23: 'Immigration: How we lost count'
Panorama's Richard Bilton goes to the immigration hotspot of Slough
where new arrivals pitch up daily and the local council says it can't balance its
books.

August 06: 'Keeping Britain Dry'
Panorama asks how much the floods have cost the UK and how much more we
are prepared to spend to defend the country from future downpours.

August 13: 'On a Knife Edge'
As the number of youths killed on the streets of London this year rises, with
more victims across the country, *Panorama* profiles two 15-year-old boys on the
fringe of gang culture.

August 20: 'Return to Gaza'
Six weeks after the release of Alan Johnston, *Panorama* returns to Gaza to examine what has become of the place now the world has looked away again.

September 03: 'Real Apprentices'
Britain's booming, says Gordon Brown – so how come so many young people
can't – or won't – get jobs? *Panorama* meets four young men from Swindon
trying to break the habit of unemployment.

September 17: 'Wasting police time'
Police officers tell *Panorama* how paperwork and pressure to meet government
targets is making it harder to do their job.

September 24: 'Give Us Your DNA'
A specially commissioned opinion poll for *Panorama* has revealed that two
thirds of people would be in favour of a national DNA database.

October 01: 'How I became a Muslim extremist'
Panorama talks to Shiraz Maher, a former member of the Muslim extremist
group Hizb ut-Tahrir which campaigns for an Islamic state.

October 08: 'Sub-prime Suspect'
Panorama finds out if the miss-selling of mortgages to those with bad credit records could cause a financial crisis in Britain.

October 15: 'Is America Ready For A Black President?'
Panorama asks whether the US is ready for a black president. Barack Obama has been described as a political sensation – but can he overcome racial divisions?

October 25: 'Alan Johnston Kidnapped: The Alan Johnston Story'
The *Panorama* Special tells the extraordinary story of the BBC correspondent's 114 days held in captivity by the Army of Islam in Gaza.

November 05: 'Taking on the Taleban – The Soldiers' Story'
Panorama follows a unit of British soldiers in Afghanistan during a tour that ended with one of them dead and 12 seriously wounded.

November 19: 'The Mystery of Madeleine McCann'
Gerry McCann speaks in a personal video of his belief that his family was watched in the days before his daughter vanished.

December 10: 'Plume of Smoke Near Vehicle – The Battle for Basra Palace'
Jane Corbin returns to Iraq as Britain hands over security control for Basra Province and tells the story of the last British fight in southern Iraq.

December 17: 'Jane Corbin in Little Iraq Basra: The Legacy'
As British troops hand over security control in southern Iraq, *Panorama* asks what sort of place will British troops be leaving behind.

Self-referential (1)

July 16: 'What Happened Next?'
Panorama returns to some of the stories it has covered over the last year to find out What Happened Next?

Thus the overall figures suggest that the programme's claim to be an investigative show are weak. Ironically, despite its assertions to the contrary, *Panorama* in 2007, was doing more or less what it has always done. For by devoting more than half its programmes to what we have identified as 'News Backgrounders', it was following the programme mission, as defined by Richard Lindley in his history of *Panorama*: '. . . to explore and explain the world we live in, week in, week out'.

This in itself is hardly a criticism, but in terms of being seen as a serious outlet of investigative journalism, it did not (in 2007 at least) match its own billing. Not only were just 14 of its editions judged to be 'substantive investigations', there also appeared to be a slowing down in the pace; six were broadcast between January and April – an average of 1.5 a month and only eight in the remaining eight months up until December – an average of just one a month.

To compound the problem, some of *Panorama*'s investigations went sadly awry. Perhaps the worst example of this being an investigation by reporter John Sweeney that 'revealed' that Scientology was more cult than a religion – hardly a blinding revelation. But its real weakness lay not so much in its content but in its approach. Perhaps the title gave the game away – it was called 'Scientology and Me' – and its focus was more on the latter than the former, as the trials and tribulations of the reporter appeared to take precedence over its exposure of Scientology. Indeed, Sweeney's encounter with the Scientologists, who hounded him at every turn, climaxed, if that's the right word, with him losing control in a series of on-camera verbal outbursts which he himself described thus: 'If you are interested in becoming a TV journalist, it is a fine example of how not to do it. I look like an exploding tomato and shout like a jet engine . . . it makes me cringe'.[7]

The programme was controversial, for the wrong reasons, even before the broadcast, and not just because of the 'exploding tomato'. For the Scientologists sought to 'expose' some of Sweeney's own techniques by issuing a DVD based on their filming him, filming them. The DVD made a series of allegations against the *Panorama* team, the most damning being a sequence that appeared to show Sweeney knocking on a locked back door of a Scientology building to give the impression that the Scientologists were refusing him entrance. Although – given its provenance – it is right to question the DVD's credibility, the visual evidence appeared strong and has not been specifically refuted by either Sweeney or the BBC.

Commenting on this episode Tom Mangold, one of *Panorama's* most distinguished reporters, used it to illustrate what, he argued, was the problem with *Panorama* in its new incarnation: 'Half an hour on this kind of irrelevance and not a word elsewhere about the world impact of the current administration in Washington, or in-depth reporting on the struggles of the new candidates for the White House; nothing about Putin's new aggressive nationalism and its implications; nothing whatsoever on British politics at a time of real political change. Instead, investigations into a faulty gas boiler in Corfu that killed two British tourists . . . ho hum; and waiting in the wings a pretty unserious-sounding sociological piece about what happens when you deprive some children of television for two weeks'.[8]

Other *Panorama* investigations also went adrift in 2007. A programme about two IVF clinics in London, which both had outstanding success rates for the women they treated but were both of concern to the regulator (the Human Fertilisation and Embryology Authority), were at the time of writing (March 2008) the subject of a libel action; with *Panorama* in a weakened position following the decision by the Regulator to agree an out-of-court settlement with the clinics.

A programme about the death of the Pakistan cricket coach Bob Woolmer 'proved' that not only had he been strangled but also poisoned – alas a note on the *Panorama* website now says: 'Since the transmission of this programme, Jamaican police have attributed the death of Bob Woolmer to natural causes'.

And an 'investigation' into the alleged dangers of Wi-Fi signals in schools attracted almost universal criticism. David Gregory, the BBC's own science and environment correspondent said of it: 'I can't believe such a biased and scientifically incoherent piece of TV made it to the air. . . . frankly the April Fool *Panorama* on the Spaghetti Tree Harvest was more rooted in scientific reality'. And in a subsequent interview on the BBC's Newswatch programme the programme's reporter Paul Kenyon, on being told that one of his main sources, a Swedish scientist, had been voted by his colleagues as 'Misleader of the Year' replied, 'Did they? That's not good'. And a note on the programme's website, rather plaintively reads: 'The BBC's Editorial Complaint Unit has upheld complaints against this edition of *Panorama*.'

So the argument is that *Panorama* in its new guise is not, solely, or even predominantly an 'investigative show', at least not one that majors on 'substantive investigations'. What it now seeks to be is a factual series that deals with popular issues in as popular, some would say 'populist', way as possible, in order to maximise its audience. Since they have succeeded in increasing their audience, and broadening its appeal to younger viewers, should this not be judged a success?

Tom Mangold believes it does not: 'Why in heaven's name must *Panorama* be judged by its audience size rather than the quality of its content?' he asks, 'What is public service broadcasting about if it fails to make available serious, sensible, responsible, informative (and, yes, entertaining where possible) television journalism at a peak time for those who want more than 100-word up-sums on their mobile phones about the major issues of our time?'[9]

John Ware, another senior *Panorama* reporter who is still with the programme, has been equally scathing about the programme's current approach to investigative journalism: 'The overwhelming impression we've had . . . is that BBC1 is about entertainment and that the benchmark for current affairs would be undercover stuff. It's not very challenging to strap on a camera and go and work in a hospital and tell people how dirty it is', he said.[10]

Panorama's editor Sandy Smith has rejected criticisms that the programme has gone downmarket. 'We haven't done Tesco, we haven't done house prices, we haven't done obesity – those are the things you would do if you wanted to compete with *Tonight with Trevor McDonald*', he said. 'I have never read or had conversations with audience planners or other soothsayers who would have told me what I should be commissioning to put more bums on seats. And I think that's blindingly obvious from my story list.'[11]

But the assumption that *Panorama* sees, as its prime role, winning audiences is not based just on the gossip of former reporters, but is in fact enshrined in its own mission statement which reads that it aims 'to deliver impact either in terms of audience size or in take-up by the wider media'[12] In other words getting bigger audiences and getting noticed by other media. This is a significant statement in that it makes clear that impacting on viewers and the media is a priority, but that making an impact on public policy is not. (This obsession with headlines was responsible for the unseemly practice of BBC News on a Sunday evening regularly running *Panorama* promos as if they were substantive news items – a practice that it eventually abandoned.)

Overall, the verdict on the role of *Panorama* as an investigative programme, at least in the first year of its new incarnation, is mixed. For sure it is still undertaking some serious investigations – in 2007 they ran high-quality and revelatory investigations into the behaviour of British troops on Iraq, the poor state of the RAF's Nimrod aircraft and MI5's failure to identify London terrorists. But equally, many of its investigations appeared to be based on finding popular subjects and presenting the results in ways that put almost as much stress on production values as on editorial content, or in ways that have raised questions about the programme's editorial standards. And the fact remains that the majority of its programmes are neither investigative, but nor are they seeking to do what *Panorama* once did so well – in the words of Tom Mangold, '. . . to spend time, energy, money and true reporting talent to cover, in real depth, the big, strategic, vital issues of the day, whatever the [audience] figures'.[13]

So does it matter? Well, yes it does because democracy depends not just on citizens having a vote once every four years but also on its citizens making informed choices. And voters cannot be expected to decide between different politicians and parties if one's only source of information is the occasional leaflet that a local political party might drop through the odd letter box. Newspapers, television and radio broadcasters (and online sites that aspire to be taken seriously) have a duty to keep people informed about the overall 'state of the nation' which they do through reportage and analysis, but they also have their oft-quoted watchdog role, that of holding governments and others to account for what they do, and equally, for what they don't do. This is one of the principal functions of investigative journalism, which is why programmes like *Panorama* are important. And why its current state requires commenting on.

Notes

1 http://news.bbc.co.uk/1/programmes/*Panorama*/default.stm
2 Interview with Stephen Bonarjee by George Scott, 1 April 1980, BBC Oral History. Archive quoted in: Lindley, R. (2002) *Panorama: fifty years of pride and paranoia.* London: Politico's: 1.
3 Ibid., p. 383e
4 Ibid., p. 255
5 Gibsen, O. (2007) 'Into the Lions' Den'. *The Guardian*, 15 January 2007.

6 British Steel Corporation v Granada Television 1981.
7 Sweeney, J. (2007) 'Row over Scientology video', BBC News website, 14 May 2007. http://news.bbc.co.uk/1/hi/world/americas/6650545.stm
8 Mangold, T. (2007) 'Upmarket 'Panorama'? 'The Spaghetti Tree was more rooted in reality'. *The Independent*, 17 June 2007.
9 Ibid.
10 Quoted in: Silver, J. (2006) 'Panorama urged not to depend on stunts and secret filming'. *The Guardian*, 21 August 2006.
11 Quoted in: Lindley, R. (2008) 'Primetime Suspect'. *The Guardian*, 7 January 2008.
12 Ibid.
13 Mangold, op. cit.

Further reading

Bolton, R. (1990) *Death on the Rock: and other stories*. London: W.H. Allen.

Briggs, A. (1995) *The History of Broadcasting in the United Kingdom: Sound and Vision 1945–55*. Oxford: Oxford University Press.

Briggs, A. (1995) *The History of Broadcasting in the United Kingdom: Competition 1955–74*. Oxford: Oxford University Press.

Cox, G. (1995) *Pioneering Television News*. London: John Libbey.

Lindley, R. (2002) *Panorama: Fifty years of pride and paranoia*. London: Politicos.

Wyndham-Goldie, G. (1977) *Facing the Nation: television and politics*. London: the Bodley Head.

15

SCRUTINISING SOCIAL POLICY
An example from Channel 4's *Dispatches*

Hugo de Burgh

Channel 4's *Dispatches* in the public sphere

In 1982 a fourth national television channel was inaugurated in Britain, among the responsibilities of which were the reflection of perspectives and issues ignored by the other channels and the commissioning of programmes from independent producers rather than in-house production. In 1986, much derided by the then current affairs establishment, David Lloyd took this to 'the extreme' by deciding to commission his creation, *Dispatches*, from a different supplier every week.[1] Many hundreds of *Dispatches* have been transmitted since November 1987 and the variety of stories and treatments is possibly greater than for any other series or strand in the same period. There can be few aspects of British public affairs that have not been touched upon by *Dispatches* and, in consequence, it has upset many and found itself regularly fielding legal challenges.

A famous *Dispatches* episode is 'The Committee', which was the subject of a court case under the Prevention of Terrorism Act; 'Mother Russia's Children' won awards as a revelation of life for street children in St Petersburg; in 'Who Pays the Gas Bill?' *Dispatches* joined the race to expose the British Parliament's 'Cash for Questions' scandal; *Dispatches* claims to have been first with revelations about the effect of CJD on humans in January 1994; its 'Obscene Telephone Calls' programme resulted in British Telecom being forced to introduce systems to deal with a problem they had denied; another inquest was held after *Dispatches* investigated the pleasure boat *Marchioness* disaster (Stott, 1998). Its most controversial programme of recent years exposed corruption in the Post Office (2007) and its most dramatic contribution to our public life was a series of four programmes on torture.

In 2008, *Dispatches* classifies its programmes under eight headings: Education, Health ('Living with Aids' and a savage criticism of NHS conditions called 'On Pain of Death', for example), Natural Disasters, Public Services, Religion, Repressive Regimes ('Torture', North Korea), Society 'Secrets of the Shoplifters' and War on Terror (the largest number of programmes of any category). While the style has become increasingly faster, more dramatic and with more use of hidden cameras, the strand still evinces the high sense of purpose and intense attention to evidence that were apparent when it started.

To investigate nursing standards and care of vulnerable elderly patients in two NHS hospitals, nursing assistants wore 'hidden cameras inside their uniforms for three months: for the first time nurses are investigating nurses. . . . What they discover is a damning catalogue of inefficiency, neglect and substandard treatment'. This programme was one of several revelations by investigative journalists of unacceptable practices in the NHS (28 July 2007).

'Supermarket Secrets' investigated whether the food on supermarket shelves is 'as good as it looks, whether prices are as good as they seem and what happens behind the scenes in the production of supermarket food' (www.channel4. com). The first of two programmes illustrated conditions inside a chicken broiler house of a company which supplies all the major supermarkets. It also examined the value of the chickens produced in this way. The second looked into levels of pesticide residues in supermarket fresh produce, factory farming of dairy cattle and the relevance to nutrition of the packaging of fruit and vegetables.

'The Hurricane That Shamed America' (October 2005) questioned the response from the US government to Hurricane Katrina. *Dispatches* also screened a number of programmes which would best be described as ruminative, of which the most arresting was 'Why Bomb London?' (8 August 2005). It asked whether it was our politicians' foreign policy decisions and domestic errors that made the bombings which took place on . . . 'not so much a surprise as an inevitability'.

> The programme shows how, during the 1990s, the British government allowed known terrorists and extremists to settle in London and build up an underground network, despite the warnings from, and much to the alarm of, governments overseas.
>
> One of Osama Bin Laden's lieutenants established an office in North London and was then implicated in the al Qaeda attacks on the US embassies in Kenya and Tanzania. The Algerian Abu Doha − a close supporter of Bin Laden − also operated out of North London and was involved in terrorist plots against Los Angeles Airport and Strasbourg Cathedral on the eve of the millennium. By the end of the '90s, terrorists and extremists were allowed to live and function in London where they used British freedom of expression and civil rights tolerance to plan terror attacks abroad.
>
> The programme tracks the clerics who inspired these hardened terrorists as they spread their extremist ideology through Britain. The siren voice of the Jordanian Abu Qatada − whose sermons inspired the suicide terrorists who hit the World Trade Centre on 9/11 − inspired a

range of extremist voices and groups who sought to take over mosques throughout the UK, and create a taste for violence and for religious war amongst young British Muslims.

Inspired first by bloodthirsty tales of Islamic fighting and suffering in Chechnya and Bosnia, these same youngsters began to turn their anger directly towards Britain, their home, when British forces marched into Afghanistan and then, in 2003, into Iraq. These major and controversial foreign policy decisions suddenly put the UK onto the frontline of growing Islamist anger and frustration.

(www.channel4.com)

In 2007, *Dispatches* also conducted its own experiment to find out if road pricing is indeed the answer to congestion (12 November 2007); analysed illiteracy in schools; examined the consequences for those now young of the house price boom; covered stories in Iraq, Africa and China.

Since the classic studies of British producers (*inter alia* Elliott, 1972; Silverstone, 1985) there have been many changes in the ways in which producers operate, not least the turn to commissioning independents; yet the sense of elitism among the independent producers is scarcely reduced. They are, though, subject to all the pressures of an astoundingly competitive freelance market. One indication of just how competitive that is, is the statement by the first Commissioning Editor for *Dispatches* that he at times received twenty times as many proposals as he had slots (Lloyd, 1998a). Producers are very keen to make a *Dispatches*; the series is usually considered to be the 'flagship' strand of C4 TV, whose remit is to take risks, to champion the under-represented and to ask the questions that have not been asked (McNulty, 1996: 19). To produce for *Dispatches* is a badge of honour, as is producing for *Panorama*, its BBC equivalent. The C4 viewer is positioned as being educated, wealthy and liberal so that, possibly more than any other channel, it talks to an elite.

Dispatches and social policy

When *Dispatches* was launched, investigative journalism was largely assumed to do with what David Lloyd calls 'the gloaming' – the hidden areas of life where sordid deals between cocaine criminals and arms barons take place and where investigative journalists can practise the skills of the commando and the spy. However, while *Dispatches* continues to screen programmes with the modern equivalent of that profile, such as 'Saddam's Secret Timebomb' (1998) in which Gwyn Roberts courageously investigated the current consequences of Iraq's germ warfare programme against the Kurdish minority, its proportion of programmes dealing with topics of more immediate concern to British citizens at home has risen. This is less in response to market forces, suggested Lloyd, and more the result of a deliberate policy of using the techniques of investigation upon important issues and stories at home, such as the 1999 films on foreign prostitutes in Britain, which required elaborate stings and secret filming ('Sex Slave Trade', 29 April 1999), and a year long undercover investigation of the Animal Liberation Front ('Animal Liberation Front', 10 December 1998) both commissioned by Lloyd's successor as Commissioning Editor, Dorothy Byrne.

These are examples of investigative journalism in the traditional sense, but both Lloyd and Byrne consider that *Dispatches* is in the business of widening the conception of what investigative journalism might be. Programmes that are original in the way they counter orthodoxy are also investigative, he claims; they 'inquire anew on some area of social policy that people think they know about – but actually, when you quarry just a few layers down you find that what you are being told is at serious variance with the evidence' (Lloyd, 1998b).

Perhaps the best-known product of this approach is the series *Dispatches* made about Aids in the 1980s. Joan Shenton and her team identified an unreported analysis of the Aids illness made by scientists who denied the link between HIV and Aids and claimed that all contemporary research was wrong – and determinedly so since its direction suited the big pharmaceutical companies, among other interests (Shenton, 1990). Lloyd does not offer this example of his work when asked about the impact of *Dispatches*, though once the subject is raised he defends the programmes – which attracted more hostility than perhaps any other *Dispatches* – on the grounds that 'although the extreme thesis that there is no connection between HIV and Aids is now discredited', nevertheless there is still no certitude as to the catalytic factors. His defence of the polemical style of those programmes gives insight into his view of investigative journalism; he argues that the medical establishment at the time simply would not admit that the scientists whom he screened could or should have any kind of voice in the debate; they were excluded, as were all counterorthodox views of Aids. Now, he says, such a programme would not be necessary as the medical establishment is chastened by its failure to solve the problem and is more open to discussion and challenge.

Dispatches has transmitted many programmes on health issues; it claims to have been the first medium to demonstrate CJD transmission to humans, to reveal the major British scandal of deaths in the surgery wards at Bristol Hospital, to reveal problems of cervical screening and to show, via the story of the Yorkshire Hospital Trust, how health service reforms were not working as intended. It has also tackled the problems of British education.

A belief that the quality of school education provided to the majority of British children was inadequate and deteriorating spread out beyond the specialists in the 1980s to the extent that by the 1990s it was a major political issue, the subject of radical government policies and a central plank in the Labour Party's victorious 1997 election campaign. *Dispatches* played a part in the dissemination of this view, principally through one programme in 1991, 'Every Child in Britain', followed by 'All Our Futures'.

'Every Child in Britain' argued a view that was widely held by specialists but barely understood in the wider agora, that by virtually any measurement most British state schooling was inferior to its rivals and crippled its products through low expectations and poor teaching methods. 'All Our Futures' proposed that one of the solutions to the problem – quality vocational education for those for whom academic courses were inappropriate – had gone wrong and was as hopelessly inadequate as that which preceded it. In 1998 *Dispatches* went on to examine another of the solutions, the Office of Standards in Education (Ofsted), whose Chief Inspector wholeheartedly endorsed the analysis advanced in 'Every Child in Britain'. Chief Inspector Chris Woodhead, although appointed by the Conservatives who encouraged his radical inspection policy, was confirmed in office by the new Labour government, despite opposition within the Labour Party, and by 1998 was widely treated by the political classes and much of the media as being the fount of all wisdom in education. There was widespread agreement in society that school inspections were good and raised standards; rather than attend to the issue of principle therefore *Dispatches* interrogated the data and sought to see if Woodhead had feet of clay by questioning his methodology.

'Inspecting the Inspectors' demonstrated that:

1   Critical school inspections have a powerful effect upon schools, in one case virtually destroying the school overnight, as the parents of all bar one pupil removed their children.
2   School inspections are demanding on teachers.
3   There may be contradictions in a system in which schools may have good Inspection Reports but atrocious SATs (examination) results.
4   A review of inspectors' judgements by the Professor of Education at Durham University showed them to lack system.
5   Inspectors' attention to detail and understanding of what they are inspecting may be limited, as evidenced in the CCTV footage available to one head teacher, himself a trained inspector.
6   Ofsted appeared to accept criticism only grudgingly.
7   There were comparative studies made by Ofsted inspectors that were not published, perhaps because their findings were inconvenient.
8   The use of data in the Chief Inspector's annual report to Parliament could be questioned.
9   Ofsted was accountable only in a limited sense.

The case made against the Chief Inspector, whose interview with reporter Spiller was used extensively, was rather weakened by considerable use of his arch-opponent, Professor Tim Brighouse, which appeared to bring polemic and personal animosity into what was otherwise detached. In what senses were these three programmes investigative? First, there is the originality, the overturning of generally held assumptions; second, there is the attack on interest groups, there were undoubtedly people who did not want those questions asked; third, there is method – the careful analyses of data upon which policies and programmes are based, the investigation for alternative or supplementary sources of data and the unexpected comparisons. All these modes led to the building of cases opposed to those which people were being asked by authority to believe.

In particular there were several aspects to 'Inspecting the Inspectors' that made it investigative rather than analytical; they were points 3, 4 and 5 (see above), and to a lesser extent 7 and 8. The fact that it is possible for schools to have good Inspection Reports but atrocious SATs results is a fascinating revelation for many parents now very aware of the differences between schools that are being revealed by the high-profile inspection system; detailed information from two very different sources, academic research data plus the evidence of CCTV footage, fortunately presented to us by a head teacher who is himself an inspector, provides very strong evidence that attention needs to be paid to inspection methodology. Points 7 and 8 appeared weaker, and were more easily brushed aside by the Chief Inspector.

An analysis of the inspection system as might have been undertaken say in the *Times Educational Supplement* or a less consistently investigative series such as *Panorama*, might have examined the issue in detail without either challenging the methodology or demonstrating that flaws in that methodology had already been detected by critical observers. The level of detail into which the programme went in order to cast doubts upon the statistics used is also indicative of a investigative approach.

Example: 'Holding the Baby'

Treatment

In 1989 the producer who was to make his first *Dispatches*, 'Holding the Baby', a year later was, among other things, producing and presenting an ITV chat show series, *Night Flyte*, on controversial issues. The scouting for this threw up an article by a *Daily Mail* reporter on the business plans of a US company, Kindercare, which intended expanding into the UK. Kindercare, said the article, offered round the clock baby parking and could solve all the problems of the mother who wanted to get a job outside the home. The writer implied that this was production line, McDonalds style, baby care and, in tune with the *Daily Mail*'s editorial line, that it was reprehensible (Gerrie, 1987).

Thus 'nursery care' came to be the subject of one of the *Night Flytes*. The transmission demonstrated strong passions both on the programme itself and at audience feedback and informed the production team that there had been 'problems' with institutional childcare in the US, including maltreatment of children by care providers and claims by academic researchers that institutional childcare stunts growth. The producer, who had already worked up programmes on corruption in the Scottish law courts and bad practices in financial services for the *Dispatches* Commissioning Editor, therefore wrote up a first proposal on about a page (HTB, 1998) and sent it to the same patron. Commissioning editors view vast numbers of proposals and are moved by many considerations. One of the most important is survival – to survive they must show that they are having impact. With the BBC or ITV this is usually, though not always, proved by ratings figures. With C4, as with broadsheet newspapers, impact may equally well be interpreted as response among the target audience of opinion-formers and decision-makers. So when the *Dispatches* Commissioning Editor decided to look further at this topic, he was moved by the following:

- he had received numerous proposals in this general area and knew that producers were interested
- he believed that it would add to his series profile.

His impact upon the proposal was significant; it went in stages through a series of meetings over a period of six months when he asked for:

- evidence that childcare was a business in the UK ripe for development
- evidence that the US entrepreneurs wanted to expand into the European market
- evidence that there were scandals in the USA.

and, later:

- proof of research evidence demonstrating that children might be harmed by childcare, and
- proof that people in a position to know were ignoring such research evidence.[2]

By this time the producer was fielding a team at these meetings which included the reporter (writer of the *Daily Mail* article) and director (the first producer–director of *Hard News*).[3] The team was nervous initially that – after investing time and effort – the angle was becoming too skewed towards research, as it did not look as if there was much conclusive evidence revealing whether or not childcare was good or not for children. Although he was disappointed that there was little or no UK research, the editor decided that they should see this lacuna as a strength. He said that '*Dispatches* will argue that it is disgraceful that HMG should encourage more mothers of young children to work when the effects have not been considered' (HTB, 1998). The programme he eventually commissioned was very different from that initially envisaged by the proponents and, during the process, they had been obliged to substantiate every statement that he had hypothesised. The final documentary treatment conformed to the classic current affairs approach in which there is a victim, villain and various subplots that eventually integrate to make the case. The case was made through the media of several stories, or component elements of the long-form documentary, in order to personalise and pictorialise. They included the story of:

- a particular little girl
- a childminder
- various young mothers
- a particular nursery and its proprietor
- how the research of an academic psychologist, Belsky, had been undertaken, replicated in other countries and received in the academy.

It also featured, by way of additional testimonial:

- a US nursery that it constructed as providing impersonal mass production
- clips from secret filming of US nurseries showing neglect and malpractice by staff.

During the course of filming in a high-profile nursery, an example of bad practice occurred and was shot. The piece of film was then shown to a psychologist and she was herself filmed at the viewing showing her professional disapproval, even horror, and reinforcing the message that commercial organisations could not be trusted to deliver reliable childcare. Since she was now the object of attack, the proprietor of the nursery 'investigated' was shown the material that reflected upon her institution and was invited to respond on camera, as is usual practice on *Dispatches* – an invitation that she took up, further condemning herself by the unsympathetic interview she gave. Not only were companies in the business of childcare implied to be flawed but the childcare establishment – officials and academics – could be construed as appearing shifty and perhaps malevolent. This was partly on account of their own behaviour in refusing to answer questions directly, and partly because of the way their interviews were cut. In summary, the documentary's main arguments were:

- childcare is one of the biggest issues society faces
- for their own interests it suits business – both those that profit from child-care and those that profit from creating a market in low wage second earners – that mothers enter the job market
- these interests have used the rhetoric of feminism and choice as a cover for their interests
- they have won the support of institutions such as the CBI and of government to promote what interests them, not what is in the interests of children
- the research there is says that this is bad for small children
- yet the establishment of government advisers and managers, wanting to

exert power over ordinary people and afraid to admit that their ideas are motivated more by political correctness than by the interests of those affected, won't listen.

Discussion

'Holding the Baby' had a very high audience rating for *Dispatches* and attracted much comment, mainly hostile. It has continued to be talked about in the television profession and used as a model, not least because of Caroline Gilbey's very effective direction. The production team at the time thought that it was being very advanced, challenging and creative, while its critics read the programme as reactionary. Within the context of the emerging discourse of childcare and the subsequent development of programming on this subject, it now seems more realistic to say that the team was responding to the 'corporate expectations' (Cottle, 1995: 162) of C4 for a certain type of programme – as was the Commissioning Editor, albeit with his more strategic antennae. C4 demands the kind of programme idea that is slightly in advance of cultural change, but only just (or no one will watch it). If it is not in advance, no one will be angry about it, which would be unfortunate for C4 and for its executives' careers. This and the subsequent development of the discourses of childcare may explain the cultural locus of 'Holding the Baby'. The expert debate was over the interpretation of the social science research and in particular over two questions: was the (US) research of Belsky generalisable and did the combination of his research with a UK, a French and a Swiss study amount to a general conclusion of recent research that institutional day-care at too early an age could be damaging intellectually and emotionally? Underlying it was a further debate on the selective use of research.

Today it is unlikely that a *Dispatches* on this topic would focus so heavily upon research and, in particular, in a manner that denied the value of earlier research in comparison with current research. The focus would be on 'a dereliction of standards that are true whatever you believe about day-care' (Lloyd, 1998b). This is in part because the latest ITC protocols have made the provision of 'due impartiality' more important, as discussed in Chapter 3; 'the other side has all sorts of purchase on the piece you do' and these are formalised in statute. The advantage of this, according to Lloyd, is that it forces you to make a clear distinction between opinion journalism and investigative journalism, no matter that both are evidenced and witnessed. Without this, much can be called investigative that is not; 'in the past you could deliver a parallel argument and make it feel investigative, but this is now less easy' (Lloyd, 1998b).

The investigative journalist and the evidence

Mark D'Arcy argues in Chapter 18 that, if only by virtue of its scale and its influence on our daily lives, local administration is a fitting target for investigative journalism. The same can be said for national social policies. More public money is spent on social policy implementation than in any other area of government; demographic changes have made topics such as age[4] and child development of central importance to the UK's economic future; education is keenly argued over for the same reasons; problems from unemployment to delinquency, nutrition and health have huge consequences and constituencies and thus experts of every political persuasion. The proposals of those experts, politicians and pressure groups need to be analysed, but, more than analysed, their premises require examination, especially since they, and justifications for current policies, are usually based upon statistical data and social science research. The journalist applies the 'social scientific' method to the scientists. Indeed, as Tankard (1976: 45) has pointed out, there are similarities between social scientists and journalists. Journalists rely upon verification by observation or testimony; they aspire to making only those statements that can be corroborated or verified and thus achieve impartiality; they attribute or cite opinions or findings and they aim at internal and external validity.

While Tankard's observations are flattering to journalists, he also points out that they regularly commit errors such as generalising from unrepresentative samples, misunderstanding the methodologies employed in research and making invalid causal associations. In theory, at least, journalists argue their conclusions deductively from the evidence, although they are often attacked for the opposite, making the evidence fit as in the case of a much reviled *Panorama*, 'Missing Mum', on a similar subject to the example above (e.g. BBC, 1997).

Research methods

A knowledge of the procedures of the social sciences is essential to the investigative journalist. Social science research has driven much of the debates over the family, the underclass, welfare and schooling that have become central in UK politics – as in other rich countries. Take the UK education debate. Many research studies have been undertaken and have been used to prove this or that theory in education. A 1998 survey of education research was sceptical of the value of much of it, complaining that it was often highly biased in its premises and incompetent methodologically as a consequence (Gold, 1998). In 1996 the National Foundation for Educational Research (NFER) was commissioned by two media organisations associated with opposite political leanings[5] to undertake a study of reading skills in the UK, a study that had already been undertaken in 32 other countries and the format of which was considered uncontroversial by the customers. It had been accepted internationally, as in the UK, as telling something worthwhile about the differences between countries in the acquisition of reading skills. At the data analysis stage, however, the methods required to replicate in England and Wales the study that had been undertaken in the other countries were confusing to the NFER, and NFER's application of them was confusing to those who had designed the methods.

265

The NFER changed its mind twice about the results and their implications, and different officials offered different interpretations of them.[6]

Not surprisingly the C4 News journalists covering the story[7] found this confusing, and a verdict had to be sought from specialists at the London School of Economics and Paris University as to whether the NFER was implementing the study properly; the verdicts were only just supportive. Worse, once the NFER had finally agreed its official interpretation, it was found that luminaries of the education establishment were so opposed to the very idea of such a study that they were unavailable to comment dispassionately on the results;[8] the one finally persuaded to do so said that the results told nothing; 'The wrong things are being measured' (C4, 1996). In effect, the educationalists approached did not accept the validity of the research. In that case, and the journalists at the time felt that this was far more coloured by their prejudices than by any soundly based critique of the research, the reliability or generalisability didn't matter. Shipman (1981) discusses several controversies within social science in *The Limitations of Social Research*, including an example, as quantitative as the NFER study, which, when replicated, gave utterly different results. Some of his cases are controversial because of the methods of the researchers, others because of their biases. He cites the famous qualitative study of Samoa by Margaret Mead which deserves to be part of journalistic folklore, as it is of academic. *Coming of Age in Samoa* (1943) was fun because it dealt with sex; it was influential because journalists interpreted it as demonstrating that in our emotional and sexual practices we are constrained less by biology than by culture. Mead's findings showed that the Samoans were uninhibited in their relationships and suggested that this was more natural than Americans' (then) repressed or discriminating behaviour. However, later research (Freeman, 1984) made clear that her method of investigation was flawed; that she did not know the language sufficiently well to understand that she was being teased and that she fundamentally misconstrued Samoan society which, in reality, had many of the same rules as Western society. Methodology aside, the study was not generalisable (what can knowing about teen sex in Samoa tell us about teen sex in Wyoming?) anyway, but at the time nobody thought about that, perhaps because her views were so welcome.

Until 1997 and the publication of a new book on Alfred Kinsey,[9] Kinsey's 1947 study *Sexuality and the Human Male* was widely accepted as valid but neither generalisable nor reliable. It now seems quite clear that it was and is a farrago of little or no scientific value. In fact, the truth about Kinsey's methods had been exposed in a study that failed to seize the attention of journalists when published in 1989. By 1997–8 the media were ready, and a television documentary complemented two high-profile books on the subject. These famous examples serve to illustrate the dangers of journalists' failure to understand key conditions for reliable social research.

Statistical data

In covering topics as varied as financial affairs and defence estimates journalists are faced with data provided them by the Government Statistical Service, policy units, pressure groups, company and government agency finance officers and the university research community. We assume that all journalists gatekeep the material, but the active journalist is surely one who is able to check out the material before use.

In 1989 *Dispatches* produced a useful illustration of how politicians bamboozle with statistics in its programme 'Cooking the Books'. It showed, *inter alia*, how the then British government had recently announced that it was building '380 large hospital schemes'. The definition of a hospital scheme was not clear, nor was the fact that every building project of over £1 million was classified as a separate scheme even if it was really part of a larger, say £30 million, scheme. Thus the '380 large hospital schemes' included several car parks. Similarly, an increase in the number of hospital beds was claimed, whereas there was no net increase if the beds abolished elsewhere were taken into account (C4, 1989). It is now well established that early ideas about the dangers of Aids were based on quite fallacious statistical projections and that these projections were used to justify expensive and often irrelevant publicity campaigns as well as the diverting of health service resources from problems of much greater concern to the majority of the population. For the student examining the use of statistics in investigative journalism a number of books listed at the end of this chapter may be useful.[10]

In sum, the investigative journalist deals with the evidence of documents, fieldwork, the findings of scientific and social science studies, testimony and statistics. The problems for the investigative journalist include its provenance, methodology and checking procedures. In the face of these problems, the investigative journalist in effect applies methods developed in academic research and called 'scientific method'. He or she tries to make only those statements that can be corroborated or verified and thus be impartial; attributes or cites opinions or findings and aims at internal and external validity (Tankard, 1976); and argues conclusions deductively from the evidence. More specifically, in dealing with social research, the investigative journalist must first review the literature to understand the context of the research under discussion; a simple review of the literature on a subject will often astonish by its paucity or by its limitations. It is also useful for journalists to remember that the peer group review system is not everywhere of the same rigour and that there is a much-loved repository called the *Journal of Inconvenient Research*!

Having had a sceptical look at the environment of the topic in question the investigative journalist will want to consider reliability (is the method clearly understandable and could the same results be achieved by other researchers using the same method?), validity (does the research really reflect what was going on?) and generalisability (does this research tell us about any situation apart from the one researched?). This can be taken further. Katzer (1978) proposes what he calls 'Standardised Integrity Tests'. My own version, here, borrows from Katzer, Simon (1978) and de Burgh (1987):

Checklist for integrity testing

- The problem statement: what exactly is being defined?
- Compare the problem statement with the findings: has the researcher answered their own question?
- What are/were the research design options? Why this one?
- Are his or her operational definitions credible? In other words is not crying by infants a sign of happiness and therefore an indication that children in day nurseries do not miss their parents? (see Katzer, 1978: section 4)
- Methodology: what exactly is being measured?
- What are the potential sources of bias? (due to research plan, researcher, behaviour of subjects)
- What did the researcher do to compensate for or eliminate bias?
- What assumptions are being made about the population?
- What are the sampling procedures?
- What has been done about noise (e.g. the Hawthorne Study[11])?
- Distortion by noise/unsystematic error (e.g. the way in which teachers react to league tables test measurement is not uniform – there is random variability)
- Validity
- Reliability
- Interpretation – is it fair and correct? Does the summary do it justice?
- Causal relationships – are they wrongly assumed?
- Generalisability? Could this be a fluke? Does this research really apply anywhere else? Do the findings matter?
- Replicability? (can the research be repeated and get the same result?)
- Has the study been triangulated? (i.e. the problem looked at from two other angles or using two other methods)
- What do rivals say?

In conclusion, in evaluating evidence the investigative journalist is confronted with at least four problems: the errors of testimony, the identification of expertise, and the authenticity of documentation and filmed material are just the beginning. The limitations of social research – and, surely, 'hard' scientific research, too, – need to be clearly understood; if the meaning of statistics is too large a topic for any one investigative journalist to feel on top of, at least he or she has access to some excellent books that will support his or her scepticism with revelations of the ways in which figures can be manipulated.

Notes

1 Bored by the fear of conflict, repression of minority opinion and consensus-seeking that he regarded as typical of the UK media, the first head of Channel 4, Jeremy Isaacs, commissioned a deliberately opinionated weekly current affairs programme, *Diverse Reports*, from the company set up to produce the series by a former BBC associate. When, however, in 1986 David Lloyd was appointed from the BBC to head Current Affairs at C4 he went one step further; he decided that each week's programme should be produced by a different supplier. At the time his decision was derided on the grounds that current affairs required a resource base that no small company or individual could provide; Lloyd claimed that though he might lose because of the weaknesses of his suppliers' resources he would gain in diversity, innovation and courage. Events have borne him out.

2 In a recent talk (Lloyd, 1998a) he compared other programmes on the same subject with 'Holding the Baby' and asserted that it was superior because of its use of that evidence.

3 Namely Anthea Gerrie, Caroline Gilbey and Hugo de Burgh. The media with which they had been associated just before this project were both 'right' (*Daily Mail*) and 'left' (C4 *Hard News*) but there were never any differences of approach among the team; the 'story' took precedence.

4 By 'age' I mean not only the issue of how smaller workforces in Europe will fund larger numbers of pensioners but matters of retirement policy, age prejudice or ageism.

5 Channel 4 Television and the *Daily Mail*.

6 The files on this programme are contained in the journalism library at Nottingham Trent University. See ISPSR (1998).

7 Hugo de Burgh and Peter Morgan. The feature was transmitted on 25 July 1996.

8 Eight senior figures in the field were approached in turn to give an overview of the significance of the research, conventionally an essential element of such a feature. Finally, and with many caveats, one did agree.

9 See Jones (1997). Tim Tate (see Chapter 22) made C4 *Secret History* 'Kinsey's Paedophiles' in 1998 on the same subject; the trail had been blazed by Janet Riesman in 1986 when she published her book but orthodox opinion was probably not ready to accept what, thanks to her, was known in the academy well before 1997.

10 The Department of Journalism at City University, London offers a module for its journalism students called Quantitative Methods for Journalists, which addresses some of the issues.

11 The Hawthorne Study illustrated how research can be affected by the research process itself.

Bibliography

BBC (1997) *Biteback* [TV audience response programme], 2 March 1997. London: BBC.

de Burgh, H. (1998) Audience, journalist and text in television news. Paper delivered at the Annual Conference of the International Association for Media and Communications Research, 27 July 1998.

de Burgh, H. and Steward, T. (1986) *The Persuasive Screen: Video Applications in Business.* London: Century Hutchinson.

Channel 4 TV (1989) 'Cooking the Books', *Dispatches* (Producer: Christopher Hird). London: C4 TV.

Channel 4 TV (1991) 'Holding the Baby', *Dispatches* (Producer: Hugo de Burgh). London: C4 TV.

Channel 4 TV (1996) 'International Comparisons of Primary Reading' *Channel Four News* (Hugo de Burgh and Peter Morgan). London: C4 TV.

Channel 4 TV (1998) 'Inspecting the Inspectors', *Dispatches* (Producer: Sarah Spiller). London: C4 TV.

Cottle, S. (1995) Producer-driven television? *Media Culture and Society*, 17 (4): 159–66.

(2004) 'The Documentary as "Amplification": Holding the Baby and the Politics of Attachment', *Contemporanea: Revista de Comunicacao e Cultura*, June 2004, 2 (1).

Elliott, P. (1972) *The Making of a Television Series*, London: Constable.

Fishman, M. (1980) The perspectival nature of events: fact by triangulation. In M. Fishman, *Manufacturing the News*. Austin: University of Texas Press: 116–29.

Freeman, D. (1984) *Margaret Mead and Samoa*. London: Penguin.

Gerrie, A. (1987) Are mothers really necessary? *Daily Mail*, 12 November: 13–14.

Gold, K. (1998) Tooley, madly, deeply. *THES*, 31 July 1998: 13.

Hird, C. (1983) *Challenging the Figures*. London: Pluto.

Hooke, R. (1983) *How to tell the Liars from the Statisticians*. New York: Marcel.

House of Lords (1991) *Weekly Hansard*, No. 1498: 11/3–14/3.

HTB (1998) The 'Holding the Baby' Documents Box, containing draft scripts, research notes, meetings minutes, interview tapes, etc. of the production and subsequent research, held in the Library of the Centre for Broadcasting and Journalism, Nottingham Trent University

Huff, D. (1954) *How to Lie with Statistics*. London: Penguin.

Irvine, J. (1981) *Demystifying Social Statistics*. London: Pluto.

ISPSR (1998) *International Comparisons of Primary School Reading*, programme production file, Library of the Centre for Broadcasting and Journalism, Nottingham Trent University.

Jones, J. H. (1997) *Alfred C. Kinsey: A Public/Private Life*. London: W. W. Norton and Co.

Karpf, A. (1988) Outside the box: medical expertise and the power to define. In A. Karpf *Doctoring the Media: The Reporting of Health and Medicine*. London: Routledge: 110–34.

Katzer, J. (1978) A step by step guide for evaluation. In J. Katzer, *Evaluating Information*. Reading: Addison Wesley.

Lloyd, D. (1998a) Talk to the students of the MA Investigative Journalism course at Nottingham Trent University, 19 February 1998.

Lloyd, D. (1998b) Interview with Hugo de Burgh, London, 9 October 1998.

Lloyd, D. (1998c) Quoted by Jancis Giles in a letter and notes to Hugo de Burgh, 25 October 1998.

McCombs, M. (1976) *Handbook of Reporting Methods*. Boston: Houghton Mifflin.

McNulty, M. (1996) Dispatches rider. *Broadcast*, 18 October 1996.

Mead, M. (1943) *Coming of Age in Samoa: A Study of Adolescence and Sex in Primitive Societies*. London: Penguin.

Meyer, P. (1991) Journalism and the scientific tradition. In P. Meyer, *The New Precision Journalism*. Bloomington: Indiana University Press.

Nissel, M. (1995) Vital statistics. *New Statesman and Society*, 27 January 1997.

Shenton, J. (1998) *Positively False*. London: I.B. Tauris.

Shipman, M. (1981) *The Limitations of Social Research*. London: Longman.

Silverstone, R. (1985) *Framing Science: The Making of a BBC Documentary*. London: British Film Institute.

Simon, J. (1978) *Basic Research Methods in Social Science: The Art of Empirical Investigation.* New York: Random House.

Stott, R. (1998) [press officer for C4 *Dispatches*] Conversations with Hugo de Burgh.

Tankard, J. W. (1976) Reporting and the scientific method. In M. McCombs *Handbook of Reporting Methods.* Boston: Houghton Mifflin.

Further reading

de Burgh, H. (2004) The documentary as 'amplification': holding the baby and the politics of attachment. In *Contemporanea: Revista de Comunicacao e Cultura*, 2 (1): 139–60.

Katzer, J. (1978) *Evaluating Information.* Reading: Addison Wesley.

Shipman, M. (1994) *The Limitations of Social Research.* London: Longman.

16

JOURNALISM WITH ATTITUDE
The *Daily Mail*

Hugo de Burgh

The *Daily Mail* is a newspaper which raises hackles in polite society. This may be because its success, at a time when other newspapers look around them and despair, arouse jealousy; it may be because it is an unashamedly conservative newspaper, and the opinion-mouthing classes are more anti-conservative than pro; or it may be for other reasons, of which more later.

The *Mail*'s critics and rivals were, nevertheless, enthusiastic about its most famous story of recent years, the investigation of the murderers of teenager Stephen Lawrence, or rather its decision to name the alleged murderers as such. Lawyers did not approve, but Paul Foot of the *Mirror*, Darcus Howe, black activist and Channel 4 presenter, and Peter Preston of *The Guardian* all expressed support. 'None of these three would normally be expected to support the actions of the *Daily Mail*' (Cathcart, 2000: 286).

In essence, the Stephen Lawrence story is that, in April 1993, a black teenager was stabbed to death in Eltham, South East London. Although charges were brought against a gang of white youths, suspected of having casually murdered Lawrence for no other motives than race hate, lack of evidence made it impossible to secure conviction, notwithstanding that four of the five youths refused to provide an alibi and the fifth provided one that did not stand up. There was widespread upset and the family launched a campaign to bring his murderers to justice, even initiating a private prosecution.

Once the inquest had found that Lawrence was indeed murdered by five white men, the *Daily Mail* reviewed the evidence and decided to mount its own accusation. It published photographs of the five white youths originally charged, but acquitted, under the banner headline 'Murderers'.

There were three investigations by the Metropolitan (London) Police, an internal police inquiry into its own procedures, a secondary examination by another police force and a public inquiry, the Macpherson Inquiry, the conclusions of which included the accusation that the Metropolitan Police was 'institutionally racist' and would bring about substantial changes in police recruitment and behaviour throughout the UK. Finally, in 2007, following the application of new forensic techniques, there was a further review by the Specialist Crimes Directorate, of which there is no published conclusion at the time of going to press.

Timeline (adapted from Wright, with acknowledgments to the *Daily Mail*, 8 November 2007)

1993

Apr 22 : Stephen Lawrence is stabbed to death at bus stop in Eltham.

May : Neil Acourt and Luke Knight charged with murder.

July 29 : Charges dropped for lack of evidence.

1994

Apr : Stephen's parents launch a private prosecution. Police charge Neil Acourt and Jamie Acourt, Luke Knight and David Norris.

Aug : Gary Dobson also charged.

Sept : Charges against Jamie Acourt and Norris dropped.

1996

Apr : The private prosecution collapses.

1997

Feb : Inquest opens but suspects refuse to give evidence. Inquest jury decides Lawrence died in 'an unprovoked racist attack by five white youths'. The *Daily Mail* publishes the names and photographs of five men. 'If we are wrong, let them sue us'

Jul 31 : Home Secretary announces a Judicial Inquiry chaired by Sir William Macpherson.

1998

Sep : Sir William accuses Metropolitan Police of 'institutional' racism.

Oct : Yard apologises to the Lawrence family and pledges to stamp out racism in force.

1999

Feb 15 : Macpherson report recommends 70 changes in policing.

2000

Oct : Lawrences accept £320,000 compensation from the Police.

2001

Sept : Dobson's parents arrested amid claims they lied to police.

Dec : Norris's cousin, Darren Davis, arrested on suspicion of Lawrence' murder.

2004

May : Directorate of Public Prosecutions (DPP) says there is insufficient evidence to bring fresh charges.

2005

Apr　　: Double jeopardy rule, which stops suspects being tried for the same offence twice, is abolished.

In November 2007 the *Mail* reported that charges might once again be brought within months, as a result of a 'sensational forensic breakthrough in the case'. It investigated the current activities of the five whom it had accused back in 1993 and found that none were apparently working in any admissible calling, but lived on a combination of petty crime and state handouts (Wright, 2007). It also reported (Wright, 2007a) that the new police investigation had uncovered blunders in the original appraisal of evidence

What the *Daily Mail* did was absolutely in the tradition of campaigning popular newspapers. Its own investigations were based upon police leads; the journalism is a typical popular media combination of legwork by experts and campaigning by the medium. The historically most similar precedent is that of *The People* of 1950, when its Editor courageously demanded the arrest of a mafia-type family accused of organising prostitution in London, whose members it pictured under the banner headline 'Arrest these four men!' (see Greenslade, Chapter 19). However similarly sensational the *Mail*'s Lawrence intervention was, it can be argued though that it is not really representative of the original investigative journalism that the *Mail* undertakes weekly, several examples of which are provided below.

The tradition of investigation at the *Daily Mail*

In the early years of the twentieth century, Alfred Harmsworth, the conservative proprietor, engaged a well-known socialist, Robert Blatchford, to go to Germany to examine its armaments programme; Blatchford returned convinced by his investigations that Germany intended to attack Britain. His reports were the basis for a campaign to alert Britain to the dangers from Germany, comparable to that conducted by Winston Churchill in the *Mirror* in the 1930s. It was a stunt, but it was also investigative journalism, a combination with which the *Mail* has become adept.

In recent years the *Daily Mail*'s investigations have been neither entirely of the redtop variety illustrated in Greenslade's chapter here, nor exactly in the same portentous public service tradition of the broadsheets. As befits a newspaper classified as 'middle market' its investigations have elements of both. Thus its *Dignity for the Elderly* campaign exposed abuse in care homes, a very serious subject dealt with in graphic, even sensational, detail, and in the W.T. Stead tradition.

Today, the *Mail*'s best-known investigative by-line is Sue Reid's. She has been Special Investigations Editor at the *Daily Mail* since 2002, a job she got after an 8-year break from full-time journalism, to have a child. She had previously been 'Number 3 on the *Mail on Sunday*'. Reid completes between two and three investigations a month, publishing about 30 a year, mostly into particular angles on topic issues. For example, when the reports about bird flu in Asia, and the possibility of it reaching England, first became of general concern in 2005, Reid went to English bird markets to understand how (if) our authorities were controlling the disease.

- For this is a pet market in Stafford in the Midlands. I am here following a tip-off that somewhere, among the hundreds of cages, is a potentially deadly and illegal consignment of wild finches recently smuggled from Indonesia, where avian flu has already killed humans. The 50 birds are believed to have been secretly trafficked to Britain in a tortuous journey via the West Indies and Brussels'.

(Reid, 2005)

She had learned from zoonotics (animal–human transmission) experts that they thought there to be more likelihood of the disease being spread through illegal rare species trading than through natural migration. Coincidentally she exposed the cruelty and unsanitary conditions of the rare bird trade.

Sue Reid agrees that she had a stroke of luck with 'How Doctors lie on death certificates to hide the true scale of the appalling death toll from hospital infections' (Reid, 2008). A reader called Joan Horne telephoned her and said that, so angry had she been at the mode of her husband's passing in Barnsley Hospital to which he had been admitted for a relatively minor complaint, that she had herself done an investigation. Tape recorder in hand, Ms Horne had visited the hospital, interviewed the managers and obliged them, wittingly, to confess on tape that the reasons for her husband's unexpected death were not as stated on his death certificate but in fact the 'superbug' that was rife at the hospital, *Clostridium difficile* (C.diff). 'In 2006, almost 56,000 caught C.diff, which is spread by poor hygiene, dirty hands and soiled bedding' (Reid, 2008: 30).

In the subsequent wider investigation Reid found that the hospital managers admit that doctors often fail to declare the cause of death when it has been probable that the cause is an illness contracted in the hospital; that this is a custom now so widespread that the Chief Medical Officer has written to hospitals telling them that this dishonesty must stop; and that there are now many cases of cover up that are being exposed. As an indication of the *Mail*'s commitment to investigative stories, it should be noted that this substantial piece of work appeared on the same day as a less original, but nevertheless investigative piece, on female genital mutilation (Goodwin, 2008).

Receiving the call from Ms Horne, Reid did as every decent investigative journalist must do, she checked it out. In the north of England she has a roving legwoman for just such assignments, and Reid dispatched her to meet Joan

Horne. Horne turned out to be a 78-year-old, a former NHS worker, very sharp and to have told the truth. The tapes were listened to and her story checked with the hospital and found to be accurate in every respect (Reid, 2008a).

Just at the time when Reid was having Horne's tale looked into, a colleague on the *Mail* died in hospital and the editor received a distraught telephone call from his widow who believed that he had died as a result of a hospital-originated infection. Interest in the subject at the newspaper was greatly augmented by this personal experience. In the more conventional way, Reid contacted two lobbying organizations, the C.Diff Support UK and MRSA Support Group, and asked whether they could provide corroborating examples. She was supplied with a list of twenty people who might further verify the hypothesis that hiding the true cause of death, when it was hospital induced infection, was widespread in the UK. Reid was in email contact with most of the twenty in December 2007 and, in the course of being so, decided to go with the supplementary stories of Phil Barnes and Marion Ham in particular, although several other cases are cited. Barnes is a lawyer, specializing in medical negligence in Birmingham. Ham 'fought at seven-month battle to get a hospital and a pathologist to admit that a superbug had contributed to her husband David's death in October 2006' (Reid 2008:30). Finally she succeeded and the details on the death certificate were changed to include a reference to MRSA.

The story was one of three that Reid was working on in December, taking up in all about 5 full days employing two people; it was filed before Christmas and competed for space at the end of December, being finally selected for 3 January.

One organisation which has found itself under the *Mail* microscope is the Church of Scientology.[1] In 2001 it published 'Nicole's Nightmare':

> They wire up children to lie detectors, interrogate them about their families and denounce non-believers as enemies . . . Is this what devoted mother Nicole Kidman so fears about Tom Cruise's obsession with Scientology?
>
> (*Daily Mail*, 17 February 2001)

The article in fact concerns Astra, a 22-year-old former Scientologist and her sister Zoe. They have been taught by the Scientologists, followers of guru L. Ron Hubbard, that the outside world is full of 'wogs' (their word for non-Scientologists) and that 'state schools were all overrun by guns and drugs', according to Zoe. Kidman is brought in to give a touch of glamour and to remind us that Tom Cruise too has fallen for this curious outfit:

> Dressed in jeans and a T-shirt, perched on the sofa of her father's

modest Californian home, there is little to link Astra Woodcraft with Nicole Kidman.

The article, however, was called 'Nicole's Nightmare'!

A quickie investigation had Tanya Gold finding out what it felt like to be an obviously Muslim woman in England after London had suffered a bombing attack by young Muslim men in July 2005. In 'My Week beneath the Burqa' Gold reported on a 'strange window into a different culture':

> On the Tube home, I sit opposite a pair of French students. They gaze at me and giggle. The giggles turn to contemptuous laughter and I blush under my burqa. De-burqaed, I would curse them, or perhaps I could steal a joke from the brilliant Muslim stand-up comedian Shazia Mirza: 'My name is Shazia. At least, that's what it says on my pilot's licence' or 'Does my bomb look big in this?' but it never occurs to me to speak.
>
> (Gold, 2005)

The idea was a good one, in which she analysed her own revulsion to the burqa, her fury at the way she was treated, her fear while wearing it and the views of Muslims she consulted about it. It surely increased readers' understanding of, and perhaps sympathy for, women who cover up.

Like other national newspapers, the *Mail* at first fell for the Blair government's deceptive line on the Iraq War. It also appears to have fallen for other, in retrospect not completely credible, scare stories about Muslim plots.

> September 11-style terror attacks on the skyscrapers of Canary Wharf were thwarted, it emerged today ahead of the Queen's Speech, which will focus on security. Plans to crash aircraft into the three skyscrapers in London's Docklands were among four or five al-Qaeda strikes that security chiefs believe they have stopped. Training programmes for suicide pilots who planned a spectacular attack on the financial centre were disrupted, a senior authoritative source told the Daily Mail.
>
> (*Daily Mail*, 24 November 2004)

The story offered a titillating mixture of danger, mystery – and few facts. But, after all, this was a period, as Paul Lashmar reminds us in his chapter, when much of the media was swallowing government spin, hook, line and sinker. Journalists were gullible to the pleasures of anonymous sources and 'off the record' briefings by government spin doctors. The fact that the story was published on the same day as a Queen's Speech (government legislative programme) introducing legislation to strengthen police and security powers, suggests to the sceptical that the *Mail* was being used.

Of note have been the *Daily Mail*'s many articles on immigration, by 2007 the major concern of the British public, on account of the widespread perception that governments have failed to impose any policy or order upon immigration. The *Mail* has given space to critics of the government's lies and evasions on this subject (for example Doughty, 2007), and blamed all parties for their share of responsibility. Campaigns in the UK encouraged the French government to close its notorious holding centre for would-be illegal immigrants to the UK at Sangatte near Calais in 2002. Five years later the *Daily Mail* found that a new such centre was to be opened, which, it argued, would just encourage more attempts. And it interviewed an Afghan who had already been deported from the UK, fares paid for by the Home Office, and was trying his luck again (Drury, 2007).

It is commonplace for *Mail*-haters to imply that the newspaper is racist, on account of its condemnation of government immigration policies and approaches to asylum seekers. The newspaper denies the charge:

> We favour economic migration to this country – clearly it can bring great benefit to industry and to the NHS. But people risking their lives on trains, at the mercy of gangsters, coming in willy-nilly on boats and trains and planes, it's horrible, it's obscene. And I know that unless you get hold of this you are going to give rise to the ugly right wing. We've been saying this for years – the *Mail*'s values are consistent.
>
> (Dacre, cit. by Hagerty, 2002)

> It is quite wrong to suggest that the *Daily Mail* is anti-immigrant. We have repeatedly extolled the value of immigration. We have highlighted successful and enterprising immigrants. But we have never let up blaming politicians of all parties for permitting uncontrolled immigration, with all its deleterious consequences.
>
> (Esser, 2007)

The *Daily Mail* campaigned for six years on the dangers of a vaccine given to babies, suggesting that there was a link between the measles, mumps and rubella triple vaccine and autism. This was based upon a study published in the leading medical journal, *The Lancet* in 1998. In the event, as described in Chapter 4, the study was found to be fraudulent and the researcher, Dr Andrew Wakefield, wrong. Up to this point typical *Mail* headlines read:[2] 'Fresh safety fears raised over MMR jab', 'New MMR link found to autism', 'MMR fears gain support', 'MMR – risk of brain disorders?'

It is only fair to add, though, that much of the media was deceived by the Wakefield assertions and not only the *Daily Mail*. And the newspaper does not regard the resources put into MMR as wasted, nor the efforts as a failure, because its campaign 'raised important issues not entirely quelled by the realisation that the whole media had for a time been hoodwinked by unscrupulous medics' (Esser, 2007).

The *Mail* campaigns on the growing of genetically modified crops, illegal immigration, prostate cancer and the Omagh bomb victims; it castigates the racism of the BNP and the failings of the National Health Service. It has attracted women not merely by publishing regular Princess Diana supplements but by taking seriously issues such as rape, domestic violence and workplace discrimination. It not only employs leading rightwing writers such as Melanie Phillips (formerly of the *Guardian*) and Peter Hitchens (who resigned from the *Express* when it was bought by a pornographer) but people from very different stables such as anti-apartheid sportswriter Ian Wooldridge and left-Labour commentator Roy Hattersley. It has been generally hostile to the Iraq War and Conservative politicians have accused the *Mail* of being allies of the leftwing anti-war coalition.

> As the war on terror has progressed, we've seen a remarkable new coalition form. The nation's most powerful reactionary force, the *Daily Mail*, has become the objective ally of the British Left in the struggle of the moment – the war against America.
>
> (Gove, 2004)

The *Mail* is happy to partner television, providing funding for investigations in return for use of the material just before transmission. In 1993 it co-funded the research that went into *Primary Failings*, an example cited in Chapter 15. More recently it has published features based on TV investigations 'Babies for Sale' on the alleged Chinese market in children (Joseph, 2007) and 'The Great Bank Swindle' in which a reporter went undercover in a high street bank to expose dodgy selling practices (Egbujo, 2007).

Political investigation

It is in its exposure of the government and its friends – some would say persecution – that the *Daily Mail* has scored its biggest hits. Having been part of the media onslaught on the Conservatives which had helped bring them down in 1997 (Greig, 1992, 1994, 1994a; Postlewaite, 1996), it had no intention, unlike some other media, of being suckered by Mr Blair's Labour administration over corruption, although, in its first few years it did give the benefit of the doubt to it on policy matters, while going on hunting the hapless Tories (Cheston, 1999).

Only months after Labour's victory, the *Daily Mail* was able to run this:

Blair hands back Ecclestone cash in sleaze storm
Tony Blair last night ordered big-money donation to Labour from

Formula One motor racing boss Bernie Ecclestone to be returned in an astonishing development in the 'cash for favours' row.

(Hughes, 1997)

Ecclestone was the Chairman of Formula One Racing and the prime mover in the planned £2 billion stock market flotation of the Grand Prix. It had been found out that he had lobbied the Prime Minister to drop the Government's ban on the sponsorship by tobacco companies of motor racing. After meeting Ecclestone, and presumably learning of his enthusiasm for the Labour Party, Mr Blair decided to change the policy of not permitting tobacco companies to sponsor, causing outrage among health organisations. By coincidence, Mr Ecclestone donated £1 million to the Labour Party. And this was just the beginning of government and Labour Party corruption scandals which would be subject to relentless exposure.

Five years later, Editor Paul Dacre showed no qualms, when he explained what he was doing:

I'm afraid I feel rather strongly that we have a Government that is manipulative, dictatorial and slightly corrupt. No. 10, in particular, cannot stand dissent. It has broken the second chamber, weakened the Civil Service and sidelined Parliament.

(Hagerty, 2002)

In spring 2006 the *Daily Mail* spent many column inches on 'Jowellgate', the connection between the British Secretary of State for Culture Tessa Jowell and a £350,000 'gift' to her husband David Mills from Italian Prime Minister Silvio Berlusconi. There had been rumours about Jowell and her husband being involved in unsavoury activities at least since 1997 and C4 TV was active in the same area in 2006, with its *Dispatches* on Mills, 'The Price of Blood' (see Chapter 4). The *Daily Mail* produced what it called 'an avalanche of incriminating evidence' provided by Italian prosecutors, and headlined '10 questions Tessa must answer'. Three days later they became '15 questions Miss Jowell must answer', keeping up the pressure in typical *Mail* style. At about this time Jowell and her husband separated, in a move that was interpreted by many observers as her trying to protect her career while her husband was in very public difficulties.

The *Daily Mail* was particularly incensed by the ways in which the Prime Minister's wife – in behaviour which was without precedent in Britain – exploited her husband's privileges and opportunities for the personal benefit of themselves and their family. It relentlessly exposed she and her husband's greed for freebies – gifts and holidays – from the rich and the foreign and delightedly reported the contempt with which this behaviour was greeted abroad; in the Italian media, for example, Blair was referred to as 'the scrounger' – Lo Scroccone.

The *Daily Mail* puts it this way:

> Since 1992 the *Daily Mail* has run many stories about the corruption of members of the government and their associates. Not all involve extensive investigation; one that stirred great interest and did involve sleuthing for evidence was that which exposed Prime Minister Blair's wife relying on an established conman to advise her over property investments. Ben Brogan the Political Editor, managed to get hold of the email which proved that Mrs Blair's protestations of innocence were lies . . .
>
> (Esser, 2007)

In 2002 the *Daily Mail* demonstrated how Mrs Blair was entrusting her financial speculations to a convicted criminal and, in trying to avoid this becoming public, had obliged civil servants to make dishonest denials on her behalf. It exposed this by finding and publishing an extensive tail of emails which proved the allegations true and illustrated the exultation with which the conman revelled in his activities.

> The e-mails call into question the judgment of both Mrs Blair and the Prime Minister in surrounding themselves with a collection of 'confidantes' who include Foster, a man jailed for fraud on three continents, Carole Caplin, a former soft porn model, and her mother Sylvia, a medium who consults the dead on Mrs. Blair's behalf.
>
> (Rayner, 2007)

Much of the other national media had dismissed the story as 'just another smear on the Blairs'; the *Daily Mail* believed this to be consistent with their failure properly to investigate the government.

The *Daily Mail* has published a very large number of revelations as to how government ministers have abused their positions and has probably led the pack on the scandals of how membership of the Upper House was sold for the benefit of the ruling party, how Party donations have been made by businesses which have coincidentally obtained advantages from government, how friends have been awarded public contracts and so forth; some of these are listed in Chapter 4.

Perhaps because of the widespread cynicism about politicians in general, the exposures did not have much effect on Blair's electoral fortunes, any more than did the exposure of how he committed the UK to the war on Iraq. Nevertheless, the *Daily Mail*, like the *Guardian*, claims that it is the real opposition. Not long after the defeat of the Conservatives in 1997, *Guardian* editor Alan Rusbridger opined:

Journalism today has assumed the role of the Opposition. When you have government with such a huge majority and no effective debate going on within Parliament . . . then the role of scrutiny and opposition falls upon the press.

(Rusbridger, 1999)

And today Robin Esser says much the same:

Other media have been reluctant to delve into what has been going on; when you have a tame media and an opposition which pulls its punches, someone has got to stand up for the people, to do the job the opposition should be doing.

(Esser, 2007)

Behind today's *Daily Mail*

The *Daily Mail* belongs to a media group, the Daily Mail and General Trust plc, with a turnover of £2,180 million, mainly based in the UK but with important media businesses in the USA and Australia. It is moving into Eastern Europe; reducing its involvement in UK regional newspapers and investing successfully in digital media. Its largest unit is Associated Newspapers, publishing the *Daily Mail, Mail on Sunday, Evening Standard* and Irish and Scots versions of the Mail titles. Other well-known media businesses owned by DMGT include *Loot, Metro* and British *Pathé*.

DMG Broadcasting owns the national Classic FM (radio, TV and magazine), a national jazz music channel and 32 local radio stations. Euromoney Institutional Investor publishes 100 specialist magazines and runs training at conferences for the financial world.

DMGT is 80 per cent owned by the family of the brothers who founded it; it is the only such family business in the British media to survive since the late 1800s.

The rock upon which all this is founded is the *Daily Mail* itself, the origins of which are described in Chapter 2. The extraordinary genius of the first Harmsworth, for innovation, for stimulating and enthralling the public and for making of his newspaper what competitors could only copy, has seemingly been handed on so that, today, his creation remains a remarkable success and, notwithstanding a bad period in the 1950s and 1960s, demonstrates remarkable continuity of approach. In the early twentieth century Harmsworth created a newspaper for the new middle classes, but he also invented the banner headline, vastly increased coverage of human interest stories, invested in sports coverage and provided for women's interests for the first time in British newspapers. He also employed the first woman war correspondent, in South Africa, in 1900. However, in 1915, rather than rely on official reports or patchy coverage by war correspondents, he paid soldiers at the front for news stories, another first.

Harmsworth sponsored flying competitions (in 1906), the Ideal Home Exhibition (1908, still running) and the world's first radio concert. The *Mail* ran campaigns, for example in favour of the Boer War in the 1890s and on domestic issues such as the need for public provision of proper equipment for police and fire brigades. In the First World War, the *Daily Mail* risked campaigning against the Commander in Chief – a very popular general – and held him responsible for failures of supply, following which the government fell and Lloyd George became Prime Minister. The newspaper also attacked the government vigorously for the defeat at Gallipoli, blaming it for the heavy casualties. In the 1920s the *Daily Mail*, in an inglorious episode, published the 'Zinoviev Letter', now widely believed to have been forged, which was supposed to prove that British communists were mounting an armed revolution. This has been generally regarded as an important factor in the defeat of the Labour Party at the 1924 general election; however the *Daily Mail*'s attacks on the Conservative leadership in 1929 are sometimes credited with the victory of the Labour Party that year.

One reason for the distaste for the *Daily Mail* of many of the intelligentsia in Britain is the newspaper's support for fascism in the 1930s, under the second Lord Rothermere, Alfred Harmsworth's son. Yet, to put this episode into perspective, we should not forget that, in this period, other British newspapers were supporting, or at least giving the benefit of the doubt to, the worst tyranny in the history of humankind, that of Soviet Russia, and in the process telling the most flagrant mistruths. The behaviour of both sides did no credit to journalism. Another reason is that they find the nationalistic, sometimes jingoistic, style unpalatable:

> The discovery of alleged plots by foreigners, which are then used retrospectively to build a climate of fear, was a staple of the old *Daily Mail*. It was a formula often copied but never improved by rivals such as the *Daily Express*, owned by Lord Beaverbook.
>
> (Barnes, 2007)

Reacting to this approach, it was a Conservative Prime Minister, Stanley Baldwin, who uttered the most famous put down of newspapers, in 1930:

> The papers conducted by Lord Rothermere and Lord Beaverbrook are not newspapers in the ordinary acceptance of the term . . . They are engines of propaganda for the constantly changing policies, desires . . . personal likes and dislikes of the two men. What the proprietorship of these papers is aiming at is power, but power without responsibility – the prerogative of the harlot throughout the ages.
>
> (Baldwin, 1930)

Following the Second World War the *Mail* went through a succession of editors who either made the mistake of trying to compete with the 'top peoples' papers, or failed to realise the populism that downmarket papers needed, becoming insufficiently enterprising. The despairing proprietor is reported as having explained a new change of editors thus:

> I have tried a short fat one, now I'm trying a tall thin one.
>
> (Greenslade, 2003: 170)

The *Daily Mail* then seemed neither one thing nor the other and was predicted to be on the way out.

Makeover

By 1971, the *Daily Mail* was in financial difficulties. Its sister paper, the *Daily Sketch*, was closed and its editor David English given the task of reinventing the *Daily Mail* as a mass-market tabloid aimed particularly at a female readership.

> Was it possible, in a tabloid format, to avoid looking, sounding and feeling like them, yet incorporate their positive journalistic approach? Could a tabloid *Mail* hold the centre ground, being both serious (and therefore credible) and frivolous (and therefore entertaining)?
>
> (Greenslade, 2003: 259)

It could. The time was right. English believed in self help, enterprise, traditional family life and respect for women and their values. And many apparently wanted these beliefs reflected in their daily news. Female journalists were happy, as he employed plenty; one, Ann Leslie, has been on the staff for 40 years.

In others ways too, English understood the spirit of the times in much the way Mrs Thatcher did; he reflected the aspirations of people struggling to get on, without troubling himself to alienate those well established. He realised their frustration with the fusty 'establishment' Britain so ridiculed by the intellectuals, but reacted by celebrating ordinary peoples' desire to get on and improve their own lot, rather than pontificate on the need for revolution or more state control as the intellectuals were wont.

Under English the *Daily Mail* investigated and campaigned against pyramid selling, lead in petrol and inadequate schools. It initiated a campaign against the religious cult of the Unification Church, which led to the longest libel action in British history. Sometimes it made an ass of itself, as when its hostility to Labour made it prey to a hoaxer and it wrongly accused a whole nationalised industry and its ministerial protectors of corruption; it was on surer ground when attacking Prime Minister Callaghan for nepotism, when he appointed his son-in-law as Ambassador to Washington, the most plum posting in the Diplomatic Service.

English' success was widely acknowledged. The *Daily Mail* was once more credited with political power. At the 1992 general election, when Thatcher won her fourth election, the rival *Observer* cried 'It was the *Mail* wot won it!', playing on a famous headline by the *Sun* of a few years earlier, when that newspaper claimed to have been responsible for an election win. However, the *Observer* claimed the *Mail*'s mendacity as the cause.

> For example, a straight(ish) report on Labour [shadow chancellor] John Smith's tax plans 'to help the poor' was swiftly air-brushed for the second edition to read 'to savage high earners'.
>
> (*Observer*, 12 April 1992)

In the mid-1990s, as mentioned above, the revelations of chicanery and minor corruption which came to be known as sleaze were led as much as by the *Daily Mail*, as by the *Guardian*, with such headlines as:

> The End of the Affair (minister Mellor forced to resign) (Greig, 1992)
>
> Sleaze: Major fights back (bribing MPs) (Greig, 1994)
>
> Pushed out by the people! (minister Tim Yeo forced to resign) (Greig, 1994)
>
> Westminster Six told to pay 31 million (Conservatives of Westminster Council) (Postlethwaite, 1996)

However, the *Mail* supported the Conservative cause during the 1997 election, even though it was obvious the Labour Party would win, and despite the fact that the proprietor had declared he was for Labour. One of its stable mates, the *Evening Standard*, supported the Liberal Democrats and the *Mail on Sunday* plumped for Labour. After Labour's enormous 1997 victory English was criticised for bad judgment; it was said that he had lost touch with middle-England. But the English formula continued to work in Blair's 'New Britain'.

Paul Dacre, who became Editor in 1992, embodies the *Daily Mail* philosophy in his own experience:

> I left Britain in 1976 [to work in the USA] that was ossified by a us-and-them, gaffers-versus-workers mentality in which a tribal working class was kept in place by subservience to the Labour authorities who owned their council homes, to the unions and the nationalized industries. Mrs Thatcher, in what was a terribly painful process, broke that destructive axis, empowered the individual and restored aspiration and self-reliance in this country. And, I suppose, if there are two words that sum up the *Mail*'s philosophy, they're 'aspiration' and 'self-reliance'.
>
> (Hagerty, 2002: 16)

Although its generally conservative stance is not in doubt, Dacre was determined that his would not be a Conservative Party newspaper, and under him it
has been as critical of Tory leaders as of Labour ministers, and, some argue,
more critical. Dacre claims that the *Mail* is politically independent (Hagerty,
2002). Says Robin Esser, a former *Express* editor now Managing Editor of
the *Mail*:

> The *Daily Mail* is generally conservative but not necessarily Conserva-
> tive. Our natural inclination is to be critical of governments and
> sceptical of the claims of politicians. In the Major years the *Daily Mail*
> was fervently critical of the Conservative government, while the *Mail*
> *on Sunday* supported it. At the 1997 election the *Evening Standard*
> supported Labour, the *Mail on Sunday* the SDP and only the *Daily Mail*
> the Conservatives. At that time our proprietor Lord Rothermere sat
> on the cross benches of the House of Lords but said that were he able
> to vote he would vote Labour. The point is that if someone needs
> investigating, we don't care what their party is.
>
> (Esser, 2007)

Attitudes to the *Mail*

'I hate everything the *Mail* stands for and I am going to destroy you' said Lord
Hollick to *Daily Mail* Editor Paul Dacre when he bought the Express Group.[3]

Just as the expression 'Guardian Reader' has long been a stock term of
ridicule, so 'Daily Mail Reader' seems to have become similarly stereotyped.
Orthodox members of the establishment must eschew, if not insult it, although
(it must be assumed) from ignorance, as no elitist would wish to be seen reading
it. A list of derogatory comments can be found at http://en.wikipedia.org/
wiki/Daily_Mail.

In the hatred for the *Daily Mail* there appears to be a kind of snobbery. This
is a hugely popular newspaper which appeals to people who are moved by very
practical problems of survival that those with private money or public school
education may ignore. The importance of schooling to children's futures; the
(perhaps only perceived) competition for jobs from immigrants; the costs of
the public sector to businesses and employers; the price of necessities; social
disruption wreaked by relaxation of rules or failure to control criminality; these
are all matters which most acutely affect those struggling to advance their
children and families without the benefit of inherited wealth, but who lack the
protections afforded to the really wealthy or the well-connected.

There may be another explanation. We can speculate that *Mail* haters are
perhaps found most among those of us who have been to arts and social science
faculties of the leading universities, which traditionally have provided the civil
servants, academics and media elites. These stand to lose job opportunities and
status from the diminution of state power, the reduction in the public services,

making state schooling competitive with public schools and the freeing up of the market, for which the *Mail* campaigns.

But perhaps the critics are not snobs, or representative of producer interests, but really do altruistically wish to hold the *Mail* to account for its moral failings. Certainly the *Mail* provides them with ammunition. Its investigative journalism can reek of the sensational and the highly coloured, with more passion than detached weighing of evidence; it is rapid firing, relentlessly accusatory and fiercely moralistic; it can seem to amount merely to whatever embarrasses or infuriates the government or vested interests, an attitude of scorn for those with power. Investigative journalism perhaps; journalism with *attitude*, certainly.

Notes

1 I am indebted to Hugh Barnes for pointing out this example to me.
2 I acknowledge Hugh Barnes' research here.
3 Reported by Paul Dacre, but characteristic of his target. Dacre went on 'This fine socialist then proceeded to treat his staff like a Victorian mill owner, sacking scores of fine journalists, saw his circulation plummet and ended up selling Beaverbrook's once great newspaper to a pornographer' (Hagerty, 2002: 15).

Bibliography

Barnes, H. (2007) unpublished mss supplied to Hugo de Burgh.
Brendon, P. (1992) *The Life and Death of the Press Barons*. London: Secker and Warburg.
Cheston, P. (1999) Jonathan Aitken: I lied, I am guilty, *Daily Mail*, 19 January 1999.
DMGT plc (2006) *Annual Report and Accounts*. London: DMGT plc
Doughty, S. (2007) 4 in 5 New Jobs go to Migrants, *Daily Mail*, 11 December 2007.
Drury, I. and Allen, P. (2007) Return of 'Complacent' Reid under fire as French give green light to new welfare centre, *Daily Mail*, 14 April 2007.
Egbujo, A. (2007) The Great Bank Swindle, *Daily Mail*, 21 March 07.
Esser, R. (2007) Hugo de Burgh interview with Robin Esser, Managing Editor of the Daily Mail, 15 November 2007.
Gold, T. (2005) My week beneath the burqa (10 November 2005) reproduced in *Muslim Q News* at http://www.q-news.com/media-DailyMail-Burka.htm
Goodwin, Jo-Ann and Jones, David (2008) Barbarity in Our Midst, *Daily Mail* 030108 pp51–53
Gove, M. (2004) *The Times*, see http://hurryupharry.bloghouse.net/archives/2004/04/15/second_class_mail.php
Greenslade, R. (2003) *Press Gang: How Newspapers Make Profits from Propaganda*. London: Pan.
Greig, G. (1992) The End of the Affair (minister Mellor forced to resign), *Daily Mail*, 25 September 1992.
Greig, G. (1994) Sleaze: Major fights back (bribing MPs), *Daily Mail*, 26 October 1994.
Greig, G. (1994a) Pushed out by the people! (minister Tim Yeo forced to resign), *Daily Mail*, 6 January 1994.
Hagerty, B. (2002) The Zeal Thing, *British Journalism Review*, 13, (3): 11–22.

Harding, J. (2000) *The Uninvited: Refugees at the Rich Man's Gate*. London: Profile.

Hope, J. (2006) Alzheimer drugs for Scots – while the rest miss out, *Daily Mail*, 9 March 2006.

Hughes, D. (2007) Blair hands back Ecclestone cash in sleaze storm, *Daily Mail*, 11 November 1997.

Joseph, C. (2007) Babies for Sale, *Daily Mail*, 7 October 2007. *The Lancet*, 28 February 1998, 28:351(9103) and 647–8.

Monopolies and Mergers Commission (1994) *Daily Mail and General Trust plc and T. Bailey Forman Limited*. London: HMSO.

Pendlebury, R. (2004) BNP: The Same Nasty Bigots, *Daily Mail*, 5 June 2004.

Postlethwaite, J. (1996) Westminster Six told to pay 31 Million (Conservatives of Westminster Council) *Daily Mail*, 9 May 1996.

Rayner, G. and Shears, R. (2007) Cherie, A Crook And The Proof No. 10 Lied, *Daily Mail*, 5 December 2007.

Reid, S. (2005) Bird Flu, Special Report, *Daily Mail*, 22 October 2005.

Reid, S. (2008) How Doctors lie on death certificates to hide the true scale of the appalling death toll from hospital infections *Daily Mail* 030108 pp30–31

Reid, S. (2008a) Hugo de Burgh interview with Sue Reid, Special Investigations Editor of the *Daily Mail*, 5 February, 2008

Rusbridger, A. (1999) Hugo de Burgh interview with Alan Rusbridger, Editor, *The Guardian*, 25 May 1999.

Wright, S. (2007) Will Five Face New Trial? *Daily Mail*, 8 November 2007.

Wright, S. (2007a) Lawrence: The Vital Blunders, *Daily Mail*, 9 November 2007.

Further reading

Cathcart, B. (1999) *The Case of Stephen Lawrence*. London: Viking.

Greenslade, R. (2003) *Press Gang: How Newspapers Make Profits from Propaganda*. London: Pan.

Taylor, S. (1996) *The Great Outsiders: Northcliffe, Rothermere and the Daily Mail*. London: Weidenfeld & Nicolson.

Taylor, S. (2002) *An Unlikely Hero: Vere Rothermere and How the Daily Mail Was Saved*. London: Weidenfeld & Nicolson.

17

EXPOSING MISCARRIAGES
OF JUSTICE

An example from BBC's *Rough Justice*

Hugo de Burgh

The problem

In 1974 an IRA bombing in Birmingham killed twenty-one people; the men convicted in the subsequent trial were later found to have been convicted wrongly on the strength of flawed evidence and forced confessions. The same year, 1974, bombings in Guildford and Woolwich resulted in the conviction of four men who were to be released in 1989, having been found innocent. From very soon after the Birmingham trial, there were doubts about the convictions. On various occasions over 13 years, two Home Secretaries reviewed the case, as did two Directors of Public Prosecutions, eleven judges and four police inquiries. Over many years a journalist (and from 1987 Member of Parliament), Chris Mullin, kept presenting and re-presenting his evidence that the men were innocent and claiming not only that he knew the names of the real perpetrators, but that the police also knew. As a result of his work, the verdict of the forensic scientist in the original trial was re-examined by the Home Office and found unsafe.

Mullin, who wrote a book on the Birmingham investigation (Mullin, 1986) made no great claims for his skills. When asked how he uncovered those whom he believed had really carried out the Birmingham bombings, he replied 'by simple detective work of the sort one would commend to the West Midlands police' (Lennon, 1991). 'Most people travelling on the buses noticed that there was something wrong in these cases, Guildford and the Birmingham Six' said Mullin, wondering why the judicial system got them so wrong.

> Stupidity would be one possible explanation for the behaviour of a succession of judges, but I am inclined to the view that it is a pre-occupation with protecting the credibility of the legal system which takes precedence over a commitment to justice.
>
> (cit. in Lennon, 1991)

In the 1970s miscarriages of justice appear to have proliferated. Another famous instance was the case of Carl Bridgwater in which four men were imprisoned for the killing of a newspaper boy in 1978; after 20 years of research and campaigning by investigative journalist Paul Foot, the men were finally released in 1996. The apparently large number of miscarriages, and of course we can only speculate as to how many there really are for only a tiny number are taken up by journalists in relation to all committals, may simply be a function of the huge increase in recorded crime over the past 50 years. While there is no agreement regarding how much of this increase reflects more crime and how much better identification of crime, it is generally accepted that crime itself has burgeoned.

Whatever the wider context in which rising crime and its control can be seen; whatever the factors in the notorious cases of miscarriage of justice named above, it has long been the contention of interested journalists that there are serious flaws in the judicial system which make it essential that there be investigative journalists prepared to subject cases to scrutiny. One of these is the fact that, contrary to popular opinion, it is not easy for the convicted to get leave to appeal, in fact virtually the only grounds for appeal is error in legal procedure. The other principal accusation is that the lack of a system of independent investigation as available in France or Italy results in courtrooms being presented with evidence that has been inadequately researched, or is partial, or is presented in a confused manner because insufficient examination has been made of it before trial.

Ludovic Kennedy, involved in exposing many miscarriages of justice over many years, sees police manipulation of evidence, the 'childish' adversary system in the courts which obscures rather than reveals truth and 'cavalier' assessment of evidence by the Court of Appeal as the main problems. Among the reforms he and others have advocated is the replacement of trial by conflict with trial by discovery. He says:

> In the short term the remedy is quite simple. It is that in all cases of serious crime, murder, manslaughter, rape, armed robbery, offences for which the penalty's likely to be many years of imprisonment, the questioning of suspects be taken out of the hands of the police and given instead to an examining magistrate . . . who will direct the police in their inquiries.
>
> (Kennedy, 1991: 312)

In a short summary Tom Sargant describes the typical miscarriages of justice and how they come about, miscarriages which 'take many forms and are far more numerous than anyone in authority is prepared to admit, or is in a position to estimate' (Sargant, 1985). He also points to the accusatorial system above all because it 'is more of a battle than an inquiry into the truth and is operated under wholly inadequate safeguards and controls' (ibid.: 218).

The legal system, in other words, provided the opportunity, even the necessity, for investigative journalists to investigate. We are not talking simply about some corrupt or inadequate policemen but of a system that promotes such inadequacy to influence the trials.

Some argue (Haywood, 1999a) that it is now easier to get to appeal and that the system is much more responsive to the concept of miscarriages; the Criminal Cases Review Commission was established in 1997 and this they credit especially to *Rough Justice* which has made everybody involved in the criminal justice system more sensitive to the possibility of miscarriages and more aware of how they can come about. There is such scepticism now that, as Steve Haywood, former editor of *Rough Justice* and now responsible for C4's equivalent, *Trial and Error*, talks of:

> a whole coterie of solicitors and barristers who will work on behalf of people claiming to be victims of miscarriages plus a political band-wagon which will provide any claimant with a support group to go politicking and junketing, trying to get others interested.
>
> (Haywood, 1999a)

He points out that programmes like those on which he has worked are important because which cases go to appeal courts are not based on judicial considerations, 'politics has a lot do with it . . . if you can build up a level of public concern to the extent that the case *must* be dealt with then you stand a much better chance' (Haywood, 1999a).

Examining the cases selected by *Rough Justice* and investigative journalists working in other media, it's easy to be struck first by the extraordinarily great gulf that separated the lives of the journalists from those of the people they were investigating – whose lives were often detached from community or family or prospects for an orderly life, which made it much easier for them to be exploited by unscrupulous or incompetent police – and second by the dedication with which reporters, and a few other individuals, fight on behalf of these, very different, citizens. Peter Hill, founder of *Rough Justice*, explains his motivation as 'outrage' that people with power can do shoddy things to people without power.

Time line of some recent, publicised, miscarriages of justice in Britain

1957: Founding of the organisation Justice
1982: First transmissions of *Rough Justice*
1982: UK government reopens cases investigated by *Rough Justice*
1985: Granada TV decides to resource Mullin's search
1989: Release of the Guildford Four
1990: March – Granada TV drama documentary 'Who Bombed Birmingham?'

1991:   Release of the Birmingham Six
1996:   26 November – *Rough Justice* transmits programme on Ryan James
1996:   26 July – *Rough Justice* on Bridgwater Case
1998:   Bentley hanging conviction quashed.

BBC's *Rough Justice* [1]

Rough Justice first transmitted in 1982, examining three cases, all of which were subsequently reopened by the Home Office. The authors were influenced by the efforts that had been made over many years by the rights campaigner and founder of Justice, Tom Sargant, and by the merits of the three cases in question. In each case the convictions seemed implausible and the evidence questionable, to say the least. According to Young and Hill (1983) *Rough Justice* was typically drawn to cases where:

- defence solicitors became involved too late
- the police could not find things that journalists could
- institutions attempted to thwart the journalists.

The *Rough Justice* investigators have usually been treated with suspicion and suffered from attempts to thwart them. For example, according to Young and Hill (1983), in a modest investigation without any wider or political ramifications, they were denied access or simple help by the Ministry of Defence, British Rail, the Broadmoor Hospital authorities, the Department of Health and Social Security (as it was then), the medical authorities and the police. Sargant found great difficulties in obtaining copies of statements taken by the police, the names of psychiatrists who had examined prisoners or court transcripts (Sargant, 1985: 237). Little has changed today.

Rough Justice started after BBC reporter Peter Hill was driving in North London and found himself accused by a policeman of jumping a red light; the fury he felt at wrongful accusation started him thinking about the nature of miscarriages and he contacted Tom Sargant of Justice. The programme he and Michael Young persuaded their BBC managers to let him launch, *Rough Justice*, started with a very clear idea of what it behoved it to do. This is how Young and Hill (1983) put it:

> we chose to observe a number of constraints. The first was that the programme should deal in facts, not opinions. We would corroborate these facts as far as possible. We would authenticate any documents that we quoted or used.
>
> The second constraint was that we should not yield to the temptation to become judge and jury, to draw inferences from the conduct of the original investigation and trial.
>
> We decided, too, that the prosecution case must be fairly and fully

represented in each case. This was a third constraint. We guessed that people were going to ask, 'But just how did he get convicted?' We wanted to be able to say that all the salient facts that the prosecution had presented against the defendant had been reported in our films. We asked our lawyers to check the script on each occasion against the transcript of the judge's summing up to ensure that we had been fair to the presentation of the prosecution case.

(Young and Hill, 1983)

Allegedly the programme experienced a difficult phase in the late 1980s because of the failure of the BBC to support its reporters when they were under attack. The two most distinguished journalists of the team were given the opportunity to work on programmes other than *Rough Justice* after it was alleged in court and in the media that they had dealt unfairly with the subject of an investigation.[2]

The investigation in question was of a woman called Anne Fitzpatrick. She had picked out in an identity parade one Anthony Mycock, known to the police in Manchester, as having forced her into her flat, assaulted and tied her up before stealing from her. The *Rough Justice* team investigated the case in 1985 and became certain that no burglary had taken place; they learned that Fitzpatrick had trashed her own flat in a fit of pique with her partner and that her pretence that there had been a burglary was an attempt to explain this event to that partner. They suspected that the identification of the suspect was fraudulent and a further cover-up in that the police had not been too scrupulous in checking, since Mycock was a 'usual suspect'.

Hill and Young traced Fitzpatrick to Los Angeles and interviewed her, securing her admission. This was reported in the BBC staff newspaper *Aerial* as a great coup. The programme went out in 1985 and the case was reinvestigated by Manchester Police, although a history of antagonism between the programme and Manchester Police meant that there was little or no cooperation, indeed Steve Haywood (then producer) believes that he was intimidated by the police at that stage (Haywood, 1999a). Furthermore, he believes that the police told Fitzpatrick she was guilty of perjury and liable to a severe sentence which in reality was most unlikely, though it served to frighten her. After the programme 'The Case of the Perfect Proof' went out on 3 October 1985, Mycock was at last given leave to appeal and at the hearing it was quickly found that the case against Mycock could not be sustained. However, in the course of the hearing it was alleged that the reporters had pressurised Fitzpatrick to the point of threatening her in order to get retraction and, although this was by then tangential to the hearing, Lord Chief Justice Lane spent a great deal of time examining the two reporters and impugning their methods.

As a result of Lane's examination of the reporters, BBC managers removed them from *Rough Justice*. They also made every effort to hush up the matter, presumably because they lost their nerve after criticism in the press (e.g. the

Daily Mail); they also feared legal actions starting in the USA which were expected to follow because the BBC failed to refute the accusations made against their reporters.

Why did Lane bother, and why did the BBC fail to defend its reporters? Other journalists on *Rough Justice* at the time believe that after the early successes of the programme in reporting failures of the police and courts, those believing themselves under attack felt antagonism, fuelled by the belief that the scepticism inflamed by the programmes was harming the justice system as a whole. In an interview at the time, one of the UK's most important judges, Lord Denning, said 'it was better that an innocent man remain in prison than that the integrity of the system be questioned'. The hostility was such that the team began to believe that if *Rough Justice* was involved the subjects' chances of release were being hindered. That was the worst period *Rough Justice* went through.

In 2000

This genre of programming has a problem very particular to it: 'You only have one person to talk to you – if you cannot get to that person, you are finished' (Haywood, 1999a). This conditions the choice of topic, or at least demands particular skills. The story is told of how in the first series Peter Hill needed to speak to a woman – call her Jean – whom he was doubtful of being able to persuade to see him. He undertook to visit several people over several months on the housing estate in which Jean lived and to interview them instead; on each occasion he mentioned that he would be meeting Jean 'because she is such an honourable woman'. After a couple of months of this everyone on the estate knew that he would eventually be seeing Jean 'because she is such an honourable woman' and, not surprisingly, he did.

The ability to plan strategically in this manner and to doorstep effectively are two of the skills that researchers on *Rough Justice* require. Equally important, though, is an analytic brain. 'By sitting and reading through a case again and again you can often crack it just sitting there.' The lawyers did not manage it because of the pressure of events, because they had no time, because they're 'not as good as us' (Haywood, 1999a). Good contacts are not so significant – 'they find you' – although, since the best contacts are in the police it is useful to know how to relate to them. More important is a grasp of how the medium works, since filling 50 minutes so that people keep on watching demands many different skills. The kind of topic a producer looks for has three essential sequences. Although the format has been changing the traditional one is made up of:

- part one – **conviction**, i.e. all the prosecution evidence
- part two – **human story**
- part three – **the handful of hair**, i.e. production of the evidence which destroys the prosecution case.[3]

In sum, this is documentary-making in current affairs with the added spices of requiring a specific narrative form, much carefully sifted detail, the risks of exposure to legal action and problems of identifying and communicating with sources that would rarely be found elsewhere in journalism. Not surprisingly, therefore, it is generally held by those in the business that *Rough Justice* is quintessentially the kind of programme that requires a public service umbrella, since there must be the freedom to select topics on moral criteria, to abort programmes, and to research them to the utmost degree. There is a risk otherwise that topics will be selected only because they are already guaranteed to attract attention or where there is certainty that they can be concluded; that producers will rely upon the information provided by solicitors rather than upon their own original research. Commercial pressures, in other words, endanger quality.

When *Trial and Error*, C4's equivalent of *Rough Justice* introduced in 1993, was commissioned conditions that were quite unique at the time were written into the contract in order to protect its integrity, to take account of the fact that a great deal of research might be done only to have the programme for which it was intended pulled. The essential provision was that the 2-year contract did not stipulate the number of programmes required to be made – an unimaginable condition in any other sector of the industry. For two reasons a different type of case is now being taken up by these programmes. Audiences for this genre of television are declining and the introduction of the Criminal Cases Review Commission (CCRC) has changed the environment. The CCRC investigates miscarriage allegations which in the past would only have been undertaken by television; there are, however, some cases that they do not take up and it is among these that *Trial and Error* finds its subject matter (Lloyd, 1999).

Contractor Steve Haywood (whose company also made the C4 series *Clear My Name* in 1998) says that in today's climate it is difficult to do cases other than 'high profile' ones. He believes that today it would not be possible for him to take on a case such as that of Jacqueline Fletcher in the 1991 'Murder or Mystery'. The victim of this miscarriage was a woman, accused of murdering her child, whom he characterises as poor, unhealthy, uneducated, exploited and ignorant; 'and yet she was innocent'. Because he was sure of this, and of the injustice of the accusation, Haywood 'had a go' and eventually, with the unstinting help of the pathologist whose original error he exposed, proved that the child had probably died of natural causes. 'Lord Justice Lane was obliged to let her out.' Haywood believes that Fletcher would still be in prison if that *Rough Justice* had not been made. His defence of the programme as it was then is eloquent: 'Miscarriages of justice don't happen to people like you or me, people with large incomes or powerful friends; they happen to poor people' (Haywood, 1999a).

Example: 'Death in the Playground'

On an afternoon in May 1992 a 3-year-old child, Karl, disappeared in a play area of some cultivated and some rough and overgrown land near a housing estate. The police were called and among those who helped them search was the teenager Paul Esslemont, the last person known to have seen the child; he had been practising golf strokes on the grass at the time. When, partly thanks to Esslemont's help, the child was found in the bushes, he had been battered to death.

Subsequent police investigations included interviews with Esslemont who gave three statements over eight days, statements that contained inconsistencies. Moreover, forensic tests revealed, according to the police case, blood on all his clothes and on his golf club. He was tried in May 1993 and the inconsistencies in his statements were declared to be not lapses of memory but lies; he was found guilty and his appeal was rejected. Incidentally, his parents' home was firebombed.

Rough Justice decided to examine the story on the basis that the idea of Paul Esslemont murdering anybody was incredible. The team talked to people who knew Esslemont, including those for whom he had been a baby-sitter, and became convinced that there was neither motive nor psychological explanation. Furthermore, at least one jury member was not convinced of his guilt. Early in the programme, *Rough Justice* states that it clarified quickly that there was no motive and that Esslemont does not fit the psychological profiles of a killer, profiles that are well recognised. They noted that the police interviews had pushed Esslemont into admitting irritability with the small boy and they thought that the forensic evidence might be uncertain since Esslemont had been searching through the undergrowth with the police looking for the child, which might explain the bloodstains on him.

In fact no forensic scientist had visited the scene until *Rough Justice* commissioned one to do so (BBC, 1994). The scientist pointed out that in such cases a map of bloodstains should be made, yet none had been. The undergrowth had been mown in order to find the weapon, possibly destroying evidence. The forensic scientist commissioned by *Rough Justice* constructed a model to see how far blood could travel in the case of the child's battering. This made it plausible that Esslemont might innocently have flecks of blood on him. He went on to find that there was little or no evidence that the murder weapon was a golf club, as claimed by the police; indeed he went further and said that the weapon could not have been a golf club. He proceeded to give an innocent explanation for the appearance of blood on the tongue of the accused's trainer; demonstrated that the blood on Esslemont's jeans was not that of the victim but the accused; and showed that, while the accused's T-shirt had no blood on it, the killer's upper garment had to have blood on it, such were the dynamics of the assault. This study pointed, too, to the fact that the police had failed to follow up the lead on another possible killer who was in the vicinity at the time; they had plumped for Esslemont, perhaps because he was handy and easy to manipulate, allowing themselves to be convinced by inadequate forensic evidence. In July 1997 Esslemont was released. He had spent three years in jail.

Discussion

People involved with this genre of journalism appear uneasy about some of the cases. The distinction is commonly drawn between a case of corruption of justice and a case of miscarriage. Thus it is asserted that in at least one of the well-known bombing cases there may have been corruption but no miscarriage. It was also suggested that further examination of other recent cases might lead one to question whether there was a miscarriage of justice, or whether inadequate evidence was the problem.

The following example of the distinction was given to me. In the Sheila Bowler case, dealt with in three programmes transmitted over 1994–5,[4] in which a spinster was accused of effecting her (supposedly unable to walk) aunt's death by taking her to a river. The *Trial and Error* team argued that the proposition that the aunt might have walked the distance was never properly examined by the court, which thus made erroneous assumptions. It was on the basis of that that there was a re-trial. The programme did not prove at any time that the aunt did walk, but only that in order to have a fair trial this matter should have been explored. By comparison, in the case of Brian Parsons, accused of murder during a burglary, there was a good deal of proof that Parsons could not have done it and some evidence that someone else had. This was a true miscarriage of justice (BBC, 1996).

In either type of case, investigative journalists can be more successful in their research than the professionals of the legal system because some witnesses will speak to journalists but not to police or lawyers. Since they investigate after the event more truth may be available than at the time, and, moreover, they are usually building upon some initial police work, however flawed. Investigative journalists should be able to bring to the case a cast of mind that is quite different from that of the professionals. They have no *interest* in the case; their *professional integrity* is not impugned if the case has to be rethought, or if no villain is found, although today such a failure may have *commercial* implications.

Journalists are not bound by the rules of evidence used in court cases, by professional conventions, by considerations of career within the system they are scrutinising or (it is hoped) by the fear of spoiling relationships within that system. It is also possible that journalists may be more intelligent in the sense that they can bring to bear a different set of intellectual skills and lateral thinking from those professionally involved. They may be educated in a different manner and be more contextually aware investigators than the police or solicitors.

The work of journalists brings them in touch with the widest possible range of people, in relationships of equality equally with those who have prestige and power, or none. This often makes them sceptical of the hierarchies and pro-cedures that less free individuals use to protect themselves from examination.

Moreover, through working in a variety of other environments, they develop specific skills and knowledge that they can employ in scrutinising the justice system. For these reasons, in examining miscarriages of justice in Britain, investigative journalists act as expert check on the activities of police or solicitors, running repeat investigations, gathering new witnesses and construct-ing models.

Notes

1 While I was writing these chapters, the editor of *Rough Justice* was Elizabeth Clough and I made great efforts to meet her, to talk to her on the telephone, or to have her designate a spokesperson to tell me about the programme today. Unfortunately, because of her personal commitments and difficulties at the time I was unable to draw upon her knowledge.
2 My account of this situation derives from discussions with Peter Hill (1999), the chapter of a book he has in preparation, an interview with Steve Haywood (1999a) and the original BBC transcripts of interviews conducted by Hill and Young for the programme in question.
3 The expression 'Handful of Hair' emanates from the first series of *Rough Justice* in which there was the case of the murder of a student of Goldsmith's College, London; the conviction was overturned on the production of evidence by *Rough Justice* that the hair grasped by the murdered woman in the moment of death was not that of the convicted. 'Handful of Hair' represents the irrefutable, what the producers are looking for.
4 The first two were in the series *Trial and Error* (reporter David Jessel, producer Steve Phelps) transmitted 20 September 1994 and 9 November 1995; the third was a fly-on-the-wall of preparations for the retrial called *The Music Teacher*, produced by Steve Rankin. (Information supplied by Steve Haywood 8 June 1999.)

Bibliography

BBC (1994) 'Death in the Playground', *Rough Justice*. London: BBC TV.

BBC (1996) 'The Vet's Wife', *Rough Justice*. London: BBC TV.

BBC (1997) 'The Bordon Baseball Bat Murder', *Rough Justice*. London: BBC TV.

Haywood, S. (1999) Being an investigative journalist today. Talk given to the students of the MA Investigative Journalism course at Nottingham Trent University, 22 April 1999.

Haywood, S. (1999a) Interview with Hugo de Burgh in Blackheath, London, 6 May 1999.

Hill, P. (1999) Interview with Hugo de Burgh, 18 May 1999.

Hill, P., Young, M. and Sargant, T. (1985) *More Rough Justice*. London: Penguin.

Kennedy, L. (1985) In P. Hill, M. Young and T. Sargant *More Rough Justice*. London: Penguin.

Kennedy, L. (1991) *Truth to Tell: Collected Writings of Ludovic Kennedy*. London: Bantam Books.

Lennon, P. (1991) Meddler after truth. *Guardian*, 2 January 1992.

Lloyd, D. (1999) Information provided to Hugo de Burgh, 10 June 1999.

Mullin, C. (1986) *Error of Judgment: The Truth about the Birmingham Bombings*. London: Chatto and Windus.

Sargant, T. (1985) In P. Hill, M. Young and T. Sargant *More Rough Justice*. London: Penguin.

Young, M. and Hill, P. (1983) *Rough Justice*. London: BBC.

Further reading

Hill, P., Young, M. and Sargant, T. (1985) *More Rough Justice*. London: Penguin.

Kennedy, L. (1991) *Truth to Tell: Collected Writings of Ludovic Kennedy*. London: Bantam Books.

18

LOCAL POWER AND PUBLIC ACCOUNTABILITY

An example from the East Midlands

Mark D'Arcy

Introduction

At the turn of the last century Lincoln Steffens exposed the corruption of US local politics in his *Shame of the Cities* (cit. in Ekirch, 1974: 92); in the 1970s British investigator Ray Fitzwalter, in what became known as the 'Poulson Saga', revealed to an incredulous public how politicians of both major political parties could be bought. Today in Britain the scope of public administration, and therefore of maladministration, is greater than ever before, yet many fear that journalists are not up to the standards of Steffens and Fitzwalter. This chapter argues that monitoring the activities of the local state (which now extends well beyond elected local government) should be a principal task for investigative journalists, particularly in the local and regional media. It shows that the job is becoming more difficult because of the changing nature of the local state, and that the emphasis of reporting is now changing towards what editors see as a more reader-friendly agenda. Although based upon the British experience, the lessons are equally relevant to other countries.

English local administration

About a quarter of total government expenditure is delivered through elected local councils to provide us with services ranging from community care to highways and schools. Much of this activity is of direct and daily importance to viewers, listeners and readers of the local media. It is their children who suffer if the schools are sub-standard; it is their cars that are damaged by pot holes in the roads; it is they or their relatives who are at risk if community care services are inadequate; it is their council tax bills that rise if local politicians are corrupt or incompetent.

Local authorities are just one component of an increasingly complex and unreported local state. With opting out for schools, colleges and hospitals, power in key services is more diffuse and at the same time the potential for wrongdoing and unaccountable decision-making is greater. In my experience, the activities of Training and Enterprise Councils (TECs) are virtually unreported, except when they decide to press release something themselves. Yet these bodies take an increasing role in employment training under the Labour government's New Deal programme, so their performance directly affect the lives of thousands of unemployed people, who might lose their benefit if they do not participate in their training programmes. Police and health authorities have been reformed in the cause of 'leaner, fitter' decision-making; but this has entailed a far more closed style of decision-making, and their activities often escape systematic scrutiny. And what of the appointment and training of their members, and come to that, of local magistrates? The latter, after all, can send people to prison.

When Tony Blair became Prime Minister in 1997 he promised to abolish unaccountable quangos, or 'quasi national government organisations' which appear often to be staffed with friends of the ruling party, to be doing work that should be subject to popular scrutiny and to be spending huge amounts of public money. In fact their cost has increased by 60 since 2003 (Taxpayer's Alliance). There are now nearly 900 quangos with 30,000 members. Many public bodies including Royal Mail, Channel 4, the Financial Services Authority, the Olympic Delivery Authority, the National Health Service and Transport for London offer huge remuneration packages to their senior executives while exhibiting rather less generousity to their lower-level staff. And the performance of those organisations does not always justify the pay, pensions and bonuses their top managers enjoy. Ofcom, the broadcasting regulator, employs eleven executives in the top 100 of the rich list of public servants produced by the Taxpayers' Alliance (Chittenden, Maurice). These facts have come in for considerable criticism. Yet in November 2007, in the Queen's Speech (the annual policy statement to Parliament) seven new public bodies★ were announced.

A good principle to observe is that the use of state power and public money should be accompanied by proper checks and balances. Where an organisation can operate in the knowledge that no one is watching, all kinds of problems can quickly develop. In the late 1990s, the local state was full of faraway bodies of which we, the public, knew nothing.

Reporting the wrong subjects?

The local state, in all its manifestations, presents an obvious and legitimate target for scrutiny and investigative reporting. But if anything, the local media are reducing their coverage of local public life. Fewer and fewer papers now devote the acres of space which would once have been allocated to reporting a council

---

★ The above paragraph was added by the Editor.

meeting with quasi-parliamentary coverage of speeches and questions. Fewer and fewer local radio stations cover council committees or even full council meetings. This is perceived to be a retrograde step, a blow to local democracy. But perhaps the real story is more complex. I doubt there was ever a halcyon era in which a breathless public crowded the streets, agog to read the latest reports of their local council's Policy and Resources Committee. If there was, that era is now over; market research by focus groups has identified, apparently, that this kind of coverage of local affairs is not what the viewers, listeners and readers want.

One reason may well be that, as far as the readers were concerned, such coverage simply did not deal with their real concerns. First, it was seldom sufficiently analytical; insults traded in the council chamber would be faithfully reported, with little or no explanation of the significance of whatever was being debated. It sometimes seemed that the journalists in the council chamber had lapsed into trial-reporting mode, and were quite consciously avoiding any comment or judgement upon their story. But without some background and analysis readers would often be left with little idea of what the argument was actually about. A second issue is that much local government reporting dwells on subjects that simply don't interest the readership. In two and a half years as political correspondent with the *Leicester Mercury*, I spent much of my time covering power struggles in the Town Hall. This was investigative journalism in the sense that it involved revealing information that those in power would have preferred to keep private. There would be whispered tip-offs, careful checking with other sources, even the occasional leaked document. In retrospect, I was probably devoting too much time to reporting the micro-politics of local government, which were of limited interest to most readers. Perhaps the verdict of the focus groups was not so surprising after all. But perhaps the wrong conclusions are now being drawn from it. Many editors and policy-makers have made an unjustified leap from arguing that traditional local political reporting is too fixated on process and micro-politics, to the belief that all stories about local politics (in its broadest sense) are boring.

For instance, what I and my colleagues in other local media outlets in Leicester failed to notice, was the appalling standard of education provided by many of the city's schools. This only came to light when the county council lost responsibility for them and the new city education authority took its place close to the bottom of the government's education league tables. Here was a story with real public appeal and far more lasting importance. The local media should be ready to pounce on the failure of essential services; in practice, it seems to me that they seldom attempt to audit the performance of bread and butter services, even where doing so would produce some startling results. One starting point for this kind of reporting is The Audit Commission's Annual Performance Indicators for local services, which cover everything from exam results to the efficiency of council tax collection. These will give a clear indication when a local authority is falling behind in the standard of service it provides, and should prompt local reporters and editors to start asking why.

Such reporting still requires a specialist who can find his or her way around a town hall, who has some credibility with politicians and officials and who has a sufficient understanding of the workings of local government to spot a potential story. The trouble is that, on the principle that 'all council stories are boring', fewer and fewer local media outlets employ such a specialist – even on a part-time basis. All too often the reporter attending council meetings is some puzzled junior with little idea what is going on and who is speaking – and in many authorities there is no one there at all.

Bob Satchwell, President of the Guild of Newspaper Editors, and editor of the *Cambridge Evening News*, believes that many newspapers are consciously shifting their reporting agenda to meet the needs and tastes of their readers, as identified through focus groups and market research (Satchwell interview, 1998). He contends that the recent revival in readership figures, led by local weekly papers and now being observed in regional dailies, is evidence that this process is indeed delivering what the readers want. But he also conceded that in some cases it has led editors to concentrate on a narrow news agenda and pay less attention to monitoring the performance of public services. This can lead to important stories that would appeal to readers being missed. 'I don't decry focus groups, but the downside of using them is that you can become over-focused,' Satchwell says. 'You do have to keep some perspective, and be prepared to have people trawling through council minutes and going to meetings that don't immediately seem newsworthy, in search of the stories that may be there.' An essential part of the process, he believes, is maintaining specialists who have the background knowledge to interpret information, and can develop contacts and gain the trust of potential whistle-blowers. But he insists that most local newspapers are doing 'a very, very good job' of monitoring the local state, and he rejects the idea that there was some lost golden age of serious local political reporting.

Ed Glinert, who compiles *Private Eye*'s 'Rotten Boroughs' feature, a regular round-up of sleaze, abuse of power and municipal pomposity from town halls across the land, is less sanguine about the performance of the local media. He says most of his stories come from 'disaffected journalists, who find they can't get some stories printed, or are forced to tone them down, because they are about local councils which advertise in their paper'. Indeed *Private Eye* lacks the resources to obtain such stories itself, and his role is mainly to check the details. Often the stories he dealt with were reasonable accounts of events, which had been rejected because editors were afraid of causing offence. 'I think a lot of local newspapers are doing a really bad job, because they're so in hock to their local establishment that they never run anything that is detrimental to it,' Glinert said. He identifies a number of reasons why local papers may shy away from exposing wrongdoing in local public life:

If a story focuses on wrongdoing by a particular individual, editors will often be reluctant to risk accusations that they are conducting a witch-hunt. For some reason this seems a particularly potent response to criticism of an individual, however powerful. This may result in stories being sanitised so that names are not named.

(Glinert, 1998)

This can be risky. A story which related, for example, tales of unnamed drunken councillors misbehaving, may provoke a writ from innocent and uninvolved local politicians, who feel they have been implicated. In the case of heavyweight political scandals, there may be a cynical assumption that the readers will not understand or wish to read about some complex tale of wrongdoing. Glinert cites the example of the collapse of the Bank of Credit and Commerce International (BCCI), which had painful financial results for those councils which had invested in it. Some local papers thought the details of how their local politicians and officials had ignored the warning signs about the BCCI, and thus opened up their councils to substantial losses, were too complex for their readers.

Another barrier to investigative reporting can be a misguided local patriotism, which may induce some editors to give uncritical support to a prestige local initiative, rather than question whether it was money well spent. Glinert suggests that the English city of Manchester's bid to host the Olympics should have received more scrutiny and less uncritical coverage from the local media. Too often, he believes, the flaws in many flagship local projects only become apparent after a spectacular and expensive failure. Other examples may include grandiose regeneration projects, perhaps City Challenge schemes, or developments funded by Millennium Commission money. Typically such initiatives are hyped up as a great leap forward for a particular area; often the reality can be rather more mundane.

Financial and political corruption

Few stories confirm prejudices more satisfyingly than those about council corruption. The image of the councillor with his fingers jammed firmly in the till may be unfair (sitting in committees for hours to decide planning applications for garage extensions or whether to take a particular child into care is neither a financially, nor emotionally rewarding activity). In Britain, council corruption is mostly a small-scale, often quite pathetic affair, involving expenses fiddles, favours and patronage, rather than grand pay-offs for massive council contracts. The latter are not entirely unknown, but are not particularly widespread.

The Audit Commission's 1997 bulletin on council fraud put the cost of the 208,000 cases of fraud detected in 1995–96 at £76 million within the context of total expenditure by local government of close to £40 billion (Audit Commission, 1997). The main component was housing benefit fraud rather than corruption by councillors or council staff. In the last six years the number of corruption cases recorded by the Commission involving councillors or paid officials has varied between 20 and 60 a year. The cases included a storekeeper in a vehicle maintenance workshop who accepted gifts and holidays for placing orders with a particular supplier, and a market inspector who took pay-offs in return for allowing unlicensed stalls to trade in his market. All this hardly suggests that corruption is pervasive in Britain's town halls. But as the Audit Commission points out, corruption is difficult to detect and prosecute. These figures represent the tip of an iceberg, and the damage such cases can do to public confidence may be out of all proportion to the actual sums involved.

What is often missed is the political dimension in many corruption cases. It is not uncommon for junketing, expense-fiddling and other forms of freeloading to be used as instruments of political control by political leaders. They can be rewards for loyalty – and, if exposed, can be used to punish the disloyal. At least one political boss, on a council where many of the elected members were unemployed, was reputed to punish his critics by giving social security officials details of the attendance allowances and other payments they had received, which in several cases resulted in criminal prosecutions. Glasgow City Council has been shaken by allegations that councillors were offered places on attractive 'fact-finding' trips abroad in return for their votes on contentious issues. Here we see corruption as a political tool. Greed is harnessed for a political purpose rather than being indulged for its own sake. This kind of abuse tends to take place in one-party states – councils where the opposition is minimal or non-existent. The collapse of the Conservatives in local government in the 1990s has led to a substantial increase in the number of councils where the checks and balances provided by democratic scrutiny have ceased to function. There are signs that the Labour leadership nationally is increasingly worried by the political culture in moribund party fiefdoms. There are fears that the record of many Labour councils could be used to discredit the party and that such councils could present a soft electoral underbelly to opponents like the Liberal Democrats and the Scottish National Party. While in office, former British Prime Minister Tony Blair spoke scathingly about councillors finding themselves 'trapped in the secret world of the caucus and the party group'.

The huge range of services provided by councils offer a vast array of opportunities for corruption. In the author's experience, typical abuses may include:

Housing: big city councils typically rent out tens of thousands of flats and houses. Many thousands of people will be on the waiting list for homes that are usually allocated through a complicated points system, designed to give priority to the most deserving cases. Potential abuses include manipulating the system to provide homes for friends or families of councillors or staff – or even conniving at illegal sub-letting of properties.

Employment: councils are big employers with huge potential for nepotism. For example in 1995 Professor Robert Black QC's independent inquiry into Labour-run Monklands Council found evidence of widespread nepotism and favouritism. He found 33 council staff who were either prominent members of the local Labour Party or relatives of prominent members; among them were a window cleaner who refused to climb ladders and a gardener who did not know how to use a hoe.

Contracting out: the drive to encourage competitive tendering for council services – everything from cleaning contracts to building work – has been accompanied by strict rules to ensure fairness and honesty – but it has actually increased the potential for a range of 'sweetheart deals' with favoured companies or businessmen.

Planning: councils' powers to grant planning permission or allocate land for certain types of development are one of the most tempting areas for corruption. A stroke of a pen can transform an anonymous field from a modestly priced piece of agricultural land near a motorway junction into a valuable development site for an out-of-town superstore. The decision-making process by which such transformations can occur often goes entirely unnoticed. And the rules under which it operates are so complex that any suspicion of corruption may be impossible to prove.

Internal democracy: most councillors win office as the candidates of a political party – and control of who is nominated is one of the key props of local political power. This can lead to all kinds of abuses. Addresses may be falsified so that people can qualify to vote in a particular ward selection (which may include making illegal false declarations in order to get onto a particular electoral register). There may be mass signing-up of members who are used as a kind of block vote, or opponents may be removed from the list of those entitled to vote or stand for selection as candidates.

Perks: one of the classic signs of a public body going sour is the extravagant pampering of those in power. When leading councillors are chauffeured too and fro in plush limousines, booked into expensive hotels, enjoy elaborate meals and free drinks on a regular basis at the expense of their council, public duty has been subverted to private pleasure. Council work has always carried a few minor perks – few would object to free sandwiches at council meetings, or tea and biscuits during a committee – but constant junketing and freeloading is another matter. Often, the problem is one of definition – is it excessive to fly first class? What standard of hotel is appropriate when councillors travel at public expense? The District Auditor's report (September 1997) on the 'Donnygate' scandal gave an illuminating picture of a culture of perks: bar bills of thousands of pounds paid by council credit card; trips to Paris, Genoa and

Singapore, with hundreds of pounds spent on phone calls, videos and drinks; a chauffeur waiting for a councillor for nine hours, outside a bar. A further issue is accepting gifts or entertainment. At what point does watching the local football team from the directors' box become the corrupt acceptance of a gift? In Doncaster, councillors and officials went to Euro 96 football matches and accepted gifts of travel vouchers worth hundreds of pounds from a developer working on a flagship project with the council. The District Auditor has criticised the council's Chief Executive and Treasurer for allowing the abuse to continue. Two councillors have been jailed for expenses fiddles.

Such cases are legitimate targets for investigative journalists – but they should also be on the lookout for activities which, while they may not be overtly criminal, also represent misuse of public money or the distribution of favours for political purposes. For example, many urban councils now support extensive networks of local organisations, perhaps championing a particular community, locality or cause. These groups may be influential within a particular political party – some may even deliver a 'block vote' at local party meetings, perhaps ferrying its members to the party meeting with a minibus loaned by the council. At best, this is unhealthy. At worst it can lead to the creation of an extremely undesirable form of machine politics, in which local bosses with influence at the town hall are able to dispense favours – jobs, leisure facilities, planning permission – to what amounts to a client community. In return they deliver their supporters' votes, both at elections and in internal party contests. In an extreme form this can harden and institutionalise 'ethnic' divisions, for, in effect, the needs and concerns of a section of the electorate are filtered through a network of local bosses who may, or may not, make the effort to address them. For example in Monklands, it has been alleged for at least 50 years that the Protestant community of Airdrie has been discriminated against, in favour of Catholic Coatbridge. An even more extreme example is Mayor Daley's Chicago in the 1950s and 1960s – where the city connived at a virtual system of apartheid[1] and political careers depended on maintaining it.

In 1994 the *Sunday Times* accused Birmingham City Council of using money supposedly set aside to improve 'environmental conditions in areas of deprivation' to win middle-class votes with cosmetic schemes in marginal wards. Conservative Westminster City Council has been accused by the District Auditor of using public money to 'gerrymander' marginal wards for the 1990 Borough elections. The strategy of attempting to 'gentrify' eight key wards, selling off council homes and hostels for the homeless to move out potential Labour voters and attract in more Conservative voters, was in conflict with the council's statutory duty to homeless people, according to the District Auditor, John Magill.[2]

Masons and others

Much attention in Britain has been devoted to the activities of Freemasons and similar groups. (For example, the Monklands scandal in Scotland highlighted allegations about the conduct of councillors who were members of the Catholic Knights of Saint Columba.) In Leicestershire in 1990, a rather out-of-date Masonic handbook for the county was discovered in a suitcase bought by a Labour Party member at a jumble sale. The book confirmed that a large number of senior Conservative county councillors and senior council officials, including the then Chief Executive and the then Treasurer were masons. It didn't prove anything else – and no allegations of corruption were ever made, let alone proved. Even so, the incident generated a certain amount of unease about possible links between some of the county's most influential figures – out of sight of voters and colleagues. In another example in 1995 a leading Conservative member of Medina Borough Council on the Isle of Wight resigned, complaining of Masonic influence – he claimed twelve of the eighteen members of the council's ruling Conservative group were Freemasons. Tensions between masons and non-masons remain an important factor in the politics of many of the cities of North East England.

Another area where Masonic influence is often perceived to be pervasive is the criminal justice system. In February 1998, the chairman of Parliament's Commons Home Affairs Select Committee, Chris Mullin MP, clashed with the United Grand Lodge of England over his attempts to establish whether the police officers involved in the Birmingham bombing investigation were masons – culminating in a threat to bring proceedings for contempt of Parliament if they did not cooperate. In another case, two men were charged with assaulting drinkers in an upstairs bar in a hotel in the Home Secretary Jack Straw's constituency, Blackburn. It later emerged they had walked into a private function for police officers from a local Masonic lodge – they were set upon when they objected to being asked to leave. The two were acquitted and later received £170,000 ($272,000) in damages from the Lancashire police – but the case underlines the problems that can arise when police, solicitors and even the hotel manager were all members of a particular lodge. Masons, not unreasonably, resent the implication that membership is *prima facie* evidence of corruption and influence peddling. Commander Michael Higham, Grand Secretary of the United Grand Lodge of England, pointed out in his testimony to the Home Affairs Select Committee that wrongdoers are expelled and that masons are 'strictly enjoined' against acts that subvert the peace and good order of society. Nevertheless it is clear that such networks *can* become channels for improper influence. Knowing about such links is an important task for an investigative journalist. Increasingly, public bodies require their staff and elected members to declare membership of the masons and similar bodies – judges[3] and police officers are among the groups who are now required by the government to declare their membership.

The changing system

Reforms since 1998 have made the problem of lack of scrutiny of the local state more serious. A new tier of regional institutions has been created – including development agencies and emergency services. These are virtually ignored by the local media, despite their considerable powers. The increased use of private contractors further blurs lines of accountability, while the tendering process by which council agencies compete against the private sector for public contracts provides a rich source for investigation and revelation.

The creation of a Mayor of the Greater London area (not to be confused with the more ceremonial figure, the Lord Mayor of London) has created the most powerful directly elected official in the land, commanding a budget of £3.3 billion ($5.3 billion) at 1996 prices. The mayor has formidable powers of patronage. He personally appoints the heads of powerful executive agencies like the new transport and economic development agencies and a range of other public sector appointments and members of the proposed new Metropolitan Police Authority. And the mayor devises strategies on economic development and transport which will touch the lives of millions of people. Leaving aside the issue of whether these arrangements will make for better government, much of the decision-making remains private for far longer than would have been possible under the existing model of local government. Eventually key decisions come before the London Assembly and are debated in public, but the initial work is done by the Mayor's private advisors and the crucial early discussions happen in his 'cabinet' of key officials, again in private. In short it is a lot harder to find out what they're up to – and investigative journalists with a keen ear for gossip and sources of information inside the bureaucracy and political establishments will have a greater role in keeping the public informed.

Similar arrangements also operate outside London. Again, it is likely that these cabinets would sit in private, and that their decisions would emerge rather later in the policy-making process than under present arrangements. Councillors left outside the cabinet have the role of scrutinising its decisions and spending more time looking after their wards. They still have the power to reject or amend the council budget every year, but they do not have a direct voice – or vote – in decision-making. For a journalist this of course means fewer sources of information about what a council is really thinking, but it would be easy to overstate the *diminution in* influence wielded by backbench councillors.

In practice the new structures formalise what actually happened in many councils already. Whatever the merits of the arrangements in terms of improving the quality of local decision-making, they concentrate even more power into the hands of the kind of local oligarchies described above. For many local bosses, they mean a better salary and far less tiresome interference from critics or dissidents. They can go further, faster, in greater secrecy. Like any set of democratic arrangements, they require a powerful opposition, or at any rate a large number of independent-minded critics, in order to work properly. Unfortunately, oppositions and independent-minded critics are currently something of an endangered species in many local authorities.

One possible side-effect of the creation of high-profile, powerful elected officials to oversee local services, however, is greater public interest in their activities. Indeed, raising the profile of local government is one of the major arguments for change. Prominent council leaders of the 1980s such as Ken Livingstone in the Greater London Council, Ted Knight in the London Borough of Lambeth, Derek Hatton in Liverpool and David Bookbinder in Derbyshire certainly attracted attention to their local authorities, although the coverage they received seldom amounted to a sober assessment of the issues confronting their local authority. It would be hard to argue that the traditional model of local authority decision-making has been a resounding success; however, it is by no means clear whether the proposed changes will give the much needed 'new life' to local government.

Reforms over the last decade have already made scrutiny of the local state much more difficult. The system has become much more complex and devolved, to the point where few local newspapers or radio stations have the resources to monitor it. More unaccountable centres of power have emerged as a result.

The health service

A classic example of this kind of change is the National Health Service (NHS) which, like local government, spends well over £100 billion of public money every year. Until the late 1980s the NHS was administered through a structure of district and regional health authorities, reporting to the Department of Health. Now there are more than 400 NHS trusts, with substantial independence from the district and regional authorities. Decision-making has become much more diffuse. Matt Youdale, the BBC's regional health correspondent in the East Midlands recalls that when he took up his post in 1994, he could go to a district health authority meeting and pick up most of the significant NHS stories in that district. Any important controversies or clinical problems in the district would normally be discussed. No longer. Now he has to try and maintain contacts in a much wider range of bodies – trusts running individual hospitals or units like the ambulance service – to get anything approaching the same coverage. In addition, there are fewer meetings open to the press – all most health trusts are required to do is stage an Annual General Meeting. Since so many investigative stories depend on an initial tip-off from a trusted source, this decentralised structure constitutes a serious barrier to investigative journalism across large tracts of the National Health Service (Youdale, 1998).

Above the districts were the Regional Health Authorities (now abolished) which usually had dedicated press officers and a relatively open attitude towards the media. Where these large authorities tended to be relatively open and accessible, many of the smaller units that have replaced them are far more suspicious of the press and far less likely to disgorge even the most innocuous information.

Example: Corby

In 1994–5 the Labour Party purged almost all its sitting councillors in Corby, a small former steel-making town in Northamptonshire, England, which curiously was inhabited by the grandchildren of Scots transferred from Monklands. Corby had been controlled by a clique of local councillors for fifteen to twenty years. When the local steelworks closed in 1980, with the loss of a third of the town's jobs, these politicians proved highly effective in attracting in new employers and reviving the local economy. But ten years later the same local elite was still in place and had become the target of a wide range of allegations. These included incompetence and neglect of basic services like council house repairs, and extended to claims of nepotism and favouritism and to innuendoes of outright corruption. Labour had targeted the Parliamentary seat in three elections, but the local Conservative Member of Parliament held on by running, in effect, against the council.

At the count for a local election, a Radio Northampton reporter overheard a conversation between a regional party official and a local activist which made it clear that the national central office of the party was planning a clearout in Corby. Similar rumours reached the author, after a conversation at a new year's party. Conversations with a Labour official and a series of off-the-record meetings with local activists – who were at first reluctant to talk for fear that the local establishment would learn that they had blabbed, produced more evidence. After some reassurance they were mostly willing, indeed eager, to dish the dirt, and the result was a cornucopia of corrupt practice stories. The credibility of some of the claims was increased by cross-checking with Labour Party members in other parts of the region who had some connection with Corby. For example, one contact had been sent there to preside over an appeal hearing for a councillor who had had the whip withdrawn for complaining about the number of free trips taken by senior councillors.

My contacts also allowed me to keep abreast of Labour's timetable for action. I put some of the allegations to the Corby leadership, and their response did not seem credible. Critics were dismissed as acting out of jealousy, or stories were not denied but met with counter allegations of similar behaviour – 'if you got that from him, he's a fine one to talk . . .'. In the absence of solid evidence for most of the stories, my editors were not keen to broadcast specific allegations – not least because the level of local feuding was so intense it was difficult to distinguish the malicious allegations from the true ones. So our strategy was to report the battle to remove the local leadership, who were known to be litigious (and indeed later issued writs against the national and regional Labour Party), without going into detail about the allegations against them. This was safe, but unsatisfying. Listeners were being told about the deselections, but not the reasons for them. The local watchdog was not entirely silenced, but the bark was certainly muffled. A danger with this approach is to try and fill the yawning gap it leaves where the explanation should be. But with a generalised reference to 'council sleaze', which can be interpreted as a blanket allegation against every councillor in a particular authority, you can end up libelling far more people.

For television, the story had an additional difficulty. Aside from a few pictures of buildings involved in various controversies, there was little to film. A cameraman was dispatched to the annual Corby Highland Games in the hope of filming inebriated councillors in the official council hospitality tent; the results were not particularly incriminating, although the pictures of marching pipe bands were useful in illustrating Corby's Caledonian heritage. Permission was also secured to film a council meeting in progress. One area where it was possible to go into specifics was the extraordinarily high level of travel and subsistence allowances paid to councillors on official duties. This was because the council's annual Management Letter (an annual assessment of their financial performance which all councils receive from the District Auditor) pointed out that if Corby brought its spending into line with that of all the other Northamptonshire district councils, this budget could be cut by 85 per cent. This was a rare instance where it was possible to use solid information from an unimpeachable source.

Another issue with the Corby case was that we did not wish to become a pawn of the Labour Party officials who were leaking much of the information – so we made a point of saying the party was engaged in a purge. This made our stories an issue in the legal action that followed the deselection of the local leadership – they complained their fate was decided in advance of formal party hearings, which indeed it was, and which we reported before the hearings were held. The deselected councillors eventually ran against official Labour candidates in the 1996 borough elections, under an independent 'Corby Labour' ticket. None was elected. Investigations into the conduct of Corby Council are still going on at the time of writing.

Example: Frank Beck

The failure of dozens of local authorities to protect children in their care from sexual, physical and emotional abuse is one of the worst stains on the record of British local government. The roll call of scandals ranges from the oppressive disciplinary regime in Staffordshire, called 'pin-down', to sexual exploitation of children in care in Clwyd in North Wales, to the brutal quack psychological therapies and sexual abuse revealed in the Frank Beck case in Leicestershire. New allegations emerge almost monthly, and it is now clear that abuse of all kinds has carried on unchecked, in some cases for decades, across much of the childcare system.

Such scandals are dangerous territory for the media; there can be few more damaging allegations than to accuse someone of child abuse, so legal worries will never be far from an editor's mind. Such dangerous cases are far more safely reported from the courtroom, with the protection of qualified privilege. Moreover, complaints from former residents at children's homes – the most likely people to bring their stories to the media – might seem to lack credibility. They might have criminal records or drug problems or have been emotionally shattered by the abuse they had suffered. As a result, they might not be taken seriously, or might be thought dangerous witnesses on whom to rely if a story resulted in a libel action. Indeed, this has typically been one of the major reasons for failures by the police and other agencies to investigate complaints of abuse. The moral here is to avoid making the kind of assumptions about individuals which mean that important stories are dismissed out of hand.

In 1989 Frank Beck, the former head of a Leicestershire County Council children's home, was arrested on charges of abusing children in his care. At the time, the author was Political Correspondent for the *Leicester Mercury*. The case was to reverberate over the next seven years, with a sensational trial that revealed more than a decade of appalling crimes against children, an inquiry and official report revealing an amazing catalogue of management failure, and a hard fought and frequently harrowing compensation action brought by Beck's victims. Every stage of this process provided opportunities for investigative journalists to deal with.

Beck's arrest was completely unexpected and, because proceedings against him were active, only the barest details could be reported – but several reporters began to sniff around the case. It quickly became apparent that officials at County Hall were deeply worried by the ramifications of the case. An outside official (in this case a retired Assistant Director of Social Services from neighbouring Nottinghamshire) had been called in to prepare a report on Beck's activities. His conclusions were shocking; that Leicestershire County Council had repeatedly ignored alarming evidence from credible sources about the physical and sexual abuse of children – mostly boys – in homes run by Beck. Not only had a major child abuse scandal emerged in Leicestershire, but the County Council should have detected the problem and dealt with it long before the case actually came to light. Even when Beck was sacked over complaints that he was sexually abusing junior social workers, he was allowed to walk away despite allegations that he had also abused children. Later, he had been given a reference that allowed him to work with children.

Spotting that they might get unwelcome media criticism, the County Council began to prepare the ground. A leading local journalist – by then semi-retired – was consulted on the formation of a PR strategy. His advice to the council was that it should build up a cushion of good news about social services and that it should try to avoid the precedent set by the Cleveland case, in which a local authority was linked directly to a high profile social services failure. They did not want the case to be referred to as 'The Leicestershire Scandal'. This advice was acted on. Council press officers invariably referred to 'The Beck Case' in conversations with local journalists, and, subliminally, their terminology was absorbed and used by journalists. Meanwhile, favourable stories about the activities of social services began to appear. A team of top officials and the leaders of the three political parties (Leicestershire was then a hung council) met regularly to consider the County Council's response. In the era of the spin doctor, investigative journalists are now far more likely to encounter such tactics.

The internal report and its damning conclusions were supposed to be highly confidential, but the County Council's political divisions meant that it was soon leaked to local and national reporters. They were unable to publish while the case was *sub judice* (the *Mail on Sunday* was prepared to risk the wrath of the court by publishing during the case) but the process of contacting and interviewing key witnesses began in earnest. Many of those involved had good reason to talk: some of Beck's victims wanted their ordeal made public; some officials wanted to defend their careers, others were horrified at the failures of their management; some politicians could see votes in the affair – Beck was a Liberal Democrat councillor at the time of his arrest and the Conservatives in particular were arguing that Labour and Liberal Democrat policies had made it easier for him to abuse children, because they had made his particular home more important within the Leicestershire childcare system. Reporters were not, therefore, short of sources, but the material they delivered had to be weighed carefully in the light of their various agendas. Often, individuals were more concerned with promoting their version of a relatively minor part of the affair, for example their role in a particular instance where evidence against Beck had not been investigated. This was often at such a level of detail that it was unlikely to be reported – while journalists were much more interested in the source's information on the major events of the case.

By the time Beck's trial began, local newspapers, radio and television had all accumulated a substantial body of material about the case, and the trial provided the chance to interview further witnesses, for broadcast after the verdict. One of the pitfalls of having such a devastating report, together with appalling accounts of abuse and mismanagement, but being unable to publish them for months was that reporters became almost bored with its conclusions, even though they would undoubtedly astonish the public when they were revealed. It was important not to allow this familiarity to distort editorial judgements.

There were further legal complications. Initially, the trial judge banned all reporting of the case because it was anticipated that Beck might face a further trial or trials on additional child abuse charges after this case was completed. This ruling was overturned by the High Court after an appeal by several newspapers. And because the verdicts on the dozens of charges faced by Beck dribbled out over a period of two days, background interviews and analysis could not be published or broadcast until well after the first guilty verdict had been announced.

After Beck's conviction, the then Health Secretary, William Waldegrave, announced an inquiry into the case, to be conducted by Andrew Kirkwood QC, a leading barrister and expert in child protection law. Kirkwood decided to take most of the evidence in private, a decision he refused to revoke, despite questions in Parliament and intense pressure from the media, which included attempts to persuade some witnesses to demand that their evidence should be heard in public. But for the most part, the media were restricted to taking pictures of witnesses arriving at the inquiry. Even so, there were substantial and detailed leaks of the evidence, including some damaging accounts of Leicestershire County Council's inept and complacent management of Beck. The greatest interest, however, was in Kirkwood's conclusions. He did manage to keep these confidential until the publication of his report, but since he was not willing to take questions about them at a press conference, and would do no more than read out a prepared statement, it was hard for the media or the public of Leicestershire to make a judgement about the soundness of his conclusions – particularly when the evidence upon which they were based had been heard in private. The media were left to take the report or leave it; and of course they were in no position to leave it – but Kirkwood's restrictions had created a position where no reporter could credibly comment on his conclusions. It would be impossible to comment that a particular criticism was a bit harsh, or that a particular individual had got off lightly.

The next event in the Beck case was the struggle by some of his victims to extract compensation from Leicestershire County Council. This eventually came to court in 1996, but the negotiations and clashes between the plaintiffs and the defendants regularly featured in the local and national news. The case itself provided a sad postscript to the whole Beck affair, with witnesses recounting the abuse they had suffered and council officials being summoned to testify as to whether the County Council had fulfilled its duty of care towards the children in its homes. Amazingly, the defendants at one stage denied that they had a duty of care towards children in their care – a legal argument that deeply embarrassed officials and councillors at Leicestershire County Hall. Much of the reporting of these events amounted to a rehash of earlier coverage, but an important theme was the long drawn out and painful process by which victims of crime had to seek compensation. More than one remarked that it felt like further abuse.

Cases like that of Frank Beck provide a protracted test for the media. It is often easy to focus on the horrific details of child abuse cases, while failing to give detailed attention to the rather drier details of the policy failures or management mistakes which made them possible. But these failures ruin lives. Cases like these should be as much the territory of those who investigate the local state as of crime reporters. What the proliferation of child abuse scandals demonstrates is that there are plenty of catastrophic failures in public policy and management out there for reporters to expose.[4]

Process

Leaks and tip-offs are the stock in trade of the investigative reporters covering the local state. But when dealing with political organisations they will need to be more than usually careful about the motives of their sources and the spin attached to the information they receive. It is an iron law of politics that there's always an opposition; if there are no opposition parties, internal divisions inevitably surface. Factional tensions and personal hatreds are among the main reasons for significant leaks and any information received should be weighed in that knowledge and should be cross-checked in some way. Relying on a single source may mean that the reporter ends up parroting the party line of some individual or faction. This discredits the reporter and fails the reader.

As well as bias, there is also the danger of manipulation. A leaked Labour Party document[5] advised local organisations to 'use a backbencher or loud mouthed staffer' to let the press know 'what you really think'. In other words, that candid unofficial source may simply be feeding out another subtle version of the party line, with the full knowledge of the people at the top. The same document also urged the use of smear tactics against opponents: 'check their declarations of interest and their records. Find one flaw and smear them all. Go negative until swamped by complaints. Then do it again . . .'. So beware of the spoon-fed exclusive about a political opponent; the Westminster cult of the spin doctor is spreading and local journalists will not escape its touch. Fortunately, some politicians are not only immoral but also infantile, as this document reveals. No really sophisticated would-be Machiavelli would ever be foolish enough to write such things down − but for many the urge to boast about how tough and unethical they are can be irresistible. So when they start boasting in the bar, believe them.

Earlier in the chapter I referred to the need for reporters to understand the structure and workings of local councils, if they were to investigate their conduct effectively. The same applies to political parties. Labour, for example, has an elaborate structure of district and regional parties that comes into play when corruption or misconduct is alleged. These little-known bodies may be the forum in which the most serious and far-reaching allegations are discussed and action decided. They may also be a useful 'one stop shop' at which a reporter can seek information about a wide variety of stories or potential stories, across a wide geographical area.

It is noticeable how few of the recent tide of council corruption stories have been brought to light by local reporters (there are of course honourable exceptions, Doncaster for one). One of the dangers of traditional council reporting is that the journalist becomes a prisoner of his or her contacts, and becomes unwilling to antagonise them. But a more substantial reason is the reluctance of editors to commit the time and take the legal risks inherent in investigative journalism. And even where investigations do reveal something, there may be little enthusiasm for the resulting story – 'too parochial, readers in other council areas won't be interested . . .', 'Who cares, everyone assumes they're on the take anyway', 'It's too complicated . . . people won't understand it'. There are other outlets – *Private Eye*'s 'Rotten Boroughs' feature, for example. And some national newspapers and television or radio programmes are willing to pick up local stories that the local media fear to print. This however, hardly amounts to the classic role of a local watchdog – often it seems safer for the watchdog to bark by proxy.

Notes

1 For an account of the politics of Chicago in this era see Royko, M. (1971) *Boss: Richard J. Daley of Chicago.* Dutton and Co.
2 Report on Westminster City Council, John Magill, District Auditor, Deloitte and Touche, 9 May 1996.
3 Out of 5400 Judges, 200 declared themselves to be freemasons and 50 refused to answer the question. Written reply to a parliamentary question by Geoff Hoon MP, then Minister of State, Lord Chancellor's Department, 22 March 1999.
4 For a fuller account of the Beck case see D'Arcy and Gosling (1998).
5 'Beating the Liberals', internal Labour Party document quoted in *Red Pepper*, October 1998.

Bibliography

Audit Commission (1997) *Protecting the Public Purse.* London: HMSO.
D'Arcy, M. and Gosling, P. (1998) *Abuse of Trust: Frank Beck and the Leicestershire Children's Homes Scandal.* London: Bowerdean Publishing Company.
Ekirch, A. (1974) *Progressivism in America.* New York: Viewpoints.
Fitzwalter, R. *et al.* (1981) *Web of Corruption: The Story of John Poulson and T. Dan Smith.* St Albans: Granada.
Glinert, E. (1998) Interview with Mark D'Arcy, 19 November 1998.
H. M. Government (1998) *A Mayor and Assembly for London.* CM 3897. 25 March 1998. London: HMSO.
H. M. Government (1998a) *Modern Local Government: In Touch with the People.* CM 4014. 30 July 1998. London: HMSO.
Satchwell, R. (1998) Interview with Mark D'Arcy, 16 November 1998.
Youdale, M. (1998) Interview with Mark D'Arcy, 17 October 1998.

Further reading

Burke, R. (1979) *The Murky Cloak: Local Authority Press Relations.* Croydon: Charles Knight.
Clarke, M. (ed.) (1983) *Corruption.* London: Frances Pinter.
Doig, J. (1983) You publish at your peril – the restraints on investigatory journalism. In M. Clarke (ed.) *Corruption.* London: Frances Pinter.

Franklin, B. and Murphy D. (1991) *What News? The Market, Politics and the Local Press.* London: Routledge.

Franklin, B. and Murphy, D. (1997) The local rag in tatters? The decline of Britain's local newspapers. In M. Bromley *A Journalism Reader.* London: Routledge.

Murphy, D. (1976) *The Silent Watchdog: The Press in Local Politics.* London: Constable.

Murphy, D. (1983) Journalistic investigations of corruption. In M. Clarke (ed.) *Corruption.* London: Francis Pinter.

19

SUBTERFUGE, SET-UPS, STINGS AND STUNTS

How red-tops go about their investigations

Roy Greenslade

Introduction

Serious investigative journalism has rarely been in evidence in Britain's most popular newspapers from 1993 onwards. As one former investigative journalist with a successful track record said: 'The tradition has been lost' (Harrison, 2007). The inexorable movement in editorial agendas away from information to entertainment, away from news-to-use towards news-to-amuse, has squeezed out more serious journalistic content from the populars. Similarly, the reduction in editorial budgets, and the consequent reduction in staffing, has made almost all investigative journalism within such papers uneconomic. Even had editors wished to leaven the preponderance of celebrity copy with what has been traditionally called 'hard-hitting investigative journalism' they would have found themselves constrained by inadequate resources. The pressure on reporters to produce copy on a daily basis leaves little time and space for a journalism that depends on lengthy periods of supposedly 'unproductive' work.

But popular papers do have a rich history of investigative journalism, which I have attempted to rescue. It is also true that, though the content has become more trivial, those papers have also continued to use investigative techniques in order to satisfy a changed agenda. The first section offers a very brief summary of that history while the second is devoted to methodology with examples that encompass serious investigations – exemplified by *The People* from the 1950s onwards, and the work of the *Daily Mirror*'s Paul Foot throughout the 1980s and early 1990s – and the increasing penchant from the late 1980s onwards for celebrity sex-and-drugs investigations, as pioneered by the *News of the World*, plus the 'stunt journalism' taken up so enthusiastically by all red-tops in the past decade.

Please note that I am restricting myself to the 'popular' category as defined by the Audit Bureau of Circulations. It designates the *Sun*, *Daily Mirror* and *Daily Star* as daily national popular titles and the *News of the World*, *Sunday*

Mirror, The People[1] and the *Daily Star Sunday* as Sunday national populars.[2] In modern journalistic parlance, these papers are called red-tops (due to their red front page mastheads), a nickname that helps to delineate them from the 'middle market' *Daily Mail* and the *Daily Express*. The appellation is rather new, and in their former broadsheet formats, *The People* and the *News of the World* would not have been described as red-tops.

The history

It is noticeable that the earliest example of investigative journalism cited in this book, W. T. Stead's 'The Maiden Tribute of Modern Babylon' (Chapter 2: 38–40), contained all the elements that were to feature in the majority of popular newspaper investigative-cum-campaigning stories some 60 years later. It was sensationalist, explicit, revelatory, appealed to the emotions of its readers and placed the journalist at the centre of events. It was also justified as being of service to the public and, most important of all, it was viewed unashamedly as a device to boost the *Pall Mall Gazette*'s circulation. The oddity is that the Stead formula was not taken up immediately by the popular newspapers, most of which were launched in the aftermath of his series, in the late nineteenth and early twentieth century. Instead, *The People* largely gained its huge audience in the 1920s and 30s because its editor, Harry Ainsworth, introduced confessional first-person series that ran for weeks on end (Minney, 1954: 186–8; Richards, 1997: 136). The *Daily Mirror* was devoid of pro-active journalism of any kind before the Second World War (Cudlipp, 1953; Hagerty, 2003). The *News of the World* built its sales success of the late 1930s largely on its coverage of crime and salacious court reports. (Bainbridge, 1993: 85; Somerfield, 1997: 44). It wasn't until the late 1940s that anything approaching Stead-style investigative journalism emerged as a regular feature in editorial pages, and then only in one newspaper, *The People*, due entirely to the influence of Sam Campbell, who controlled the content as managing editor before becoming editor in 1958 (Edwards, 1988: 40). He pioneered weekly investigations, usually about crime, targeting price profiteers, ration-dodgers, petrol thieves and racketeering landlords (Cudlipp, 1976: 87).

Campbell also turned one reporter, Duncan Webb, into a journalistic hero figure. Webb lived a kind of fantasy life, talking in code, concealing his identity, claiming to live in perpetual fear of attack from gangsters (Kersh, 1990: 46; Manifold, 2007). A *Time* magazine profile of Webb dubbed him 'the greatest crime reporter of our time' (*Time*, January 10 1955). Whether true or not, Webb's reporting abilities cannot be doubted. He combined two important investigatory skills: he formed good relationships with police *and* villains, and he also mastered documentary research techniques. His most famous exposé – 'a Homeric undertaking' (Kersh, 1990: 46) – was the 'evil traffic' of prostitution in London's Soho that was organised by a Maltese family, the Messinas. Campbell risked the libel laws to publish pictures of the Messina brothers under the headline 'ARREST THESE FOUR MEN!' (*The People*, 3 September 1950). He was a master of sensationalist spin, turning a single story into a long-running saga, and created the legend of Webb as an intrepid crime-fighter, letting it be known that Webb's office was protected by bullet-proof glass and that he had eight locks fitted to his front door at home. Campbell is also credited with having invented the phrase that was to become synonymous with Sunday newspaper journalists when they found themselves in delicate situations: 'I made my excuses and left' (Edwards, 1988: 44). What made many of his investigative articles so readable was the detailed narrative of how his reporters had carried them out, making them read 'almost like police court depositions or detectives' reports' (*The Times*, 3 February 1966).

Rival Sunday titles saw the virtue of investigations and hired reporters happy to imitate Webb's approach. In 1952, the *Sunday Pictorial* (renamed the *Sunday Mirror* in 1963) hired Harry Procter as its 'special investigator' and he became famous for exposing criminals, from drug peddlers to slum landlords, from white slavers to phoney doctors and headmasters (Procter, 1958: 137; Greenslade, 2004: 95). The *News of the World* was slower off the mark, due in part to complacency by its owners and also to a succession of uninspiring editors. Sales fell away sharply until Stafford Somerfield was given the editorship in 1959 and introduced kiss-and-tell stories as a major attraction. But he also realised why Campbell was having success with *The People*. 'It was the day of investigative journalism, the story behind the story', he wrote. 'It was not enough to print straightforward court reports' (Somerfield, 1979: 111).

Even so, the *News of the World* did not get into its investigative stride until a story broke in 1963 that was to prove a watershed in British newspaper history: the Profumo affair (Greenslade, 2004: 174–92). The Secretary of State for War, John Profumo, was forced to resign for telling a lie in Parliament by denying a sexual relationship with a young model, Christine Keeler. It transpired that she was also sleeping with a Soviet secret service agent, a dual liaison, arranged by a man called Stephen Ward. The scandal had all the necessary ingredients to attract readers: sex, spies, politics, the aristocracy, low crime and high drama. Amidst an unprecedented media feeding frenzy the Sunday populars unleashed their investigative reporters in a competition to see who could obtain the sleaziest, and most saleable, stories (Knightley, 1987). Trevor Kempson was a 21-year-old freelance when the story first broke and went so far as to break into Ward's country cottage and steal two photographs of Ward and Keeler (Summers, 1987). He joined *The People* soon after and competed for stories with the *News of the World*'s urbane Peter Earle (Bainbridge, 1993). The popular daily press got involved too, assigning reporters to dig wherever they could.

The details of those investigations need not detain us. The significance of all this activity was that several popular newspaper editors got a taste for investigations, particularly on the Sunday titles. The other important factor was a journalistic enthusiasm for a secret service approach to their job. They began to acquire an intense interest in investigatory techniques, such as the use of subterfuge, and in surveillance technology. It is ironic that the major journalistic outcome of a 'spy scandal' was the formation of the journalist-as-spy phenomenon.

After Campbell's death in 1966 *The People* continued to make the running with its investigations, and almost none of the best-known examples had anything to do with sex. The new editor, Bob Edwards, had inherited 'a skilled investigative team led by a remarkable figure, Laurie Manifold, who would have made an inspired and incorruptible police chief' (Edwards, 1988: 159). Everyone I have interviewed about Manifold speaks of him in similar glowing terms (Thorne, 2007; Entwistle, 2007; Lester, 2007; Gadd, 2007). It is no exaggeration to describe him as the father of modern popular paper investigative journalism. He trained scores of journalists in a range of investigatory techniques, which they went on to practise in other newspapers, such as the *News of the World*, and on television, most notably with *The Cook Report*. For more than 20 years Manifold oversaw a range of investigations, many of which were complex and took months of painstaking work. A description of his methods is discussed in the following section, but even if one knew nothing of Manifold, his record and its range speaks for itself. He oversaw the exposure of religious racketeers, the ill-treatment of the elderly in old people's homes and the exploitation of schoolboy footballers. One of Manifold's first major scoops came in 1964 when his reporters exposed a football bribes scandal (see next section). Many *People* investigations involved relatively minor rackets or scams, but these were regarded as one of the paper's strong selling points because its own readers were targets for the assorted con artists it exposed. By far the most important investigation of Manifold's career, and arguably the most far-reaching ever to be published by a popular newspaper, was the exposure of Scotland Yard corruption (see next section).

Edwards's finest moment came with the publication of an investigation that revealed the massacre of 25 villagers in Malaya by British soldiers in 1949 (Edwards, 1988: 164–5; 'Horror in a nameless village', *The People*, 1 February 1970). The award-winning story was of genuine public interest, but it drew fierce criticism from politicians – the incoming Tory government refused to hold an official inquiry – and it upset many readers, causing cancellations. (Manifold 2007) This aspect of popular paper investigations is a reminder that not only not are they guaranteed circulation-builders but can often depress sales (Chibnall, 1977: 161). From 1966 onwards, *The People* faced stiff competition because two of its key investigative staff, Trevor Kempson and Mike Gabbert, defected to the *News of the World* and began to turn in a string of exclusives for their new paper. Gabbert masterminded a drugs inquiry into the Rolling Stones in 1967 (Bainbridge, 1993: 236). The following year Kempson revealed a case of mass rape and murder in Brazil carried out by members of the Indian Protection Service (Taylor, 1991: 210–13). Kempson's most controversial investigation came in 1973 when his inquiries caused the downfall of two Tory ministers, Lords Lambton and Jellicoe. To obtain proof that Lambton, a junior defence minister, was consorting with a prostitute, Kempson and a photographer concealed a camera behind a two-way mirror in the bedroom of the prostitute, along with a tape recorder (Bainbridge, 1993: 237–40; *UKPG*, 11 June 1973).

Both Manifold's team at *The People* and Kempson's at the *News of the World* were given time and space to pursue their investigations, often going weeks at a time without anything being published. *The People* continued its run of investigative triumphs in the 1970s, under the more cautious editorship of Geoff Pinnington, publishing one of its most memorable investigations about vivisection cruelty (see next section). By contrast, even though Edwards took over the *Sunday Mirror* editorship he never managed to build a successful investigative unit. He appointed an investigations editor, and a couple of reporters to work under him, but what was wanted were serious stories that could be turned round in a couple of weeks rather than in-depth investigations (Barker, 2007).

By the early 1970s the *Daily Mirror* had also begun to develop a taste for investigations. Its 'shock issues' on social questions tended to be 'sub-topical' journalistic exercises without the essential bite of genuine investigations (Engel, 1996: 193). But one writer who cut his teeth on shock issues was John Pilger, a journalist who became synonymous with the paper's more serious and socially committed agenda during his 23 years with the paper (Pilger, 1998: 376). He was more of a campaigning journalist than an investigator, though much of his output read like investigative material. He often spent weeks and months researching his pieces, usually working abroad, becoming famous for his searing reports from Vietnam during the American occupation and his graphic report about Pol Pot's Cambodian genocide ('Death of a nation', *Daily Mirror*, 12 September 1979). Subsequently, he revealed Britain's own shady relationship with the Khymer Rouge (Pilger, 2004: 140–5).

Revel Barker was a young *Daily Mirror* district reporter in the north of England in the early 1970s when he attended the bankruptcy hearings, held in Wakefield, involving an architect named John Poulson who could not account for £250,000 that had passed through his hands for building contracts. Several prominent names were mentioned as possible recipients, including that of Reggie Maudling, the Home Secretary and deputy Prime Minister. Barker was assigned by the *Mirror*'s northern news editor, Leo White, to devote all his time to what had become known as the Poulson affair (Barker, 2007).

When Poulson's trial on charges of bribery and corruption began in November 1973, Barker took to joining Poulson in the canteen at Leeds crown court and, by buying him cups of tea, managed to get him to talk. Thus, after Poulson was jailed for five years at that trial (with a further two years added at a subsequent hearing) Barker's articles on the scandal were imbued with a truly exclusive inside knowledge ('Poulson, the toppled giant', *Daily Mirror*, 12 February 1974). Another self-starting *Mirror* reporter, Richard Stott, came in on the tail of the Poulson affair, writing about Maudling and a corrupt ex-minister, Ernest Marples (Stott, 2002: 143–59, 166–7). His greatest reporting success led to the disgrace of England's football manager, Don Revie, who had paid bribes to fix matches. He resigned after fleeing to the United Arab Emirates, disguised in Arab robes. Stott was named Reporter of the Year and Revie was banned from English football for ten years (Stott, 2002: 173–81).

The only truly memorable *Sun* investigation of modern times also involved football bribery, and it proved to be very controversial. The paper accused the former Liverpool goalkeeper, Bruce Grobbelaar, of fixing matches to bene-fit a betting syndicate. Its informant, who was paid by the paper for his story, was Grobbelaar's former business manager, Chris Vincent. The *Sun*'s main evi-dence was a videotape of Grobbelaar accepting £2,000 from Vincent for supposedly agreeing to throw a match for his new club, Southampton, and appearing to admit that he had previously thrown a match ('Grobbelaar took bribes to fix games', *The Sun*, 9 November 1994). Grobbelaar was charged with conspiracy to corrupt, along with two other footballers and a Malaysian busi-nessman. After two trials, in both of which the jury could not agree on a verdict, all four were cleared. Grobbelaar went on to sue the *Sun* for libel and was awarded £85,000. The paper appealed and lost, but the House of Lords ruled in January 2001 that, though the specific allegations had not been proved, there was adequate evidence of dishonesty. They reduced the award to Grobbelaar to £1, the lowest libel damages possible under English law. He was also ordered to pay the *Sun*'s legal costs, estimated at £500,000. Unable to raise the money, he was declared bankrupt. He has consistently asserted his innocence ever since ('Triumph and despair: Bruce Grobbelaar', *The Observer*, 5 June 2005).

The methodology

One of investigative journalism's central controversies is how reporters go about obtaining their information. It has always been an ethical and legal grey area, in which journalists have often stepped over the boundaries in pursuit of stories. Before editors drew up a code of ethics in 1991 as part of a reformed press self-regulatory regime in the wake of the Press Council's demise, there was relatively little guidance to reporters on how they should behave. They tended to abide by a rough-and-ready application of 'custom and practice', with individual editors deciding what was fair and what was not, usually on a story-by-story basis. Some decisions were made purely on the story's appeal to readers, and therefore the likelihood of it selling more copies. However, editors also kept in mind a public interest justification. In many instances, if they believed the story warranted it, they would turn a blind eye to questionable behaviour. Though they disliked Press Council rulings against them, and fought tenaciously to avoid being censured, most were openly contemptuous of their decisions (Somerfield, 1979: 143–5). If there was little fear of the Council, all were certainly aware of the legal constraints, such as libel and contempt of court.

In the years since the foundation of the Press Complaints Commission in 1991, and its policing of the Editors' Code of Practice drawn up in advance of the PCC's formation, the guidelines have been much more clear-cut (Shannon, 2001). There has also been a sea-change in the way editors treat the Commission, never openly criticising its findings. The Code has also been amended several times down the years, most notably to prevent phone hacking and to restrict the use of subterfuge (http://media.guardian.co.uk/pressprivacy/story/ 0,,2112589,00.html). Investigations, even controversial ones in the *News of the World*, have led to few complaints, and most of those have not been upheld. However, since 1991, there have been two successful libel actions against the *News of the World*, by a Scottish politician, Tommy Sheridan, and by one of the men accused of the Beckham kidnap plot, discussed later. (At the time of going to press Mr Sheridan was facing a charge of perjury in relation to this libel settlement.) The paper was also fined £50,000 after being found guilty of contempt of court in July 1997 for publishing an investigative story about a gang planning to distribute fake currency. These are relatively rare examples of newspaper investigations leading to trials.

Popular newspaper editors take advice from in-house lawyers who will sometimes go to the lengths of consulting barristers. This has always been the case. In the 1960s and 70s, with *The People* being in the forefront of investigations into criminal activities, its editors were alert to the dangers of failing to obtain unimpeachable proof of wrongdoing. The paper was helped by the fact that its deputy editor for a time, Nat Rothman, was also a lawyer. *The People* and the *News of the World* have also employed shrewd in-house lawyers, and the man generally accepted as the most astute of them all in modern times, Tom Crone, has worked for both titles. Both Richard Stott and Paul Foot were full of praise for the *Daily Mirror*'s legal eagle, Hugh Corrie ('Hugh Corrie, the lawyer journalists loved', *Press Gazette*, 17 November 2006). It is, of course, helpful if journalists can foresee the legal problems when first gathering evidence. That, according to all the former *People* reporters I have interviewed, was one of Laurie Manifold's special skills. 'He had a mind like a steel trap', said Frank Thorne. 'He could see the pitfalls from the beginning' (Thorne, 2007).

In order to overcome some of the problems he witnessed in his early years at *The People*, Manifold devised a set of rules for both staff and freelance reporters. These ranged from commonsense matters, such as a ban on drinking while on the job, to specific injunctions about how to negotiate drug deals without taking possession of the drugs. Manifold expected reporters to sign up to the rules and said: 'I never asked anyone to do anything they didn't want to do. If they refused I didn't hold it against them' (Manifold, 2007).

Meanwhile, at the *News of the World*, reporters were also groomed in the dark arts of undercover investigations by a variety of executive journalists, such as Charles Markus, Bob Warren, Eddie Jones, Rodney Tyler and Stuart Kuttner. Though none were as methodical as Manifold, they passed on experiences that helped to educate journalists into investigative techniques. The methods they used were dictated by the specific requirements of each story, but there were some general principles. However, the best way of illustrating how papers go about their work is by giving concrete examples. Regardless of how stories begin – with identifiable informants (whistleblowers), anonymous tip-offs, through trusted contacts, gut instinct, the emergence of a suspicious behaviour pattern, some form of documentary disclosure (such as the Freedom of Information Act) – they have to be verified.

The key to a successful investigation lies in mounting enough evidence to ensure that the story can stand up to any attack, especially in a courtroom. There must be sufficient evidence to satisfy the in-house lawyer. To that end, newspaper informants often find themselves required to do much more than merely tell their story. They have been used in a variety of ways, such as making covert tape-recordings, being 'wired up' when meeting the 'target', making phone calls to the target with a reporter present, and luring the target to a public meeting in order that it can be witnessed and/or photographed.

At least one method, both of obtaining a story or verifying it, is illegal, namely telephone bugging or eavesdropping. Despite that, there have been instances where popular paper journalists have attempted to listen into private conversations via bugging devices or through tampering with telephones, intercepting answer-phone or text messages, and obtaining mobile phone accounts to discover who called who and when. Most of these intrusions into privacy are fishing expeditions (see below) in order to see if anything vaguely worthwhile might crop up. It was this kind of activity that led in August 2006 to the arrest of the *News of the World*'s royal editor Clive Goodman, and his accomplice Glenn Mulcaire, on charges of conspiracy to intercept voice-mail messages and several counts of intercepting messages. They were jailed in January 2007 for four months and six months respectively (*The Guardian*, 26 January 2007. At http://media.guardian.co.uk/pressprivacy/story/0,,1999274,00.html). On the day the pair were sentenced the paper's editor, Andy Coulson, resigned. He had not known about the illegal activity, he explained, but felt he must accept responsibility.

One example where an editor was able to justify his staff listening into calls, and taping them, occurred in July 1992. *The People* revealed the contents of phone conversations between a cabinet minister, the Heritage Secretary David Mellor, and his mistress, Antonia de Sancha (*The People*, 19 July 1992). The paper had not committed an offence because the phone was bugged by the man who owned the house and had rented the line (Greenslade, 2004: 574). Two months later, Mellor was forced to resign after it was revealed – during a libel action against *The People* over an investigation it had published two years before – that the daughter of the Palestine Liberation Organisation's finance minister had funded a holiday for him and his family in Spain. The investigation into Mellor's extra-marital relationship with de Sancha was considered to be of public interest because he was threatening to introduce a privacy law which was viewed by journalists as an attack on press freedom.

However, the practice of newspaper reporters listening in to one side of a phone call made by an informant is now very common and is not illegal. When the *News of the World* suspected that politician Lord (Jeffrey) Archer had had relations with a prostitute called Monica Coghlan she was persuaded to call him in order, to quote one of the reporters involved, 'to listen to how he sounded when a Shepherd Market hooker called him stone cold out of the blue' (Brown, 1995: 19). She made several more phone calls over the following two weeks, always with a reporter listening in, until Archer made an error of judgment by agreeing to fund a holiday for her. The *News of the World* swung into action, fitting Coghlan with a bugging device when she turned up at a train station to meet Archer's emissary where she was offered, and refused, an envelope of money ('Tory boss Archer pays vice girl', *News of the World*, 26 October 1986). Though Archer won a libel action against both the *News of the World* and the *Daily Star* the following year, the papers were vindicated in 1999 when the *News of the World* revealed that Archer had concocted a false alibi at the libel trial ('Archer quits as we expose false alibi', *News of the World*, 21 November 1999). Once again, this story had been verified when phone calls between the informant – the man who had previously agreed to lie for Archer – and Archer were monitored by the paper's staff. Archer was later jailed for four years for perjury and paid back considerable sums of money to both papers.

There is no law in Britain that prohibits anyone from taping a call to another person without informing them, though it is illegal in several American states, which has caused problems for British tabloid journalists on occasion (Roy Greenslade, 'The Sun's side of the story', *The Guardian*, June 7, 2004; Brian Flynn, *The Sun*, 13 February 2004). What then is legal? Here is a definitive list:

(i) Extracting confessions

The *Sunday Pictorial*'s Harry Procter, working in the days before tape-recorders and video cameras, had to convince his investigative targets to make and sign confessions. He rarely used subterfuge, depending instead on his gift of the gab and bluff (Procter, 1958: 156; Greenslade, 2004: 95). Perhaps Procter was lucky. His straightforward method would be unlikely to work nowadays. Instead, journalists tend to apply pressure in order to encourage a confession. A classic example was the *News of the World*'s exposé of the TV presenter Frank Bough for indulging in sex and drugs parties. The paper had obtained evidence from a drug-dealer, two prostitutes and alleged partygoers, but a jury was unlikely to take their word against Bough's. Nor did the paper have any photographic or video evidence that linked Bough to the prostitutes. But the *News of the World* had, in effect, thrown a stone into the pond and it didn't take long for the ripples to reach Bough's ears. Convinced that the paper was about to publish a scandalous story, he took steps to head them off. But he made a bad error by consulting a friend, Bernard Falk, who foolishly advised him that, in order to ameliorate what the *News of the World* might publish he should make a 'limited confession'. In return for holding back some of the more lurid allegations, Bough agreed to own up to being a weak victim of manipulative people. It was the equivalent of a plea bargain deal, which the *News of the World* gleefully accepted (Brown, 1995: 245–69). These two gambits – the throwing of a stone into the pond followed by the coaxing and cajoling of a person to make a confession in return for watered-down coverage – was honed by the *News of the World* into something of an art form.

(ii) The playback technique

Manifold claims to be the journalist who devised this method when his reporters were trying to break the 1964 football bribes scandal. Recounting the whole episode, as related by Manifold, gives an insight into how *The People* went about its investigatory tasks (Manifold, 2007). Through one of its sports reporters, the paper knew that the football authorities were on the brink of charging a goalkeeper with letting in goals in return for money, so there was little time to act. Manifold, suspecting that the keeper was a small fish, instructed a freelance to turn up on the player's doorstep, tell him that the paper knew he was about to be charged and offering him £300 to give his side of the story. He swiftly agreed and named a former player, Jimmy Gauld, as the main fixer. 'He sounded a much tougher job', said Manifold, 'so there was no point in waving money in front of him. I gave it some thought and came up with the playback technique'.

It began with reporters visiting Gauld, telling him they knew everything about his game-fixing activities, as did the authorities, and that he was about to be charged. But there was still time for him to make a large sum of money if he cooperated with the paper. It was suggested to him that he should contact the players who had accepted his bribes and ask them to meet him urgently, in secret, after dark, in his car. He would get a fee – of £1,000 or £2,000, Manifold can't recall the exact figure – for every player he entrapped. He was primed to tell each player the same story: the police are on to the fact that you took money from me; if they visit me I'll say nothing; if they visit you, you must say nothing either. The car was wired so that the reporters could tape the conversations in which the players were clearly admitting to accepting bribes.

Manifold then completed the playback procedure by having a reporter visit each of the players in turn to read them the transcripts of the tapes of them talking to Gauld and asking them to own up by signing a statement admitting what they had done. Honesty, they were to be told, would stand them in good stead. Manifold specifically chose Mike Gabbert for that task because of his 'Machiavellian skills'. Not every player fell for Gabbert's line but some did and Manifold later suspected that Gabbert went far beyond his brief by pro-mising players to cooperate on the understanding that the editor would be so impressed with their honesty that he would downplay their part in the venture.

The upshot was that *The People* landed one of the biggest stories of the decade with evidence so conclusive it was impossible for anyone to deny its authenticity (*The People*, 12 April 1964). 'We had it from beginning to end on tape and with signed statements', said Manifold. Gauld did not profit because the judge at his trial fined him the same amount, £30,000, that he had received from the paper. He was also sent to jail for four years. Ten other players served between four and 15 months for conspiracy to defraud. Varities of the playback technique have since been used by several newspapers.

(iii) Uncovering documentary evidence

An informant's word alone is never good enough nor, in the early 1970s, could tape-recordings be adduced as proof. It was considered essential to get some kind of documentary back-up. *The People*'s Scotland Yard corruption revelations are a case in point. The starting point was a passing mention to Manifold by a freelance reporter with good underworld contacts who said that the head of the Flying Squad, Commander Kenneth Drury, had been on holiday to Cyprus with a pornographer, James Humphreys, who had paid for the trip. That information was nowhere near sound enough to publish. Even though Humphreys confirmed it to Manifold, documentary proof was required. Their word in court would never have stood up. So Manifold sent a reporter, Sid Foxcroft, to Cyprus to see if he could check the register, and he immediately had an amazing stroke of luck. On arrival at Nicosia airport, the Greek Cypriot taxi driver recognised Foxcroft as a former comrade in the 8th Army and offered him help. Within minutes of getting to the hotel the driver persuaded the manager to show his old friend the register, which recorded the fact that Drury and Humphreys, and their wives, had stayed at the hotel at the same time. But it did not show who paid the bill because it was a package tour pre-paid in Britain. Manifold guessed that the package tour operators were unlikely to provide a copy of a receipt if approached straightforwardly. He told me: 'I thought there's only way to get this, and we've got to break the law. You've got to take a chance sometimes'. So he hired a man he had used before, an ex-army officer with a shady past he knew as 'Matt', to bluff the clerk at Cook's in Regent Street by pretending he was Drury's accountant and that he'd lost his receipt. The clerk accepted the story and supplied him with a duplicate, which confirmed that Humphreys had paid for Mr and Mrs Drury's holiday. The result was a sensational front page: 'POLICE CHIEF AND THE PORN KING: Was it wise of Commander Drury of Scotland Yard to go on holiday with this old lag?' (*The People*, 6 February 1972).

Within days the paper soon discovered it had turned over a stone. Informants suddenly came forward to reveal widespread corruption within the force. Three weeks later, a single sentence in *The People* broadened the accusation beyond a single rogue policemen: 'Police officers in London are being systematically bribed by dealers in pornography' (*The People*, 27 February 1972). As with so many investigations, especially once charges were laid, it proved to be a long drawn-out affair. Eventually though, as the Metropolitan Police Commissioner, Sir Robert Mark, got to grips with the situation, it resulted in the suspension and early retirements of 90 officers, and the conviction of 13 policemen, who were sentenced to a total of 96 years (Cox, 1977). Drury was sentenced to five years for taking bribes from Humphreys, and in 1977 Commander Wallace Virgo, chief of the Obscene Publications Squad, received a 12-year jail sentence for accepting bribes, which was overturned on appeal. Nevertheless, he had been disgraced. Manifold and his team were recognised with a special *What The Papers Say* award (*UKPG*, 30 January 1978). The paper's determination to get documentary evidence had paid off.

(iv) The set-up

This involves the informant being used to lure a target into the open. There are two reasons: it helps to prove that the informant genuinely knows the target and it provides an opportunity for a taped conversation and also for photographs or video footage. The classic example involved a Chief of the Defence Staff, Sir Peter Harding. The wife of a Conservative MP, Lady (Bienvenida) Buck, approached the *News of the World* in the hope of being paid a large sum to tell of an affair with Harding. The paper therefore encouraged her to prove her story by contacting Harding, despite their relationship having ended some time before. She did so, luring Harding to a hotel so that he could be photographed with her on the steps. The paper came up with a public interest justification – about a possible breach of security – and got its story ('Chief of Defence in sex and security scandal,' *News of the World*, 13 March 1994). This particular example is nothing more than a glorified kiss-and-tell, and may not fall into the investigative journalism category, but the set-up technique is often used by popular paper investigative journalists.

(v) Going undercover: 'living the news'

The use of subterfuge is widely regarded with suspicion, but there are many occasions where it is demonstrably impossible to obtain a story unless it is employed. A public interest justification has always been essential. Going under cover is certainly not as romantic as it might sound. One former *People* reporter, Lee Lester, found it hard going when working for six weeks on a ship repair gang at the London docks in order to expose restrictive practices (Lester, 2007). Two female reporters working from *The People*'s Manchester office took jobs as volunteers at a mental hospital in an investigation into alleged promiscuity among patients. For their trouble, they were censured by the Press Council for an 'improper use of subterfuge' that 'did not serve the public interest' ('Paper's method of inquiry condemned', *The Guardian*, 19 February 1979). Another *People* reporter, Frank Thorne, told of his nervousness when, as a 22-year-old freelance he had to pose as a junkie, in scruffy jeans and a filthy t-shirt, to buy drugs (Thorne, 2007).

One of the most successful examples of 'living the news' undercover work was carried out by Mary Beith for *The People*. One of several reporters detailed to work under cover at various animal research laboratories, she obtained a job with ICI. She could not produce her insurance cards, because they would have given away her journalistic background, so she pretended they had been mis-laid. The company gave her three days to find them or face instant dismissal. Under time pressure to produce, she soon witnessed dogs trussed up and forced to inhale 'safe' non-nicotine cigarettes, called New Smoking Material. Manifold then arranged for a darkroom to be set up in a van parked near the lab and Beith was given a tiny camera, which she concealed in her bra, to take photo-graphs. The results were unusable. So the following day she took the risk of smuggling in a larger camera and managed to snap a picture of the 'smoking beagles' that ranks as one of the most iconic images ever published by a paper ('Misery of the captive chain smoker', *The People*, 26 January 1975. At http:// myweb.tiscali.co.uk/acigawis/smoking_beagles_at_ici.htm).

In 2003, the *Daily Mirror* pulled off one of the most spectacular undercover exercises when one of its reporters, Ryan Parry, spent two months working as a footman at Buckingham Palace, resulting in a 15-page report with pictures (*Daily Mirror*, 19 November 2003). The reporter was pulled out on the eve of an official state visit by American President George W. Bush, and the paper justified Parry's actions by pointing to the security lapses which had allowed him to obtain a job after responding to an internet advert by using fake refer-ences. The pictures included shots of the Queen's breakfast table, and the suite the President was due to occupy. The paper's editor, Piers Morgan, said: 'We employed very basic subterfuge and got incredible access' (*The Guardian*, 19 November 2003. At http://media.guardian.co.uk/mirror/story/ 0,,1088497,00.html). Two days later the Queen won a court order preventing the *Mirror* from publishing further revelations. Within a week the paper agreed to pay £25,000 towards the Queen's legal costs and agreed not to print any further material obtained by Parry. In return the Queen's lawyers dropped a breach of confidence claim.

Again, there may be questions about whether this story deserves to be rec-ognised as an investigation. Aside from the security angle, and some embarrass-ing revelations about what the Queen has for breakfast, there was no genuine story. It is true that undercover operations to expose failings in security appear frequently in tabloid newspapers. In 2004, for example, a *Sun* reporter, Anthony France, went undercover to work as a cleaner in a hospital to expose what were claimed to be dangerous levels of the 'superbug' MRSA (*The Sun*, 22 March 2004). This did not arouse the same kind of publicity as Parry's – which did involve the head of state after all – but it is possible to argue in both cases that these kinds of investigations are little more than well-executed stunts (see below).

(vi) The sting (or entrapment)

The technology of surveillance has grown ever more sophisticated over the years. Tape-recorders have become easier to conceal. Almost undetectable pin-hole cameras not only enable still pictures to be taken, but can record video footage too. Directional microphones can be used outside buildings to hear what is happening inside. Mobile phones have opened up a new path to discovering secrets. The internet not only provides information, often opening up avenues for investigation, but it allows reporters to draw unsuspecting targets into scenarios. In the years following the decline of *The People*'s investigation team, especially once Manifold retired in 1986 and his team began to break up, the *News of the World* became the leading investigative newspaper, and its reporters took full advantage of the developing technological advances to enhance their reporting.

However, its editorial content from the late 1980s onwards began to differ markedly from *The People*'s and it also moved on from the one it had itself employed in earlier years. Crime remained an important component, but sex and celebrity began to dominate, and investigations reflected that agenda. In order to uncover secrets about people the paper also pushed at the ethical boundaries. Subterfuge became the norm, as did the use of concealed audio and video recorders. Several of its investigations led to charges of entrapment and *News of the World* reporters happily spoke of their skill at 'sting operations'. Far and away the best-known operator of these increasingly controversial methods was Mazher Mahmood, who eventually became the paper's investigations editor. His penchant for dressing up in Arabian-style robes also earned him a memorable nickname, the 'fake sheikh.' Like Duncan Webb in the 1950s, he was the central actor in the dramas he wrote about and cultivated an image of being a marked man within the criminal underworld. Unlike Webb, he refused to allow his picture to be used, successfully fending off attempts by the rest of the media to preserve his anonymity until losing a court action in April 2006 ('Judge lifts ban on Galloway photos of "fake sheikh" reporter', *The Guardian*, 6 April 2006). Mahmood, who worked briefly at *The People* and has acknowledged his debt to Manifold, earned his spurs at the *News of the World* with several investigations into the activities of illegal immigrants, especially those who entered into bogus marriages, and he also played a leading role in exposing men who preyed on children. His stories are said to have resulted in more than 130 people being convicted (Coulson, 2006).

But many of his high-profile investigations that have ended up in the courtroom have been heavily criticised by judges and lawyers. In 1999, the Earl of Hardwicke was convicted of supplying cocaine to Mahmood but he received a suspended sentence after the jury, in a highly unusual move, handed a note to the judge saying he had been a victim of entrapment. The judge remarked: 'Journalists in general, and those involved in this case in particular, should carefully examine and consider their approach to investigations where it involves no police participation, or indeed until after the trap has been sprung and the story reported in the press' (*The Guardian*, 23 September 1999. At http://www.guardian.co.uk/drugs/Story/0,2763,201032,00.html).

Defence lawyers made a similar complaint in a case involving television actor John Alford, who was convicted in 1999 and jailed for nine months for dealing in drugs. The following year Rhodri Giggs, the brother of football star Ryan Giggs, was cleared of a charge of supplying cocaine to Mahmood after the prosecution conceded that the Crown Prosecution Service had 'serious concerns' about the taped conversations between Giggs and Mahmood that formed the main evidence ('Reporter may face charges in Giggs case,' *The Independent*, 17 March 2000). In 2006, three men who had featured in a Mahmood investigative scoop which claimed they were trying to buy 'red mercury' to construct a 'dirty bomb', were cleared at the Old Bailey of three terrorism-related charges. The key to the defence's argument was that they had been manipulated by Mahmood's informant (BBC online, 25 July 2006. At http://news.bbc.co.uk/1/hi/uk/5176522.stm). In these so-called 'stings' and many more celebrated examples – such as those involving two Newcastle United FC directors (1998), the Countess of Wessex (2001), Princess Michael of Kent (2005) and Sven-Göran Eriksson (2006) – Mahmood used variations of a well-tried method. The target was approached with an offer that was, in effect, too tempting to refuse, usually a lucrative business deal, in order to lure them into a trap. Though Mahmood, as the 'fake sheikh' of newspaper legend, generally made the first approach, other members of his team sometimes wore the robes. Among his trusted colleagues, composed mainly of freelances and, in one notable case a cousin, were also two men – Gerry Brown and his son, Conrad – who had mastered the surveillance technology that was the hallmark of all his evidence-gathering (Brown, 1995).

Mahmood's techniques came under the greatest scrutiny following an investigation which led directly to the arrest of five men by armed police who believed they were about to kidnap Victoria Beckham, famous in her own right as a former member of the Spice Girls pop group and the wife of English footballer David Beckham, and hold her to ransom ('Posh Kidnap: We stop crime of the century', *News of the World*, 3 November 2002). The story proved to be sensational long after its publication. When the men finally appeared in court, after spending seven months in jail on remand, an embarrassed prosecution lawyer had to announce that the case was being dropped because the main witness not only had several convictions to his name but had also been paid £10,000 by the *News of the World*. He was therefore an unreliable witness ('Truth behind the Beckham "kidnap" plot', *Observer*, 8 June 2003. At http://observer.guardian.co.uk/uk_news/story/0,6903,972961,00.html).

Mahmood and the *News of the World* stuck by the story, despite the judge referring the case to the Attorney General and threats by some of the men to sue for libel. But no action was taken, and a Press Complaints Commission inquiry declared that the *News of the World* had not breached the Code of Practice (*The Guardian*, 11 July 2003. At http://media.guardian.co.uk/medialaw/story/0,,995846,00.html).

The story refused to go away. One of the accused, Adrian Pasareanu, spoke at length about the affair, claiming that they had all been 'set up' by a Kosovan Albanian who had befriended them, Florim Gashi (*The Guardian*, 9 June 2003. At http://media.guardian.co.uk/mediaguardian/story/0,,973258,00.html). Another of the five, Alin Turcu (aka Bogdan Maris), sued the paper for libel. While that wound its lengthy way towards the courts, the Gashi trail went cold. Then, in the summer of 2005, Gashi made phone calls to Scotland Yard and to me, saying that he was eager to talk about Mahmood. I flew to Croatia, as did three Yard detectives, to interview Gashi. We met him separately but he told us the same astonishing story. He claimed that he had acted, at Mahmood's instigation, as an agent provocateur to inveigle the men into the Beckham kidnap plot. Conversations he had filmed with a hidden camera that formed the basis of the evidence against the men were not as they seemed. He had engineered the discussions to make it appear as if they were involved in a genuine plot, but they were merely indulging in a fantasy. Material that would have shown them as innocents had been edited out. The footage had been doctored to ensure the inclusion only of incriminating statements. Other key 'facts' were also manipulated. There was no gang. A visit to 'case' the Beckhams' home was not genuine because the men did not realise where they being taken. The gun the men were seen holding on camera was supplied by Gashi. The supposed getaway driver – Mahmood's cousin – was introduced to the men by Gashi. Though some of the men had been involved in a robbery, and were eager to sell off their ill-gotten gains, others were completely innocent.

Gashi's statement dovetailed with the claims of both Turcu and Pasareanu, but it was anything but conclusive proof that Mahmood had misbehaved. As the *News of the World* was quick to point out, it showed once again that Gashi could not be replied upon as a witness. He had a track record of dishonesty. Gashi did not restrict himself to the Beckham story. He also claimed to have been involved in various roles in several other Mahmood investigations, originally as an informant and later as part of Mahmood's team of 'actors'. For example, he alleged that he had persuaded a young mother to sell her baby for £15,000 at Mahmood's behest ('Baby For Sale Plot', *News of the World*, 20 March 2005). Again, it was entirely plausible to argue that Gashi had fooled Mahmood.

The police inquiry into Gashi's claims was inconclusive and no action was taken ('Police probe News of the World stories', *The Guardian*, 17 October 2005). Similarly, it looked as though the libel action was also bound to fail. A High Court judge rejected the claim, clearing the paper of libel ('Judge throws out libel claim in Beckham "kidnap" case', *The Guardian*, 5 May 2005). The following year Turcu was given leave to appeal and Gashi agreed to give evidence on his behalf ('Accused to appeal against NoW Beckham libel ruling', *Guardian*, 26 May 2006. At http://media.guardian.co.uk/presspublishing/ story/0,,1784093,00.html; 'Journalist complicit in Beckham plot, court told', *Guardian*, 26 July 2006. At http://media.guardian.co.uk/presspublishing/story/ 0,,1830658,00.html). In the months leading to the appeal Turcu's lawyers found what they believed to be corroborative evidence for part of Gashi's claim, securing a statement from a man who said he had supplied Gashi with the gun supposedly obtained by the 'gang'. But no evidence was given at the appeal hearing because the *News of the World* announced in court that it was apologising to Turcu and accepted that he had not been involved in the kidnap plot ('NoW apologises in Beckham case', *Guardian*, 14 February 2007. At http://media.guardian.co.uk/presspublishing/story/0,,2012823,00.html).

Though it was a significant climb-down by the paper, it did not negate the entire story nor affect Mahmood's status within the paper. His investigative work continued, as did the controversies surrounding his methods. Were the offers held out to targets too tempting? Were people unfairly manipulated to commit crimes? Was the persistent use of subterfuge really warranted? Was there a genuine public interest in every instance? Despite considerable hostility towards Mahmood's techniques, his successes ensured that they were used by other *News of the World* journalists and, to a lesser extent, by reporters on other papers too. The ethical questions remain, but he did set the investigative standard for Britain's popular papers from the mid-1990s onwards.

(vii) Fishing expeditions

Though the Editors' Code of Practice does not use the phrase, it is considered wrong for journalists to engage in subterfuge in the hope that something might turn up. In a ruling in 2001, the Press Complaints Commission censured the *News of the World* for covertly filming a private Christmas party given for the cast of a television series, Emmerdale. The PCC ruled that the partygoers' right to privacy had been infringed and the paper had no prior evidence to suggest that anything might have occurred that would have been of public interest. The PCC's director, Guy Black, said: 'The code isn't there to stop legitimate investigation; it is there to stop fishing expeditions' ('News of World censured for secret video', *The Guardian*, 17 April 2001; PCC Report 53. At http://www. pcc.org.uk/news/index.html?article=MjAyOQ=). That effect-ively closed the door on journalists setting off on undercover investigations merely on a hunch or a whim.

(viii) Drip-drip-drip discovery

When Paul Foot died in 2004 he left behind voluminous files in the offices of *Private Eye*, where he had done so much of his work. However, a great deal of

335

the material touched upon investigations he had carried out in part for the *Daily Mirror*, where, for fourteen years, he wrote a column that was truly unique because, unlike investigative journalism elsewhere, it meant Foot had to fulfil a weekly commitment of revelatory story-getting. He was hired in 1979 by the then editor, Mike Molloy, 'to put some balls into the paper' despite his own concerns 'about bringing to the paper a Trotskyist and member of the Socialist Workers' Party' (Hagerty, 2003: 154; Ingrams, 2005: 83). Foot later explained that they had an 'unspoken and unwritten agreement' that he would not make political propaganda for the SWP. Instead, his page would 'take the side of the poor against the rich, public enterprise against private enterprise, Labour against Tories, wrongly convicted prisoners against the judiciary, and so on' (Foot, 1990: xiii). Giving Foot a full-page column was to prove an inspired decision. Under Molloy and his successor, Richard Stott, Foot was able to pursue all manner of stories. His range was remarkable. He took up relatively small, localised stories while mounting long-run inquiries into stories of inter-national importance, such as the Lockerbie air disaster. As one of his *Mirror* colleagues noted, he displayed a 'defiant doggedness and ferocious attention to detail, leavened by wit' (Rostron, 2004).

Foot's investigations were inevitably transformed into campaigns as he sought to overturn miscarriages of justice. Stott recalled that in 1986, Foot sent 13 Christmas cards to the men and women he believed were then serving life sentences for murders they did not commit: 'It took time, but every single one of them was eventually cleared and freed' (Stott, 2002: 19).

The hallmark of a Foot investigation was the drip-drip-drip discovery and recording of evidence, over months and often years, in short pieces in the *Mirror* or *Private Eye*. In some celebrated instances these led to books that pulled together all the details to devastating effect, illustrating incompetence and/or malfeasance by the authorities (Foot, 1983, 1986, 1989). His advantage in having a regular page was that he could publish a couple of incisive paragraphs to flush out yet more information. In sifting through one file, about the 1988 bombing of the plane over Lockerbie in which 270 people were killed, it became clear to me that he was a mixture of magpie, picking up all manner of possibly import-ant material, and terrier, never letting go once he was on to a story. His interest was initially piqued when the Transport secretary Paul Channon told six lobby journalists that arrests were imminent but subsequently denied it in the Com-mons (Tam Dalyell, 'Lord Kelvedon obituary', *The Independent*, 31 January 2007). From that moment on, Foot became convinced that the official inquiry was tainted by political pressure and went on to chart how the finger of suspicion that first pointed at Syria and a Palestinian connection switched suddenly to Libya (Rostron, 2007). He then tore apart the official narrative, showing how governments, aided by a compliant or quiescent press, were responsible for convicting innocent people (Foot, 1994).

Foot's greatest source of stories were distressed people who felt they lacked the power to right a wrong. They were, in the words of one of Foot's *Mirror* team 'ordinary people [who] wrote to him with the most extraordinary stories'. They found a ready ear in Foot, who memorably wrote: 'There's only one thing worse than believing people who are telling lies and that is not believing people who are telling the truth' (Foot, 1990).

(ix) Stunt journalism

This is really pseudo-investigative journalism, a cheap and easy substitute for the real thing. As I mentioned earlier, the *Daily Mirror*'s reporter-in-the-Palace story was really a stunt (and also, arguably, a fishing expedition). But the *Mirror* then caught the stunt journalism bug by regularly employing an age-old gimmick of 'testing security' by having reporters plant devices on public transport ('We plant "bomb" on nuke train', *Daily Mirror*, 21 July 2006). When caught in the act on one occasion, thereby proving the efficiency of security arrangements, the paper then had the impertinence to complain at the alleged ill-treatment of its staff ('Mirror journalists arrested over fake bomb', *Guardian*, 24 July 2007. At http://media.guardian.co.uk/presspublishing/story/0,,2133828,00.html; 'Mirror slams "fake bomb" arrests', *The Guardian* 25 July 2007. At http://media.guardian.co.uk/presspublishing/story/0,,2134379,00.html).

Popular newspapers, citing a public service ethic, have made a habit of this kind of 'investigative journalism' to expose security lapses. Here's a random sample. In 2000, a *News of the World* reporter claimed to have boarded a passenger jet at Birmingham Airport by posing as a pilot (*News of the World*, 19 November 2000). In 2001, shortly after the 9/11 attacks in New York, a *Daily Mirror* reporter managed to enter a hangar at Stansted airport and get inside the cockpit of a passenger plane (*Daily Mirror*, 2 November 2001). In 2003, a *News of the World* reporter boarded a plane at Gatwick airport carrying a replica machine gun. He was later arrested (*News of the World*, March 16 2003). In 2004, a reporter from the *Sun* used bogus references to obtain a baggage-handling job at Birmingham airport and then assembled a fake bomb in the toilet of a plane bound for Majorca (*The Sun*, 17 August 2004). A month later, a *News of the World* reporter walked into a restricted area at Heathrow airport holding a fake bomb in a bag (*News of the World*, September 12 2004). In 2004, a *Sun* reporter who had obtained a waiter's job in the House of Commons smuggled in a fake bomb ('Sun bomber in Commons', *The Sun*, 17 September 2004). Shortly before the 2005 wedding of Prince Charles and Camilla Parker Bowles, *Sun* journalists drove a van carrying a brown box marked 'bomb' into Windsor Castle ('Gatecrasher in the Castle', *The Sun*, 7 April 2005). Two months later a *Sun* reporter – bylined 'The Investigator' – strolled around Sandhurst military academy with a fake bomb during Prince Harry's cadet training ('Harry was a sitting duck', *The Sun*, 16 June 2005). *The People* got into the stunt business in 2007 when some of its staff drove a van with the obligatory fake bomb into a secure area at Manchester airport (*The People*,

18 June 2007). In 2007, a *Daily Mirror* reporter tried to obtain a post as assistant to the Conservative Party chairman, but her infiltration attempt was thwarted ('Undercover Mirror journalist exposed as she tries to infiltrate Tory Party', *Mail on Sunday*, 19 August 2007). It is little wonder that a BBC journalist was moved to observe: 'Those who regularly read a red-top newspaper might be forgiven for asking if there is really anything left to infiltrate' ('Do newspaper security stunts work?' BBC online, 16 June 2005. At http://news.bbc.co.uk/1/hi/uk/4098402.stm).

Conclusion

The two latter examples – the fake sheikery and the stunts – are virtually the only extant form of regular investigative journalism now published by popular papers. Though content does not necessarily negate the techniques they employ, the public interest justification for much of it seems threadbare. Manifold, the grand old man of the trade, sees it very differently. He believes the problems stem more from the lack of resources. With newspaper profits so squeezed and editorial budgets cut back, no editor – even if he or she wished to do so – could allow journalists the time to spend on investigations of real merit. They are obliged to work fast and that inhibits proper in-depth reporting. Moreover, they cannot afford the luxury of failing: they have to come up with something worth publishing. Furthermore, newspapers cannot match the huge resources deployed by television companies for investigations, nor the appealing quality of the results. 'It's all TV now', said Manifold. 'Newspapers can't possibly compete' (Manifold, 2007).

Notes

1 *The People*'s name has changed backwards and forwards several times from *The People* to the *Sunday People*. To avoid complications, I have stuck to *The People*.
2 There are other titles designated as populars. I have ignored the *Daily Record* and *Sunday Mail* because, as Scottish titles, they do not circulate across Britain. I have ignored the *Daily* and *Sunday Sport* because they do not sell widely enough.

Bibliography

Bainbridge, C. and Stockdill, R. (1993) *The News of the World Story*. London: HarperCollins.

Barker, R. (2007) Email to Roy Greenslade, 30 September 2007.

Bromley, M. and O,Malley, T. (eds) (1997) *A Journalism Reader*. London: Routledge.

Brown, G. (1995) *Exposed! Sensational True Story of Fleet Street Reporter*. London: Virgin.

Chibnall, S. (1977) *Law-and-Order News*. London: Tavistock.

Coulson, A. (2006) We can do without lessons in ethics from Roy Greenslade, *Independent on Sunday*, 23 April 2006.

Cox, B., Shirley, J. and Short, M. (1977) *The Fall of Scotland Yard*. London: Penguin.

Cudlipp, H. (1953) *Publish and Be Damned!* London: Andrew Dakers.

Cudlipp, H. (1976) *Walking on the Water*. London: Bodley Head.

Edwards, J. (2007) Emails to Roy Greenslade, 27/29 September 2007.

Engel, M. (1996) *Tickle the Public*. London: Gollancz.

Entwistle, C. (2007) Emails to Roy Greenslade, 28 September 2007.

Foot, P. (1983) *The Helen Smith Story*. London: Fontana.

Foot, P. (1986) *Murder at the Farm: Who Killed Carl Bridgewater?* London: Sidgwick & Jackson.

Foot, P. (1989) *Who Framed Colin Wallace?* London: Macmillan.

Foot, P. (1994)) 'Taking the blame', *London Review of Books*, 6 January 1994.

Foot, P. (2004) The Great Lockerbie Whitewash, 1989–2001. In John Pilger *Tell Me No Lies: Investigative Journalism and its Triumphs*. London: Jonathan Cape.

Gadd, G. (2007) Emails to Roy Greenslade, 30 September 2007, 2, 3 October 2007.

Harcup, T. (2004) *Journalism: Principles and Practice*. London: Sage.

Harrison, F. (2007) Phone interview with Roy Greenslade.

Ingrams, R. (2005) *My Friend Footy*. London: Private Eye.

Kersh, C. (1990) *A Few Gross Words*. London: Simon & Schuster.

Knightley, P. and Kennedy, C. (1987) *An Affair of State: The Profumo Case and the Framing of Stephen Ward*. London: Jonathan Cape.

Krais, M. (2007) Phone interview with Roy Greenslade, 28 September 2007.

Lester, L. (2007) Emails to Roy Greenslade, 3, 4 October 2007.

Manifold, L. (2007) Interview with Roy Greenslade in Andover, Hampshire, 5 October 2007.

Minney, R.J. (1954) *Viscount Southwood*. London: Odhams Press.

Procter, H. (1958) *The Street of Disillusion*. London: Allan Wingate.

Richards, H. (1997) *The Bloody Circus*. London: Pluto.

Rostron, B. (2004) 'This star of England', *British Journalism Review*, 15 (3), 2004: 70–73.

Rostron, B. (2007) Email to Roy Greenslade, 22 September 2007.

Shannon, R. (2001) *A Press Free and Responsible*. London: John Murray.

Somerfield, S. (1979) *Banner Headlines*. Shoreham by Sea: Scan Books.

Spark, D. (1999) *Investigative Reporting: A study in technique*. Oxford: Focal Press.

Summers, A. and Dorril, S. (1987) *Honeytrap: The Secret Worlds of Stephen Ward*. London: Weidenfeld & Nicolson.

Sutherland, J. (1983) *Offensive Literature: Decensorship in Britain, 1960–1982*. Totowa, NJ: Barnes & Noble.

Thomas, D. (2006) *Villains' Paradise: Britain's Underworld from the Spivs to the Krays*. London: John Murray.

Thorne, F. (2007) Phone interview with Roy Greenslade, 29 September 2007.

Webb, D. (1953) *Crime Is My Business*. London: Frederick Muller.

Webb, D. (1955) *Deadline for Crime*. London: Frederick Muller.

Further reading

Edwards, R. (1988) *Goodbye Fleet Street*. London: Jonathan Cape.

Greenslade, R. (2004) *Press Gang: How Newspapers Make Profits from Propaganda*. London: Pan.

Hagerty, B. (2003) *Read All About It! 100 Sensational Years of the Daily Mirror*. Lydney: First Stone Publishing.

Seymour, D. and Seymour, E. (eds) (2003) *A Century of News*. London: Contender.

Stott, R. (2002) *Dogs and Lampposts*. London: Metro.

Taylor, S.J. (1991) *Shock! Horror!* London: Bantam.

20

PILLAGING THE
ENVIRONMENTALISTS

The Cook Report

Hugo de Burgh

In this section we look at two phenomena, widespread concern about the environment with reference to the problems and opportunities this poses investigative journalists; and how *The Cook Report* has made investigative journalism into popular theatre. Taken together they focus our attention on how complicated scientific issues can be dealt with by the media, and the risks of trivialisation, of tendentious sourcing and of misinformation.

The media and the environment

Environment issues became mainstream news in the 1970s; in the UK the industrial correspondents started to disappear and were replaced by environment correspondents. Their popularity may now be on the wane as readers and viewers become inured to doom-mongering or at least more sceptical as to whether environment reports have immediate relevance to them. Research has shown that citizens of rich countries, especially women, have until now evinced much concern about the environment; the spectacular burgeoning of pressure groups which, in some cases, have developed from being eccentric fringe protesters into large, wealthy and sophisticated policy pushers, is one indication of the trend. However, there is little agreement on the role that the media have played in this (Anderson, 1997: 171). One model of communication effects is perhaps pertinent here. Anderson (following McQuail and Windahl, 1981) suggests that:

> ... individual opinions are highly dependent upon what is perceived to be the 'majority' view on any given issue ... individuals gain clues as to the relative prominence of particular points of view. If an individual's own position does not seem to accord with the dominant view

then they are seen as being much less likely to express their opinions than if they are perceived to have wide support.

(Anderson, 1997: 78)

Thus opinion polls, reported in the media, influence people's behaviour; high-profile campaigns such as that for lead-free petrol (see Chapter 12) have a dual function; they may achieve the stated objective, say a change in government policy, but they do this in part because the very prominence of the issue created by the campaign has convinced many people that the campaigners' assessment of the situation is the dominant view and that they should come on board. Brosius and Kepplinger's (1990) ideology diffusion model shows how pressure groups have their influence extended through specialist magazines, which then have their articles picked up by general magazines whose concerns are picked up by the popular media from which they diffuse into the general public. Other studies cited by Anderson (1997: 179) suggest that the influence of the media on the general population in respect of environmental issues is small; the impact that they have is upon policy-makers. This ties in with theories of media influence described by Wayne Parsons (1995). Other research (Bell, 1991) tells us that only if people already have awareness of the issue in question do they learn anything more from the media. Climatic change resulting from ozone depletion and global warming became an international political issue in the 1970s. Bell (1994) has studied its treatment by the media in New Zealand, the economy of which is particularly sensitive to climate, as well as the effect of this reporting upon the populace. Bell's findings on treatment of the issue are salutary for journalists. He shows how scientists' views have been distorted by journalists and he shows the processes through which the information they provide to journalists goes, and why it ends up so distorted. Five techniques are applied:

1   'illocutionary force' is used to *assert* what scientists prefer to *speculate* upon;
2   overstatement;
3   proposition of imminence, presenting phenomena as certain or imminent;
4   imaginability, picturing the topic graphically so that a strong and memorable impression is created;
5   confusion, the blending of information such as that on ozone depletion or the greenhouse effect are, for example, merged into one great awfulness.

As a result of the application of these techniques readers may see a multifaceted catastrophe all around them; they may be taught to believe that a given phenomenon, upon which scientists are merely speculating might touch us in hundreds of years, is certain and imminent, if not already here (ibid., 1994). Another reaction is that they may cease to believe anything on the subject at all.

Sources and the problems of sourcing

That sourcing may pose problems for journalists is very well illustrated by Matt Ridley's salutary essay collections, *Down to Earth* I and II (1995 and 1996). In them he looks afresh at the environmental issues of the moment: acid rain, fisheries policy, fuel resources, culling of pests, population, famine warnings, rising sea levels, dangers from sunlight and so forth, and either questions the science upon which the scares are based or questions the proposed solutions, intentionally taking a sceptical or 'contrarian' (as he calls it) view. He shows on many occasions that the fashionable view is not necessarily that of the scientists closest to the issue in question, for example on acid rain and the melanomas supposedly resulting from greater exposure to sunlight. He provides a convincing reminder that it is easy for journalists to get sucked into fashions if they do not carefully examine their bases. An illustration of this not cited by Ridley is the way journalists have, over some 35 years, failed to interrogate the overpopulation scare. This has been the most famous and long-running series of apocalyptic predictions for which journalists have fallen; the result of failure to question the evidence adequately or to consider alternative views in the scientific community have been policies that have affected the lives of millions (Simon, 1992; Kasun, 1988).

Ridley accounts for gullibility on environmental issues by blaming the pressure groups who use hyperbole, he says (Ridley, 1996: 79, 87, 101) in the competition for funds.[1] In dealing with the environment, journalists are faced with some wealthy and powerful interest groups, public relations officials and campaigners, and he recommends knowing the sources of your information and the background of your informants.

Shoemaker has argued that it is not the justice of a source's case that affects journalists' selection of sources but the source's extroversion, assertiveness, credibility (assigned to them by the journalists!), accessibility and quotability (Shoemaker, 1996: 182). In the UK the most active environmentalist operations are Greenpeace and Friends of the Earth. There are several hundred other bodies, from the Nature Conservancy Council to the Royal Society for the Protection of Birds and the National Trust. Some of these organisations are believed to be both rich and influential, with policies and monetary interests to defend. Greenpeace is suspected by some of launching some of its campaigns to boost membership rather than to call attention to a real problem (Ridley, 1996); it has been argued that the National Trust, Britain's best established conservation body, has argued to serve sectional interests while presenting itself as altruistic (C4, 1994). Their weapons are those of all pressure groups and include briefings by plausible experts, press releases in print, video or audio form, pseudo events and contacts in the worlds of the decision-makers and the opinion-formers. Journalists on the whole like sources that seem established and mainstream; in a study of the coverage of environmental disasters by newspapers, it was found that journalists were more likely to rely upon government sources than upon scientists (Hornig, 1991).

The Cook Report

Central Broadcasting is one of the fifteen regional Independent Television (ITV) companies in the UK (London has two) and is part of Carlton Communications, which has two ITV licenses: (weekday) London and the Midlands (Upshon, 1997). In its portfolio Carlton also has substantial percentages of Meridian TV, the London News Network, GMTV and Select TV. Central Broadcasting's franchise covers a quarter of England with a population of nearly 9 million. The conditions of the franchise require that Central supply certain types of programmes, in particular regional programmes and news, although the core schedule, as with other ITV regions, is provided by the Network Centre to which Central is a substantial contributor of programmes.

Its network output is large and famous; perhaps the most famous are *Family Fortunes*, *Inspector Morse* and *The Cook Report*. *The Cook Report* was started in 1985 by Roger Cook, the New Zealander who had been the creator of the BBC's investigative programme *Checkpoint*.[2] Among other things, the series has exposed child pornography, protection rackets in Northern Ireland, baby trading in Brazil, loan sharks, the ivory trade, war criminals in Bosnia and the Russian black market in plutonium. 'A number . . . have been followed by successful police prosecutions of the villains or major changes in the law' (Central Television, 1997). Cook is proud of 'our after-sales service' by which he means giving evidence in court that will convict the villains and cites among the programme's achievements legislation on child pornography, an extradition treaty between the UK and Spain and the closure of a Hong Kong refugee camp.

> What we are trying to do is to reveal what we think is damaging to the public, whether it be child pornography or gangsters. And taking people off the streets who shouldn't be there like the members of the UDA [Ulster Defence Association] who were making money through extortion of building companies. It was our evidence got them convicted. The object is to take the case of the victims as far as you possibly can; I see investigative journalism as public service broadcasting at its best.
>
> (Cook, 1999)

The Cook Report is expensive to produce, over £180,000 a programme, and needs a star presenter of courage and initiative. In 1996 the Network Centre (which takes *The Cook Report* from the ITV company making it for the national ITV network) considered abolishing the programme as part of a revamp of current affairs, notwithstanding that it achieved remarkably high viewing ratings for current affairs.[3] However, it thought better and *The Cook Report* remains in the form of hour-long specials approximately every two months. The hallmarks of *The Cook Report* are that a popular topic is selected, in the example below canned lion hunting with its implications of cowardly killers parodying the noble hunter of yore, set within a theme that triggers off some satisfying emotions such as, in this case, those associated with the battle to defend the environment, and endangered species. The story form is employed and as layer upon layer is revealed you can almost hear the master storyteller whispering 'and then?' as each twist in the tale is made to increase your involvement. The viewer expects, and gets, the elements appropriate to the genre: a righteous champion (Mr Cook), a villain, assumed identities, a sting, a chase, victim or victims who will be vindicated, even rewarded. In other words, the drama narrative style is typical, rather than the upturned pyramid of straight reportage.

That characteristic of *The Cook Report* has been copied by other programmes since, but when first used was very remarkable, as were the atmospheric effects including the hand-held camera and eerie music (Beckett, 1995). Viewers at home anticipate a dramatic confrontation; according to audience research they 'like to be made to sit on the edge of their seats' (Cook, 1999). Criticisms have focused on whether these narrative methods diminish the seriousness of the issues under consideration, or make it impossible to tackle some issues. Tim Tate, formerly one of *The Cook Report*'s producers, jokes that editorial meetings revolved around the question of 'who's going to hit Roger this time?' (Tate, 1997). Cook denies this vehemently. For all his modesty, however, *The Cook Report is* the man; he is a hero to many, known to have received death threats, and seen on screen being assaulted by indignant villains as he braves their wrath.

To draw attention to the artefact is not to diminish the work of investigation nor the public service motivation of teams who seek to right wrong and overcome evil. In the Cook investigation into the pop music business (Central, 1997b), the fact that Cook managed to hold our attention for two programmes on the subject was surely due both to the narrative skill and to the research; research that revealed suspected but hitherto unproven naughtiness in the manner in which 'successes' in the pop records charts could be effected by the spreading of a little money here and there. Cook found an attractive but otherwise ordinary girl, created a pop group for her, produced her song and promoted it in order to demonstrate the entire process of manufacturing pop celebrity. The programmes were entertaining and, like some other Cook Reports but unlike some other investigative journalism whose shelf-life is limited to the duration of the topic in question, would likely hold interest as repeats.

The programme has been fiercely criticised from time to time, never more so than over its two programmes on cot deaths (1994) and one that investigated monies donated to help the strike of the National Union of Mineworkers

(1990). In March 1990 *The Cook Report* combined with the *Daily Mirror* in what the *Mirror*'s proprietor, the late Robert Maxwell, described as 'classic investigative journalism'. The investigative journalists exposed not only that the National Union of Miners (NUM), which had been battling with the then government for ten years over restructuring of the energy industry, had been in receipt of foreign funds during its strikes, but that some of the money donated by Soviet miners and Colonel Ghaddafi of Libya had been used to make life more comfortable for senior officials of the NUM.

In his book on the issue, Seamas Milne argues not only that the details were wrong but that the journalists involved were the dupes of the miners' leaders' political enemies and of the notorious secret services who planted ideas and clues and provided surveillance reports and convenient interpretations of them to the reporters (Milne, 1995). These accusations are rejected entirely by the journalists involved. Suggestions that the programme was 'manipulated by the Secret Services' are risible, says Cook. Allegations made in the programme were all at least dual sourced and all facts thoroughly checked (Cook, 1999). *The Cook Report* was attacked in another television programme, this time C4 *Dispatches*, which also used the trademark Cook doorstepping technique on Cook himself. It was successfully shrugged off by Cook, whereas by common consent its use on NUM leader Arthur Scargill had been damaging to Scargill, who was seen at a disadvantage, uttering what seemed to be legalistic phrases about requiring notice to questions. The *Daily Express* described it as 'trial by television' (Milne, 1995: 49).

The cot deaths programmes put forward a theory from a leading consultant scientist that the fire retardants recommended by the government for use in the manufacture of baby mattresses could, in some circumstances, produce poisonous gases. According to one commentator, there followed a panic among parents of young children who bought up new mattresses in large quantities and expressed their fears in tens of thousands of letters and telephone calls to the media and to advice sources (Beckett, 1995). The BBC's science programme, *QED*, examined the claims by *The Cook Report* and attacked them. Cook defends his programme on the grounds that it gave a platform to the views of the most respected scientific authority, views that have never been disproven as one of the causes of cot deaths, that its attackers used research that was itself flawed and that, regardless of the mechanisms which connected mattresses and deaths, the withdrawal of the mattresses resulted in a further decrease in cot deaths (Cook, 1999).

These two serious criticisms must be seen within context. If you accept that investigative journalism must happen, then you accept that there will be opponents of it and that, from time to time, the research will be characterised as selective, the authorities as eccentric, the researchers over-enthusiastic, the managers as failing to make the right checks and for failing to spot the hidden hand of outside interests. In the long career of *The Cook Report* it is hardly surprising to find some carping.

Example: 'Making a Killing'

The public interest basis for this programme is that, while there is an international agreement to protect species that are facing extinction – rhinos, turtles, elephants, tigers and so forth – thanks to mankind's taking over more and more of the Earth's surface, this agreement, CITES or the Convention on International Trade in Endangered Species of Wild Flora and Fauna is known to be widely flouted. Evidence of this has been obtained by, for example, the Environmental Information Agency (despite its official sounding name, a pressure group of activists with skills in video production and investigation) (Grundy, 1996) and in this case by journalists. 'Making a Killing' tells the story of a chase: how Roger Cook got evidence of the trade in species supposedly protected by CITES, how he recorded the illegal and cruel killings of such species and then took his evidence to the South African High Commission (Embassy) to demand action on behalf of us all.

The transcript of this programme is self-explanatory and relatively short. I have therefore decided to incorporate it, slightly edited, and am grateful for permission of Central Television to do so. Readers should, in reading this script, note:

- the tease at the start that suggests you will see a kill
- the gradual accumulation of evidence, some obtained with covert filming
- the appeal to our sympathies and to our anger at the dastardly customers
- the sting on the dealers
- the build-up to confrontation
- the confrontation
- the declaration to the world.

'Making a Killing'

Generic montage of dramatic shots of guns, chases . . . exciting music . . . Cook driving a 4-wheel in Africa . . .

ROGER COOK   Tonight, hunting down the hunters – we expose the men who make big money from the killing of protected and endangered animals.

South African 'gamekeeper' beside stuffed lion.

SANDY MCDONALD   Two-thirds down, one-third up, right on the shoulder blade. Smoke it in there and he'll bounce around and make a lot of noise and run off and die probably . . .

Montage ends with the generic 'Cook confrontation' picture, cut to overheads of Kruger National Park.

ROGER COOK   This is the Kruger National Park, perhaps the world's best known reserve for wild animals running free in an area the size of Wales.

Here, millions of tourists, the majority of them British, have enjoyed seeing the well-protected big game that gives South Africa its reputation as a safe haven for the continent's endangered species. Our investigation has uncovered the shocking truth these tourists have not been told – no animal here is safe, even the King of the Jungle. We've discovered that even lions are being stolen from under the noses of game wardens to die at point-blank range and end up on some rich man's wall.

Change of scene, general views Costa del Sol.

Spain's Costa del Sol, playground of the wealthy is where *The Cook Report* has come to uncover the unacceptable face of big game hunting – the wealth is conspicuous, less obvious are the unscrupulous middle men who cater to the basest of instincts – middle men like José Iglesias and Luis Gomez, on the face of it legitimate sportsmen, but for the right money, they'll arrange for you to shoot anything you like, any way you like, anywhere in the world – however endangered.

Change of scene – meeting.

ROGER COOK   Within minutes of meeting Mr Gomez, *The Cook Report* undercover team was offered the illegal shooting of gorillas, tiger and jaguar. As his credentials, he offered this video of a jaguar hunt in Bolivia complete with posturing client and prohibited kill.

Change of scene – company office.

Back in Marbella, we set up a bogus company, we pretended to be agents for rich people who wanted hunting trophies, no matter how illegally obtained.

Cook to camera:

This is a story of cruelty and greed. From an office in this country renowned for its devotion to hunting in all its forms world wide, we set up a cover company which offered rich rewards to game hunters who could arrange for our clients to shoot anything at all. The response was astonishing. The Spanish hunters recommended South Africa for the sort of hunting we were interested in.

Change of scene – back to Africa.

ROGER COOK   Our team found this ranch run by professional hunter Chris Sussens on the edge of the famous Kruger National Park. The distressing pictures you're about to see, taken on a legal Sussens hunt, were to massage his French client's ego.

Hunter shown killing a lion in the bush.

It was a short trek but a slow death for this lion. It took several minutes and six more shots than we're going to show you for the lion to die. They didn't want to spoil the trophy by shooting him in the head.

Covert filming.

Sussens can also arrange the illegal shooting of big cats in small enclosures in what's called a canned hunt.

Covert filming.

CHRIS SUSSENS   The only time I can actually guarantee an animal, it's going to be like a canned animal which I don't like doing and that's normally not done in this area, we have to go up towards the Free State, we'll give the odd operator there that's got lions in big camps and you can go into a big camp and you can shoot a lion there. Basically, this camp where this chap's got the lions is about a 20 hectare camp.

Change of scene – young man in view.

ROGER COOK   Bruce Hamilton was once a farm manager on what he thought was a lion breeding project. When he discovered the speciality was actually canned hunting, he left in disgust having taken this video.

Actuality of lioness beside wire, cubs other side, unhappy.

The lioness has been separated from her bewildered cubs who still follow their mother's steps on the other side of a wire enclosure. As they look on, a German hunter is preparing for the kill.

BRUCE HAMILTON   It's totally disgusting what happens here in South Africa. A lot of wealthy game ranch owners make a lot of money out of shooting lions which have been bred in cages and purely for that purpose. They take them out either by darting or by baiting them out of these cages and an overseas client will come in sitting on the back of a Land Rover or on foot and just shoot it for his own pleasure.

ROGER COOK   Roy Plath is the wealthy man who owned that lioness. We contacted him to see if he'd sell us another of his tame lions for a canned hunt. Keen to take our client's money, he lets us film examples of the prey without showing the wire enclosures to preserve the illusion of a fair free-range hunt. We asked him to record a personal invitation to our bogus client. He was happy to oblige.

Pitch to camera by:

ROY PLATH   Mr James Rogers, nice to meet you, look forward to meeting you in South Africa. I'd like to say, as you can see, it looks like we've got just the lion here for you and we look forward to you being able to come out and shoot this lion and have a trophy for your office or home as it pleases you.

We see the lion.

ROGER COOK   Mr Plath had also wanted to kill this young lioness, Shamwari, because she had rickets. Conservationists stepped in, and one of South Africa's few lion sanctuaries is now her home. Safe from what the owner regards as a barbaric practice.

SIMON TRICKEY   Canned lion hunting is like shooting fish in a barrel, it's unethical, it's bloody easy, and it's earning a lot of people a lot of money.

Airport scenes.

ROGER COOK   For the moment, away from lion hunting to a different quarry in London as Luis Gomez, the Spanish middle man, arrives to explain how his plans for the illegal gorilla hunt are progressing. We meet him at Heathrow and take him to the man we've told him is the brother of a hugely wealthy client.

Covert filming of a meeting between Cook and dealers.

Gomez, on the left, has already offered us gorilla but is guarded in front of our interpreter but he confirms we'll get exactly what we want and wants another 12,000 dollars to smuggle the gorilla's head out of the country.

ROGER COOK   And in the meantime, what I'm going to do, just to keep you going, I'm going to give you 2,000 dollars in advance . . . Gomez refuses to give a receipt but will supply the coordinates of the hunting ground in Cameroon so we can fly out undetected.

Scenes of gorillas.

ROGER COOK   The hunt in prospect horrifies gorilla experts like Ian Redmond who says there are only 12,000 of these imposing animals left.

IAN REDMOND   *(Interviewed)* They are almost human and to go and shoot one, it's I guess, it's a . . . it's a sickening insight to the kind of species that we belong to.

Back to the covertly filmed meeting.

ROGER COOK   Gomez says we can also hunt endangered tigers in Malaysia using his corrupt contacts.

Tigers in wire enclosures . . . splendid tigers.

But why risk being caught hunting endangered tigers in Malaysia when you can shoot captive ones in a private canned hunt in South Africa for 100,000 dollars apiece? This is another wealthy businessman, Farnie Roberts, his farm has Bengal tigers, black leopard and jaguar. Like Roy Plath, he's eager to hide the wire enclosures from our wealthy clients and even cuts a hole in the wire for our camera. No hunting permit would ever be given to shoot these cats and certainly not in the canned conditions Mr Roberts has on offer.

Covert filming.

FARNIE ROBERTS   I have got enclosures which are like 100 metres by 100 metres. Something like that. Where you and your clients and the tiger can't come out.

Undercover researcher in discussion with Roberts.

FARNIE ROBERTS   And this one is available to shoot . . .

Picture of a jaguar.

ROGER COOK   This beautiful jaguar is surplus to Mr Roberts requirements so for 100,000 dollars, our client can shoot him too. We showed our evidence to actress Virginia McKenna who's been devoted to the wellbeing of the big cats of Africa ever since she starred in *Born Free* with Elsa the lioness in the 1960s.

McKenna testimonial at her home.

VIRGINIA MCKENNA   I don't think anyone except someone with a sick or warped mind could call this kind of hunting sport and from the evidence that I have seen on your programme, it should be banned from this moment onwards.

Lions in shot.

ROGER COOK   South Africa again and more doomed lions. This time it's hunter Mossie Mostert who runs another outfit operating on the edge of the Kruger Park. He wants to sell our client one of his 86 caged animals for hunting including his rare white lions in 5 years' time when they've bred enough to spare.

White lions.

But it's in Kruger National Park, the world's best known conservation area that the King of the Beasts is quietly and secretly disappearing.

Cook looking at elephants.

In 3 days in Kruger, we've seen lots of wildlife but neither hide nor hair of a lion, the very symbol of this national park. One good reason perhaps why lions are less often seen than they used to be is that they're being lured across the border and into the sights of the canned hunters.

Taxidermists' operations.

ROGER COOK   It's easy to see why the pressure is on to provide big game hunters with a steady supply of prey – the Americans alone spend 110 million dollars a year in South Africa obtaining trophies like these and it's a market which is growing rapidly as the taxidermists of South Africa work round the clock to send their wealthy customers their bloody souvenirs.

Covert filming in McDonald's office as she counts her money.

TRACEY MCDONALD   So many are allowed to be exported because they feel that they're endangered, which is also a load of nonsense.

ROGER COOK   This is Tracey McDonald, who runs what she claims is one of the biggest hunting outfits in Southern Africa with her husband Sandy. Last year, she boasts her company arranged the shooting of more than a thousand animals but we've discovered many of the most profitable ones are actually stolen.

Once again, we pay a hefty deposit and, captured by our secret camera, she explains how the tourist and the South African government are being cheated as Kruger Park lions are stolen for canned hunting through the boundary fences.

TRACEY MCDONALD   You just dig a little bit under the fence and you leave her a little piece of rotten meat on that side and then you drag it with the blood running through and that lion picks that scent up so easy and it just comes through.

Back in the bush.

ROGER COOK   Stealing lions from Kruger these days is literally a pushbutton job. One, to turn off the electric fence and the other, to start the lion call tape on your ghetto blaster. It doesn't take long for the lions to answer the call and come right under the fence. And this is the fate a Kruger lion will face – death in the closely controlled-conditions of a canned hunt. Bruce Hamilton explains how the lioness met her end.

Lioness and cubs again.

BRUCE HAMILTON   The lioness had three cubs. We took her out of the camp that morning into a hundred hectare enclosure, which is not legal, and she was still running up and down the fence, she wouldn't leave the cubs even though a bait was used to try and lure her away from the fences so that . . . the hunter wouldn't see the fences and be caught up in the illusion.

Over shots of violent death of lioness:

ROGER COOK   Some illusion.

Gunshot.

BRUCE HAMILTON   Even though she wouldn't leave the fences, he still shot her. You could see the cubs on the other side of the fence but that didn't bother them. Even when the lioness was skinned and the milk was pouring out of her teats, it didn't bother the hunter nor the professional hunter that

351

she was still producing milk for those cubs and now they didn't have a
mother.

VIRGINIA MCKENNA   Just unbelievable isn't it really? To separate a lioness
from her cubs, to wound the animal so that she dies in agony; how anyone
could actually find pleasure in that kind of hunting so-called must be really
sick, that's all I can say.

Change of scene – hotels etc.

At lunch table with friends/targets.

ROGER COOK   In Barcelona we're about to meet José Iglesias and Luis
Gomez who think they're collecting 40,000 dollars from us for the illegal
gorilla hunt in Cameroon. All the animals they've offered us in perfect
English are protected by international law under what's called the CITES
convention.

   I think you should know something – I am a television reporter and you
have been offering us three animals, protected to shoot. We can shoot
gorillas pictured in this book which you've just shown me, the gorillas that
we could shoot, you're offering us jaguar, that's CITES too, that's illegal.
You've offered us tiger, you are offering us the opportunity to kill CITES
1 animals, this is illegal. Illegal animals to kill.

Gomez/Iglesias, rather surprised, forget how to speak English, mumble, rise to go;
Cook shows he's miked up.

ROGER COOK   And what's more, you speak perfectly good English. . . .
What's more, Mr Iglesias, I've been recording you speaking perfectly good
English on that microphone . . . Iglesias and Gomez beat a retreat but
they'll be hearing from the Spanish authorities now we've passed on a
dossier of their illegal hunting activities.

Change of scene – South Africa and a hunt – Cook in hunting gear.

ROGER COOK   The South African hunters think they are taking businessman
James Rogers, alias Roger Cook, for a ride. He's not meant to know this is
a canned hunt. In fact, we're conning the hunters by recording the event
for what we say is a vanity video. Wheezing and puffed up to play the part
of an incompetent and unfit hunter, in need of all the help he can get, and
easy prey for Mossie Mostert who owns the land and Sandy McDonald
who runs the hunt.

SANDY MCDONALD   It's not too bad once you're here, it's on the road you
know, it's pretty bad out there. Let's step inside, having something to drink
and go through a bit of a procedure here and what . . .

A park house, McDonald the 'gamekeeper' beside a stuffed lion.

Voice-over scenes in 'Gamekeeper' training room

ROGER COOK   They split the 18,000 dollars being paid for this one-hour expedition. No television programme has ever before got this far inside the secret and sordid world of canned hunting but first, a quick lesson in lion killing.

SANDY MCDONALD   Being a park lion, he's not too wary about humans, cars and that sort of stuff which means he's pretty relaxed, but once he's stood up we've got his attention, it's very important, the shot placement is very important, our first shot is the most important shot. After that we'll sort any problems if there are any. And what you've got to remember Mr Rogers is that we want to try and break a limb, that's the most important thing on any cat. Now he's got . . . just follow his leg up, two-thirds down, one-third up . . . is the vital spot and to break a leg. We really want to get him that, if it so happens that he'd be wounded, he's got one leg less which makes it a hell of a lot easier for us. It's easier on the dogs, it's easier on everything else. Now he'll have a bigger mane than this, maybe a bit longer this way than this one. So, it's important that mentally, you don't take the mane for his chest, remember that . . .

SANDY MCDONALD   . . . remember that his chest inside there, it's behind. All you need to do is when he's either looking straight at you, which is probably what he'll do, if you shoot him just under the chin here. Just shoot him in there . . . because he'll be looking down at us, because the grass is thick. It's hot, he's in a cool place. Side on, two-thirds down, one-third up, right on the shoulder blade. Smoke him in there and he'll bounce around and make a lot of noise and run off and die probably and they're not difficult animals to kill, they're soft skinned, they have a very highly developed nervous system which means that all the shock effect from the bullet is taken into their body and absorbed and it hurts them.

ROGER COOK   McDonald admits he's offering us a Kruger Park lion but he's not telling Mr Rogers what he told our undercover team earlier on.

Covert shots filmed earlier.

SANDY MCDONALD   It's a canned lion, make no mistake, but it's a very nice size but it's at a bait and it's going to be fairly easy for him to have a first shot at it.

Back to the main story and the hunting expedition.

ROGER COOK   Every part of the crooked business is recorded on tape as Mr Rogers' cameraman filmed their so-called client's expedition.

SANDY MCDONALD   What we'll do is we'll go to the camp and let your have a few shots at a target.

Cook does target practice – and he's good at it. They look at the target he's hit.

ROGER COOK   What you mean two went through there?

SANDY MCDONALD   Two went through there which is really good because you can . . .

Target practice over, the pretence of tracking a roaming wild animal resumes. Music.

The vehicles drive over the park, stopping every so often to find the spoor of the lion (!)

Covert shots filmed earlier.

SANDY MCDONALD   From our side it's all fixed, you guys . . . and I'll keep him happy, I know what to say at the right time and all the rest of it.

SANDY MCDONALD   Right, basically what's been happening is that, er, this area is adjacent to the Kruger National Park and what we have is a movement of usually old male lions that come out. Once they come in here, we keep them in by virtue of the fact that we have a pretty good bait out there and being an animal that is lazy by nature, he's going to stick around by the bait and this is a really good time to get him then because he's lying at the bait.

ROGER COOK   The conspiracy continues as we move closer to the lion now dazed by drugs and unable to escape.

Covert shots filmed earlier.

SANDY MCDONALD   I've tranquillised it, it's a hell of a nice lion . . . nobody will suspect a thing.

UNDERCOVER RESEARCHER   Right.

SANDY MCDONALD   We do a lot of them.

In the vehicles.

ROGER COOK   Out in the bush the hunters go through charade of tracking down the prey, although they know precisely where it is. All this is just for show.

They 'find' the lion. Cook's voice-over:

And here he is, after 20 minutes of circling the same small area of bush, we find our Kruger lion. Lured from the reserve with meat, then drugged, to give the hunter the chance to kill it at close range without the slightest risk to himself.

SANDY MCDONALD   (*instructs his client*) I want you to look at him through the scope. I want you to find his eyes. I want you to follow his neck down, then shoot him where the mane ends, on his shoulder. Shoot him and, take your time, do a good shot. Remember it's a lion. It's hot, he doesn't want to move away, but if we get out of sight, the wound is bad. You have to shoot him from here.

ROGER COOK   (*changing tone and confronting McDonald who for several minutes fails to understand what is going on . . .*) Well, let me tell you why I'm not going to shoot this lion, he doesn't stand a chance and you know he doesn't and I'm not a businessman, I'm a television reporter making a programme about canned hunts, and that's what this is, isn't it?

SANDY MCDONALD   There is your lion.

ROGER COOK   This is a canned hunt isn't it? I'm not shooting that lion, it doesn't stand a chance. It's been drugged, you told us earlier, you know it has. My colleagues are all from the same television company, let this sink in. This is a canned hunt, I am not shooting that lion, and neither are you. It doesn't stand a chance. It's been tranquillised. It's a lion that's come across or been baited across . . .

SANDY MCDONALD   (*his predicament has still not sunk in*) It has been baited.

ROGER COOK   . . . it's been baited across, from the National Park . . .

SANDY MCDONALD   Yes. Yes.

ROGER COOK   . . . So he actually belongs to somebody else.

SANDY MCDONALD   No, he belongs to here.

ROGER COOK   . . . and he's been baited and that's not ethical is it?

SANDY MCDONALD   No, that's ethical.

ROGER COOK   He's been darted, that's not ethical. He's been shot from a vehicle, that's not ethical.

SANDY MCDONALD   He's from the park.

Let us end here. . . .

ROGER COOK   No, we're not going by foot, we're turning round and going back, I'm paying for this. We're not shooting that lion. Caught red-handed McDonald pressured us to hand over our tapes, then, when we tried to leave the Mostert Farm with them, the mood turned ugly.

ROGER COOK   We found a road-block of heavily armed men, stopping us reaching the safety of the public highway.

Covert filming of armed thugs menacing Cook's party.

Even when the police arrived, they wouldn't let us go. Eventually the gate was opened, but the hunters made it very clear they still wanted our tapes of the canned hunt. During an hour of negotiation, we smuggled out the tapes, and got a stern warning from the police not to return.

Change of scene – Trafalgar Square, London

ROGER COOK   Back in Britain, we took our dossier on canned hunting to the South African High Commission. Our findings shocked the New Republic's Deputy High Commissioner.

DEPUTY HIGH COMMISSIONER – HAPPY MAHLANGU   Look, I'm really appalled, I'm really appalled that something like this is still going on in my country. I promise you, I'm saying to you after this I'm going to be talking to some people from the environment, in the ministry and make them aware of what you guys found out and ask them if they could look into this because, it must be stopped and it must be stopped immediately.

ROGER COOK   Sadly that will be too late to help our drugged canned lion. Before we left, the hunters told us he would only survive until the next wealthy foreigner came to take his life – for money.

Discussion

Critics say that *The Cook Report* over-dramatises mundane matters, goes for small-time, accessible crooks and doesn't understand the wider implications of its stories. These critics miss the point. Successful communication reflects the cultural values of those with whom you wish to communicate. Successful communication, transforms 'what you already know' by providing a new cast within a trusted format or genre just as the epic poem in the ancient world could be peopled with different warriors or lovers but deliver the same satisfactions because of its use of familiar techniques and its grounding in shared outlook. In other words, as a vehicle for popular investigative journalism, *The Cook Report* knows its audience. Yes, the topic is one that he can be sure the viewers will be in sympathy with, it is in no way counter-orthodox. A less conventional theme would be, as Ridley might say, how the CITES convention itself endangers the survival of the species, but a story based on that would be very complicated and although it might expand viewers' horizons, it might also come up against the communications difficulties identified above. The goal of this particular *Cook Report* is a lesser one, but it is well achieved: it demonstrates how regulations, international, national and local, are flouted by people prepared to plunder everybody's heritage for the sake of personal enrichment, and it does so very effectively. Villains have been nailed, their villainy evidenced and reported.

The programme performs another unusual task. In investigative journalism the gulf between what is aimed at the broadsheet market – serious investigations with public interest dimension – and what is aimed at the tabloid market – exposure journalism, is large. *The Cook Report* bridges the two by doing subjects of public interest in a popular format.

Notes

1 Ridley himself is not, as he admits (1996: 41), without a point of view; he argues that it is property rights that defend, rather than ruin, the environment, a view contrary to that held by many international and national agencies.
2 For his own gripping account of his life and adventures, see Cook, R. (1999) *Dangerous Ground*. London: HarperCollins.
3 Various conversations over 1998 with David Mannion, former editor of *The Cook Report*.

Bibliography

Anderson, A. (1997) *Media Culture and the Environment*. London: UCL.
Beckett, A. (1995) Looking for Mr Big. *Independent on Sunday*, 21 May 1995.

Bell, A. (1991) *The Language of News Media*. Oxford: Blackwell.

Bell, A. (1994) Climate of opinion: public and media discourse on the global environment. *Discourse and Society*, 5 (1): 33–63.

Brosius, H. and Kepplinger, H. (1990) The agenda setting function of television news. *Communication Research*. 17 (2): 183–211.

Central Television (1997) 'Roger Cook'. Briefing sheet supplied by Central Television Department of Current Affairs, June 1997.

Central Television (1997a) 'Making a Killing', *The Cook Report*. Nottingham: Carlton Central Television.

Central Television (1997b) *Putting the Record Straight*. Nottingham: Carlton Central Television.

Channel 4 (1994) 'J'accuse the National Trust', *Without Walls* (reporter: Stephen Bayley). London: Fulmar for C4 TV.

Cook, R. (1997) *The Cook Report*. Talk to students on the MA Investigative Journalism course at Nottingham Trent University, 30 October 1997.

Cook, R. (1999) Interview with Hugo de Burgh, 14 June 1999.

Grundy, R. (1996) *How Do They Do That?* London: Environmental Investigation Agency.

Hornig, S. (1992) Framing risk: audience and reader factors. *Journalism Quarterly*, 69 (3).

Kasun, J. (1988) *The War against Population*. San Francisco: Ignatius.

Lowe, P. *et al.* (1984) Bad news and good news: environmental politics and mass media. *Sociological Review*, 32: 75–90.

McQuail, D. and Windahl, S. (1981) *Communication Models*. London: Longman.

Milne, S. (1995) *The Enemy Within: The Secret War Against the Miners*. London: Pan.

Parsons, W. (1995) *Public Policy: An Introduction to the Theory and Practice of Policy Analysis*. Aldershot: Edward Elgar.

Ridley, M. (1995) *Down to Earth I: Combating Environmental Myths*. London: Institute of Economic Affairs.

Ridley, M. (1996) *Down to Earth II: Combating Environmental Myths*. London: Institute of Economic Affairs.

Shoemaker, P. (1996) *Mediating the Message*. White Plains: Longman.

Simon, J. (1992) *Population and Development in Poor Countries*. Princeton: University of Princeton Press.

Tate, T. (1997) The making of *Laogai*. Talk to students of the MA Investigative Journalism course at Nottingham Trent University, 6 November 1997.

Upshon, L. (1997) Interview with Hugo de Burgh, 10 June 1997.

Further reading

Anderson, A. (1997) *Media Culture and the Environment*. London: UCL.

21

GRAVE-DIGGING

The case of 'the Cossacks'

Hugo de Burgh

Background

From 1989 to 1993 a historical investigation became news in tabloid and broadsheet media alike as argument raged over the merits of the combatants in a struggle over who might have done what over a few days in 1945. The case of 'the Cossacks' has been perhaps the single most prominent example of historical investigation to be turned into journalism, not only in the acres of newsprint devoted to the story and based upon the several books on the subject but also in a programme in the BBC historical series, *Timewatch*. We will come to the part played by *Timewatch*[1] shortly; first, the background.

A month after the Second World War ended in May 1945, British troops in occupied Austria appear to have contravened orders and deported large numbers of defenceless people to their enemies for certain suffering and likely death. The case has been much discussed in the British, and latterly the Russian and North American press, ever since a book by Nicholas Bethell was published in 1974, *The Last Secret*. The case achieved international prominence when a libel action was brought in 1989 by a British retired officer who had been accused of ordering the deportation. Exactly why it was done and who was responsible has not been finally established. However, many influential and well-known people in Britain have been involved in the controversy, and there have been charges of conspiracy to suppress the evidence as well as charges against the integrity of both sides.

The case is interesting to journalists for the following reasons. It is generally agreed that an injustice was done to many thousands of people in May 1945 (the story is told below) and thus there is, to any journalist, a case worth investigating. When it is argued that the injustice was committed against the express orders of the highest authority, the case becomes intriguing. The difficulties of establishing the truth because of the passage of time, the apparent evasiveness of some of those in a position to help, the death of witnesses, the complexity of the written records and the strong emotions conjured up by the story are all stimulating to the hunter.

The investigation of the incident was initially carried out primarily by two writers, Nicholas Bethell and Nikolai Tolstoy, and provides an ideal illustration of the problems of complex data trawling in several countries' archives and using several languages. Problems of obtaining evidence from public bodies appear to have been exacerbated through intentional obstruction and, it is claimed, illustrate how well-connected parties can obfuscate the work of the researcher and how official files can be weeded before being put in the records (Faulkner, 1998).

At the time of initial research, Russian and some German archives were not accessible; they now are and are claimed to throw new light upon the case (Tolstoy, 1997); this may demonstrate how research interpretations can be stymied because of partial sourcing. The arguments over the libel case have already shown how important access to documents at the right time can be in determining judgement (Mitchell, 1997: Appendix A).

Both writers have come up against opposition merely for tackling the study, and Tolstoy has been vilified. Tolstoy's involvement in the case drew him into a series of court actions, the first of which bankrupted him, and the subsequent ones have been draining without achieving any satisfactory result (to him). The case is widely thought to have illustrated flaws in the British legal system, in particular Britain's notorious libel laws. Aspects of it have also made legal history.

The story

In May 1945, after the total German surrender, British troops occupied much of what is now Austria. There was no more fighting, but there were considerable problems involved in keeping the peace and ensuring communications and supply of necessities to the population.

Western Europe was awash with refugees, known then as Displaced Persons, who were put into Displaced Persons Camps for screening, that is checking for war criminals or potential sources of information. Refugees included the millions of slave labourers brought to Germany by the fallen government; members of minorities persecuted in Poland and other countries of Eastern Europe; escaped prisoners of every variety; German colonists in flight from revenge; participants in the ill-fated armies of liberation that had sought to free the East from the Soviets but found themselves exploited by the Germans; families and camp-followers who joined the fleeing German armies in their stampede West.

At a meeting at Yalta between Stalin, Roosevelt and Churchill in 1945 it had been agreed that former Soviet citizens among these should be repatriated. However, down in the camps it was not always easy to ascertain who was a former Soviet citizen; moreover it was generally recognised by the Allies that anyone so deported might be liquidated.

In these circumstances, Harold Alexander, Allied Commander in Chief in

Italy, in concert with Prime Minister Winston Churchill, decided that the refugees should not be deported. This was particularly pertinent in Austria, where British troops looked after large numbers of refugees not very far from the border with the Soviet occupied zone. They tend, and tended, to be referred to as 'the Cossacks', although actually how many were Cossacks, recruited by the Germans in an anti-Soviet crusade, as opposed to other kinds of refugees is unclear. Over half of them were women and small children and most were easily identifiable as never having been Soviet citizens. Many were expecting to be able to emigrate to Canada or Argentina while others waited clearance to return to their homes in France or Germany. In these circumstances, and because of deteriorating relations with the Soviets, Alexander and Eisenhower, the Supreme Commander, agreed that the refugees should be moved further from the Soviet border. This was a concrete decision such that an allocation of resources was made and 800 trucks were supplied.

These facts were well known to the officers of the British army of occupation, although in the 1980s and 1990s it was to be suggested that this was not so. In May 1945, very shortly after Alexander's order had been issued and those vehicles been released to enable the refugees to be transported to safety, an operation began to hand over the refugees to the Soviet side. US troops sent by General Patten to protect the refugees were rejected by the British. The vehicles obtained for their release were returned to sender. The question that has exercised researchers since is why, and on whose initiative was this action carried out.

It could be circumvented. For example, the Sixth Armoured Division under General Murray oversaw around 50,000 Cossack refugees in the Drau Valley, of whom at least 11,000 were old, women or children. Once Murray's officers knew that force was about to be used on the refugees some of them warned them to flee (de Burgh 1995).[2] Murray himself remonstrated with the command, on the grounds that many of the refugees were not Soviet citizens, but he was overruled. There was, therefore, an impetus behind the initiative that would not be gainsaid. Many refugees were savagely beaten by British troops before they could be forced over the border to the Soviet side where whips and bullets were ready for them.

What has intrigued researchers is that the person or persons responsible not only deliberately disobeyed the instructions of the Commander in Chief but also quashed requests by senior officers that the task be reconsidered, ignored the well-known fact that many of these people were not appropriate for repatriation, and turned a blind eye to the known fate that would befall them. Malice of this kind seems implausible, so that commentators have proposed a 'banality of evil' explanation – that it suited the career aspirations of an officer and an official so well that they were prepared to contradict the Commander in Chief.

While Bethell's book apportioned no blame, elsewhere it was suggested that Brigadier Toby Low (Lord Aldington from 1962) had been involved;

subsequent publications with which Tolstoy was concerned went further and suggested that Low, who would shortly leave the army to fight a parliamentary seat, was keener to please his political patron than his Commander in Chief. His party patron was Harold Macmillan, then Political Adviser at the Allied HQ for the area, and an important politician whose influence would presumably be useful to Low, just starting out in politics. Macmillan would later be British Prime Minister.

If this is to be believed, then some motivation has to be ascribed to Macmillan; thus far Tolstoy has not convinced many that he has successfully explained this motivation. Unfortunately those who object to Tolstoy's view (Horne, 1998; Johnson, 1990) have not themselves come up with a satisfactory attribution of responsibility or explanation of motive.

Timeline of story and legal case

1945   In May 1945 an officer or officers in the British army of occupation in Austria, apparently contradicting written orders from superiors, initiates an operation, grossly inhumane, that results in the savage treatment and/or murder by Russians and Yugoslavs of many refugees under British protection.

1957   Polish historian Josef Mackiewicz publishes *Kontra*, an account of a brutal handover of Cossacks by British troops. Nikolai Krasnov, great-nephew of Don Ataman Krasnov, is released from prison in the Soviet Union and publishes *Hezabyvaemoe* [The Unforgettable].

1962   Ataman of the Kuban Cossacks Vyacheslav Naumenko publishes Volume 1 of *Velikoye Predatelstvo* [The Great Betrayal]; the second volume is issued in 1970.

Toby Low is created Lord Aldington.

1973   US writer Julius Epstein publishes *Operation Keelhaul* based on US documents of the case.

The British Public Record Office receives the files for 1945 from the Foreign Office and War Office, and makes them available.

1974   Lord Bethell publishes *The Last Secret*.

1977   Count Tolstoy publishes *Victims of Yalta*.

1978   Tolstoy discovers that relevant UK Foreign Office files have been destroyed; obtains duplicates from Washington.

1981   Aldington claims he left Austria on 25 May 1945.

1985   Tolstoy publishes *The Minister and the Massacres*.

Nigel Watts, for reasons not connected with the case, publishes a pamphlet critical of Lord Aldington. *Inter alia*, it refers to Aldington as the officer responsible for the infamous initiatives of May 1945. He had consulted Tolstoy on the detail of the case.

Lord Aldington brings an action for libel against Watts. Tolstoy, sure of his case, asks to be included in the indictment.

1987–8   Aldington prepares his action; his costs, it emerges, are to be underwritten by the Sun Alliance Insurance Company; he gets access to files denied to Tolstoy.

1989   Main trial from 2 October to 30 November; Tolstoy found culpable and Aldington awarded damages and costs totalling £1.5 million, the largest ever libel award.

1990   Tolstoy appeals; Aldington proposes the appeal be subject to Tolstoy proving he has funds to pay costs; Registrars of the Court of Appeal reject this; Aldington appeals against this decision and wins; Tolstoy is required to deposit £124,900 which he cannot do; appeal dismissed. Tolstoy declared bankrupt.

In Strasbourg Tolstoy appeals to the European Court of Human Rights that the award to Aldington violated his rights to freedom of expression under Article 10 of the Convention.

1991   The BBC makes a film in the *Timewatch* series, 'A British Betrayal'. Before it can be released, Lord Aldington writes to the BBC 'reserving the right to sue on the grounds that it is libellous'. BBC goes ahead and shows the programme (once).

An injunction is taken out prohibiting Tolstoy from speaking publicly or writing about the case.

1993   Tolstoy applies to the Court of Appeal for leave to adduce new evidence. Application rejected.

1994   Tolstoy issues a writ against Aldington in the High Court, applying for an order to set aside the 1989 judgement on the grounds of fraud.

Mr Justice Collins strikes out the writ as abuse of process. He then, in a decision which made legal history, orders Tolstoy's *pro bono* lawyers to pay 60 per cent of Aldington's costs, thus effectively ensuring that Tolstoy will be unable ever to find lawyers to help him again.

In Strasbourg the European Court of Human Rights declares that the award to Aldington violated Tolstoy's rights to freedom of expression under Article 10 of the Convention.

1996   In February Tolstoy attempts to appeal the High Court judgement. Refused leave to appeal.

The data sources used by researchers

From 1957 to 1970 several memoirs of the events were published in Russian, and one in Polish. German survivors of the war were also writing their memoirs, and these included those who had served with the so-called Army of Liberation. For those interested in the case and with facility in those languages (which both Bethell and Tolstoy have) there was a good deal of raw material already available on the case in general.

However, as interest began to focus more and more on the responsibility and the motivation for the initiative, and once Bethell and Tolstoy had realised how orders had been ignored that the initiative might be taken, then the data sources which mattered were those of the Allied forces. Details of these sources may be found in the references in Tolstoy's books, and a discussion of them, and of those which mysteriously disappeared when needed in evidence during the 1989 trial, are described in the appendices to Mitchell (1997).

The extraordinary story of how an ostensibly impartial inquiry was undertaken into the issues raised by Tolstoy (the Cowgill Report); of how Lord Aldington obtained special help over the documents from party political contacts, help that was denied Tolstoy; of how the Foreign and Commonwealth Office lost files when they were most needed and then found them when it was too late is described elsewhere, particularly in Mitchell (1997).

If Aldington was indeed the officer responsible then Tolstoy must prove that he retained his command, Brigadier General Staff for V Corps, on the days when certain orders were given. Two key orders were given pertaining to the operation on the afternoon of 22 May and on 23 May, and they were given on the authority of the Brigadier General Staff for V Corps. Although on earlier occasions Aldington had said he had left Austria on 25 May, by the time of the trial he was saying that he had left before the fatal order of 22 May, so that he could not have been responsible for it (the military title would have applied to his successor), and that he had left before a meeting at which it was decided to shoot at those resisting deportation.

These matters might have been cleared up had it been possible for anyone to get access to eight hour's tape-recordings of interviews Aldington undertook for the Imperial War Museum in 1990. When an attempt was made to gain access to them it was found that only Aldington could give permission, which he refused with the comment that 'I do not want to complicate affairs by having on record for the public any statements different from those I made on oath in the courts'.[3] Although he is dead his family continue the embargo.

Because of the absence of documentation and the vagueness with which those involved have answered questions about dates, it has not been possible to finalise this issue. Tolstoy has not proved his case.

The work of investigation

Why did these two men undertake this investigation? For many years after the Second World War the full extent of what the Germans did to their subject peoples, and in particular to minorities, was not generally or fully understood. Even once it was understood, it was not universally agreed that all those involved in the vast project of cruelty should be held to account or that it was necessary to put resources into finding them. The competitive spirit of the Cold War encouraged the Allies not to do anything that would besmirch the Allied side. Thus, war criminals from Germany or those countries now part of 'the West' who had worked with the Germans were often left in peace. The goodness attributed to the Allied cause in the Second World War was now transferred to the 'West' in the Cold War. To suggest otherwise could at times be dangerous, as the McCarthy period in the USA illustrates.

These factors may account for the failure to question how the Allies found it expedient to cooperate with criminals from among their former enemies, or indeed to question the Allies' own conduct during the Second World War. Times change. The Case of the Cossacks was always known to enough people, and enough people who felt ashamed, that it was never forgotten. They believed that this was 'Britain's war crime' and, while it might appear insignificant beside the horrors inflicted by the Germans, it should not be allowed to be forgotten.[4] If there be a guilty party then he must be revealed so that justice may be seen to be done, even over 50 years after the crime. There were survivors who longed for their loved ones' sufferings to be recognised and for some explanation of the deed.

Bethell was one of those who had always been aware of the case and who directed his attention to the documents dealing with the place and the period as soon as they were made available in the Public Record Office. Tolstoy, an established historian before becoming a public figure as a result of this case, was more emotionally involved with the story. Having been brought up in part in the White Russian émigré community in England, he was familiar with the tale from an early age. Furthermore, one of his childhood heroes, Ataman Krasnov,[5] was killed as a result of the deportations. Tolstoy wanted to find an explanation for this, and his sense of chivalry revolted against the manner of his hero's treatment (Norman, 1990).

In making what Aldington has argued is an unjust and unsubstantiated allegation that has besmirched his reputation, Tolstoy has inflicted tribulations upon himself too. After losing the 1989 libel case his supporters set up a Forced Repatriation Defence Fund (Norton-Taylor, 1990) to enable him to appeal. However, the trial judge, Mr Justice Michael Davies, froze that fund. This meant that in future he would not be able to pay lawyers and he at first decided to conduct his own case; when, in 1994, in a further action, lawyers agreed to conduct his case *pro bono*, Mr Justice Collins ruled that those lawyers should pay 60 per cent of the costs of the other party's lawyers, in effect fining them heavily for helping Tolstoy. It is not perhaps surprising that Tolstoy believes that every opportunity is being taken by highly prejudiced judges to make it impossible for him to make his case.

The *Timewatch* documentary

Timewatch is the BBC's historical strand, with a remit 'to cover, in a succession of one-off, predominantly 50-minute films on BBC2, historical issues, ideas and stories from twentieth and pre-twentieth century history'. Its objectives are to 'excite the viewer about pre-twentieth century history and show the resonance of the distant past to today' as well as to ignite debate, as in its programmes about Second World War bombing or the history of immigration (BBC, 1999). Its rival is Channel 4's *Secret History* strand.

'A British Betrayal' is a good example of British documentary art. Not only does *Timewatch* here tell the story clearly and systematically, but it does so with well-selected footage used without redundancy. It contains archive material that either shows the story as it unfolds or illustrates excellently the tenor of the times.

It starts – and this assertion is repeated towards the end – by stating that the libel trial completely vindicated Lord Aldington, but that this does not mean that interest in the case itself is reduced. Late in the programme it notes that Tolstoy's defeat was based upon his having made a mistake in the date of Aldington's departure from Austria, and therefore wrongly attributing blame. It nowhere mentions the controversy surrounding that date, or the fact that Aldington is alleged to have changed his mind about it. In this sense the programme can be said to accept the verdict of the libel trial, namely, that Aldington was not to blame. It nowhere suggests that the trial was anything but fair.

Aldington's position is put by his allies and associates, Brigadiers Tryon-Wilson and Cowgill. Cowgill's claims of operational necessity are given due space and respect. Sir Charles Villiers, a partisan specialist in the Second World War and later a very distinguished industrialist and writer, can also be said to be on the Aldington 'side' in the sense that he explains the initiative in terms of the prevailing political and military climate. He does not, however, subscribe to the view that the refugees were deported out of fear of imminent war with Tito's Yugoslavia, one of the arguments in defence of the initiative.

While being scrupulously polite to the Aldington case therefore, the producers do not in any way disguise the belief that the initiative was shameful and not worthy of an army that had claimed to be on the side of truth and justice. An array of testimonials attest to the dishonesty practised on the refugees in arranging their deportation and the brutality with which it was executed. British officers of different ranks and backgrounds and regiments admit their part, supporting the evidence of survivors. One, a mature woman from Scotland, had been in Auschwitz concentration camp as a young Polish girl. Getting away during the German collapse, the 12-year-old joined herself to some Cossacks and their families for safety but found herself being beaten and shot at by British troops as they tried to thrust them over the border towards their would-be executioners. A very moving witness, she was one of the few who escaped in the chaos as the troops coerced the refugees into accepting deportation.

Everything is done by the programme makers to avoid legal action, and to be impartial in the manner required by the *BBC Producers' Guidelines* (BBC, 1996). For example, in defence of the initiative it has often been said that there was chaos in Austria at that time, or that the British authorities were under extreme physical, political and administrative pressure. Although these claims are not always borne out by the recollections of British survivors (de Burgh, 1995), the programme nevertheless repeats them, presumably in an attempt to be fair to those responsible for the initiative. Moreover the British troops are put in as favourable a light as possible; the stress some of them felt at having to comply with orders requiring them to be dishonest and brutal is emphasised. One officer tells how he wrote a critical report of the proceedings, mentioning the distaste his soldiers had for them, which he was ordered to repudiate in a later report (Nicholson, speaking in BBC, 1991), reminding the viewer that not all documents are factual, even if they are old and official.

The question of responsibility is examined carefully. No explanation is presented as to how it was that clear policies by superiors Churchill and Alexander should have been ignored at the executive level. British officers on the ground 'knew there was something wrong . . . many of them had no connection with Russia' in the case of the identifiable Cossack units (Davies, in BBC, 1991); about a thousand separately encamped Germans were handed to the Russians (about 80 per cent allegedly died in slave labour) following an order of 24 May which included Germans and camp followers (i.e. women, children, the elderly) although it was known to all the British that they were not Soviets; the Yugoslavs deported against precise orders from Prime Minister Churchill appear to have been butchered as they anticipated and as their British guards expected. The man who negotiated with the British and then organised the mass slaughter is interviewed arrestingly, as is one of the British officers who, with repugnance, lied to them so that they could be tricked into deportation (Nicholson, speaking in BBC, 1991). The mass graves are found and filmed. Official documents, location shots and primary testimony are woven together well to create a convincing case.

No one is named a war criminal, nor is anything negative attributed to any named person, with the exception of the Yugoslav officer who condemns himself. The producers have been extremely careful to obey the BBC's guidelines which stipulate, 'We must not use language inadvertently so as to suggest value judgements, commitment or lack of objectivity' (BBC, 1996: 7).

Lord Aldington is himself treated with kid gloves. He is introduced as 'a bright young officer who, at 30 years of age, was the second youngest Brigadier in the army' (BBC, 1991). When, later in the programme, there is a description of the deception practised upon the women and children to ensure that they also be handed over, the narrator gives Aldington's own justification:

> Despite the fact that those civilians were not told where they were going, Brigadier Low (now Lord Aldington) said at the libel trial that he felt that he had probably let them accompany the men out of compassion.
>
> (Commentary, BBC, 1991)

The treatment is not at all sensationalist, yet is sensational in the sense that its witnesses are moving – those who suffered as well as those who are ashamed of carrying out the orders which caused them to suffer. What is telling is the failure of the more senior officers, the decision-makers of the time or their defendants, to acknowledge any kind of responsibility or even admit the enormity of what was done, although this may be a producer's device.

The impartial viewer would, I believe, come away with the strong belief that a wrong was done and that someone somewhere is not coming clean. The fact that the accusations have not stood up to scrutiny does not mean that there is no villain, or villains. Although describing Tolstoy as discredited, in allowing him to explain why the case matters the producers demonstrate that this is an important story: 'I'm not saying that what I say is the truth, but if somebody doesn't fight for the truth to be investigated and recognised, and that's what I want, terrible events like this will be repeated' (Tolstoy in BBC, 1991). Ruthless men, in other words, must know that they will be held accountable for their actions even 50 years later; the rules of decency apply just as much to the victors as to the vanquished; the same type of criminal person can appear in every society if he be but given the opportunity or if he thinks he will not be found out; the representation of unbesmirched British honour must not be defended with lies and evasions; in this case ideals such as justice and compassion were betrayed and it is necessary to know why.

Discussion

For British society, the most immediate lessons of this case have been legal ones. In various legal actions to which he was party, Tolstoy was allegedly treated without the respect accorded to Aldington, a disrespect amounting to partiality. There were failures to take account of evidence, failure to acknowledge the damage caused to Tolstoy's side by the 'disappearance' of evidence and the failure to keep (or supply) transcripts. The size of the award against Tolstoy was extreme; at the time it was the largest ever such award. It was unfair in that it was clearly calculated to destroy Tolstoy; Lord Aldington's case was being underwritten by the Sun Alliance Insurance Company (an interesting issue in itself, but one mainly for the shareholders of that company).

At a conference of lawyers and senior journalists in September 1990 the Tolstoy–Aldington case was cited as demonstrating that 'the present legal arrangements [in libel cases] were unreliable in the extreme and should be reformed' (Norton-Taylor, 1990). Charles Gray QC, Aldington's barrister when he won £1.5 million damages from Tolstoy, stated that he believed juries should not be used at all in libel trials. Another leading lawyer, Michael Beloff, 'called for a curtailment of judges' powers to ban reports of court proceedings, powers which were unknown in America or continental Europe' (Norton-Taylor, 1990).

There were alleged obstructions to Tolstoy's attempts to appeal which have been detailed above. The ban on discussion of the case has also excited interest. As a consequence of a decision of the Court of Appeal in 1987, it is held that an injunction 'against one is for all' (Welsh and Greenwood, 1999). The injunction put upon Tolstoy in 1989 not to disseminate his views was, after 1991, regarded by the BBC as extending to 'A British Betrayal', screening of which would apparently be in contempt of court; when the Series Editor (and Producer of 'A British Betrayal') was invited to speak about the case to students he regretted that he could not, because of the injunction. Moreover it is technically contempt of court for Tolstoy to carry out research and supply information to the media.

There are more general lessons from the case. A few years ago, before the Birmingham Six, Guildford Four, Scott Inquiry and so on, it was hardly credible to British people, first that connivance in covering up could be possible, and second that judges could be so biased, ignorant and wrong. The Tolstoy libel case has probably further undermined faith in the system. It has also focused attention on the cavalier way in which elected politicians can deal with public records in Britain, and on the need for rules and systems to prevent this. Many people regretted that the issue came to light because of how it reflected upon British chivalry, and some allowed their regret to cloud their sense of justice; others gloried in the undermining of what they saw as a nonsensical myth. Neither attitude is very laudable. However, they do point up the emotions aroused and the issues raised by the investigation of history. Historians are forever reinterpreting history, knowing that each period's history is influenced by the passions, prejudices, policies and limitations of its time. They can bring to bear new evidence, new techniques and new attitudes. They are not necessarily aiming at a permanent solution, but may be trying to challenge the prevailing interpretation because that is a worthwhile contribution to debate in itself. Not all historical reinterpretation will be of immediate influence upon us; Joseph Needham's empirical researches for Science and Civilisation in China have both changed our understanding of science and trade history and challenged our Eurocentrism, but it may take generations for these to permeate daily life. Emmanuel Todd's theories of development and political process may be in the same category. Of more immediate relevance, in 1999 an amateur Irish historian produced a startling piece of research, the evidence of which was meticulously transparent and respectfully applauded in reviews; he demonstrated from the historical evidence that the image of Oliver Cromwell as the butcher of Drogheda, an image so powerful in Irish history as to have been almost a justification in itself for the existence of nationalist terrorism, is a myth. Moreover, it was a myth invented intentionally by an identifiable individual in the nineteenth century, whose ghost (we must suppose) has since had the satisfaction of seeing the nonsensc he created being repeated by eminent historians and political propagandists alike.[6] That is the rethinking of history with immediate relevance.

Investigative journalists are interested in the here and now of the past. The investment of time and resources is such that they will usually select topics which they believe will have, or can be made to have, wide general interest, perhaps a mass audience. They can appeal to the thrill of dark secrets; to the sense of triumph which comes from overturning assumptions. They can make use of availability of documents earlier kept classified or the accessibility of people who, either because circumstances have changed or because they themselves have changed, are willing to talk. They can build on memories kept alive by resentments and anguish.

The story of the Cossacks did all this. Part of its fascination is that guilt has not been finally ascribed.

Notes

1 Laurence Rees, editor of *Timewatch*, was not able to make himself available to discuss his team's work, hence the limited information on *Timewatch* itself. Nevertheless it seemed to me that the story has been so very prominent, and has so many aspects of interest to investigators, as to be the obvious example.
2 John de Burgh MC was a young officer of the Ayrshire Yeomanry, recently recovered from wounds sustained at Monte Cassino, and a very fine horseman. As such he had an immediate bond with the Cossacks and German cavalrymen camped around the Drau Valley with their families. They raced, played bareback games and foraged for food over several months. He was called in one day by his Commanding Officer and told that they would soon have to shift the refugees, who were of course to be told nothing.

> It was obvious that they were to be forced, and forced into the hands of the Russians. There was only one thing to do, and I was pretty sure that this was what General Murray expected, too. I immediately mounted and rode down the valley to our friends. Women in the fields waved at me and the children ran beside me.
> I was at the senior officer's tent at about 2 in the afternoon. I said to him 'at dawn tomorrow troops will arrive to move you'. He asked me 'to where?' you see they thought they were going to England or Australia. I said 'to where you do not want to go'. He took my hand and he looked into my face for a few minutes. I remember it very well. He said to me. 'Thank you Mr de Burgh. We will get to work'. As I rode back the mothers were calling their children in. The next morning we paraded early and arrived at the camp to carry out the orders, but the camp was empty.
> (de Burgh, 1995)

3 Aldington, Lord (1993) Letter to Mrs Margaret Brooks, Imperial War Museum, 26 August 1993.
4 I believe that this is a reasonable summary of the position of some of Tolstoy's partisans, including Sir Bernard Braine, Viscount Cranbourne, Nigel Nicolson, Chapman Pincher, Alexander Solzhenitsyn and Roger Scruton.
5 Krasnov was a Russian soldier who held out against the Bolsheviks during the Civil War of 1917–1920; after the White defeat he fled to France. Following the German invasion of the Soviet Union he helped inspire an Army of Liberation that was intended to free Russia initially from the Communists, and then from the Nazis. Krasnov was one of those in the Displaced Persons camps who would be handed over and killed.
6 Doubtless this subject will be revisited, but in the meantime Tom Reilly (1999) seems to have the best of it. See also R. Dudley-Edwards (1999).

Bibliography

BBC (1991) 'A British Betrayal', *Timewatch* (Producer: Laurence Rees). London: BBC.

BBC (1996) *Producers' Guidelines*. London: BBC.

BBC (1999) 'Timewatch Remit'. Notes supplied by *Timewatch* office.

Bethell, N. (1974) *The Last Secret*. London: André Deutsch.

Booker, C. (1997) *A Looking Glass War*. London: Duckworth.

de Burgh, J. (1995) interview with Hugo de Burgh at Oldtown, Naas, 12 May 1995.

Dudley-Edwards, R. (1999) The Good Soldier. *Sunday Times*, 23 May 1999.

Faulkner, R. (1998) Tolstoy Pamphlet. On the internet at www.tolstoy.co.uk.

Horne, A. (1988) *Macmillan, Volume 1: 1894–1956*. London: Macmillan.

Horne, A. (1998) Letter to the *Times*, 30 October 1998.

Johnson, D. (1990) A vindication that came too late. *Times*, 19 October 1990.

Mitchell, I. (1997) *The Cost of a Reputation*. Lagavulin: Topical.

Needham, J. with Ling, W. (1954) *Science and Civilisation in China*. Cambridge: Cambridge University Press.

Norman, M. (1990) 'I loved the romance of the Tolstoys': Count Nikolai Tolstoy: a childhood. *Times*, 11 August 1990.

Norton-Taylor, R. (1990) Tolstoy conducts his own libel appeal. *Guardian*, 11 January 1990.

Rayment, T. (1996) The massacre and the ministers. *Sunday Times*, 7 April 1996: 2.

Reilly, T. (1999) *Cromwell: An Honourable Enemy*. Dublin: Brandon.

Todd, E. (1987) *The Causes of Progress*. Oxford: Blackwell.

Tolstoy, N. (1977) *Victims of Yalta*. London: Hodder and Stoughton.

Tolstoy, N. (1986) *The Minister and the Massacres*. London: Century.

Tolstoy, N. (1997) Investigating the forced repatriation of the Cossacks. Talk given to the students of the MA Investigative Journalism course at Nottingham Trent University, 13 November 1997. Tolstoy@enterprise.net OR http://www.uvsc.edu.tolstoy.

Welsh, T. and Greenwood, W. (1999) *McNae's Essential Law for Journalists*. London: Butterworths.

Further reading

Mitchell, I. (1997) *The Cost of a Reputation*. Lagavulin: Topical.

Rayment, T. (1996) The Massacre and the Ministers. *Sunday Times*, 7 April 1996.

22

INTERFERING WITH FOREIGNERS

An example from *First Tuesday*

Hugo de Burgh

The idea of the universal journalist

Anglophone journalists tend to believe that there are only two types of journalism, good and bad. Thus, David Randall:

> There is no such thing as Western journalism . . . there is only good and bad journalism. Each culture may have its own traditions, each language a different voice. But among good journalists the world over, what joins them is more significant than what separates them . . . Good journalists, universally, agree on their role.
>
> (Randall, 1996: 2)

Journalists from cultures that lack some of the underpinnings of Anglophone journalism – journalists from African or Asian countries, for example, where the legal, cultural and political premises can be different – often agree that they are underdeveloped, and make efforts to conform to Anglophone norms (Golding, 1977). Journalists in countries as diverse from each other and from the Anglophone world as Italy, Turkey and Germany have waged heroic struggles to have this vision of journalism accepted. The key tenets (after Allan, 1997) of this vision are as follows:

- Objective reality exists out there to be apprehended and reflected by journalists, and it is the relationship of the journalist to this objective reality – in which relationship he or she applies certain principles – that is the touchstone of being a *real* journalist rather than stooge, PR person or partisan.
- Journalists who do not behave as journalists should are not yet up to the mark, or are perverted by ideology, usually forced upon unwilling journalists by politicians.

- What Anglophone journalists adhere to is not, they believe, an ideology, but a group of tenets that reflect the essence of journalism. The question here begged, however, is whether there exist 'facts', or 'objective reality'. Is there such a thing, or does reality depend upon the observer? In journalism, as in academia today, not everyone agrees. What is agreed in journalism studies is that the media prioritise different aspects of reality, depending upon:

    - who owns them (the *Sun*, a British tabloid with the largest circulation in Europe and a very distinct set of priorities, is a product of Rupert Murdoch's particular genius)
    - the political system surrounding them (compare China with the US)
    - the audience for which journalists mediate, the expectations of which may be different, and their own education and social background
    - the resources currently available from camera teams to information sources
    - the news context, i.e. what stories are thought necessary to provide a good mix that particular day, how often similar stories have appeared, etc.

If all these are influences upon what bits of reality become news, then the ideal of the universal journalist as impartial and disinterested truth-finder can seem compromised.

The organisation of the global media

It has often been observed that the world's principal suppliers of news, the news agencies, and the main buyers of news are Anglophone corporations and that this gives an Anglophone bias to the selection and depiction of events.[1] Not only do the stringers and agents on the ground, the ultimate sources for news, strain to sell to their masters what their masters will perceive to be news but the editors and schedulers gatekeep the information received; the significance of this system in political and cultural life is debated and the evidence is contradictory (Tracey, 1985: 30–1).

The news agencies are the wholesalers of the world media; suppliers such as CNNI, BSkyB, Fox, StarTV and BBC World Service Television (WSTV) are the retailers. Boyd-Barrett (1997) argues that, for all of them, Anglophone definitions of what constitutes news are paramount; that the news provided originates in the Anglophone capitals and responds first to their own rich domestic markets. News aside, that the world market in entertainment provision is also predominantly Anglophone has been much observed (Tomlinson, 1997: 134ff and 143ff), as is the fact that the Anglophone countries are virtually impervious to non-Anglophone cultural products (Tracey, 1985: 30).

Going further, Chambers and Tinckell (1998: 15) suggest that the so-called global media are agents of Anglophone values which privilege norms of 'competitive individualism, *laisser faire* capitalism, parliamentary democracy, consumerism'. They see the presentation of the English language as international as a further feature of Anglophone dominance. People are, they suggest, defined according to their relationship to Anglophoneness. Those who are not quite 'wasp', but nearly, are 'subalterns', that is the English-speaking Irish or Indians or Jews, compared to the real Anglophones who are Australians, Americans and English.[2] Their assertions are complemented by a number studies (Smith, 1980).

Concern about this cultural imperialism transmitted by the media has been expressed regularly over the past 30 or more years. In the 1970s it was identified in the promotion by UNESCO of the idea of a 'New World Information Order' that would provide more impartial (or more positive?) information on non-Western countries; more recently it has seen expression in the arguments over GATT, in which some countries (e.g. France, China) have sought to defend their cultural integrity by banning imports of foreign media products. These matters are discussed thoroughly in Tomlinson (1991).

How foreign countries are seen

Edward Said has argued for many years that the west has created images of 'the Orient' that have then been used as bases for political, economic and foreign policy decisions, to say nothing of informing culture generally (Said, 1995). He has written mainly of the Arab world, but the West's image of, and therefore attitudes to, China, as expressed in contemporary culture, have changed markedly over the centuries in accordance with its own self-perceptions (Christiansen and Rai, 1993).

The magic Tartary of a splendour and technical superiority that Europe could not match (fourteenth and fifteenth centuries) gave way to Voltaire's China, in which philosophers eschewed superstition, ruled according to reason and had meritocratic institutions. This was useful at a time when Europeans of the Enlightenment were confused at the decline of the old certainties. Then came the China of silk and ceramics and superiority in arts and crafts so popular in the early stages of Britain's industrial revolution. This image of China ceded place to the grotesque and contemptible tyranny that could not withstand either modern might or manifest destiny during the imperial period of say the 1870s to 1930s; she became pitiable, weak and easy to exploit by adventurers, open to spiritual reconstruction by missionaries, tricked by politicians. During the Second World War, China was admired as a plucky ally against Japan; during the Cold War that followed, excoriated as the 'Empire of the Blue Ants'. In the 1960s the European left hailed the communes as a 'new civilisation' while the right discussed the Yellow Peril; by the 1980s China was once again loved for its quaintness and for the business opportunities it offered ('the last great market'); after Tiananmen China was condemned as the world's moloch – rival, giant and thug.

The dynamics of how other societies are depicted today have been looked at in particular by Galtung and Ruge (1965) who found that foreign news is reported in various categories and in part conditioned by our own cultural prejudices. Evans (1997) has given an example in his description of how Soviet President Gorbachev's test ban announcement was treated by the US media in 1985. Although the test ban was unilateral and real, it was consistently represented by all the media as propaganda, demonstrating not only gullibility to political spin but unwillingness to check facts when the facts might not suit the belief. During the Gulf War the *Guardian* examined the language being used by the press in one week, and reported:

> We have Army, Navy and Airforce; they have a war machine . . . We dig in; they cower in their foxholes . . . We launch [missiles] preemptively; they launch without provocation . . . Our missiles cause collateral damage; theirs cause civilian casualties . . . Our men are lads; their men are hordes . . . Our boys are professional; theirs are brainwashed . . . Ours resolute; theirs ruthless . . . Our boys fly into the jaws of hell; theirs cower in concrete bunkers . . . We have reporting guidelines; they have censorship . . . We have press briefings; they have propaganda.
>
> (cit. in Leapman, 1992: 266)

Keeble, in a book that dissects our assumptions about the Gulf War which, he suggests, are made up of a whole collection of myths and half truths, also draws our attention to research on the way in which the *Sun* and *Star* newspapers used war news selectively to make convenient points (Keeble, 1997: Chap. 16) and Hume suggests that the 1999 war in Yugoslavia should be seen as self-projection (various articles, Hume, 1999). A study of the 1997 handover of Hong Kong to China in the UK and Chinese media shows that 'the reporting of both countries has sharply different perspectives and therefore each presents equally different perspectives to their respective readers' (Cao, 1998: 15). According to Cao British accounts are infused with a 'history-oriented nostalgia for the empire and present-oriented myth of democracy' whereas Chinese accounts are infused with the myth of victimhood and reinforce the myth of the Communist Party (CP) as saviour of the Chinese.[3] An interesting aspect of Cao's study is that whereas the homogenous view of the Chinese media might well be anticipated from the fact that it is centrally owned and directed, the UK media are not, and yet on this story at least are similarly homogenous in their approach. This point (ibid.: 16) appears to bear out the argument that the influences of culture are very powerful. Thus, empirical research of media content complements the research on news agencies.

Ethical imperialism or human rights?

On page 268 I listed a number of the conditions within which journalism is practised and by which it is moulded. Beyond these, it is widely acknowledged

(Shoemaker, 1996) that the conventions of journalists and their work practices determine the limits of news, selecting certain types of events rather than others for processing, privileging certain themes and then shaping events into pre-specified formats such as the TV news package, so that they become elements which make up a conventional news programme.

The exact relationship between these various influences, which are the more powerful or more explicit, is probably impossible to determine. Nevertheless culture, meaning 'the social practices and beliefs of a given group of people who share them' (Jandt, 1995) is surely fundamental. A central message of cultural scholarship over the past few decades has been that 'what you see depends both upon what you look at and what your previous experience has taught you to see' (Jandt, 1995: 157). Stuart Hall and others have shown how our culture affects the ways in which we represent others – other individuals, societies, institutions and so on – according to where we ourselves are situated. Where we are situated may mean our degree of prosperity, our gender, our cultural identity and so on.

So, when can a foreign story tell us about the society reported and how much is it a reflection of our own culture? It may appear to others not as truth but as 'their reality', or even *ethical imperialism*. I first heard the term used nearly ten years ago by the then Turkish ambassador lambasting the BBC for reporting British Liberal politician Lord Avebury's concern over the Kurds. He sneered that Avebury was behaving like a typical British colonial governor and used this term *ethical imperialism* as abuse. He touched a nerve, for there is unease, if not among journalists, then among media academics, as to whether we have the right to investigate other countries, declare some aspect of their society wanting according to our lights and demand that they conform. Child labour, political imprisonment, industrial diseases . . . these are among the ills that offend the Anglophone sense of human rights and, *prima facie*, require investigation and condemnation. Some people in the investigated, and therefore perhaps labelled and demonised, societies may disagree. The matter of their disagreement may, of course, be opportunism; some have attacked the Anglophone media on the grounds of offending their values when in fact they resent interference in their own nefarious activities. However, let us assume for the sake of argument that resistance to Western journalism is disinterested.

The notion of human rights transcending those of institutions is fundamental to Anglophone attitudes today, yet when critics of the Anglophone media, or of politicians' raising human rights issues make their criticisms, they commonly refer to the colonialist antecedents of these notions, presenting them as arrogance, a kind of imperialism of the heart.[4] Prime Minister Blair's crusading zeal in the bombing of Serbia and Kosovo in 1999 has doubtless reinforced such reaction and may be seen by non-Anglophones as contradicting simultaneous claims of promoting human rights.

Over the last 30 years in Anglophone societies it has been widely declared that different cultures must be respected, that the Anglican way of life is no more valid than that of the Sikh, the Rastafarian or the Sufi. Those who do not respect other cultures but seek homogenisation through language, media, commerce or political domination are cultural imperialists. Despite this, to non-Anglophones, what we see as the defence of human rights is simply a manifestation of that very imperialism. Moreover, journalists who have a missionary conception of their calling and seek to reveal wrongs are simply the servants of Anglophone interests, dressed up as morality. Outside of the Anglophone world the idea of the journalist as missionary, defender of the defenceless, sceptic and critic of the way things are is probably held by few. Even where, as in China today, an investigative role is acknowledged for the journalist, it rarely extends to interrogation of the leadership or virtual political opposition. Critics of the Anglophone conception share the widely-held belief that journalists are partial; that the selection of events as newsworthy and the processing of those events into stories (conflict seeking, counter-factual, identifying victims and villains) are culturally biased and reflect the needs of the observers' culture rather than the 'objective reality' of the observed. More sophisticated critics reject the very concept of objectivity as anything more than a professional device to evade responsibility. Some observers from poorer countries believe that the news needs of their communities and those of the rich and developed ones are different and that the Western 'construction of reality' is positively harmful. Anthony Smith quotes an Indian journalist:

> In our environment there is, and there will be for a long time to come, much that is ugly and distasteful. If we follow the Western norm we will be playing up only those dark spots and thus helping unwittingly to erode the faith and confidence without which growth and development are impossible.
>
> (Smith, 1980: 94)

Smith adds 'A journalist would have to share the commitment to the ideology of development before he would see the objective story in a developing society'. Going further along this path the English political thinker John Gray has suggested, as a fact upon which to base mutual respect between incompatible systems, that some rights that we value little are better defended in other cultures. He is thinking of the right to community, to economic security and to freedom from chaos (Gray, 1995: 140).

Coverage of China: the ultimate other

This however comes perilously close to saying that the Chinese, for example, are so different that we cannot apply any of our values. At the extreme this ends up in claiming that, for example, the Tiananmen massacre was an invention of the Western media because what was going on was something too Chinese for our scandal-hungry media to understand. This view has been criticised by Zhang Longxi (1992) but as he acknowledges in two interesting essays, although it might seem absurd it has a distinguished pedigree. For, as we have already mentioned, China has indeed often been reported by Westerners in terms that revealed their own longings, prejudices and political assumptions. For generations, writers up to, in our own time, Foucault and Borges, have helped to perpetuate the China that is 'the image of the ultimate other' in the manner in which, as Edward Said has so well demonstrated of the Middle East, the West created 'the Orient' (Zhang Longxi, 1988). More prosaically, a group of Chinese academics and journalists, all claiming to have gone to study in the USA filled with admiration for their host country, have published a bitter book full of impressive evidence of the misrepresentation of China, which they call 'Demonising China'.[5] So we should always look at a text on China and say: what do we understand about ourselves from this?

Example: 'Laogai': inside China's gulag

Harry Wu is a Chinese man who spent 19 years in prison camps in his homeland and who has made it his life's purpose to expose the extensive penal system of the People's Republic of China.[6] He is the author of several books on Chinese prisons and the head of a foundation researching them (Wu, 1997). His ability to provide first-hand information, his contacts, courage and eloquence have all ensured that he has been taken up by the Anglophone media and that his story has become famous, particularly since 1995 when he was released from prison, apparently so that the wife of the US President might be prevented from cancelling a visit to China at the instigation of human rights activists.[7] The style of his writing is rather sensational:

> The American passport was tucked into the pouch on my belt. Occasionally I would reach for it the way a cowboy in a Western movie might feel for his six-shooter, just to know it's there. Everybody wants an equaliser. It was June of 1995, and I was riding in a taxi through a remote corner of Kazakhstan, trying to slip into China. I felt a shiver, half-love, half-terror. My US passport would not protect me if they caught me inside my homeland. China has a most wanted list, and I was on it.
>
> (Wu, 1997: 3)

Description of the programme

The film 'Laogai', transmitted by Yorkshire Television on the national ITV (commercial) network in August 1993 for the *First Tuesday* strand,[8] argues that pressure should be put on China to reform its penal system, and that this should be done by shaming it in international fora such as the UN and by the trade authorities of Western countries refusing to accept imports that have originated in forced labour camps.

Wu and his wife disguised themselves as business visitors or tourists, depending on the occasion, and used US passports. They filmed with hidden cameras in the vicinity of several camps; on one occasion Wu donned police uniform to get nearer and on another represented the family members of a prisoner to get access. There are testimonial interviews on the extent and general harshness of the camps with Robin Munro of the human rights pressure group Asia Watch and on individual cases of brutality with several former prisoners of different generations.

The treatment is dramatic. 'Laogai' starts with a sequence showing illegal immigrants 'on their journey to freedom' being picked up by (then British) Hong Kong police and, probably incorrectly, allows the impression that these immigrants are largely political refugees. At various points in 'Laogai' we see the careful preparations made for undercover filming. There are many shots of the grim landscapes in which the camps are situated and there is one risky encounter with guards, from which Mrs Wu flees.

As to the quality of the information contained in the programme, the main corroboration comes from Munro of Asia Watch. We are told that there have been approximately 25 million political prisoners since 1949; that the population of the camps may now be as much as 10 million; that 10,000 activists were arrested after the 1989 massacre in Beijing, of whom 'many are still behind bars'; 'inside these walls are prisoners whose only crime is to think' we are told at one point, and it is suggested that they may comprise Tibetan independence activists, students and priests. We learn that many prisoners are working in 'cruel and degrading conditions', exposed to toxic chemicals; there is torture; the ethos is that of the Nazi camps.

The second part goes into detail on the economic significance of the camps whose products are exported to 30 countries, we are told, although China has been obliged to sign a pledge to the effect that gulag exports have ended. Harry Wu is seen setting up a sting in Hong Kong to see if he can buy from Chinese government brokers goods that originated in the camps. He signs the contract and it is then confirmed by US Customs that the subjects of the contract are indeed the products of prison labour.

Wu goes to Congress to present his findings to sympathetic politicians who will use them as ammunition in their battle with China over human rights and trade. He then turns his attention to the UK and the case is made that much of the tea consumed in the UK may come from prison farms, notwithstanding the fact that as long ago as 1897 the UK banned all prison-made products. At the end, as earlier, Wu makes an impassioned case for action by the West, explaining his motivations as the urge to make up for the youth that the camps took from him, the hope to see an end to the system that devoured his friends and the longing for an end to communist power in his country.

Critique of the programme

The programme can be faulted on three grounds. One is that it exaggerates the importance of the issue selected, i.e. lacks real truth by being selective and that it does so on the basis of incomplete (if understandably incomplete) data; second is that it takes no account of the changes for the better that have taken place since the 1970s, in other words it lacks context; third is that it panders to Western prejudices and interests.

There is no reason to doubt the veracity of the cases described or of the descriptions of the camps visited. It is possible that the overall figures quoted for the size of the prison system are correct, although in the absence of authoritative statistics, judgement must be suspended. 'Around 10 million' is a prison population of 1 per cent; the proportion of political prisoners appears to be entirely speculative.

As to treatment, it is very likely that brutality exists in these camps since there are no institutions that can inspect or expose them. It is quite comprehensible that former prisoners will have passionate views, but it is equally possible that they are not representative. It is also arguable that the number of people being maltreated is not as important a fact as that some are being maltreated. Nevertheless, if the overall impression given is one that contributes to prejudice rather than to enlightenment, then the journalist is open to criticism. Such criticism is answered by Tim Tate, producer and main author of the programme after Wu himself, with the point that if a wrong is wrong, then demanding detailed statistics is asking the wrong question; what matters is that the main thrust is right (Tate, 1997).

Grant McKee, Executive Producer of 'Laogai' when at Yorkshire Television, says that such a programme would be most unlikely to be made now. A few years ago ITV did many foreign stories. Why 'Laogai'?

> We'd been going for easy targets such as multinationals based in the West, and a totalitarian regime such as China and Russia presented a challenge. After all, it's easy to go after malfeasance in democracies, every so often we ought to do something a bit more difficult! Also it was very relevant at the time because China was being considered for most favoured nation status and the question of what kind of relations we should have with a country which had such a poor human rights record was being discussed everywhere.
>
> (McKee, 1999)

He was scathing of the suggestion that his programme was part of systematic demonisation of China.

> The reaction of the Chinese is an indication of great insecurity. I am proud of being English but I would not have the slightest hesitation in

exposing or seeing exposed the murky corners of my country. Are they suggesting that what Harry Wu saw should be kept hidden in the cause of some greater balance? Well, I do not wear that. Human rights are universal. Should we not show that people are stoned and tortured to death in Africa or Arabia? Of course I understand that if you are African or Arab and do not have a long-standing tradition of press freedom and human rights behind you then it is rather galling that it is always foreigners exposing things; but we are not trying to be imperialistic. We are just saying 'look this is going on, don't you want to know about it?'

(McKee, 1999)

The context in which this programme is made and filmed is one of trade war between major powers, disagreement between China and the USA on international issues and a fear of eventual rivalry between the USA, currently the sole superpower, and China. China sees the USA as a threatening military force moved by ruthless business interests and irresponsible politicians; indeed, there are interests in the USA that want to see China tamed for commerce and weakened politically. Thus the characterisation of China as an abuser of human rights, its demonisation, serves political purposes as well as being a contribution to enlightenment. In such circumstances investigative journalists would probably do well to consider whose interests they serve; they will still expose, but they might expose with more circumspection.

Channel 4 has transmitted some unrelentingly critical programmes about China's most sensitive aspects: the population programme, the treatment of non-Chinese citizens, the nuclear project and its effects upon ordinary people. Head of News and Current Affairs David Lloyd, questioned about his attitude to China, considers that 'you have to judge a country by its worst aspects' (Lloyd, 1998). He makes an analogy:

If 5 per cent of the Royal Ulster Constabulary are bigoted persecutors of Catholics, they must be followed up, even if 95 per cent are not, because the damage is being done by the 5 per cent. . . . Investigative journalism very properly looks for the worst case; investigative journalism stands for human rights, transparency, ability of people to have some control over their futures . . . it is, if you like, the people's tribune.

(ibid.)

China is a 'big story' both because it is becoming a big economy and because of the discrepancy, to Western eyes, between its economic ambition and its political system. There are two ways of factually representing China to people; witnessing the unfolding of real life, for example through an observational documentary series such as the lyrical *Beyond the Clouds* or the much admired portrait of a big city, *Shanghai Vice*; and investigation. Lloyd denies being

Anglocentric: 'We are not Martians, we have to relate China to British perspectives, we have to mediate for British people'. Taken to task for spreading, through C4's investigations in China, a partial view of China that has great impact for its sensational revelations, he says that he 'speak[s] as someone who must hold the torch of investigative journalism' and that C4 has also covered many aspects of China in ways that are not investigative (C4 has also transmitted Chinese opera, modern films, features on Chinese economic successes). Coverage of China is, however, like that of other countries 'intermittent and not coherent', partly because of the attitude of the Chinese government and partly because of the scepticism among British broadcasters as to whether international subjects can win audiences.

Discussion

There is an established British tradition of investigating and reporting on other countries; in addition to the general current affairs series already mentioned there are programmes exclusively dealing with foreign countries, such as BBC *Assignment*, C4 *Correspondent* and BBC *Foreign Correspondent*. These media, and the broadsheets, usually home in on some aspect of foreign countries that excites reproof or even condemnation; individual reporters, in particular John Pilger and Martin Gregory, have concentrated upon the responsibility of their own society for the issue in question. How do we account for Anglophone journalism's interest in other societies? We can point to the idea of social responsibility and see travelling abroad as an extension of that. Our present interest in suffering in other countries then appears to be the heir to a noble tradition of concern, from anti-slavery to women's rights. There is the one-world view which sees no man as an island; we are all our brothers' keepers. These are arguments that could be used to defend the missionary moralism of Spanish priests in sixteenth-century Latin America or Protestant pastors in nineteenth-century China. Then there is the camp of ethical relativism, using this kind of argument: 'Anglophones and Africans have different cultures and therefore different standards; we mustn't be judgmental'. This is also the defence of those who want to preserve the *status quo* in, for example, Africa.

More pragmatically it can be argued that we are not justified in investigating foreign countries and revealing what we consider to be abuses simply because we understand so little about them. It is often observed how few correspondents know the languages, let alone have a deep knowledge of the cultures of the countries they report; indeed this is often regarded as a disadvantage for a correspondent. In such conditions the journalist can encounter many problems in trying to understand another society, and probably often gives up, whether allowing others to mediate for him or her or simply accepting that his or her perspective is the limited one of seeing that society only insofar as it touches upon the political or economic interests of his or her own.

At its worst, foreign reporting is merely the use of exotic locations to show up squalor, with the underlying message that the reporter's society is superior; furthermore, in a culture with different traditions, in which not only is the reporter ignorant of the culture but also the host society is unaccustomed to the reporter's style of journalism, the case for the defence may never be put. The report is then subject to less stringent standards of fairness than would be possible at home. To some extent, these problems could be resolved by education of journalists, sensitising them to other societies; however such sensitising might be seen to go against the ideology of social responsibility and the professional values of Anglophone journalism, exemplified in the quotation from Randall, above. John Pilger (1999) responds to the critics thus: 'To a great extent they are right. The reach, monopoly and power of the Western media is a new form of imperialism which interprets countries to themselves in the light of Western interests as well as seeing them only in the light of those interests'.

More aware critics will recognise though that nationalism should be separated from the right of people to know, no matter from where that knowledge comes, and that both Chinese and Western journalists 'speak culturally'. [As far as the Western journalist's investigations are concerned] if you do not do it in your own country then you have no right to do it in foreign countries. As to the demonisation argument, the reporting of Russia today is typical; we see the horrible things but we never understand why. For if you do not place your investigation within the political context, explain it, then you are at risk of demonising. 'Laogai' therefore raises a number of issues in the Anglophone reporting of other societies.

Notes

1 The largest news agency in the world is quite possibly Xinhua (New China), but its influence on the media outside China is probably negligible.
2 Interestingly, they see two attempts to escape from this as confirmation of the trend: the efforts to create International Cultural Studies they see as a further example of Anglophone cultural imperialism, imposing Anglophone categories; and the introduction of the norms of multiculturalism and hybridity in the UK, Canada, USA and Australia they see as further reinforcing the dominant position of the Anglophone majority.
3 Both the Chinese myths are debatable; it is quite possible to see China as a victim of itself rather than of Western imperialism as the Communist Party (CP) has sought to portray it; many Chinese by no means subscribe to the myth of the CP as saviour. No less suspect are the British myths. Whereas the British media criticise China for its society today, the Chinese media are defensive, perhaps acknowledging in so being that in a world whose ethical leadership is Anglophone there is no mileage in attacking its assumptions.
4 In the early imperial period there was a hierarchy in which many non-white people were seen as having different or conditional rights. Conrad's novel of the exploitation of the Congo, *Heart of Darkness*, puts this point, although it may also be the case that the notion of universal human rights was strongly felt at least among British colonial officials in the twentieth century. This may account for the many attempts to

ameliorate the lot of subject peoples, particularly where such amelioration was against the interests of the colonial rulers, for example in the attempts to eradicate paederastic sodomy and clitoral circumcision in West Africa.

5 Xiguang, L. and Kang, L. (1997) *Yamohua Zhongguo de Beihou* (Behind the Demonisation of China). Peking: Zhongguo Shehui Kexue CBS.

6 Accounts of Wu's life appear to originate exclusively from him and, as far as I am aware, are not corroborated by disinterested sources. To say this is not to denigrate him, but to utter a caveat.

7 Wu was by this time a US citizen and had returned to China specifically to make a film there which was sure to stimulate the wrath of the authorities.

8 *First Tuesday* was ITV's flagship documentary series from 1983–93, screening monthly a highly acclaimed range of programmes of many different kinds and winning many international awards. The highest ratings ever obtained were 12.5 million for 'Katie and Eilish; Siamese Twins' (August, 1992); the most controversial arguably was 'Windscale: the Nuclear Laundry' (November, 1983). In its ten-year period it had two Series Editors, John Willis and Grant McKee. Information supplied by Chris Briar, Group Controller of Factual Programmes, to Hugo de Burgh by telephone on 4 November 1999.

Bibliography

Allan, S. (1997) News and the public sphere: towards a history of news objectivity. In M. Bromley and T. O'Malley (1997) *A Journalism Reader*. London: Routledge.

Boyd-Barrett, O. (1997) Global news wholesalers as agents of globalisation. In A. Sreberny-Mohammedi (ed.) *Media in Global Context*. London: Edward Arnold.

Cao, Q. (1998) Discourse, ideology and power: a comparative study of the reporting of the handover of Hong Kong in the British and Chinese printed media. Paper delivered at the 21st Conference of IAMCR, Glasgow.

Carlton TV (1994) *Death of a Nation* (Reporter: John Pilger). London: Carlton TV.

Chambers, D. and Tinckell, E. (1998) Anglocentric versions of the international: the privileging of Anglo-ethnicity in cultural studies and the global media. Paper delivered at the 21st Conference of IAMCR, Glasgow.

Christiansen, F. and Rai, S. (1993) *Theories and Concepts: shifting views of China*. Coventry: University of Warwick PAIS Working Paper 117.

Evans, H. (1997) Prometheus unbound. Iain Walker Memorial Lecture, Green College Oxford, May.

Galtung, J. and Ruge, M. (1965) The structure of foreign news. In J. Tunstall (1970) *Media Sociology*. London: Constable.

Golding, P. (1977) Media professionalism in the third world: the transfer of an ideology. In J. Curran, M. Gurevitch and J. Woollacott (eds) *Mass Communication and Society*. London: Edward Arnold.

Gray, J. (1995) *Enlightenment's Wake*. London: Routledge: 140.

Hall, S. (1997) The spectacle of the 'Other'. In S. Hall (ed.) *Representation: Cultural Representations and Signifying Practices*. London: Sage.

Harrison, P. (1996) *News Out of Africa*. London: Shipman.

Hume, M. (1999) The war against the Serbs is about projecting a self-image of the ethical new Britain bestriding the world. It is a crusade. *Times*, 15 April 1999.

Jandt, F. E. (1995) Culture's influence on knowledge. In *Intercultural Communication*. Thousand Oaks: Sage: chap. 9.

Joseph, C. (2007) 'Uncovered by the makers of Dying Rooms, the scandal of how China's brutal single child policy leads to . . . Babies For Sale' *The Mail on Sunday*, 7 October 2007.

Keeble, R. (1997) *Secret State, Silent Press*. Luton: John Libbey.

Leapman, M. (1992) *Treacherous Estate*. London: Hodder.

Lloyd, D. (1998) Interview with Hugo de Burgh at Nottingham Trent University, 19 February 1998.

McKee, G. (1999) Interview with Hugo de Burgh, 17 May 1999.

Pilger, J. (1999) Interview with Hugo de Burgh, 29 June 1999.

Randall, D. (1996) *The Universal Journalist*. London: Pluto.

Said, E. (1995) *Orientalism: Western Conceptions of the Orient*. London: Penguin.

Sandford, J. (ed.) (1990) *Gunther Wallraff: Der Aufmacher*. Manchester: Manchester University Press.

Shoemaker, P. (1996) Influences on content from outside media organisations. In P. Shoemaker *Mediating the Message*. White Plains: Longman.

Smith, A. (1980) *The Geopolitics of Information: How Western Culture Dominates the World*. London: Faber and Faber.

Tate, T. (1997) The making of 'Laogai'. Talk to students on the MA Investigative Journalism course at Nottingham Trent University, 6 November 1997.

Tomlinson, J. (1991) *Cultural Imperialism*. London: Pinter.

Tomlinson, J. (1997) Internationalism, globalization and cultural imperialism. In K. Thompson (ed.) *Media and Cultural Regulation*. London: Sage/Open University Press: 117–62 (chap. 3).

Tracey, M. (1985) The poisoned chalice? International television and the idea of dominance. *Daedalus*, 114 (4): 17–56.

Wu, H. (1997) *Troublemaker*. London: Village.

Yorkshire TV (1993) 'Laogai: The Chinese Gulag' (Director: Tim Tate. Reporter: Harry Wu), *First Tuesday*, Leeds: Yorkshire TV.

Zhang Longxi (1988) The myth of the Other: China in the eyes of the West. *Critical Inquiry*, 15 (Autumn).

Longxi, Z. (1992) Western theory and Chinese reality. *Critical Inquiry*, 19 (Autumn).

Further reading

de Burgh, H. (2007) 'Looking at China, Looking at the Chinese Media', Introductory article to Cao Qing (ed) 'Reporting China in the British Media', Special Edition of *China Media Research*, 3 (1), January 2007.

de Burgh, H. and Xin, X. (2006) 'News Probe: What does it tell us about Chinese journalism today?' in *Medien Journal*, 30 (2–3), 2006.

de Burgh, H. (2006) *China: Friend or Foe?* Cambridge: Icon.

de Burgh, H. (2003) *The Chinese Journalist Mediating information in the world's most populous country*. London: Routledge.

Gray, J. (1995) *Enlightenment's Wake*. London: Routledge: 140.

Hall, S. (1997) The spectacle of the 'Other'. In S. Hall (ed.) *Representation: Cultural Representations and Signifying Practices*. London: Sage.

Tomlinson, J. (1991) *Cultural Imperialism*. London: Pinter.

INDEX

National Archives and Record
   Administration (US) 144
National Car Parks 217, 235
National Commission on Standards in
   Public Life 220
National Council for the Training of
   Journalists 131–2
National Foundation for Educational
   Research 265–6
National Health Service 310–11
National Institute for Computer Assisted
   Reporting 155
National Security Agency (US) 168
National Security Archive (US) 144
National Trust 342–3
National Union of Journalists 27, 158
National Union of Mineworkers 344–5
National Whistleblower Center 28, 155
Nazism 61, 150
Ndaywel è Nziem, Isidore 145
Needham, Joseph 368
Neil, Andrew 175, 216, 218, 225
nepotism charges 284, 306
Network Centre 343–4
New Deal 301
New World Information Order 373
New York Times 147, 203
New Yorker 204
New Zealand 341
Newcastle United Football Club 333
Newmont Mining Corporation 148
Newnes, George 46–7
news agencies 372
news agenda 13, 44; *see also* agenda setting
news databases 163
News of the World: Bough 327–8; call girls
   54, 58; Editors' Code of Practice 325;
   Greenslade 9; on Harding 330;
   investigative journalism 319, 332–5;
   libel action 325; Press Complaints
   Commission 334, 335; Profumo 54;
   reporters 322–3, 325; sales 321;
   security lapses 337; sleaze 66
newsgathering 6, 34, 103
Newsnight 243
News-Press 102–3
newsworthiness 13, 14–15, 162–3, 303
Nicholls, Lord 114, 117, 118, 122n3,
   126n37
Night Flyte 261
Nightingale, Florence 40
Nixon, Richard 140

Nolan Committee 63
Non-Governmental Organisations 146
Northcliffe, Lord 129n80
Northern Echo 44
Northmore, D. 226
Norton-Taylor, Richard 206
Nottingham City Council 12
Nottingham printing company 239–40
nuclear power 56, 59
nuclear weapons 141, 206, 217, 231
nursing standards 257

objectivity 42–4, 100, 371
Oborne, Peter 19, 71, 83, 84
Obscene Publications Squad 330
Observer 64, 77, 197, 285
Ofcom 28, 87, 301
Office of Standards in Education 260
Official Secrets Act 59, 130–1
Omagh bombing 76, 115, 116, 124n16
Omar, Abu 192–3
O'Neil, Onora 71
Online Policy Group 109
Open Democracy Advice Centre 154–5
open sourcing 184
opinion polls 341
Optical Character Recognition 152
Orwell, George 191
outsourcing 232
overpopulation 342
ownership of media 372

paedophilia 58, 64
Page, B. 57, 226
Palestine Liberation Organisation 326
Pall Mall Gazette 44, 175, 320
Panorama 65–6; audience 90, 245, 254;
   Carrickmore IRA roadblock 244;
   Church of Scientology 92; drug trials
   146; Edwards 14, 65; elderly 77; 'A
   Fight to the Death' 88–9; Gaber on 8;
   on Gilligan 202–3; history of 243–4;
   immigration 81; as information source
   254; investigative journalism 244,
   251–2; Iraq war 202; libel action
   252–3; 'Missing Mum' 265; new
   backgrounders 248–51; news
   backgrounders 246, Omagh bombing
   115; populist investigations 245–6, 248;
   programmes classifed 245–6; re-launch
   of 245–54; Scientology 91; self-
   referential programmes 246, 251;

Lightning Source UK Ltd.
Milton Keynes UK
UKOW06f0904280515

252444UK00004B/28/P